A YEAR OF DAILY MEDITATIONS FOR WOMEN

God bless you with a More Abundant Life!
Renetta Brovont

RENETTA BROVONT

ISBN 978-0-9885434-0-9

All scripture references, unless otherwise noted are from the *Holy Bible: King James Version*.

Printed in the U.S.A.

Design and layout by Lindsey Vroma

Dedicated to all my sisters
in our home congregation
near Scottville, Michigan
past and present.

God bless you
with a *more abundant life*.
I love you all!

Acknowledgments

My first thanks goes to our great God who compelled me to begin this book when I thought I was far too busy to start a project of any kind, much less one of this magnitude. And for giving me the gentle nudges along the way that I needed to keep going. His grace is sufficient and His blessings are abundant.

My family deserves a heart-felt thank you for putting up with seven years of having a wife and mother who at times forgot she was suppose to be fixing a meal or doing the laundry because she was completely absorbed in writing these devotionals. Thank you for all the times you pitched in so I could keep writing. You were patient and supportive and I appreciate it!

A special thank-you to my husband, Jeff, for being the number one proof-reader of each of these. Even on the evenings when you were tired and I had to be patient and wait for you to "read it in the morning!" Your support and encouragement during this long project means a lot to me.

I want to thank Bill & Kathy Mustard; Don & Nina Miller; Galen & Ronda Bowman; my parents, Willard & Ruth Wrightsman; and my sisters, Rachel Brubaker and Rita Miller for reading each devotional and giving me the feedback that helped to make this book what it is. You are greatly appreciated.

A special thank you to Bill & Kathy Mustard for your encouragement and time spent helping me along the way. Thanks, Bill, for loaning me your sermon notes countless times and for always being there to patiently answer my many questions. This book would not be the same without your input. God bless you for your service to Him.

There are other ministers, also, from various church fellowships, who have answered questions and loaned or given me their sermon notes. God bless you for your willingness to help even though you may not have understood exactly what I was doing with your notes!

I also want to give a very special and heart-felt thank you to Fred Miller of Christian Light Publications for your faithful work in editing this book. It was a big project for you, too, and I appreciate all you did for me. This book definitely would not be the refined, polished work that it is without your experienced help. God bless you richly for it.

A big thank you to Rinck and Lindsey from InnerWorkings for all your time and patience as we worked together to bring this project to its conclusion. Lindsey, you took my humble manuscript and turned it into a beautiful book! God bless you both for using your talents and skills in His honor.

And finally, many thanks to all of you who gave me permission to use the stories of your personal experiences and for proofreading the resulting devotional for me before I filed it. You are too many to list but you know who you are. God bless you for your kindness. This book wouldn't be what it is without your testimonies in it.

Introduction

This book is the culmination of nine years of work. God prompted me to begin writing devotionals in 2003 when I had seven children, six still at home, one still a baby. We lived on a dairy farm and were home-schooling. I resisted, thinking I didn't have time for anything of the sort! Maybe someday... But one weekend He impressed clearly on my heart the difference between life, an abundant life, and a *more abundant life*. I got out of bed that night and wrote down the thoughts that were swirling through my mind. (A trait inherited from my dad!) I looked at the finished result and thought, "Uh-oh. That looks like a devotional!" So I submitted to God's call and began writing as He inspired. Some of these devotionals were written early in the morning while it was still quiet. Some were written late at night after it became quiet. And some were written during the day with phone calls interrupting, toddlers getting into things, baby fussing, someone on my lap wanting to "help," and even a curious toddler jerking the cord out of the outlet and causing me to lose what I had just written! I confess, my words and actions were sometimes a sad contrast to what I was writing. Sometimes weeks went by without any progress. Many times I just didn't feel like writing. Sometimes I resisted writing what I knew God wanted me to share because I didn't want anyone (much less *all of you)* to know how I sometimes feel and act! But I also knew that if I could help anyone who is struggling, to know and *feel* that she is not alone, it would be worth it. So, with God's inspiring, nudging, grace, and patience, little by little, my file grew thicker.

These devotionals cover a seven-year span of my life. When I started writing, we were a large family on a dairy farm. In 2007 we sold the cows and the farm. We opened a Bent-N-Dent grocery/bulk foods/Christian book store in 2008. So you will read about both the farm and the store. Three of our children are out of the nest now so life has changed a good bit since I started this book in 2003.

I cannot begin to explain how I have been blessed in working on this project. My goal to begin with was to be a blessing to other women through this book. I had no idea how deeply I would be blessed myself. Hearing and using the testimonies of others has made a big impact on my life. The effort of putting a sermon into a "nutshell" was a task that made the message more real and meaningful, as one has to *understand* a message before one can *share* it. I only pray that anyone who reads this devotional book will also experience the richness of God's blessings as they live out the *more abundant life*.

January

Read: John 10:1-18 January 1

The More Abundant Life

"I am come that they might have life, and that they might have it more abundantly."
- John 10:10

Are you alive? Of course you are. If you are reading this you are a living, breathing being, created by God. He has given you life to live as you choose. You have "life."

Do you believe in God as your Creator, and as the Supreme Being of the universe? Do you have fellowship with other believers within a Body of Christ? If so, you can have an "abundant life."

But it takes a personal relationship with Jesus Christ to have a "more abundant life." That quality of life is available to all, but forced onto no one. Sadly, many people miss out on that "more abundant life" because they feel that belief in God, and fellowship with other believers is all they need.

Get to know the good Shepherd who lovingly tends His sheep! Pursue a personal daily walk with Jesus, and tap into that "more abundant life." Listen as He speaks to you through His Word. Commune with Him in prayer during your quiet time and as you go through your day. Share with other believers your struggles and victories. Satan is waiting, we know, to kill our desire for spiritual growth, to steal away the peace in our hearts, and to destroy the relationship we have with this Shepherd. The more you pursue this more abundant life, the more determined he becomes to stop you. As you grow closer to the Lord, however, and your daily walk with Him becomes more intimate, you'll find that the "more abundant life" becomes an "ALL abundant life." Jesus will meet your every need and you'll have life more "abundantly" than you ever dreamed possible. He loves you and was willing to lay down His life for you. As we strive to follow His leading, we are blessed over and over in countless ways. As we are blessed, we find ourselves with a desire to share what God is doing in our lives, and to pass on those blessings to others. This brings about the blessing of heart-to-heart fellowship with other believers–a vital and precious aspect of The More Abundant Life.

- Am I actively pursuing a more intimate relationship with Jesus?
- How could I spend adequate time in daily Bible reading and prayer?
- *Lord, lead me into a closer relationship with you and a more abundant life.*

Read: I John 1

My Mirror Image

"So God created (woman) in His own image, in the image of God created He (her)."
- Genesis 1:27

Most of us spend a fair amount of time in front of a mirror each day. We brush our teeth, comb our hair, and wash our face. Then we use a full-length mirror to make sure our clothes hang evenly and aren't wrinkled or stained. We may even get another mirror to check the back view. When everything suits us, we're good to go.

Now imagine for a moment that you had a special mirror hanging on your bedroom wall that allowed you to see yourself as *God* sees you. Would this mirror reflect your face, hair, and clothes? I don't think so. Would it reflect the image of Christ that we *want* it to reflect? Hmmm. Mirrors are painfully honest and I'm afraid I'd want to turn this one to the wall and avoid it. I think I'd see an x-ray image of my heart and everything hiding there that others can't see.

Now be brave with me for a moment and look straight into this mirror. Look carefully for any blemishes of ***selfishness.*** Self-centeredness is an ugly blemish that needs to be cured, not just covered with "make-up." It's a dark shadow of pride and causes more spots of discontent. It does not fit into a Christ-like image. Look for a "rat's nest" of ***guilt.*** Guilt is to the conscience as pain is to the body. It warns you that something is wrong, needing to be dealt with. Guilt is draining and disheartening. We can't reflect God's love with guilt plaguing us.

What about wrinkles of ***meaninglessness?*** A life without meaning leads to depression and feelings of worthlessness. Stains of ***hopelessness*** mar our image and cripple our witness.

Now step back. Do all the smudges and smears in the mirror seem overwhelming? Are you wondering if this image can ever be changed? **YES, it can!** Today's Scripture passage assures us that the smears of sin can be erased by the blood of Jesus and the image you see in the mirror ***can*** be His image. The promise, however, is preceded by a command. In order to receive this cleansing, we must repent of our sins and confess to Him that these ugly blemishes exist in our hearts. If we do this, "*He is faithful and just to forgive us our sins, and to cleanse us from all unrighteousness.*" (v. 9) This is not just a one time cleansing that is then no longer available. I John tells us in verse seven that "*if we walk in the light...the blood of Jesus Christ his son cleanseth us from all sin.*" As we look into the mirror of God's Word, and walk with Jesus in confession, we can experience His cleansing throughout every day.

- What do you see when you look into this "mirror?"
- Do you truly desire to have a clean heart before Him?
- *Lord, I hate the sin I see in my heart and in my life. Cleanse me with Your blood and make me pure.*

Of Pizza Stones and Sweaters

"Delight thyself also in the Lord;
and He shall give thee the desires of thine heart."
- Psalm 37:4

A young friend of mine shared with me how God had blessed her one day. The pathway of her life, as a young adult, had gone through some unusual valleys, but she was steadfastly committed to submitting to God's will in her life. On this day, God had shown her clearly that He hadn't forgotten her, and that she was still precious to Him.

On various occasions, she had looked at pizza baking stones and thought she'd like to have one someday. Another thing she'd found that she really liked was a black Chenille sweater. Knowing that these items were only desires, not needs, she hadn't purchased either one.

Shortly after her next birthday, she received two packages in the mail. They were both gifts, and when she opened them, she found that one was a pizza baking stone, and the other was a black Chenille sweater! In speaking with the givers, she confirmed that neither one knew of her desires. Feeling God's love wrapped around her like a warm blanket, she knew that this was more than just a coincidence.

Since I happened to be the one who had sent her the pizza stone, the story blessed me too! I shared with her that as I was looking for her gift I was drawn to the pizza stone and really didn't know why. But I bought it, hoping she would like it. I was humbled and amazed once again at God's leading and so glad I'd followed. Often we don't know what blessings we miss out on when we don't follow His leading, but the blessings we experience when we do are sweet and worth the efforts.

While we can't expect to have our every desire satisfied, God does show us in special ways that He cares. He knows just what we need to encourage us along the way. It's easy to chalk things up to coincidence. But if we think a little further about those "coincidences," could it be that God is telling us something?

- Do I recognize the special ways God shows me that He cares?
- Do I praise Him for His love for me and my family?
- *Lord, help me never to forget how much you love and care for me as one of your children.*

 Read: Luke 22:31-62

To Shake A Tree

"But I have prayed for thee,
that thy faith fail not."
- Luke 22:32

Have you ever seen a tree severely shaken? We live in one of Michigan's "fruit belts" with fruit trees all around us. To harvest tart cherries, the farmer brings in a machine that clamps onto the trunk of the tree and vibrates it. Cherries, dead leaves, and small branches rain onto a tarp that is spread on the ground under the tree. The cherries are then dumped into a large tank of cold water for the trip to the processing plant.

It takes a pretty sturdy tree to withstand the vigorous shaking. An unhealthy tree would snap right off at that kind of treatment. But for a healthy, fruit-bearing tree, a good shaking is a good thing. And for a healthy, fruit-bearing Christian, a good "shaking" can be a good thing too, even though it doesn't *feel* good at the time.

A good shaking awakens the tree and it can awaken us too. It may seem like a rude awakening, but sometimes that's just what we need! A severe shaking can be devastating enough that we have nowhere to look but straight into the eyes of our Savior. Peter had that sort of experience when he denied Jesus three times and then heard the rooster crow. When he looked up into the disappointed eyes of his Master, he remembered, and "went out and wept bitterly."

After we "wake up," we can begin to bear fruit. Peter had a renewed zeal for Jesus and His ministry after the resurrection. Going through hard times in life can bring out the best in us also. Going through trials can produce in us compassion and understanding for others that we didn't have before. It strengthens our faith and builds patience. When we've been through hard times ourselves, we become stronger in ministering to others for Him.

Shaking a tree causes dead limbs, leaves, and rotten fruit to fall. A shaking experience can remove "dead areas" of our lives, too. Time we spend in unproductive activities seems insignificant and worthless. Unbelief, cowardice, and doubt disappear as we see God working His will in our lives. Pride tumbles as we are humbled through circumstances beyond our control. Hard hearts are softened as we repent of the sin in our lives.

As the limbs lose their burden they lift higher and higher, reaching to the sun for the light they need to live. As we bless others with our "fruit," and get rid of the dead "leaves and limbs" in our lives, our hearts and minds are lifted higher too. Keeping our eyes on the Son, we receive the Light that we need to live and learn and love for Him.

- Do the trials I endure serve to awaken and strengthen me?
- What areas in my life need to be shaken out as dead leaves and rotten fruit?
- *Lord, I don't enjoy the shaking, but I desire to be awake and bearing fruit for you. Show me where I need to change.*

Read: I Peter 1 January 5

Redeemed!

"Ye were not redeemed with corruptible things...
but with the precious blood of Christ."
- I Peter 1:18, 19

The word redeem means "to buy back" or to "rescue." To understand a little better what Christ's redemption of His saints means to you personally, imagine yourself a Hebrew woman many years ago. The Hebrews were just like we are in many ways. Although their lifestyle was quite different, they felt what we feel. Cold, warmth, pain, fear, happiness and sadness were a part of their lives, too.

Imagine that you are a young Hebrew woman named Jochebed. You've grown up in a good home and are now happily married with three small children. One day your husband becomes very ill and, as there is no medical care available, he worsens and dies. Along with the crushing grief, you are alone. You have children to support and no welfare system to help you. You could glean in your family's field for food, but you have no family. So, you choose your only option and borrow money for food. You have no hope of repaying, however, and eventually the lender comes for his money. Now the lender has two options. He can either take you as his slave or he can sell you to another as a slave. He decides to sell you and your children to a harsh taskmaster. You have gone from a happy life of freedom to a cruel life of slavery. You and your little children work hard, but it's never enough. Heartbrokenly you comfort your little ones in the evenings, putting salve on wounds from the whip's lashes, and you try to soothe their little hearts. Day after grueling day you exist with no hope for the future.

Then one day a stranger stops by unexpectedly and asks the master if a "Jochebed" lives here. He's your dead husband's cousin and is looking for you! He makes a generous offer to your owner, hands over the money, and kindly takes you and your children home with him. You can hardly believe that you are *free*. You have plenty to eat, a beautiful warm home, and plenty of clothes. Best of all...your children are safe. Your redemption is priceless.

Like Jochebed, we have been redeemed from a harsh taskmaster--*sin*. Under this cruel master there is no hope for the future and no way to escape on our own. Only the life and death of God's Son can save us from eternal punishment. Our Redeemer paid for us--not with pocket change--but with His own precious blood. *What a priceless redemption!* May our hearts overflow with a sincere desire to please our Redeemer in every area of our lives.

- Do I truly understand the depth of what Christ's redemption of His saints means for me?
- How could I change my life to better show my gratitude for what He has done for me?
- *Lord, it's difficult to fully understand what You have done for me, but I want to love and praise You for it.*

Read: I Timothy 2:1-13

Heart Health: A Weak Heart

"Thou therefore, my (daughter), be strong
in the grace that is in Christ Jesus."
- I Timothy 2:1

Most of us have a strong, healthy heart that is faithfully pumping the blood through our bodies at about 70 beats per minute, and much faster if needed. Our hearts work day and night from soon after conception until death. During a lifespan of 76 years, the heart will beat nearly 3 billion times and pump 179 million quarts of blood.

But not everyone is blessed with a healthy heart. Some start out healthy, but become diseased for one reason or another. There are many types of heart disease and many solutions for the problems. Hearts aren't plagued with only physical ailments, however. Spiritual conditions can also affect the heart.

A person with a weak heart will lack the energy he needs to live a normal life. A weak heart may pump sluggishly, as it tries in its weakened condition, to keep up with the needs of the body. If the heart becomes too weak, a heart transplant may be needed to keep the person alive. If so, his name is put on a transplant list and hopefully he will receive a donated heart before his gives out completely. A replacement heart, if not rejected, will give the patient a chance to live a healthy, normal life again. Sometimes one has to wait a long time, being bumped down the list because of health or other issues. We can't even imagine the blessing of receiving a healthy heart after being so sick, unless we've been there.

We have all experienced, however, a spiritual weakening of our hearts. Some sort of disease creeps in, maybe just from neglect. We fail to keep our hearts strong with daily exercise; reading God's Word, communing with Him in prayer, and quietly listening for His voice. We're too busy to spend time with Him, or we think He doesn't really care about us anyway. It doesn't take long for neglect to weaken the heart and we become tired and sluggish; lacking the energy to face the trials of life. Satan will take full advantage of times like this and strike while we're weak. Before long we find ourselves in bad need of a transplant. But there's good news! We don't have to be put on God's transplant list. We don't have to wait for an available heart knowing someone else has to die for us to live. Our transplant is available now. Jesus has already died so that we can have access to a changed heart at any time and as many times as we need it. Don't put it off. If your heart is failing you today, spend some time alone with the Master Surgeon and ask Him for a transplant. You're already at "the top of the list" and a new outlook on life is yours for the asking.

- Am I facing life today with a weak heart that is draining the energy from my body and spirit?
- What "exercises" do I need to be doing that would strengthen my heart?
- *Lord, transplant in me a new heart today and help me to keep it strong with daily spiritual exercise.*

Heart Health: A Heart Murmur

"And suddenly there came a sound from heaven as of a rushing mighty wind."
- Acts 2:2

A heart murmur is common and often found in adults and children alike. It's simply an extra whooshing sound, made by the blood as it passes through the valves in the heart that can be heard through a stethoscope. It may indicate that there is something wrong with the heart, needing immediate attention. Most of the time, however, it's a normal sound produced by normal blood flow. Heart murmurs produce different sounds that can help a doctor determine whether there is a serious problem, or if it's just an innocent murmur. The normal blood flow sounds like water running through a garden hose. A hole in the "hose" will cause the blood to leak out, producing a whistling noise of varying intensities, depending on the size of the hole. A narrow valve will cause the blood to become turbulent trying to squeeze through and will create a heart murmur. A leaky valve doesn't close completely, allowing some of the blood to flow back, causing the extra sound. These problems need to be addressed in some way, but normally a heart murmur is labeled "innocent" and of no concern to the patient. It's been described as sounding like the wind through the forest, a flowing stream, a swarm of bees at work, or a faint, roaring sound.

Does that definition sound familiar, like something else you've read about? Acts 2:2 describes the coming of the Holy Spirit at Pentecost as sounding like a rushing mighty wind. So this heart murmuring is not necessarily a heart defect! A Spiritual "murmur" can be the sign that something is amiss or it can be a sign of the Holy Spirit flowing through our hearts. Maybe it means we have a "hole" in our heart and what we learn through reading, teaching, or preaching just leaks out, doing us no good at all. Maybe we have "narrow valves" that restrict what comes in because of past hurts or a lack of concern about spiritual matters. Maybe we just have "leaky heart valves" that only retain what we want to hear; what makes us feel good about ourselves.

It could be, however, that this "roaring" is the sound of the Holy Spirit, alive and well, flowing through your life, like the wind in the forest; inspiring you to be as busy as a bee in your work for Him. Wherever God has placed you, no matter how insignificant or important the work may seem to you, a life that is filled with the murmur of His Spirit will please the Lord and will be much richer than one with a serious type of heart murmur.

- As I sit quietly before the Lord, do I detect a "heart murmur" of any kind in my life?
- What areas of my life are determining the type of "murmur" that I'm sensing?
- *Lord, show me where I need to change my life to turn the serious "murmur" I have into the flow of the Holy Spirit.*

Read: Genesis 26:12-33

Heart Health: A Plugged Heart

"A new heart also will I give you...I will take away the stony heart...and...give you an heart of flesh."
- Ezekiel 36:26

Sometimes our hearts will become plugged by "disease," stopping the flow of God's blessings, just as Isaac's wells were plugged by his enemies, stopping the flow of water. When the Philistines filled up the wells Abraham had dug, it was a sign that the newcomers were not welcome. It was actually an act of war. The Gerar area was desolate and water was precious. Digging a well there was staking a claim to the land and plugging it up was a serious crime. Instead of striking back, however, Isaac moved on after Abimelech asked him to. They dug a well there and his enemies plugged it up with dirt. Isaac peacefully dug another well and they plugged it, too. Finally, after digging the third well, they left it alone. Isaac was blessed for his patience with plenty of water and with his enemies coming to make peace.

A plugged well in Isaac's time was serious. No water meant death for people and animals. It was essential that the well be unplugged or another well be dug immediately. Allowing our hearts to become plugged with sin is a serious thing also. We need God's love and blessing in our lives, and it is crucial that whatever is blocking that flow be cleared out at once. Being cut off from God results in spiritual death.

The Philistines used dirt to fill wells. Possibly the dirt was already piled there from digging the well and it was easy filler. We have "filler" all around us too, and Satan has no problem using anything to plug our hearts and cut us off from God. *Guilt* is a very effective filler. *Temptations* trip us up; filling us with guilt and a reluctance to face God with yet another failure. *Busyness* crowds out time we should be spending with the Lord, clearing the dirt from our lives and unblocking the flow of communication with Him. *Worry* fills our minds with dark thoughts and fears, and blocks the peace that God has for our hearts. *Meddling* and interfering in another's life can actually block God's plan for him and certainly will not be healthy for us. *Anger, bitterness*, and *offense* are each a huge shovel-full of "dirt" that Satan loves to pitch into our lives. *Pride* will fill us up with ourselves until we can't even see the blockage itself. Don't be deceived. Satan will use absolutely *anything* to block the flow of God's love to you, and he will never give up on his mission. That's why it is so vital to our Spiritual health to keep our hearts free of all impurities and open to God's love and will for our lives. The blessings will flow and our lives will be like a well-watered garden, blessing others as well.

- What "fillers" are plugging my heart today, blocking the flow of God's blessings into my life?
- Am I truly willing to let these things go and allow God to cleanse my heart and bless my life?
- *Lord, show me the fillers that I'm allowing in my life and give me a longing for a pure heart to serve You.*

The Course of Life

"I have fought a good fight, I have finished my course, I have kept the faith."
- II Timothy 4:7

For a certain number of miles in the Boston Marathon, the course is fairly flat, gentle terrain. Then it becomes hilly, getting more rugged until finally a runner comes to Heartbreak Hill. By now, he's likely tired, maybe hurting, and this hill is going to take all the endurance he can muster. But he is determined to push on to the finish line.

We can think of our life as a race. Paul tells us in Hebrews 12 to "Lay aside every weight... and run with patience." Are we carrying extra baggage? Are we holding onto bitterness or anger toward another? Are we stumbling under a backpack full of pride, or tripping over a bad habit that we need to break? We can also get off track if we focus on someone else's course instead of our own. Her course may seem much smoother and brighter than ours. Generally, if we could see the whole picture, we would see that it is not.

It takes endurance to complete this race. We encounter fatigue, pain, and tears. We fall, get up, and go on. And at times, we find ourselves at the foot of Heartbreak Hill. But we don't run alone, and everyone wins! Jesus is there to remove the weights and pick us up when we fall. He'll carry us to the top of Heartbreak Hill. And at the finish line, if we have run faithfully and patiently, He will welcome us into His kingdom. He will give us a crown and we will live eternally with Him. Don't give up!

- What baggage am I carrying that I should surrender to Jesus today?
- How could I better keep my focus on my own course?
- *Lord I thank You for running this race with me and giving me the strength to go on to the finish line.*

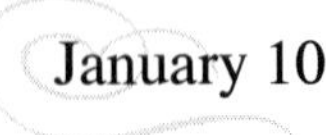

January 10

Read: Psalms 119:33-40

Committed... Or Devoted?

"Stablish thy word unto thy servant,
who is devoted to thy fear."
- Psalm 119:38

I've been meditating lately on the difference between commitment and devotion. My dictionary defines commitment as a responsibility or an obligation, while devotion is defined as commitment with a deep love, dedication, and loyalty. So... devotion is commitment with deep positive feelings attached.

It seems that commitment can actually be a hindrance to devotion. We can be deeply committed to many different causes--good causes that glorify the Lord and further His Kingdom. We can go out of our way to prove our commitment to Him through good works. But if we're lacking in *devotion to* the *Reason for* our commitments, we're going to find ourselves working in our own strength; lacking the power, wisdom, and resources that He has available for us.

Our discipleship is based on devotion to Jesus, not on devotion to causes, beliefs, or creeds. Our commitment to these works and beliefs is born out of our devotion to Jesus Himself. To work effectively in any serving role, whether close to home or across the sea, one must be absolutely dependent on God. This allows us to be used in whatever way He chooses without becoming resentful, discouraged, or bitter. It keeps us serving even when we feel we are not appreciated or properly repaid. When we love Him personally, passionately, and devotedly, we can be used in building His Kingdom in ways that we have never even dreamed of.

Satan loves to confuse us in this concept. If you find yourself feeling discouraged or disenchanted in your walk with the Lord, search your heart. Could it be that you are focusing on your *devotion* to Him rather than on *Jesus* Himself? Remember--the bedrock of Christianity is a personal passionate love for our Lord Jesus Christ Himself. If our lives are completely devoted to Him, He will guide our commitments; and our lives of service will be pleasing to Him, bringing glory and honor to the One who is worthy of all praise and devotion.

- Am I so busy fulfilling my commitments that I'm neglecting my devotion to Jesus?
- Am I willing to allow God to work in me, changing my heart to better please Him?
- *Lord, search my heart and show me where I'm lacking in devotion to You.*

God Our Deliverer

"The Lord is my rock, and my fortress, and my deliverer."
- Psalm 18:2

"Do you know what it is that you're afraid of?" I asked our struggling 13-year-old son. I was sitting on his bed and we had just had a long discussion about a bad choice he had made and was planning to follow through on. I could tell he was weakening, and most likely changing his mind. However, after we ended our discussion with a hug, I sensed that all was not well. He was afraid of his room and the dark…very unusual for him.

I went downstairs and shared with my husband what was going on. Our son came down, too, still afraid and puzzled about his feelings. We explained that Satan was not happy with his change of heart and was probably attacking him with a spirit of fear. He was very willing when we offered to pray with him.

After a time of hands-on prayer, rebuking Satan, the fear left and he was okay again, ready to go back to bed and sleep.

As parents, we need to pray for wisdom to recognize opportunities to show our children God as their deliverer. Growing up is not easy and it seems that teens, especially, are vulnerable targets for Satan's arrows. They are not spiritually mature enough to recognize the enemy's schemes and can fall prey to him without even realizing it. As adults we don't always see it, either! Satan is sly and will attack us in any way he possibly can to cause us to stumble and fall. We have to be on guard at all times, ready to resist the devil and cling to our Rock and Fortress. Pray diligently for His protection from the enemy. God cares and will give us a sensitive heart to understand our own fears and those of our children or others we may be called on to help.

- What experiences have I had that would illustrate God as my deliverer?
- Am I willing and able to help others through struggles they may be going through?
- *Lord, the enemy is so subtle. Open my eyes to see the danger before it overwhelms me.*

 Read: Psalm 16

Clouds

*"For thy mercy is great above the heavens:
and thy truth reacheth unto the clouds."
- Psalm 108:4*

Clouds...in the sky. Sometimes they cover the sun. They are black and foreboding, racing and swirling across the sky. They send down sheets of cold rain and streaks of lightning on a dark, dreary day. They shut out the light, making the world seem a dismal place.

But there is another side to clouds, too. They can be beautiful. White and puffy against an azure sky. They can give us a cool respite from the blazing sun on a hot day. They make a sunset beautiful. They cleanse and refresh the earth with sparkling raindrops. Without clouds there would be no life on this planet!

Clouds...in my life. They seem to cover the Son. Dark and ominous, they swirl through my days, causing hot tears to fall like rain. Pain stabbing through my heart like lightning, making me stumble, and shaking my faith. Can there possibly be any beauty in these clouds?

Yes, there can. We can give these clouds over to Jesus and allow Him to work in our hearts. Praying can bring a peace and comfort that is beautiful beyond measure. Meditating on Scripture can still the tempest raging in our hearts. Our tears can glisten as they gently cleanse our souls. Just as the sun's rays can shine through the darkest clouds, so the Son's love can shine through our darkest days.

- Are there clouds in my life that I need to allow the Son to shine through?
- In what ways could I allow Jesus to shine through these clouds?
- *I praise You, Lord, for shining through the clouds, and I ask You to shine in my life today.*

Read: Matthew 25:31-46 January 13

Encouragement

"Inasmuch as ye have done it unto one of the least of these my brethren, ye have done it unto me."
- Matthew 25:40

I was stressed and exhausted, at the "end of my rope." I had a new baby, a toddler, and another pre-schooler. Plus three more that I was home-schooling. Or at least I was supposed to be. At this point, it was not going well at all. I felt like a complete failure, unable to carry out any of my responsibilities successfully.

As I was sitting in our bedroom one day, sobbing out tears of despair, my husband came in with the mail and handed me an envelope. Shakily, I opened it to find a card of encouragement from a dear sister. She had written a personal note at the bottom which read in part: "you are not a failure."

Although it brought a fresh flood of tears, I felt a healing balm spread over my heart. Someone cared! God cared enough to prompt her to send a card and she cared enough to follow His leading. How could she possibly have known? It couldn't have come at a better time. When I expressed my appreciation sometime later, she said that the card had actually lain on the desk for several days before it was sent. We both marveled at God's timing.

A card, a note, a phone call, a hug, or just a simple "I love you and I care." We may never know the results as we respond to God's promptings, but as we willingly follow His leading, we encourage others, and possibly give them the courage to "keep on keeping on." The encouragement also comes right back to us as God blesses us for our obedience.

- Am I sensitive to God's promptings to respond to someone else's need?
- Do I recognize encouragement from others as a gift from my loving Father?
- *Lord, I thank You for the encouragement You send to me through other people.*

 Read: Acts 3

A Forever Difference

"And he gave heed unto them,
expecting to receive something of them."
- Acts 3:5

Acts 3:1-11 tells the story of a lame man who was carried every day to the gate of the temple. He would spend the day begging from the people going in and out. As Peter and John passed him on their way into the temple to pray one day, he asked them for money. When Peter told him to look at them, he did, expecting to receive something from them. He didn't get what he expected but received something much better! Because Peter had received the gift of the Holy Spirit, he was able to reach out and touch the lame man; giving him the Holy Spirit's healing touch. The man was completely healed, and as he went into the temple rejoicing and praising God, people were amazed and God was glorified. This lame man expected a natural gift of money. What he needed--and received--was a supernatural blessing of healing that made a "forever difference" in his life.

As believers, we have received the gift of the Holy Spirit, also. He wants us to live with the awareness of His presence. Through the Word of God, prayer, and the power of the Holy Spirit, we have access to all the resources we need to "reach out and touch a lame man." If we keep our eyes and hearts open, God will lead us to these "lame men" who may be just waiting to receive something from Him. A lonely elderly person, a sick child, a weary mother. Perhaps you know a hurting teen, a grieving family, or a struggling teacher. We don't have to look far to find someone who deeply needs the healing touch of the Holy Spirit; a supernatural gift that could make a "forever difference" in that person's life.

It's not just others who can receive these supernatural gifts, however. You can too! Is there "lameness" in some area of your life? Is Jesus saying to you, "In the name of Jesus Christ rise up and walk?" Through faith in His name, we can experience the Holy Spirit's healing touch in our lives, too. He can make a "forever difference" if we ask for His help just as the lame man was asking for Peter and John's help. We may be completely amazed at the healing He wants to give us!

- Whom do I know that could use my encouragement or help today to make a "forever difference?"
- Is there an area in my life today that needs a supernatural touch from the Holy Spirit?
- *Lord, help me to be open to Your healing touch today; restore me so that I can minister to others.*

Under His Shadow

"He that dwelleth in the secret place of the most High shall abide under the shadow of the almighty."
- Psalm 91:1

The teacher at our small private school has spent some time with his family at their church's small mission post in Kenya, Africa. As he and the school children were studying through Psalm 91 in their morning devotions, he told them this story:

A woman living in a small mountain village in Kenya near the mission post had a drunken husband. She had been a drinker, too, until she gave her life to the Lord and was baptized. However, she continued to make and sell homemade liquor that she would brew up in her little still. Finally, God convicted her that what she was doing was wrong, and she found another way to make a little money. She would ride a taxi down the bumpy mountain roads into a larger village, buy some chickens at the market, take them back to her home village, and resell them. This was much more difficult than brewing liquor at home as she also had a baby to carry along, but she persevered, knowing she was making an honest living.

One day as she walked into the market to buy her chickens, she had a strong feeling that she was not to buy those chickens. She was quite puzzled as she had just spent a lot of time and money just to get there. But the feeling persisted, so she got back on the taxi, with her baby, to go home empty-handed. As the loaded-down truck labored back up the mountain, they came to a notoriously dangerous stretch of road. As they chugged along, they were attacked by a small band of thieves. The woman was terrified as she had all her "chicken money" with her. Having no time to think about what to do, she stuffed it into her baby's diaper! The passengers were ordered to lay on the ground and were searched by the thieves. It was a frightening experience but her money was safe, and she and her baby were unharmed.

This woman had made a choice, probably a tough choice, to give up her old life and to "dwell in the secret place of the most High." His shadow of protection was covering her as she obeyed His voice in the market, went home without the chickens, and as she lay on the ground with her hidden money. She could have lost it all.

The same shadow of protection is available to you, wherever you live and whatever your circumstances. Staying within His will keeps you under the shadow of His protection.

- Is there any area of my life that I know deep in my heart is outside of God's will for me?
- How can I resolve these areas to bring myself more completely into the center of God's will?
- *Lord, show me any unprotected areas of my life and lead me back into Your full protection.*

God's Wealth

"Ask, and it shall be given you; seek, and ye shall find;
knock, and it shall be opened unto you."
- Luke 11:9

In II Kings 7, we read the story of four lepers who sat outside the gate of Samaria. Because of attacks on the city by the Syrian army, there was no food in Samaria. The lepers knew they were destined to die. So they decided to go to the camp of the Syrian army and surrender. Perhaps they would be killed but just maybe they would be allowed to live.

Imagine their surprise when they arrived at the camp to find it deserted! God had caused the Syrians to hear a great noise that sounded like horses and chariots. Since the Syrians thought they were being attacked, they fled. Although the lepers could hardly believe their eyes, they went from tent to tent, eating and carrying out money and clothes. It must have seemed like a gold mine! Then they went back to Samaria with the good news of what they had found, sharing the wealth with the rest of the city folks.

Can we, as God's people, tap into wealth such as they found? Yes, we can. By taking hold of God's Word---by reading and applying it to our lives. And through prayer, asking in faith and allowing God to work His will in our lives. Then we can share with others our experiences, answers to prayer, and nuggets of truth we have uncovered. The riches are there, available to all, just waiting to be discovered and shared!

- Am I earnestly searching for the riches of God through Bible study and prayer?
- Am I willing and ready to share those riches with others in my life?
- *Lord, I thank You for sharing Your wealth with us. Help me to recognize opportunities to share with others.*

Sharing The Wealth

"Their eyes stand out with fatness:
they have more than heart could wish."
- Psalm 73:7

This Scripture is speaking of the wicked, but we can possibly apply it to ourselves a bit more than we'd like! I read an article recently which reported that the country of America contains just five percent of the world's population, but is blessed with fifty-four percent of the world's wealth. And American Christians have eighty percent of the wealth of the world's Christian population. It's sobering to think that while we are feasting at our bountiful carry-in meals, in countries like Thailand, some people are thankful for the protein from a meal of roasted rat! Many of the world's people eat a diet consisting mostly of rice and beans and wear clothes we would consider rags. The modern conveniences we consider necessities are unheard of in these places.

Just what are we doing with the wealth God has given us? What does God want us to do with it? Are we willing to do with less ourselves so that we can share with others? Perhaps God is prompting us to help someone with a gift of money, provide a meal for a new neighbor, or transportation for the elderly. Or maybe a gift for the new baby at church, or school supplies for the local mission. With a willingness to share and follow God's promptings, we can bless the lives of others in countless ways. In addition to blessing the lives of others, those blessings come back to warm our sharing hearts and lives as well.

- Do I think of all my blessings as "wealth" from God?
- How can I share with others the wealth with which God has blessed me?
- *Lord, I thank You for all with which You have blessed me, and I want to be willing to share it with others.*

What's Gotten Into You?

"If we live in the Spirit,
let us also walk in the Spirit."
- Galatians 5:25

Have you ever looked at one of your children, or your husband, or a friend and asked, "What's gotten into you?" Has anyone ever asked you that? This question can be asked in amusement or joy, but also in frustration or anger. What's "gotten into you" can be any number of things that are causing you to act in a way that's different from the norm, drawing the attention of those around you. This may be a good thing or a not-so-good thing depending on what it is that's "gotten into you!"

There is something that has "gotten into" every believer that is a good thing. We have the Holy Spirit dwelling in us causing us to act in a way that's different from the worldly norm. This way of living is the *fruit of the Spirit* produced by the Holy Spirit working in us. This fruit is the manifestation of the character qualities of Jesus shining through us that are noticeable to others.

Paul says in this chapter that the fruit of the Spirit is ***LOVE***...a feeling that is sacrificial, warm, and compassionate in our dealing with others. ***JOY***...an emotion of great happiness or pleasure not only for circumstances in our own lives, but in the lives of others also. ***PEACE***...a mental state of calmness and serenity, even in the midst of turmoil. ***LONG SUFFERING***...patiently enduring wrongs or difficulties in your life. ***GENTLENESS***... being kind and gentle in nature or manner. ***GOODNESS***...a quality of virtue, kindness, and integrity. ***FAITH***...a belief in and devotion to God. ***MEEKNESS***...being mild, gentle, and humble in nature. ***TEMPERANCE***...moderation and self-control in the face of temptation.

This fruit is not something we can get just by trying. If we want the fruit of the Spirit to grow in us, we must yield our lives to Him. In order to fulfill the great commands of loving God and loving man, we must *know Him, love Him, and submit our hearts to Him.* Being rich in the fruit of the Spirit enables us to fulfill these commands. As we submit every aspect of life to God, the Holy Spirit is given freedom to overflow our hearts in blessing to others.

- Does my life reflect the fruit of the Spirit?
- Which of these qualities do I want the Spirit to produce more fully in me?
- *Lord, my desire is that these qualities shine through me in all areas of my life. Mold me into Your very likeness.*

God, Our Protector

"For he hath said, I will never leave thee, nor forsake thee."
- Hebrews 13:5

While we were on a trip to the West Coast, our oldest son and I had gone to a laundromat while my husband stayed in the motel with our other children. While we were there, alone, we were "visited" by a strange man. I felt some fear as he stood between us and the door, talking with a slurred voice and asking for money for food. He told us he'd been in jail for harassing a woman and had just gotten out! I sent up some heart-felt prayers as I offered him a package of cookies from the van and watched him stagger across the street to a gas station. I was quite relieved when the kind laundromat owner returned, and I shakily told him what had happened. I was further relieved when he assured me he would stay until we were finished. Later, as we watched police officers search the strange man, hand-cuff him, and take him away, I thanked God for His protection.

During the same trip, our three-year-old once wandered away from us, unnoticed, in a two-story motel. After some frantic searching, we found him downstairs with the friendly employees behind the check-in desk, our van keys in his hand! Once again, we thanked God for His protection.

Although most of us have had experiences where we have felt God's protection, we don't always know when or how He is protecting us. We can be sure, however, that He will never allow anything to happen to us that is outside of His will. We can be assured that He will keep His promise to "*never leave, nor forsake us.*"

- What situations have I experienced that revealed God's protection in my life?
- Do I recognize God's protection in my life and thank Him for it?
- *Thank You, Lord, for your promise of protection every day of my life.*

 Read: Ephesians 4:17-32

Toss Those Rocks, Part I

*"And be renewed in the spirit of your mind;
and that ye put on the new man."
- Ephesians 4:23,24*

Paul was telling the Corinthian brethren in this letter that, since they were no longer Gentiles, they should be living as Christians, not the way they had lived in the past. We must discard the old life as you would throw away a filthy, old coat. Since our words and actions all begin in the mind, Paul tells us we need to be renewed in the spirit of our minds. We should put on our new life of righteousness and holiness as we would put on a clean, new coat. God wants each one of us to be completely filled with His Spirit, allowing Him to work through us to bring glory to Himself and to influence others to live for Him. Any sin that we're harboring will block His Spirit and keep us from living a true Spirit-filled life. Let me illustrate.

Picture with me an empty pitcher that represents your life. Now picture a small pile of large stones beside it with words painted on them. Words like *anger* (hostile feelings) *malice* (a desire to harm another), *wrath* (intense anger or rage), *clamor* (loud demands or complaints), *bitterness* (harsh resentment), *lying* (deception of *any* kind), *stealing* (taking *anything* that isn't yours: including reputations, by damaging them through gossip or slander), *evil speaking* (deliberate insults and cutting words), *corrupt communication* (any filthy talking), and *grieving the Spirit* (by ignoring what you know is God's will for you). And finally, think of a pitcher of water sitting at the side with "Holy Spirit" written on it. Now, being completely honest with yourself, pick up any of these or any other stones that represent sins you are allowing in your life. Put them into the empty pitcher marked "my life." Now pick up the pitcher of water and slowly pour it over the rocks until the container is full. There. Now "my life" is filled with the "spirit," right? Let's find out. Pour out the water into another pitcher of the same size and shape. Is this container full? If it is, praise the Lord! You've conquered the sin in your life and are living in victory. If it's not (which will be the case for most of us) we need to examine those rocks, remove them and toss them far away. Now that sounds pretty easy but how, exactly, do you do that when the "rocks" are actually sin in your life? God has provided a way! First, you need to recognize those rocks and acknowledge them as sin. True repentance and confession to God and anyone else involved will empty your life of those sins and allow you to be completely Spirit-filled.

- What "rocks" can I identify in my life that need to be tossed out?
- Am I willing to take them out, examine them, and get rid of them through repentance and confession?
- *Lord, my desire is to live this Spirit-filled life. Please help me get rid of these rocks and fill me with your Spirit.*

Toss Those Rocks, Part II

*"And be renewed in the spirit of your mind;
and that ye put on the new man."
- Ephesians 4:23,24*

As we sit quietly and observe the container of rocks and water, we have a desire to remove the rocks so that the water can fill the container. The desire spreads to our hearts, and we know that we also want to get rid of the sin in our lives so that the Holy Spirit can completely fill us. We know God has provided the way. We know we must recognize the words on those rocks--meaning the sins in our lives. We know we must acknowledge those sins and repent of them. But what exactly *is* this way that God has provided? Just what are these sins we're looking for?

These sins are like rocks. They are the *hard* areas in one's life that are *unyielded,* such as refusing to yield my entire life to God. My time, my finances, my body, my talents, and my family, should all be given to Him to do with as He pleases, even if His will doesn't line up with mine. Areas that are *unrefined*, such as our manners or speech. Do they glorify God at all times? Maybe there's an area where I'm just plain *stubborn*. Submission to my husband is an area where I face this test. Especially if I'm quite certain I'm right on a matter! At times we know that God is asking us to change something in our lives and it's pretty easy to be stubborn. "Not now, Lord, what would people think? Maybe later when I'm older or circumstances have changed."

These hard areas don't always show up as glaring faults. Satan doesn't want us to recognize them at all. But we can identify them by reading God's Word, letting it speak to us personally and allowing the Spirit to convict us of the areas in our lives where we have failed to live as we should. God has a way of making those "rocks" appear. Then we must acknowledge that we *are guilty* of these sins. As we pick up these rocks from our lives and repent of them, He will forgive us and toss our sins "as far as the east is from the west," (Psalms 103:12) and He will not remember them any longer. (Isaiah 43:25) Each confessed sin makes room for the Holy Spirit to dwell in us more fully.

Now a warning. Don't pick those rocks up and allow them back into your life! If you drop a rock into the water filled container, water will flow out the spout. And so will the Holy Spirit be squeezed out of your life with every rock of sin that you allow back in. Don't let those rocks keep you from being a new person. Read, discover, acknowledge, repent, and be made new by the life transforming power of God's Holy Word.

- Am I searching my heart in an open honest way to find any "rocks" hidden there?
- In what ways can I allow God to show me how I must change to become a new woman?
- *Lord, I want to be a new woman before You. Please reveal the rocks and help me toss them out of my life.*

More Lovable Than A Pig?

"And hath raised us up together, and made us sit together in heavenly places in Christ Jesus."
- Ephesians 2:6

I recently read the testimony of a friend who had an experience that opened her eyes a little more to how little of God's love our minds can truly grasp. She was standing on the bottom rail of the fence, out at the barn, looking down at the dozens of upturned dirty little snouts of the pigs. They had come running over, delighted for a new diversion, and were all watching her with wary little pig eyes. As they stood there and looked at each other, she wondered what was going through their minds. She thought of all she knew that the pigs didn't. They didn't even know where they came from, where they were going, or why. They did know where their food and water was and where to find their beds, and they had their pecking order established. Unable to comprehend a world or intelligence above their own, the pigs were quite satisfied that they knew all there is to know.

With riveting clarity she saw something of how we must appear to God and she was again amazed at the utter awesomeness of Who He is. She tried to imagine loving those pigs as God loves us--crawling into the pen with them, sharing their food, and attempting to help them. How unthinkable to love them enough to allow them to turn on her with mindless vengeance and kill her when it was in her power to prevent it.

If we feel more lovable than a filth-encrusted pig, it is because we don't know how abhorrent a sin-covered soul appears to a Holy God! We even tend to act like pigs, running around in our daily lives, content that we know all we need to know about Him and His ways. In spite of all our ugliness, Jesus loves us enough that He came to earth to live among us, share our food, and help humanity in a multitude of ways. Then, in an act of supreme love, He allowed mankind to turn on Him with a vengeance and kill Him, even though He had the power to prevent it. We can't begin to comprehend the marvelous love that lifts us up out of the pigpen, cleanses us with His own precious blood, and invites us to sit together in heavenly places in Christ Jesus. And it is all ours if we only accept it.

- Do I see myself as the sinful creature I really am?
- How deep is my comprehension of how much God loves me?
- *Lord, I thank You and praise You for Your incredible love for me, a sinful creature. Help me to sense it more fully.*

Returning Good For Evil

"But I say unto you which hear, love your enemies, do good to them which hate you."
- Luke 6:27

A friend of mine was sharing with me something her young daughter had recently experienced. She had a couple of friends at school that she normally played with. One day, however, she kindly chose to play with another little girl who looked lonely. One of her other friends, it seems, didn't appreciate the switch in loyalty. The girl was unkind and told her that they hated her. She was crushed, and as she and her mother talked about it, they came up with a plan. They would have a tea party and invite this unhappy little girl to the party!

Our little friend was up at 6:00 a.m. that Saturday morning to make cookies and other refreshments for her guests. The tea party was a big success. The girls had a wonderful time playing games and eating their refreshments. And before she left, the little girl who had been unkind returned an invitation to a party of her own! Their wounded little hearts had been healed and they were friends again.

I was deeply impressed. As mothers, it's hard to see our children go through painful experiences and easy for us to get angry and bitter toward the wrong doers. Jesus, however, says to love our enemies and do good to those which hate us. What a lesson it is to our children and others, when we obey that command and witness the blessing of good results. This mother could have reacted angrily and taught her daughter the wrong response. Instead she chose to act in a way that would teach her daughter the way Jesus would have responded. Either way will have lasting effects on our children or others around us. Which way will we choose?

- How do I respond to someone who is unkind to me or to someone I love? Do I become bitter or respond kindly?
- Am I taking the time to teach my children the things that really matter?
- *Lord, this can be a hard thing, but I want to be a good example of Your love to those around me.*

Read: Acts 1:1-11

Kingdom Advancement

"But ye shall receive power…and ye shall be witnesses unto me…unto the uttermost part of the earth."
- Acts 1:8

After God created the earth, He created man to live on it. The earth belonged to man. Then, Satan entered the scene and, through the fall in the Garden, stole the earth from man. But God, in His great mercy, has provided a way for man to return to Him, and even today Jesus is taking the world back, one soul at a time. Are you helping Him?

Randy was a friendly, robust 51-year-old man who was found dead in his bed by his daughter just last week. He was the only child of his still-living parents. Our minister, a good friend of Randy and his parents, was sitting in his study on Saturday afternoon preparing for the next day's message when he got the phone call about Randy's death. Could he come to be with the family? Now he had a choice to make. Sunday was coming and he needed preparation time, but his friends needed him too. Both good things to do, but he didn't hesitate. He went to his friends.

God wants to advance His Kingdom through you, whether it's as a missionary in a foreign country, in your own home raising children to someday be Kingdom advancers for Him, or simply encouraging others along the way. As Christians, we should desire to be vessels fit for the Master's use. We should *want* to be about the Master's business, but it all has to start with *us*. We must believe that we are no longer "in the flesh," but we are *believers in Christ*. Kingdom advancement begins in our hearts and takes God's power to do His work. He uses those who are willing, and He will supply all the resources needed whether it be money, time, energy, or just plain courage. He wants to use *you*!

Death is a sobering event that should bring a sense of urgency to our hearts. Randy's life is over. No longer can he work in God's Kingdom. Neither can he receive encouragement from others. Most of us don't spend much time thinking about death. We naturally dwell on *life* and all the happenings going on around us. Our family is in the midst of planning a wedding, and the evidence is all through the house. We're thinking about *life* not death! But just one simple phone call could immediately change our thoughts and actions. And the fact is…we don't know how long we have to live. The time to be God's witness is *now*. Stay in tune with Him. Be aware of His nudges and requests for your help. When you need to make a choice, choose the top priority and *go*, trusting Him to supply all your needs.

- Am I willing to be a vessel fit for the Master's use?
- What is God asking me to do today that will further His Kingdom?
- *Lord, my desire is to be a helper in Your Kingdom. Show me what to do and supply me with what I need.*

Bring Your Vessels, Not A Few

"But my God shall supply all your need according to his riches in glory by Christ Jesus."
- Philippians 4:19

The first seven verses of II Kings 4 tell the story of a widow who was so poor that she had no money or food in the house. All she had was a pot of oil. Have you ever read this story putting yourself in her place? Imagine the despair she must have felt with a man at her door demanding money. And the panic when he said he'd take her two sons and sell them as slaves to pay the debt! It must have been a deep relief to be able to confide in Elisha. But I wonder how she felt about his command to borrow all those pots. Did she feel a bit foolish, wondering how she'd explain this odd request if nothing happened? I admire her faith in deciding to trust God and do as Elisha said. I wish I could have seen the looks on their faces as she and her boys watched that oil flow and flow, never stopping until the last pot was full. And we can only wonder at the gratitude to God she must have felt for meeting her need in such a way.

What a blessing to know that God still wants to meet our every need. He wants us to bring all our vessels to Him. Bring your pain, your loneliness, your guilt, your weariness, and your frustrations. Bring all your problems large or small. Then open your heart so that the oil of God's love can fill you rather than just coating the outside. God's supply of oil will never run dry as you allow Him to fill all the empty places in your life.

- What empty vessels do I have in my life that I could allow God to fill out of His sufficiency?
- Do I really believe that He can fill them to overflowing?
- *Lord, teach me to allow you to fill my empty vessels with your love.*

January 26 *Read: Philippians 2:12-18*

An Attitude Adjustment

"Now our Lord Jesus Christ himself...stablish you in every good...work."
- II Thessalonians 2:16-17

Whack! "Mutter mutter." Punch! "Grumble grumble." I was kneading dough for the pizza pockets my husband had requested. Snap! "Now cut that out, you're getting pizza at young folks." I told my teenager. Slap! "Stop that! Just get down and go play. I'm busy," I snarled at my preschoolers.

My husband was oblivious to the storm going on in the house. He had no idea that I'd planned to finish sewing a dress that Saturday. Or that I was already frustrated with all the delays and interruptions from the baby and the other children. When he innocently suggested, on his way to the barn, that pizza pockets sounded good, the battle raged inside over what I knew I *should* do and what I *wanted* to do. But I finally just gave up. I shifted into my "wounded martyr mode" and I made those pizza pockets. But I was not happy. Later, ignoring his sincere comments of appreciation, I silently tried to let him know just how much I'd sacrificed and suffered...though it didn't seem at all like he was catching on.

The next morning God spoke to me through a devotional about guarding my attitude. *Uh-oh*. He reminded me that quiet, willing service from a sincere servant is much more pleasing to Him than the noisy, begrudging work of a sour one. *Gulp*.

Convicted and ashamed, I confessed my bad attitude. After receiving forgiveness from God (who knew all about it) and my husband (who really hadn't caught on!), peace reigned in my heart once again. Even though we try our best to live a life of sincere servanthood, unfortunately, we need an attitude adjustment now and then. How amazing is the tranquility our hearts can experience when we humble ourselves in repentance and make restitution with those we have wronged.

- Do I willingly submit my heart to an attitude adjustment when necessary?
- Am I allowing any bad attitudes to affect my thoughts and actions today?
- *Help me, Lord, to guard my attitude toward any service that You ask of me today.*

True Riches

"Lay not up for yourselves treasures upon earth...But lay up for yourselves treasures in heaven."
- Matthew 6:19,20

We are dairy farmers, and we rely on the two milk checks we get each month to pay the bills and supply our needs. Sometimes milk prices are good and there's enough money to stretch and some left over. But right now prices are low; in fact they've been low for too long, and the money doesn't reach as far as we wish it would. My husband sits at his desk shuffling bills and punching numbers into the calculator and tries to decide who gets what this time. It's easy to get discouraged. It's easy to think "We don't *have* money to tithe." It's easy to spend too much time thinking of ways to make a little extra and spend a little less. It's too easy to lose our focus on what's really important.

The right focus, however, became more clear again as we heard a message at church yesterday on true riches. The minister didn't preach a sermon on making money, either! He talked about *contentment, faith, and generosity*. Wealth is not a bad thing; after all, it was God's idea. All the wealth in the world belongs to Him and He distributes it among the people on earth as He sees fit. More important than how much money we have, of course, is how we use what God has given us. Paul reminds us in this chapter that we need to be content with what we have, realizing that none of it will be of any use to us when we reach the end of our lives anyway. We need to be careful about what we'll do to get more money and be willing to freely share what we have with those in need.

Verse eleven of this chapter lists the true riches that we should be seeking after. God's storehouse of riches will never be empty. Money and valuable possessions can be stolen and never seen again, but no one can take these true riches from us. The love of money is the root of all kinds of evil such as envy and selfishness but desiring God's treasures is godliness and great gain. Many rich people die lonely, unhappy, and fearful, having never experienced the true peace and happiness of laying up their treasures in heaven. A large bank account doesn't guarantee peace.

Examine your heart. Do you love people more than money? Do you love God's work more than money? Does money really provide you with security? Invest in God's riches and watch your spiritual bank account grow beyond anything you ever expected!

- What is my true attitude toward money?
- Am I satisfied with what I have, or do I crave more and think about it often?
- *Lord, help me to remember that true riches come from You and to focus on that instead of what I don't have.*

Transformation

"And be not conformed...but be ye transformed by the renewing of your mind."
- Romans 12:2

On a cold, quiet morning, Ronda looked out her window to a winter wonderland. It had snowed during the night, and the front yard was a place of ethereal beauty. All the normal, mundane things of the world were covered in pure, sparkling white. The sunlight bounced off the pristine loveliness, shattering into millions of diamonds. As Ronda stood there drinking in the sight, she thought about how much this was like the transformation of a soul in Christ Jesus. The muddy ruts and brown dead-looking grass of our lives are dressed in a robe of pure, spotless white.

As Ronda watched, a truck drove up the lane. The snow cover was not thick, and behind the truck appeared two muddy tracks, scarring the portrait of unblemished beauty. Looking at the ugly, dirty lines that bisected her view, she realized that the purity was only an illusion. Beneath it, the same dirt still existed, just as the dirt of sin can remain in our lives under a thin coating of righteousness. Paul tells us in Romans 12 to be transformed by the renewing of our minds. Through Christ we are made clean from the inside out. What a blessing that the cleansing we receive through Jesus is a complete transformation, not just a light covering easily brushed away by the circumstances in our lives. Then as we draw near to God daily, *"The peace of God, which passeth all understanding, shall keep our hearts and minds through Christ Jesus."* (Philippians 4) What a lovely picture of a wonderful promise God has given us!

- Have I allowed Jesus to truly renew my mind and heart, or do I have only a "frosting" of righteousness?
- Am I more concerned that I look righteous or that my heart is pure?
- *Lord, change me completely; make me a new creature in Christ.*

Prayer Is The Bridge

"Consider and hear me,
O Lord my God."
- Psalm 13:3

David was in total despair. It's hard for us to imagine a life of running and hiding from enemies. David's Psalms clearly show us the intense emotional ups and downs he experienced, fleeing from Saul. He battled times of fear, anger, and exhaustion as well as times of confidence, elation, and joy.

This Psalm opens with a clear picture of deep weariness and discouragement. Four times in the first two verses David cries, "How long?" He feels cut-off from God and forgotten. He is depressed and tired of trying to figure things out. He is completely worn out from being on the losing side.

Three verses later, David is praising God in complete confidence of His mercy and deliverance! He is singing and rejoicing in the bountiful goodness of God.

What was the bridge between the protests and the praise here? It was *prayer.* In the middle two verses, David's prayer turns from protest to petition. He pleads for God to send help quickly lest his eyes be closed forever in death. Unless the tide turned, David's enemies will soon be rejoicing in their triumph over him.

By expressing his feelings to God in prayer, David is reminded of His goodness and His unwavering faithfulness. He chooses to continue trusting God to bring him through.

In times of despair it can be much easier to give up than to hold on. We protest our situation and feel the same impatience David felt when it seems God is moving too slowly or not at all. But we, like David, can choose to trust that God is working things out for good in our lives. We can let prayer be the bridge from our protests to our praises. We can quit fretting and start praising! It may not change our circumstances as it likely didn't change David's right away, but it can change our outlook and give us a peace that comes only from complete faith in God.

- Do I truly understand the power of prayer?
- What distressing situation in my life could be made easier by changing my protests to praise?
- *Lord, praising is difficult when I feel like protesting, but please accept my feeble attempts at praising You.*

January 30

Read: Acts 13:1-12

How To Be God's Echo

"And when they had fasted and prayed...
they sent them away."
- Acts 13:3

Each one of us is an echo. The way we live our lives; the way we think, speak, and act is either an echo for God or an echo for our enemy. I like to think that my life is a clear, distinct echo of God. But if I think about it a little longer and a little more honestly, I have to admit that my echo gets dim, hazy, and wobbly all too often. It can go from clear to faint in a day; sometimes in an hour or less. How many times do I speak sweetly to a friend on the phone, encouraging and supporting her; then hang up and scold my children harshly for their behavior; or give my husband the silent treatment? (Of course I hang up the phone first. I wouldn't want my friend to *know* my echo isn't perfect!)

None of us wants to be an echo for Satan. We want to be a clear, effective echo for the Lord. So, how do we *become* that echo? Acts 13:2 tells us that before Saul and Barnabas were sent off on their missionary journey, they were together ministering to the Lord. They were *worshiping, fasting*, and *praying*. They were *open and receptive* when the Holy Spirit spoke to them. They were *obedient,* leaving to follow God's plan after more fasting and prayer. They left, filled with the Holy Spirit; under His *influence,* with the *authority* He gave them, and in the *direction* that He sent them. Bar-Jesus, on the other hand, was under the influence, authority, and direction of Satan. When he opposed Paul and Barnabas, Paul boldly rebuked him in the name of Jesus.

If we want to be a bold echo, many of us will have to be *willing* to change our ways. God calls us to set our minds on the things of the Spirit, "bringing into captivity every thought to the obedience of Christ." (II Corinthians 10:5) We can't do this in our own strength but, with God's help, we can follow the example of Paul and Barnabas. Living in a spirit of worship and prayer, fasting, and searching His Word opens doors to the Holy Spirit's leading.

Are you willing to be God's echo, glorifying Him and turning people's hearts to Him? Thinking a little deeper; are you willing to change your ways--maybe spending more time seeking Him in Bible study and prayer, through worship and fasting? Being a clear echo for the Lord requires a price. But the blessings and the richness you'll experience from it will repay that price many times over!

- Am I enjoying the blessings that come with being an effective echo for the Lord?
- In what ways could I be more open and receptive to the Holy Spirit?
- *Lord, my heart's desire is for You to show me how to become a clearer, more distinct echo in Your service.*

Grieving God

"Let no corrupt communication proceed out of your mouth, but that which is good to the use of edifying, that it may minister grace unto the hearers. And grieve not the Holy Spirit of God."
- Ephesians 4:29-30

I was intrigued by the concept of grieving God as I listened to a friend share what she had experienced. In talking with her sons, she had related an incident concerning a friend of hers. The story drew mild explosions from the boys as they verbally attacked and tromped on her friend. Since she loved this person and had not meant to be critical or unkind, their reaction grieved her.

As she pondered what had happened, she was struck by a sobering thought. How often do we grieve our Heavenly Father by what we say? How often do we verbally or even mentally attack another person? That person is God's creation just as we are! It must grieve Him to hear us assault anyone else. How about when we complain about the weather? God knows that without rain we couldn't live, and He meets an important basic need when He sends it. Yet we grumble about a rainy day and wish for the sun. It must grieve Him to hear that. Or when we grumble about our daily duties as wives and mothers. God gave us our husbands and children as gifts, and it must grieve Him to hear us complain about caring for them. We'll surely be happier if we praise Him for His goodness rather than grieving him with our grumbling!

- What attitudes do I need to change that would help me to praise more and complain less?
- Am I willing to face those attitudes and work at changing them?
- *Lord change my complaints and criticism into praise and adoration.*

February

Beating Back The Wilderness

"Be ye therefore followers of God,
as dear children."
- Ephesians 5:1

The pioneers of our country had an enormous job in carving their homesteads out of the wilderness. I can only imagine how strong those women must have been or how weary and discouraged they must have felt at times. Imagine arriving at your new home after an exhausting journey with small children. Now you're standing on your home site and all you see is trees and brush and rocks to be cleared before you can even build a little cabin or plant your crops.

Months pass as you work beside your husband felling trees, clearing land, carrying rocks, and planting the precious seeds you brought with you. You dream about a real house as you continue to live out of your covered wagon or possibly in a tiny, dark dugout with a sod roof and dirt floor. The crops must go in first, you know. Finally, one glad day, you move your belongings into your brand new cabin. You rejoice as you stand outside with your husband and children, gazing contentedly at the tidy little homestead. All your hard work has paid off.

Along with the feeling of satisfaction, however, is the knowledge that much hard work lies ahead to keep the wilderness from reclaiming the little farm. Small trees and brush must be cleared away every spring and rocks carried out of the field before planting. Farmers today face the same challenges to keep their fields clear and productive. Slacking off just a little will result in losing valuable ground. Rocks must be cleared from the fields, sometimes every spring. There's a never ending battle with weeds and other invaders threatening to take over the land.

As Christians we fight a similar battle. When we first invite Jesus into our hearts, His blood cleanses us and makes us pure and clean from all the trash and debris that had been polluting our lives. It is a wonderful feeling, but we don't dare just sit back, relax and enjoy it! Just as the wilderness tried hard to reclaim the settler's land, so our enemy tries hard to reclaim our souls. It gets discouraging at times as we face those rocks of bitterness, pride, and negative thoughts. We sweat as we chop away at the roots of materialism and moral failure. Our spiritual muscles ache from fighting back the giant weeds of anger and discontent. It's a hard life of battling the enemy of our souls. But, just as the settlers enjoyed the deep satisfaction of their hard work, so we can enjoy the rich beauty and deep blessings of a life in Christ. The peace and contentment of a life lived in His service is priceless. Don't miss out on it!

- What do I see creeping into (or already growing in) my life that threatens to overtake my peace?
- What steps do I need to take to get rid of these invaders?
- *The wilderness gets so thick at times, Lord. Please give me the strength and courage to keep beating it back.*

February 2 *Read: Matthew 5:38-48*

What Would Jesus Do?

"Be not overcome of evil,
but overcome evil with good."
- Romans 12:21

"I just threw a snowball over the schoolhouse roof. You didn't have to come around there and hit me hard with an ice ball!" The angry words flew as I listened to my sons "explain" what had happened at school that day. They were not happy and each was hoping I would take his side.

"I didn't hit you that hard, and you sure didn't have to throw your ping-pong paddle at me! Now I have a big bruise on my leg. I did not deserve it, and your paddle is going to disappear tonight, and you won't see it again, ever!" His brother fired back determined to get revenge.

The next morning the ping-pong paddle was indeed missing, but the owner found it in his brother's book bag and revengefully hid it in his own closet. Then he gleefully told me about it.

"Son," I said. "I know how you feel, but you are both in the wrong, and revenge will not give either one of you peace. Think about what Jesus would do and try His way. I'd like for you to take that paddle, apologize to your brother, and tell him he can have it."

Well, that went over like a lead balloon at first, but after discussing it some more, my son decided to follow my counsel. Later that evening, he apologized and gave up the paddle. He was forgiven and ended up having the ping-pong paddle returned to him!

A bit surprised myself at how it had turned out, I had to think that often our natural reaction, after we have been wronged, is to get even. But Jesus said we should do good to those who wrong us, to love and forgive them. This is the only way to have true peace in our hearts.

- Am I willing to forgive and pray for those who wrong me?
- Is there anyone in my life that I need to forgive today?
- *Lord, my desire is to forgive anyone who has wronged me.*

Blocking The View, Part I

"See that ye love one another with a pure heart fervently."
- I Peter 1:22

Satan's goal is to block our view of Jesus in any way he can so as to confuse us, discourage us, and get us headed down the wrong road. We're much easier to manipulate if we are not focused on Jesus and following His plan for us. It's a challenge to stay focused ourselves, but it's also a challenge to live so that we don't block the view of Jesus for someone else.

One obstructive way to block another's view of Jesus is through ***criticism or gossip***. Unfortunately, when we've been criticized or treated unfairly, it's easier to focus on the offender than to see past the hurt and focus on Jesus, the Healer. We want to strike back, and we do so in our minds even if we never would in action. I've held many useless, spiteful conversations in my head that didn't go any further. All they did was wear me out and leave me beaten down and discouraged. And unfocused. Then I wonder…how many times have I caused someone else to lose their focus through my careless speech or actions? How many times have I blocked the view of Jesus?

On the other hand, we can magnify the view by building others up. By an encouraging word or note when we know a friend is going through a rough time. By praising our children when we see them obeying cheerfully or treating their siblings lovingly. We can be a friend to young adults, loving them unconditionally, accepting them where they are. We can encourage others in their life of service to the Lord, wherever He has placed them. We can let the love of Jesus shine through us and spread out, touching everyone with whom we come in contact. Ask God to reveal any critical spirit within you and to give you the strength to break a habit of criticism. Ask Him to show you where you can build up, strengthening His Kingdom and making a difference for eternity! God will bless you for it.

- Do I struggle with a critical spirit, possibly wanting to put others down to make myself feel better?
- How could I encourage someone today, allowing Jesus' love to shine through me?
- *Lord, I fail so often, but my heart longs to magnify others' view of You, rather than blocking it by criticism.*

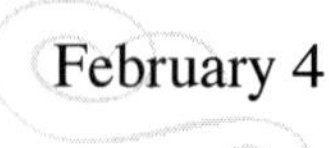

 Read: II Timothy 1

Blocking The View, Part II

"Be not thou therefore ashamed of the testimony of our Lord."
- II Timothy 1:8

Most of the ways we block another's view of Jesus is by something we *do*, but there is one way we can keep others from seeing Him by what we *don't do*. By *hiding our testimony* we are actually missing an opportunity to give others a glimpse of Jesus and what He can and longs to do for all of us. We disappoint Him when we ignore His nudge to share His goodness, to give Him glory, or to bless the lives of others. We have no way of knowing just how our story may affect someone else. Whether it's an inspiring thought that God brought to your mind, an insight into something puzzling, a little miracle that He did just for you, or an amazing solution to a major problem. Maybe it's just simply God's faithfulness day after day as He helps you over one hurdle after another. Life gets wearisome, monotonous, and sometimes lonely. Hearing someone's testimony can be like a ray of sunshine in your cloudy day. It can inspire you to go on, with fresh reassurance that God loves you, too, and is right there for you. Maybe we just need to look for those little miracles and recognize them as being from God. We may need to get back to our habit of quiet time with Him, listening for His voice and praising Him for all He's done. And the testimony of another may be just the nudge we need to do that.

I confess, I write this with a hesitant, even reluctant, heart. Share my testimony? Well, maybe to one person…whom I know will "get it"… if it just happens to come up in a conversation…and if I have the courage. But in a group? To someone who may just look blankly at me, wondering where I'm coming from? *Gulp*. I can come up with a lot of excuses in a very short time! And I've argued with God when I felt His nudge to do so. (It's a one sided argument, He just waits patiently for my choice to share or not to share.) But I've also experienced the peace and blessing that follows sharing a testimony, even if it's only a smile and a simple "The Lord bless your day!" Offering to pray with an elderly shut-in while you're visiting can bring tears of gratitude to their eyes and bless your day, too. A sister who's discouraged may deeply appreciate hearing about a time when you were struggling and what God taught you through that time. Conversations take on a new depth as we move from surface chit-chat to sharing glimpses of Jesus that we've had and allowing others to glimpse Him through us. Don't be afraid to share your testimony!

- Do I feel comfortable talking about God's goodness to me?
- How could I share a glimpse of Jesus with someone in my life today?
- *Lord, I don't want to block anyone's view of You. Give me the courage to share my testimony and glorify You.*

Blocking The View, Part III

"Be thou an example of the believers, in work, in conversation, in charity, in spirit, in faith, in purity."
- I Timothy 4:12

The ***example*** we show in our day-to-day life can very effectively either block the view of Jesus or it can let His love shine through us, magnifying the view that others see of Him. This is true whether we are mothers, dealing with the daily stresses of children, or rubbing shoulders with the world in the workplace, or wherever we are. Unless we choose to be a hermit, we're going to be in contact with other people. The way we treat others, or maybe even more importantly, the way we react to stressful situations, will either block or magnify the view of Jesus.

A friend of mine remembers an incident that made a big impression on her. When she was a young girl, she babysat in a home where the mother was constantly screaming at her children. This actually seemed rather normal to her and she didn't think too much about it. But another family she babysat for had a different sort of mother. She watched once as one of the children accidentally spilled a glass of milk, making a mess of the table, chair, and floor. Mother calmly reassured the child and wiped up the puddles. Amazed at the time, she knows now which children saw Jesus. And I cringe. I don't like to think too much about whether or not my children are seeing Jesus through their mother! I fail so often.

What about others? Am I too busy to care when someone needs help? It's pretty easy to think someone else will surely take a meal to a family with a new baby. "Surely someone closer will help clean that house for the ones who are moving into it." "There have to be others visiting the lonely shut-in, besides, I'll have more time next week." We not only miss a chance to be a blessing to someone, we also miss a chance to give our children a glimpse of Jesus through our willing service. We can be good examples to others who may be looking on by our cheerful willing service to our husbands or the employer at work. We can be a helpful, neighborly neighbor. Let's live the message we speak!

- What kind of example am I showing in the way I live?
- Which areas do I really need to work on to leave a better example to those around me?
- *Lord, I fail so often but I do want to be a good example so that others can see You through me.*

Blocking My Own View

"When thou saidst, Seek ye my face; my heart said unto thee, Thy face, Lord will I seek."
- Psalm 27:8

We've been thinking about how we can block someone else's view of Jesus, but we can also block our own view of Him. Actually, that's probably even easier. We're probably more of a threat to ourselves than to others! How often self gets in the way. Do you ever struggle with self-pity? How about guilt, misplaced or real? Have you ever become so fearful that you're afraid to trust God for the outcome? I'm afraid I'm guilty on all counts.

Self-pity is a destructive thought pattern that comes straight from Satan. It will drag you down into the pit of despair and keep you there. It's terribly hard to keep your focus on Jesus when you're feeling sorry for yourself. We're also in no shape to be used by God when we are wallowing in the muck of self-pity. We're not about to step outside of our little "poor me" box for fear of being bitten. It takes much effort to recognize the sin of self-pity, to repent of it and to ask God for forgiveness. But once we have asked God to cleanse our hearts and minds and allowed Him to blow away the clouds surrounding us, we can *see Him once again* and be useful in His Kingdom. What a blessing that is!

Guilt is a very real part of a woman's life. Sometimes it seems there is no end to the reasons to feel guilty! Some guilt is very necessary to lead us to repentance and confession, but much of the guilt we feel is completely misplaced. All it does is make me feel like a bad person. And it can hinder my view of Jesus. After all, why would He be interested in guilty me? I can't seem to do anything quite right, and I really don't deserve His time or attention. Guilt is just another cloud obscuring our view. Repentance and confession will erase real guilt, and misplaced guilt can be removed by asking God to fill your heart with peace when there is no reason to blame yourself.

Have you ever been so fearful that you're even afraid to trust God? It's hard to completely trust Him with our children or other people dear to us. It's difficult to let go of situations that may change our lives forever, depending on how they turn out. We want so badly to *help* God work out these problems. Trust takes *faith* and it's so hard to have faith when you just can't see any solution. But fear blocks our view of Him and clouds our vision. Choose to give it all to Him in faith. He'll give you peace in your heart even if you still can't see the outcome.

- What areas am I struggling in that are blocking my view of Jesus?
- Am I willing to give everything to Him and let Him help me to victory?
- *Lord, I allow myself to become unfocused so often. Show me where I need to change and give me the courage I need.*

To Be Content

"I have learned, in whatsoever state I am,
therewith to be content."
- Philippians 4:11

It took only a split second. One moment I was skating gracefully along the ice, feeling pretty good about myself, a 49-year-old grandmother of four...*ice-skating!* The next moment I was lying on the ice in an ungainly heap, having fallen *hard* on my knee and shoulder. I managed to hobble off the ice but by the time we arrived home, I could no longer put any weight on my left foot or move my right arm more than a little. Thus began a long recuperation period that included an X-ray showing a kneecap broken into three pieces. Days on the couch feeling helpless. Six weeks in a knee brace keeping my leg straight day and night. A wheelchair...crutches...a cane...and finally just an awkward stiff-legged walk. Then weeks of patience and working to limber up a joint stiff from inactivity. After a few months my shoulder was healed and after about seven months, my knee only occasionally reminded me that I had mistreated it.

For awhile, the forced "vacation" was rather a novelty. I had plenty of time to read and write and relax in my nest on the couch. After awhile, however, it wasn't so much fun. It was back to life as normal but with a definite handicap. It was *hard.* I got tired of it and thought I'd never get out of that brace.

One day when I was feeling particularly grumpy about it, I arrived to help at our Discount Grocery store, where I got a much needed attitude adjustment. At the check-out counter stood a man on crutches. One of his legs ended mid-thigh. He shared with us that he had been building a chimney which had somehow shifted and fallen on him. He felt blessed to have lost only his leg and not his life. Even though life was difficult now for him and his family, his good attitude and cheerful acceptance were amazing and inspiring.

Needless to say, I was no longer grumping about my *temporary* handicap. I had so much to be thankful for. It could have been so much worse. Thanks to our surgeon friend, we were able to get through the whole ordeal for a fraction of what it could have cost. Caring friends brought in meals, and others helped along the way. My husband and children pitched in, helping with housework and taking care of me. And best of all... my knee *healed.* Maybe now I can be more content through the bumps of life.

- Do I struggle with being content regardless of what happens in my life?
- In what situation could I use an attitude adjustment today?
- *Lord, sometimes life gets hard, but I want to be like Paul... "content in whatsoever state I am."*

 Read: I Kings 20

Full Surrender

"My Lord, O King, according to thy saying,
I am thine, and all that I have."
- I Kings 20:4

My mind was on all the work waiting at home as I pulled into the driveway of an elderly widow one Monday morning. Our daughter had spent the night with a friend who was living there as a care-giver, and I was there to pick her up.

"Come on," I thought impatiently. "I don't want to have to come in and get you." Tapping my fingers on the steering wheel, I sensed God gently telling me to go in and say hello to "Grandma." I often wished I had more time to spend with lonely people and here was an opportunity. The previous day's sermon on "full surrender" also came to my mind. So, choosing to ignore the waiting work, I went on in. She was delighted, and we had a lovely little visit. What an inspiration she was as she talked about the Lord and her desire to be with Him. But also her willingness to serve Him here until then. She was touched when I told her that I prayed for her. But when God spoke to me again saying "Pray with her now," I balked.

"Oh really, Lord? Do I have to? I've never prayed *with* her before. That's a bit out of my comfort zone!" But hard on the heels of those thoughts came another reminder of the "full surrender" message. So I asked her if she would like for me to pray with her before I left.

"Oh, yes!" she said eagerly, gripping my hand. Minutes later, as she thanked me with tears in her eyes and a gentle hug, I was reminded once again that full, minute by minute surrender to God's gentle promptings brings blessings far greater than getting the work done at home.

- Do I recognize God's promptings in my life as opportunities to serve Him?
- In what ways could I become more fully surrendered to Him in my daily life?
- *Lord, create in me a deeper desire for full surrender to your will in everything I do.*

Listening For God

"And it shall be, if he call thee, that thou shalt say, Speak, Lord; for thy servant heareth."
- I Samuel 3:9

Eli's sons were grown men who refused to listen to God, even though they knew better. (Samuel 2:22-25) Samuel was just a child, but he faithfully served the priest. When God called to him quietly in the night, little Samuel heard Him and responded immediately, even though he thought it was Eli.

Have you ever thought about how loudly God may have to call to get the attention of your children some day? How loudly or how often do you have to call to get their attention? Some days at our house I'm thinking the call would have to be quite loud to be heard above the din of daily life. Some days, I'm afraid, He has a hard time getting *my* attention.

The way we train our children to listen and respond to us now will reflect in how they listen and respond to God as adults. It will make a difference in whether God will be able to speak softly, as He did for Samuel, or if He has to call loudly to be heard. Or if He's simply ignored or not heard at all.

Perhaps we need to begin with ourselves. Do we quiet ourselves before the Lord on a daily basis? Do we give Him a chance to speak to us through His Word and through prayer? Do we really listen? As we train ourselves and our children to be quiet, to listen, and to respond promptly, God will bless our lives in ways that are not possible if we are too busy or noisy to listen for Him.

- How can I rearrange my days so that I can have adequate quiet time?
- What can I do today to help teach my children to listen and obey promptly?
- *Lord, help me to have the desire to listen to You and to teach my children to listen, also.*

 Read: Genesis 16:1-6; John 11:38-46

Roll Away That Stone

"Said I not unto thee, that, if thou wouldest believe, thou shouldest see the glory of God?"
- John 11:40

Abram and Sarai were puzzled. God had promised Abram an heir but how was that going to happen? They were too old to have a baby. Abram thought that possibly Eliezer, his steward, having been born into his household, was to be his heir, since that was the law at that time. But God said "No," that he would have a son to be his heir. (Genesis 15:2-4) Now, we know that it is hard to just trust when something looks impossible. And this promise looked impossible to Abram and Sarai. Surely God must expect them to help Him out. So Sarai suggested, and Abram agreed, that they should have a son by her handmaiden, Hagar. Their plan worked, however not only did they see their mistake in a very short time, but the results of that decision are still being seen today in the conflict between the descendants of Ishmael and Isaac. It never pays to run ahead of God, thinking that He needs help!

In another instance, recorded in the New Testament, Jesus was standing in front of Lazarus' tomb. The opening of the cave was sealed by a large stone. The weeping group was astonished when Jesus told them to roll that stone away. It was unthinkable! Lazarus had been in there four days, and it would not be a pretty sight or smell. But at Jesus' command the stone was rolled away, and at His call Lazarus came forth, alive and well.

Abram and Sarai took matters into their own hands trying to help God fulfill His promise to them. At the tomb, a large stone stood between the mourners and the miracle Jesus was about to perform. Can you identify with these folks? How many times have we wanted to help God out with a situation that looks impossible to us? We *know* that all things work together for good to them that love God, and we *know* that He loves us and wants only the best for us. On the other hand, there's this big "stone" in the way and how is He ever going to "roll it away?" And what kind of a "stench" is it going to cause if He does? We don't think about how our interference, or even our unbelief, may be hindering His progress in this very situation. God wants us to patiently and quietly wait on Him, allowing the Holy Spirit to work *through* us, not *with* us, in working out His plan to our good and to His Glory. Allow Him to roll away the stones in your life and perform the miracles that He has planned for you.

- What situations do I have in my life that I'd like to help out with?
- What "stones" can I identify that I'm afraid to allow God to "roll away?"
- *Lord, help me not to make a mess of things by trying to work them out in my own way but to give them fully to You.*

Our Vision, Part I

"If any man will come after me, let him deny himself, and take up his cross daily, and follow me."
- Luke 9:23

Our minister gave us a good explanation of this verse as being our vision as Christian disciples. Our greatest foe and hindrance to living a godly life is self. We are all familiar with self-denial. We deny ourselves certain foods or pleasures, knowing they are not good for us. But denial of self is a different story. It's a complete giving of our lives to God and His will for us. It's doing what we know we should do rather than what we want to do. And it's taking the time to seek God's will before we rush headlong into a situation. We may desire to live a life that denies self, staying safely within the will of God, but it takes self-discipline to remain there. Many people love the Kingdom and rejoice in Him, but few actually bear His cross and suffer for Him.

Taking up our cross daily is Christian discipleship. It is Christ's ministry working through our lives. To be effective in His Kingdom, we must have His Word abiding in us, equipping us to teach. Being familiar with the Bible is essential in being able to teach others about Jesus. Prayer can be a ministry of worship and intercession, affecting the lives of others in ways that we may never know. Fellowship with other believers strengthens our awareness of Jesus and deepens our longing to abide in Him. It also gives us the opportunity to sense struggles in the lives of others, to nurture them, and to help bear their burdens as they have need. Jesus wants us to be a witness for Him. He doesn't seek a group of people to hide in, but one to shine through! That God has provided mutual fellowship and support in Christian brotherhood is a blessing without measure.

- In what ways do I deny myself daily?
- Does my life fit the description of Christian discipleship?
- *Lord, I desire to live a life denying myself, and I ask You to show me how to be a better disciple.*

February 12

Read: Luke 9:23-27

Our Vision, Part II

"If any man will come after me, let him deny himself, and take up his cross daily, and follow me."
- Luke 9:23

Living a successful, victorious life requires a focus on several different areas. First of all, we must recognize **ONE** LORD as our first priority. This is our vision, that we strive in all ways to please God and to further His Kingdom. We must also carefully maintain **TWO** RELATIONSHIPS: the *vertical* relationship we have with God, through a daily quiet time with Him; and the *horizontal* relationship we have with people, always acting in a way that would allow Jesus' love to shine through us. We need to make and live out **THREE** COMMITMENTS: to deny *ourselves*, *take up our cross*, and *follow Him*. We need to regularly practice **FOUR** DISCIPLINES: spending time in *God's Word* on a daily basis; *praying* in faith that He hears, He cares, and He will answer our prayers in His time; regular *fellowship* with other believers to encourage and be encouraged to press on; and *witnessing* to those around us through our daily walk with the Lord. And finally, we engage in **FIVE** AREAS OF MINISTRY: as we *share God's Word*, teaching our children or others about Jesus; as we *fellowship with others* nurturing or being nurtured; through *prayer,* worshiping God and interceding for those around us; *following God's leading* in different ways of being a witness for Him; and by loving *acts of service* whenever we see a need.

Keeping this kind of a vision through our daily life is not easy, but the rewards are great. It makes the difference between an abundant life and a more abundant life.

- Am I willing to make the sacrifices needed to experience that more abundant life?
- Which of these areas can I improve in today?
- *Lord, I thank You for the opportunity to live a victorious life, and ask for guidance today.*

A Helpful Husband

"The effectual fervent prayer of a righteous man availeth much."
- James 5:16

A friend once shared an amusing incident with a small group of us ladies as we were discussing the power of praying for each other as husband and wife. She was feeling rather put-out one evening and was in the kitchen muttering audibly as she grumped about here and there, cleaning up. Her husband came in and kindly asked if there was anything he could do for her.

She just looked at him and said, "Well yes, there is something you can do for me. Don't touch me and get out of the kitchen!"

Undisturbed he just said kindly, "I do know of something I can do for you, dear," and he left.

"Humph," she thought irritably. "Now he's gone off to pray for me." She continued her grumpy clean-up, but very soon she felt her spirits lifting, and a peace once again spread through her heart like sunshine burning away fog! The rest of the evening was much more pleasant for all of them with Mom in a better mood.

Sometimes the best practical help we can give to a loved one is to stop and pray. It is so much easier to react with sharpness and criticism ourselves, but that only makes things worse. Stopping to pray rather than reacting negatively can make a big difference!

- Do I think to pray for someone who's acting grumpy, or do I react with grumpiness myself?
- How can I remind myself to respond properly in these situations?
- *Lord, help me to be a blessing rather than being critical to someone who is feeling down.*

 Read: John 4:7-21

Our Father Always Loves Us

"Herein is love, not that we loved God,
but that he loved us."
- I John 4:10

God always loves me. Each of us has an earthly father. There are some who do not know who their father is and even more who know *who* he is, but don't really *know* him, having little or no relationship with him. Others have a heart-felt desire to know their father but have felt the deep pain of his rejection through the years. Still others have a loving, close relationship with their father that thrives and grows deeper with time. No matter how loving an earthly father is, however, none is perfect. As humans they, like anyone else, will fail.

Each of us has another Father who *is* perfect and will *never* fail. *God always loves us with a perfect love.*

God first revealed His love for mankind at creation when He tenderly formed Adam from the dust of the earth and Eve from a rib out of Adam's side. In His ultimate expression of love for us, He sent His only, beloved Son to die for us to save us from our sins. His love for us right now is shown in His living within us, filling us with a love for Him and for others. Because of His love, we have no need to fear the future. We can look forward to an eternity with Him in Heaven.

God doesn't love us because we loved Him. He loved us when we were dead in sin. He loves us despite our human, sinful nature. He loves us with a perfect love.

Such great love toward us should deliver us from all fear, allowing us to rest in His perfect plan for us. It should create in us a sincere desire to share His love with others, filling us to overflowing and spilling out to those around us in a way that clearly reveals His presence in our hearts and lives. If we truly love Him, we will love those who are created in His image.

- Do I fully understand the love that God has for me?
- How can I better reflect that love to those around me?
- *Lord, Your love for me is so immense. Help me comprehend that and share Your love with others.*

Banyan... Or Banana?

"That ye might walk worthy of the Lord unto all pleasing, being fruitful in every good work."
- Colossians 1:10

There's an old Indian proverb that says, "Nothing grows under a Banyan tree." Have you ever had an opportunity to observe a Banyan tree? Our daughter had one in the back yard of the house where she lived in Florida one winter. It was amazing. A large cluster of trunks grew together with some of them leaning to the side and putting down aerial roots into the ground forming new supporting trunks along the main trunk! A Banyan tree bears a small red fruit that is not edible. Seeds from the fruit are dropped by birds into the tops of palm trees where they germinate and send down roots that embrace, and eventually kill, the palm tree. These trees are native to India and can grow to huge proportions. But, under the tree the ground is barren, just dirt and dried leaves. "Nothing grows under a Banyan tree."

A banana plant, however, is a different story. It bears bunches of nutritious bananas after just eighteen months. Each bunch of bananas weighs twenty-five to forty pounds and is composed of many bananas. While it is growing to maturity, its roots are sending up shoots all around it that are also maturing quickly. After bearing fruit, the banana, an annual plant, soon dies. The offshoots are replanted, and their growth is so rapid that the fruit is usually ripe after just ten months. On and on it goes, each plant putting out more shoots to take its place when it dies.

The Banyan tree is an interesting specimen that takes up a lot of space and lives a long time, but it is useless. The banana plant takes up little space. It lives a short time, but it is very productive. A Banyan tree kills its "support," while a banana plant produces its own "support." A Banyan tree bears a small fruit that is no good. A banana plant produces bunches of fruit that look too large and heavy for its small trunk. The fruit is delicious and nutritious, and it is exported all over the world to feed the hungry. A Banyan tree allows nothing to grow under it. A banana tree sends out new sprouts, sheltering, nurturing, and encouraging them to maturity, so they can take their place in bearing fruit for the use of others. A Banyan tree looks massive and strong, but it only destroys. A banana plant looks thin and frail but produces and reproduces.

Maybe it is time to search our hearts and see if there are any characteristics of the Banyan tree lurking there. We don't want to just be "interesting" Christians who produce no usable fruit and even eventually "kill" the spirits of those who support us! If we ask God, He will show us how to *become a banana tree!*

- Do I have any characteristics of the Banyan tree showing up in my life?
- What are they and how can I allow God to change my life to destroy these negative traits?
- *Lord, I want my life to be productive and fruitful for You. Show me where I need to improve today.*

 Read: Ephesians 2

Who? What? When? Where?

"For we are His workmanship,
created in Christ Jesus unto good works."
- Ephesians 2:10

WHO am I? Ephesians 2:10 says that I am God's workmanship. That is quite remarkable and sobering, considering the raw material He has to work with! In Christ I become a new creation, a masterpiece of God.

WHAT is my vision? As God's masterpiece, my vision should be God's vision for me, as a woman in His service. Whether I am a wife, a mother, or serving Him in other areas, my vision should be to follow His leading in every area of my life.

WHEN am I accountable to God? Romans 14:12 says that I will give account of *myself* to God. I am not accountable for the actions of others, but I am accountable for *my* actions today and every day.

WHERE do I spend my time? Do I spend most of my time in an environment that is friendly and supportive, encouraging me in my spiritual life? Or are the people I spend time with discouraging, possibly even hostile or deceptive, causing me to questions God's leading, and dragging me down? God's workmanship is perfected more readily when His masterpiece is in a godly environment.

HOW should I order my life? Isaiah 35:8 tells of a Highway of Holiness for God's people. As I order my life according to His plan for me, I can be assured of His presence and protection along this Highway.

WHY do I falter? "I find then a law, that when I would do good, evil is present with me." (Romans 7:21) It's a sad fact that Satan will do all he can to keep me from this Highway of Holiness. He is determined to destroy God's workmanship in my life. But with the help of Jesus Christ, who has conquered sin once and for all, I do not have to give in to sin. I can resist the devil and live victoriously, experiencing the more abundant life that Jesus came to give us!

- Do I feel in my heart that I am a masterpiece of God?
- In what ways should I work on changing the "order of my life" to better follow in His ways?
- *Lord, I thank You that You are still working in me, creating the masterpiece that You want me to become.*

II Timothy 2:15

"Study to shew thyself approved unto God, a workman that needeth not to be ashamed, rightly dividing the word of truth."
- II Timothy 2:15

I remember choosing this verse for our family to memorize when I was just a little girl at home. It didn't mean much to me then, I just liked the way it sounded! But I've often been glad since then that I have it memorized. It has a lot of meaningful instruction and becomes more clear and dear to my heart as I get older. Recently I felt blessed to hear it broken down and explained in a worship service.

STUDY... is an active verb. To study Scripture is more than just reading it. It is digging in and using reference books to learn the meaning of words, passages, or customs of the day. It is finding out what God has in it for you. To *SHEW*...means to show evidence of having learned the lesson intended. *THYSELF*... you, not someone else. No one else can take your place before God. *APPROVED* unto God... we seek our approval from God, not from others around us. A *WORKMAN*... not just a reader, a student, or a teacher, but a doer! That needeth not to be *ASHAMED* (embarrassed about carelessly handling Scripture) --- being ashamed is in direct contrast to having God's approval. *RIGHTLY DIVIDING* the Word of Truth... breaking it down into bite-sized pieces, to understand its meaning, making it easier to apply these truths to our daily lives. It is pretty easy to just rush through a morning reading and be off to begin our day. But as we study His Word and strive to apply the principles we find there, with God's help, we will be blessed beyond measure.

- Do I make time to study God's Word each day, even if it's just a short time?
- Am I actively applying what I learn to my daily life?
- *Lord, help me to carve some time out of each busy day to study Your Word.*

February 18 *Read: Romans 12*

Given To Hospitality

"Distributing to the necessity of saints;
given to hospitality."
- Romans 12:13

As our family was traveling in Florida, we called some friends of our son, whom we had met a couple of times. We reached one of the two grown sons who lived together in a little house. He welcomed us warmly and urged us to stay overnight with them. We weren't sure about that...our plans had been to just stop by for a short visit. To us it seemed rather overwhelming for a family of eight to stay with two bachelors! But they treated us as honored guests, showing us to the room and bath that they keep available for visitors. They shared with us that they feel blessed to host anyone that God sends along to them. A couple from Germany had stayed with them just the night before!

We smiled at the sign on the front door that said "The House of Grace," and discovered how true it was. "Anything we have is yours," they said. "It's not much but make yourselves at home." We felt very welcome, enjoyed the sweet fellowship, and were deeply blessed by our visit.

The next day we located their widowed mother and two sisters who live together. They also greeted us warmly and, even though it was mid-morning, offered us a meal or other refreshment. After a short time of fellowship, they directed us to a good place to spend the afternoon at the Gulf of Mexico. They offered us towels, toys, sunscreen, and water. We were blessed again by their warm hospitality.

As we later returned the borrowed items, I had to wonder... have I always made our guests feel so welcome? God wants us to exercise hospitality without grudging. (1Peter 4:9) Serving guests willingly is richly rewarding and can result in deep bonds of friendship. If we offer our hospitality grudgingly, our guests may sense our lack of welcome, and we will miss out on the blessing that could have been ours.

- Can God count on me to be hospitable to anyone He sends along?
- What could I do to make our guests feel more welcome and loved?
- *Lord, I want to represent You to every guest who enters our home.*

Just A Little Prayer

"O thou that hearest prayer,
unto thee shall all flesh come."
- Psalm 65:2

A visiting minister was preaching an inspiring sermon on prayer to the little congregation gathered in central Florida. My heart was touched as he shared a personal testimony. At a time when he was struggling to understand the full scope of prayer, he wondered just how interested God is in the small cares of our lives. With just a little time to spare one day, he entered a huge department store for one item...a can of Fix-A-Flat. His search up and down the aisles of the automotive department proved to be fruitless. A bit frustrated he thought, "Now some people would pray about this. But does God really care about a little can of Fix-A-Flat?"

"Lord," he prayed as he walked into the next department, "I don't know if this really matters to you or not, but if you do want us to pray about these small things could you just have the Fix-A-Flat at the end of this aisle on the left side?" He was admittedly skeptical as he started down that long aisle and wondered if he should even look. But there at the end of the aisle...on the left side...sat several cans of Fix-A-Flat...at eye level! Amazed, he knew that God does, indeed, care about the little things. His conviction deepened as he checked on several return visits and found no Fix-A-Flat on that shelf.

God doesn't answer every little prayer in that manner. But you can be assured that He does care about you, and He wants you to pray about any little perplexity that you encounter in life. The power of prayer is difficult to comprehend. We don't begin to utilize the power that is available to us. It takes practice for prayer to become a habit just like it does for any other habit we cultivate. As we begin to experience the blessing of prayer, however, it will become a normal part of our daily life. Don't miss out on that blessing!

- Do I believe God is interested in every area of my life?
- Am I in the habit of taking everything to the Lord in prayer?
- *Lord, remind me today when I need to ask for your help rather than just relying on myself.*

Read: I Samuel 17:38-47; II Kings 6:15-17

Go Forth And Conquer

"For the weapons of our warfare are not carnal, but mighty through God to the pulling down of strongholds."
- II Corinthians 10:4

To be successful in spiritual warfare, we need a plan as in any battle. Here are a few points to consider.

1) ***Use what is familiar to you...*** (I Samuel 17:38-40) As David prepared to go against Goliath, Saul put his own suit of armor on him. But it was all too big and cumbersome, and David took it off, preferring to use weapons that were familiar to him, that he had already proven. He took his staff, shepherd's bag, sling, and five smooth stones with him to meet Goliath. Pretty flimsy protection compared to Saul's heavy armor, but with God behind him, he slew the giant.

We'll be more effective, too, using what we are familiar with. Scripture verses that we have memorized or studied carefully are swords to "slay the giant." Simple prayers and simple faith in God's protection may arm us far better than armor that someone else may find useful. Just use whatever is familiar to *you.*

2) ***Engage the battle before the battle...*** (I Samuel 17:45-47) David actually won that battle in his heart before he ever cast the stone from his sling. He had complete confidence that God would protect him from Goliath and would destroy the enemy even though it looked impossible. "*For the battle is the Lord's and he will give you into our hands.*" We can have this confidence in our minds too. That is where most battles are fought anyway! Know in your mind and heart that God *will* fight for you, and choose to allow Him to do it.

3) ***Be aware of spiritual power and conflict...*** (II Kings 6:15-17) Elisha's servant got up early one morning and, to his dismay, saw that the Syrian army was surrounding the city. But *Elijah prayed*, his servant's eyes were opened, and seeing that God's heavenly army was around them also, he was no longer afraid.

When you are facing difficulties that seem impossible, remember that God's resources are there even if you can't see them. Look through your eyes of faith and let him show you what they are! Then rest in Him, unafraid.

4) ***Stand, wearing the whole armor of God...*** (Ephesians 6:10-13) This is talking about the armor that God provides for us. Any armor we try to put on that is not of God will be heavy and unwieldy. But the protection that God covers us with is light and fits perfectly. The way to put on this armor is with prayer. Through prayer we engage the battle, determine enemy strategy, and win the victory. Go forth and conquer!

- Am I aware of the spiritual battle that I'm engaged in as a believer?
- Do I spend quality time in prayer, preparing for the battle on a daily basis?
- *Lord, show me where I can be more effective in this battle against the enemy, and thank You for being there for me.*

Reasons We Fail In Spiritual Warfare: Sin In The Camp

"O Israel: thou canst not stand before thine enemies, until ye take away the accursed thing from among you."
- Joshua 7:13

Joshua's armies had just experienced a major victory in defeating Jericho. God had delivered the city into their hands in a miraculous way. Now they were facing Ai, a small city that looked like an easy take. Joshua sent only about three thousand soldiers for whom things did not go as planned. These men "fled before the men of Ai." The enemy soldiers chased them back home, killing thirty-six of them.

Joshua was shocked! What had happened? He mourned, fell to the earth on his face, and cried to the Lord, asking *why* He had brought them over the Jordan just to destroy them. He wished they had been content to just stay on the other side of the river! He wondered what he was going to say when the other cities found out what had happened, lost their fear of them, and attacked!

"And the Lord said unto Joshua, get thee up; wherefore liest thou thus upon thy face?" Then God told him that there was sin in the camp. Someone had taken some things from Jericho after the battle there, which God had specifically told them not to do. They had lied about it and had hidden the stolen goods "among their own stuff." And that is why the Israelites could not stand before their enemies but turned their backs and fled.

So the next morning, Joshua determined who had sinned. Then Achan, with all of his family and possessions, including the stolen items, were stoned, burned with fire, and buried under a heap of stones. And when the Israelite army set out again to conquer Ai, God gave them the city. Defeat turned into victory.

Sin will cause us to be defeated, too. This defeat can be collective, as in a congregation, but it can also be personal. We're only as effective in our spiritual life as the thoroughness with which we eradicate sin from our hearts. Once sin is dealt with, forgiveness and victory can be ours. With God's guidance we don't need to be discouraged or burdened with guilt. Sin gives Satan an inroad into your life, but destroying the sin will give you the power to stand against the enemy as Joshua and his army did.

- Can you identify any sin in your life that is keeping you from victory in your spiritual warfare?
- Are you willing to allow God to forgive this sin, freeing you to live a victorious life?
- *Lord, I ask You to reveal any unconfesssed sin in my life and help me to be willing to give it up.*

 Read: Acts 4:32-5:11

Reasons We Fail In Spiritual Warfare: Failure In Total Devotion

"Commit thy works unto the Lord,
and thy thoughts shall be established."
- Proverbs 16:3

The early believers lived in community and shared their possessions. Those who had land sold it and gave the money to the apostles who distributed it to those who needed it. They were able to live this way because of the unity they experienced by the Holy Spirit working in and through their lives.

Not everyone, however, was totally devoted to this structure. Ananias and Sapphira sold a possession, but they decided to secretly keep part of the money for themselves, and they lied about it. Immediately, Peter knew what Ananias had done, and he told him that he had lied to God, not to them. Before Ananias could even defend himself, he fell down dead. In great fear and amazement, the young men wrapped him up, took him out and buried him.

Then, about three hours later, Ananias' wife came in with no idea what had already happened. Imagine her astonishment when they told her. She didn't have long to think about it though because she died, too, and was carried out and buried beside her husband. God had clearly shown His displeasure at the deception seen in the lack of total devotion of Ananias and Sapphira. The new believers were shocked, with a new respect for God's judgment.

Dishonesty and covetousness are destructive, keeping the Holy Spirit from working effectively through us. It ruins our testimony for Jesus, turning others away rather than drawing them to Him. We don't live the way the early believers did, but there are many ways we show a lack of total devotion. We hold back a part of our money, not wanting to use it for someone else or for His work in the mission field. We guard a part of our heart, reluctant to open up because of the pain it would cause, or we are just wanting to hang on to the sin we're harboring. We turn over only part of our plans (You can plan my day Lord, but please don't mess it up); our family (Our children are yours God, but I'll deal with this rebellious teen myself); our occupation (My life is Yours, but Lord I need this job, *please* don't take it from me). Look deep within yourself. Are you giving your all? Allow God to show you where you are holding back. Satan certainly doesn't want us living in total devotion to the Lord. He will defeat us any way he can. Give it all to Jesus and live victoriously in this battle of spiritual warfare.

- What part of my life do I struggle with releasing to God?
- Do I see how I'm letting Satan have control and that I need to just give it to Jesus?
- *Lord, show me where I'm holding out on You and help me to be willing to surrender my entire life to You.*

Reasons We Fail In Spiritual Warfare: Failure To Recognize Jesus In A Storm

"They all saw Him and were troubled...And...He...saith unto them, Be of good cheer: it is I; be not afraid."
- Mark 6:50

The disciples had just spent the day with Jesus. They were exhausted and had tried to get some rest, but the people had seen them and were coming from all the cities nearby to hear Jesus teach. As He looked out at them, they seemed to Him like sheep without a shepherd and, though He was weary, He had compassion on them and taught them many things. (v. 34) In the evening the disciples assisted Him in feeding the multitude. Then he sent the disciples away in the boat, told the people to go home, and went up into the mountain to be alone, rest, and pray.

From where He sat He could see the disciples in the boat, and sometime later He noticed that it was getting windy, and the sea was getting choppy. The disciples were struggling to row the boat through the waves, and the situation was getting dangerous, so Jesus went to them. He didn't need a boat Himself, He just walked toward them on top of the water. Now, the disciples must have been feeling quite anxious just trying to manage their boat in the storm. They probably didn't know where Jesus was at that point and likely weren't even thinking about Him. Their concentration was on their survival. Imagine looking up and seeing, through the misty darkness, a figure walking toward you on the water! They panicked, all of them, thinking they were seeing a ghost. As close as they were to Jesus, as well as they knew Him, in their distress and struggle to survive, they didn't recognize Him. But He immediately calmed their fears...and the storm.

The storms we face can make us as fearful as the disciples were. We struggle to "keep our boat afloat" and strain to see the future through the darkness. It's during these times when we need Him the most that we are the least likely to recognize Him for the storm; but He will be there. Maybe in the form of another person, but we will be afraid to share our struggles, not seeing Him in their concern. Maybe He will speak comfort to us through the Scriptures or give us that peace that passes understanding. Look for Him through the storm. He'll be there saying, "Be of good cheer, it is I; be not afraid." He'll give you the courage and strength to go on to victory in this spiritual battle.

- Am I in the midst of a "storm tossed sea" looking for Jesus but not seeing Him?
- In what ways could He be ministering to me and I'm not recognizing Him?
- *Lord, I'm "clinging to my boat," and ask You to show Yourself, giving me comfort and peace in my heart.*

 Read: I Kings 18:16-40, 19:1-8

Reasons We Fail In Spiritual Warfare: Inconsistency In Practice

"How long halt ye between two opinions? If the Lord be God, follow Him: But if Baal, then follow him."
- I Kings 18:21

Elijah was a fearless, valiant prophet as he challenged the prophets of Baal on Mount Carmel. "You go first," he told them. "Put your sacrifice on the altar and call on your gods, see if they send fire to burn up your sacrifice." When nothing had happened by noon, he mocked them. "Cry louder, your god must be busy! Maybe he's on a journey, or maybe he is sleeping and you need to wake him up!" But of course, their god didn't answer. It couldn't, it wasn't real.

Then it was Elijah's turn. He confidently prepared the sacrifice. He built an altar, dug a trench around it, and put the wood and sacrifice on top. To make the victory even more amazing, he had water poured over the altar until the trench was full. And then he prayed. Immediately God sent fire from heaven to burn up not only the sacrifice, but also the wood, the stones, the dust, and even the water in the trench. And in a final act of fury, Elijah took those four hundred and fifty prophets down to the brook and killed them all. What a day! What a triumph. What a man of God.

But look what happens next. When Ahab, who had been present at the contest, told his wife Jezebel what Elijah had done to her prophets she was livid. She sent an angry message to Elijah that he would be dead within twenty-four hours. Elijah panicked and ran. While his reaction is perfectly understandable, we do have to wonder what happened. He had complete faith that God would protect him and win the victory on Mount Carmel, but now, a short time later, he was running for his life and begging God to just let him die. As he lay under the Juniper tree completely dejected, an angel came twice and ministered to him with food and drink. It was the encouragement he needed to go on.

I don't think we should be too hard on Elijah. I'm afraid, if we just look close enough, we'll be able to see trends like this in our own lives. Sometimes it's easier to trust Him through the big trials when we have nowhere else to turn. But then a smaller test comes along and we panic. We want out, we see no way through and we're miserable. We forget all the times that God has carried us through the hard times. No problem is too small for Him, or too big, either. To be victorious in this battle of spiritual warfare, we need to be consistent in our faith that God will always fight our battles for us whatever they may be, if we just trust Him.

- Do I struggle with trusting God to fight all my battles for me?
- What am I facing today that He is just waiting to help me through?
- *Lord, I fail so often to just trust You but my longing is to allow You to work through every situation in my life.*

Reasons We Fail In Spiritual Warfare: Entertaining Worldliness

*"And the cares of this world...choke the Word,
and it becometh unfruitful."*
- Mark 4:19

Sowing seed was quite different in that time than it is today. The farmer walked across his field, throwing handfuls of grain from a large bag that he carried over his shoulder. These plants didn't grow in nice, neat rows like they do in our fields planted with machines. The farmer also had no way to keep some of his seeds from falling on unfertile ground. It drifted to the wayside and landed on rocks or among thorns. Some of it was carried off by the wind. He scattered it generously, though, and enough fell on good soil to ensure a harvest.

Let's think about the seeds that fell among thorns. With plenty of rain and sunshine, the little seeds would sprout and grow. They may have looked quite promising at first, but as they grew, the thorns were growing, too. While the tender little plants were probably growing straight up toward the light, thorns have a way of twisting and twining around anything in their path. Eventually, they will take over, crowding out the little plants, blocking the sun and soaking up all the moisture. The life is choked right out of the plants and they bear no fruit.

Jesus is talking here about the people who hear the Word but allow the cares of the world to choke it out of their lives. We can go to church two or three times a week, having plenty of opportunities to hear the Word of God. But it takes effort and discipline to keep daily life from taking over our thoughts and actions. We become preoccupied with the cares of the world. These cares can be the love of riches, worry, peer pressure that keeps us from being satisfied with what we have, or anything else that closes our hearts and minds to what God would have for us. These "thorns" block the Son and soak up the moisture of His Word, choking the Life out of our lives and rendering us unfruitful. Our hearts must be a fertile soil, receiving the seed of His Word, understanding it, and putting it into practice. Only then will we become a fruitful vine, bringing forth fruit for His Kingdom. Only then will we defeat Satan in his devious plans to destroy our witness for Jesus.

- What areas of my life could possibly be "thorns," choking God out of my life?
- How can I change my life, beginning today, to make me more useful in His Kingdom?
- *Lord, I want to be a fruitful vine for You, not allowing Satan to destroy my witness for You in any way.*

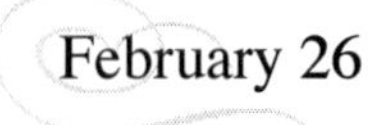

February 26 *Read: Judges 2*

Reasons We Fail In Spiritual Warfare: Failure To Obey

"Thou shalt not go aside from any of the words which I command thee...to go after other gods."
- Deuteronomy 28:14

When Joshua died, the Israelites lost their strong leadership and began to flounder. They started losing their focus on God, finally abandoned their faith altogether, and worshiped the pagan gods around them. The Canaanites had gods for almost everything. Jehovah was just another god to them. Worshiping these gods of wood and stone required terrible atrocities. Human sacrifice, the burning of babies, and moral wickedness was a way of life to the Canaanites. The Israelites soon became accustomed to that and joined right in. They arranged marriages with the foreigners, directly disobeying God and further provoking His anger. (Judges 3:6)

Time after time this happened, and each time God punished the Israelites by allowing them to be overrun by enemy nations. These people were still in the land because the Israelites had not obeyed God in driving them out. When the oppression got too heavy, the children of Israel would cry out to the Lord, begging for mercy and deliverance. And each time the Lord would raise up a judge to lead them, not only to military victory, but also back to obedience to God. They would live in peace for awhile, enjoying God's blessings until the judge died. Then it wouldn't be long until they were losing sight of God again and sliding back into the habits and customs of their pagan neighbors. In Judges we read that this cycle repeated itself six times during the approximately three hundred years after Joshua died.

We wonder, "What was wrong with those people? You would think they'd learn that it wasn't worth it, teach their children not to stray from the Lord, and their troubles would be over." Whoa...we'd better stop a minute and think about our own lives! The Israelites *knew* God and what He wanted from them. We can *know* God and what He wants from us too. We have His Written Word to teach us, His Holy Spirit to guide us, and fellow believers to encourage us; but how many times do we fail to obey? Maybe we think, "If only I knew what God wants me to do now." Do we *really* not know what He wants? Or do we possibly not *want* to know? He has promised to "direct our ways if we trust in Him and lean not to our own understanding." (Proverbs 3:5) Spending time in His Word and in prayer is essential to knowing His will, and a willingness to obey His revealed will is a key to victory in the spiritual warfare of daily life.

- Can I see a tendency in my life to cycles of disobedience similar to the Israelites long ago?
- What is God asking of me today that I need to be willing to obey?
- *Lord, I don't like the thought of disobedience in my life but it is there at times. Help me to always be willing to obey.*

Attic Or Parlor

"If we confess our sins, he is faithful and just to forgive us our sins, and to cleanse us from all unrighteousness."
- I John 1:9

Is your heart an attic or a parlor? We all know what most attics are like. They are full of dusty boxes containing unused stuff. Miscellaneous unnecessary items clutter up the room, and mice congregate to feast and make their nests. Many of these boxes and things have been there collecting cobwebs for years. We just continue to kick them further back into the dark corners and leave them there. After all, what would we do with all that stuff?

A parlor, however, is a room that is kept ready for visitors. It is tidy with nice furniture attractively arranged. The atmosphere is pleasant and there is no dust in sight. Pretty wallpaper and beautiful rugs make it cozy, and a fire in the fireplace keeps it warm. An inviting place for anyone.

My heart does not always feel like a parlor. Sometimes it begins to feel like an attic. Not exactly a pleasant place to entertain a guest! I stash a box of bitterness along one wall. I toss a pile of pride onto a sagging shelf and kick a clump of unforgiveness into the dust balls in the corner. A bag full of anger sits ready for a mouse's nest and discontentment covers it all like a thick layer of dust.

Then I have a choice. I can leave it all there. Let the spiders spin their webs around it, and the mice come out to chew on it. Or I can choose to invite Jesus into my heart to clean house. His blood will cleanse all the ugly stuff in my heart and change it from an "attic" into a "parlor." A clean, bright, pleasant place to entertain such an important Guest. We are much happier and more effective in God's kingdom if we allow Jesus to clean house for us. Take each "box of clutter" as you come to it, confess it, and allow Him to remove it from your heart and discard it for you. You'll stand amazed at His ability to "clean house!"

- What clutter do I have in my heart that I could allow Jesus to clean out for me?
- Do I truly believe that He is willing and able to do this cleaning?
- *Cleanse me, oh Lord, from mine iniquity. Make me pure to do Thy will.*

 Read: Isaiah 32:9-20

Mothball Christians

"Rise up, ye women that are at ease;
hear my voice ye careless daughters."
- Isaiah 32:9

A minister recently told us about a large fleet of ships which make up what they call the "mothball navy." These ships are anchored in various harbors around the country and kept in readiness for service. They receive regular maintenance, being repainted periodically and receiving frequent electrical impulses to slow down the process of rust and corrosion. Moisture content of the air in their inner compartments is kept at a proper level with giant humidifiers. These ships can be readied for combat on a very short notice, but at the present time they just sit there doing absolutely nothing. The only purpose they serve right now is to provide jobs for those responsible for the upkeep.

It sets us thinking about "mothball Christians." How many do you suppose comprise that fleet? They are being preserved somewhat through the ministry of concerned friends. They consume incredible amounts of time and energy in local churches. Periodically someone must try to reactivate them. Their talents and abilities are not being used for anything constructive. They are on the church roll and perhaps feel snugly harbored because of it. They receive lots of attention and loving concern but rarely give anything in return. They are served, but not serving.

We can see a legitimate reason for our government to maintain our "mothball navy." National security is at stake. But there is no excuse for a believer to remain inactive. The energy and manpower needed to win the world is sidetracked--used up on those who should be involved in helping reach the world. Every Christian is responsible to use his God-given abilities for the salvation of the world.

If you examine your own life, what do you see? Are you a "ship in the midst of the battle?" Or are you a part of the "mothball navy," sitting at ease, being maintained by your fellow believers. Are you actively serving others, or are you content to be served by those "more talented" than you? Do you feel "safely harbored" by your church membership, not feeling the need to use your talents in service to the Lord? We all need times of rest--a time of refreshment and being served. But there is no excuse for staying there. The mothball navy is a stagnant part of the fleet, presently useless to anyone. A stagnant Christian is of no use to God or to others. Which "fleet" do you want to be a part of? Remember, Jesus said and demonstrated that "it is more blessed to give than to receive."

- What do I see as I examine my life?
- Am I a "mothball Christian," or am I actively and willingly serving the Lord in the way He calls me to?
- *Lord, it's so easy to just float in the harbor. Show me what You would have me to do, and give me the courage to do it.*

Sources Of Encouragement

"Who comforteth us in all our tribulation,
that we may be able to comfort them."
- II Corinthians 1:4

God provides comfort and encouragement for His people through various sources. He knows exactly what we need at different times in our lives. Isaiah 40:29-31 says that everyone gets weary at times, but God's strength is always available. He will renew our strength when we seek Him, listen for Him, and allow Him to help us rise above the difficulties of life.

Acts 9:31 tells us that after Paul was converted and no longer persecuting Christians, the church enjoyed a time of peace. They "walked in the fear of the Lord and in the comfort of the Holy Ghost were multiplied." God often comforts us through ***His Spirit***. You may find yourself humming a song and realize the words are just what you need. Thoughts and Scriptures come to mind to soothe and encourage. A feeling of peace in the midst of the storm... Recognizing the comfort of the Spirit is a wonderful source of strength.

We can find encouragement in ***God's Word***. "That we through...comfort of the Scriptures might have hope." (Romans 15:4) Many passages provide encouragement for the weary. Learning more about what God has done in the past gives us confidence that He will care for us in our present situations. God wants to lead us to verses that speak to the particular need we are facing.

He also provides support through ***other believers***. "Wherefore comfort yourselves together, and edify one another..." (I Thessalonians 5:11) As we share experiences, show our love and concern, and let others know we are praying for them, we build each other up. Encouragement plants seeds of hope, further encouragement nurtures that hope, and as an added blessing, encouragement encourages the encourager! As we share the fruits of that loving support, we ourselves will be further built up and strengthened in the Lord.

When you feel that life is crushing you down and you simply don't have the strength to go on, turn to the help God provides. His sources of encouragement will never go dry!

- Am I tapping into the sources of encouragement God has provided for me?
- Whom do I know that could use support from me today?
- *Lord, show me where I need to accept Your encouragement or lift up someone else today.*

March

Slave Auction

*"But now being made free from sin,
and become servants to God."*
- Romans 6:22

Do you ever feel like a slave? Do you feel as though all you do is cater to others all day long with little or no appreciation or reward? What would it have been like, I wonder, to be a real slave. A slave who was taken to the auction block; surrounded by a crowd of buyers and gawkers; poked, prodded, and ridiculed. Slaves were cruelly separated from their families, sometimes never to see them again. Some were purchased by a kind owner who treated them with respect or even set them free, but too often they became the slave of a hard-hearted master. Living lives full of hatred, pain, and loneliness, they had no rights but did just as they were told. Long ago, if a master set his slave free, and he chose to stay because his family was still there, he would have his earlobe pierced with an awl to show that he was a free man. Then he would serve his master the rest of his life. (Exodus 21:2-6).

We can identify with these slaves in that we were slaves to sin. Satan is a cruel master, and a sin-filled life is dark and gloomy. But Jesus has purchased our souls at the auction block, right out of the slave market. We can no longer be sold because He has set us free, and we are His. We have been bought by Someone who has everything. He has mansions eternal, He feeds us better than anyone else could, and He lavishes us love and blessings without measure. We are no longer slaves to sin but are free to serve Him. This doesn't mean we never sin. We are human and we fail often. But sin no longer rules our lives, God does. He is faithful to forgive us when we come to Him in repentance, and He frees us from guilt. (I John 1:9) Being a servant to such a loving Master is not a duty; it's a privilege.

- Does my life show the "mark" of being free from sin?
- Am I rejoicing in my freedom and in my service for Christ?
- *Lord, I praise You for purchasing me with Your blood and for setting me free to serve You.*

Read: Jeremiah 18:1-10

Pottery

"Behold, as the clay is in the potter's hand,
so are ye in mine hand."
- Jeremiah 18:6

To mold a perfect piece of pottery, a potter must first choose a lump of suitable clay. Then he carefully prepares that lump for molding. He removes all roots, dirt, pebbles, and other substances to make the clay smooth. He adds just enough water to make a dough. He throws it on the wheel to work out the air bubbles that could later expand and cause the vessel to break. As the potter forms the piece on his wheel, he is able to see any flaws inside. Sometimes he will smash the piece and start over, even though it looked perfectly good on the outside! And when it is finished, he will coat it with a glaze and put it into the kiln for the final step of firing.

Just as the clay is in the hands of the potter, so we are in the hands of the Master Potter. He lovingly removes roots of bitterness, pebbles of pride, and other gravelly bits of sin. He adds the pressures of daily life to smooth us and greater pressures to work out the "air bubbles." At times it feels that the "heat is on" as He works to "put the finish on our souls." It takes heat to bring out the beautiful colors and the shine on the finished vessel. As the potter can see his reflection in the shine of the vessel he has created, so our Heavenly Father should be able to see the reflection of Jesus in the lives of His saints.

- Are there circumstances in my life today that God wants to use to mold me into His image?
- Do I chafe at these pressures, or do I see them as opportunities for growth?
- *Take my life, Lord, and mold it into a vessel that daily reflects the image of Jesus.*

There Is A Reason

"And we know that all things work together
for good to them that love God."
- Romans 8:28

"OK," I sputtered angrily. "So I'm worthless." In the privacy of our bedroom, I spewed out all the ugly ways my husband had been telling me that I was not worth a thing. Worthless as a wife. Worthless as a mother. A poor excuse of a housekeeper. Failing as a godly woman. "How can I possibly be worth anything to God, and what is the point of even going on if I'm a failure in everything I do?!" I finished in a huff.

My poor, baffled husband just stared at me in astonishment and assured me he was thinking no such thing! "Well then," I wondered, "if you're not *saying* all these things, why am I *hearing* them*?*" As we talked about everything that had been going on, I finally saw those thoughts for what they really were. Lies from Satan. He's the father of lies and delights in us believing them. Talking, repenting and confessing, and claiming God's truth through prayer brought peace again to replace the turmoil. No, I am not worthless. You are not worthless. No one is worthless! *"For God so loved (you) that He gave His only begotten son…"* (I John 3:16) I went to sleep wondering, "Well Lord, what was *that* all about?"

Several weeks later I had a completely unexpected opportunity to spend some time with an out-of-state friend who was visiting in our area. It was a meeting that only God could have arranged. I had been wishing I could talk with her in person but saw no possibility of that happening. Through some last minute plan changes and numerous details just "working out," there we were, alone and with ample time to talk. A few pointed questions opened the flood gates, and in the course of the conversation she tearfully poured out her feelings of worthlessness. As I shared with her my own not-so-long-ago struggle with the same feelings, she was surprised that I also feel that way at times. As God helped me reassure her of her worth to God and to her family, I no longer wondered why I had gone through that battle. God knew the experience would be good for me, and that I would be able to use it in comforting a hurting friend.

Satan's lies are vicious and they are just that; *lies*. But sometimes God allows them to be included in the tests we face to strengthen us and to fit us for further work in His Kingdom. It's not easy to thank God in the middle of the hard times, but if we can see the tests as potential Kingdom building experiences, we can patiently wait for Him to bring us through them. I was thankful that I could truly relate to my friend in her pain. God can use your struggles to strengthen you too, as you purpose to learn from them instead of resenting them.

- Can I see my struggles as good for myself and possibly for others?
- What am I experiencing now that can strengthen me for God's future work?
- *Lord, the trials aren't easy, but I want to be able to see them as opportunities for spiritual growth in my life.*

More Than Conquerors

"Nay, in all these things we are more than conquerors through Him that loved us."
- Romans 8:37

Remember the story of Abraham rescuing Lot from the armies that captured him and his family? Not only did he bring back Lot, his family, and his possessions; Genesis 14:16 says "And he brought back all the goods..." then he gave one-tenth of everything to King Melchizedek. Abraham was "more than a conqueror."

David, also, would bring back spoils from his battles. I Chronicles 26:26-27 tells us that he dedicated part of these spoils to maintain the temple. David was "more than a conqueror."

Esther rose above her fear and approached the King to save her people. She didn't know whether she would be accepted or killed. She chose to risk her life for the sake of many others. Esther was "more than a conqueror."

So how does being "more than a conqueror" apply to us today? As Christian women we can hardly go to battle as these men did or risk our lives by speaking to a King. But think about some of the dark times you've been through. Maybe the death of a loved one. A wayward child, a painful marriage, financial struggles, or a crushing disappointment. Perhaps you've been deeply hurt by a friend. Or even just the day-to-day struggles of life.

Now think about how you have grown in your Christian life. Are you more patient with daily irritations? More compassionate toward hurting people? Do you have a deeper trust in God to see you through the hard times? Have you become more of a prayer warrior for your loved ones? If so, you are not only surviving these dark times, but you are also growing in Christ-likeness and you, too, are "more than a conqueror!"

- In what ways have I grown in my spiritual life?
- Do I recognize the painful times as times of growth?
- *Lord, help me to come through the dark times in my life as more than a conqueror.*

Alive Attracts

"Likewise reckon ye also yourselves to be dead indeed unto sin, but alive unto God through Jesus Christ our Lord."
- Romans 6:11

Picture a lovely flower garden full of beautiful blooms of every color and hue. Roses... Daisies... Poppies... Geraniums... and a host of other flowers and plants among them. Well-watered and lovingly-tended, they are blooming in brilliant profusion. Freshly-painted benches and sparkling water fountains add to the beauty. Beautiful butterflies flit from flower to flower. This is an attractive scene! People drive for miles and spend their hard-earned money to walk through beautiful flower gardens, filling their senses with beauty.

Now picture this same garden... dead. Untended, unwatered, brown, drooping, weed-infested plants... completely dead. Rusted benches and dirty fountains sit in disrepair. No birds or butterflies grace this scene. This type of garden is not attractive. People have no desire to stroll through a garden like this. In fact, they will go out of their way to avoid it.

Believers who are alive with the love of Jesus Christ in their hearts will naturally attract other people. They can also have heart-to-heart fellowship with other believers, sharing trials and triumphs, building each other up in the Lord. God wants to bless us with the richness that comes with being spiritually alive.

Spiritually dead is as unattractive as a dead garden. No true beauty flows out for others to enjoy. There is no attraction to draw others to Christ, the living source of all beauty.

Don't be afraid to let the love of Jesus shine through your heart and pour out to bless others. It is an important key to the more abundant life and you will be richly blessed in return. Alive attracts!

- Am I alive enough to give others a desire to know Jesus better?
- How can I cultivate my life so that I feel more alive in Christ?
- *Lord, my heart's desire is to be alive in You, and to have Your love flowing through me to others.*

Read: I Peter 2:1-3

Of Babies And Believers

"As newborn babes, desire the sincere milk of the word that ye may grow thereby."
- I Peter 2:2

It doesn't seem to matter how many children we have, each baby's growth is a fascinating process. God has instilled a life within each child that causes that little one to grow and learn. No one has to teach a normal baby to roll over, crawl, stand, or walk. It is a process that happens naturally throughout the first year or so of life. It is essential, however, that the child is fed. A baby who is not properly nourished will not grow or develop normally.

As children get older, most of them want to grow up. They long to be like the teenagers or their parents. Along with healthy food, a good diet of training, discipline, and example is important to help them to grow into healthy, godly adults.

When we become believers we are spiritual babies. God instills in us a Life that makes us yearn to grow. If we are healthy we will have a deep desire for the pure spiritual milk of the Word. As we grow and develop, "tasting that the Lord is gracious" will whet our appetites and make us want to draw closer and closer to Him. Allowing sin in our lives will stunt our spiritual growth, while feeding on God's Word nourishes us.

As a child desires to grow more like his parents or other adults, our ultimate goal in spiritual growth is to become more and more like our Lord Jesus Christ. Studying the Scriptures, communicating with God in prayer, and worshipping and fellowshipping with other believers will help us to move closer to our goal.

- How strong is my desire for God's Word?
- Am I growing as a healthy believer, or is my spiritual growth stunted by unconfessed sin?
- *Lord, I long to grow in You. Reveal any sin in my life and increase my desire for Your Word.*

God's Provision

"Yet have I not seen the righteous forsaken,
nor his seed begging bread."
- Psalm 37:25

Our son was on his way home from Wisconsin with friends one weekend when they stopped in Chicago to see the Sears Tower. Walking the streets of downtown Chicago, our country born and raised son saw sights that he had never seen before. He saw sleeping bags and pillows under a bridge. On the sidewalks, men, though they were not shabbily dressed, held out their hands or plastic cups and begged for money. One man even asked for money so that *he* could help the poor people! Knowing what the money would likely be used for, they knew they should not give them much cash. Feeling compassion for these people and thinking of all he was blessed with in his life, our son did give one grateful man a couple dollars.

As we later discussed our son's experiences, it was apparent that the contrast between what these folks had (or didn't have) and what he enjoyed in his life was making a big impression on him. He thought of all the *things* he had wanted to buy to satisfy his teen-aged desires, when the people he had seen could not even afford a good meal or a place to sleep, much less a place to live. Thinking it over, those things he had wanted to buy didn't seem quite so important anymore.

God tells us in this Psalm that He will take care of those who follow Him and seek to do His will. David writes that in all his life he had never seen the righteous forsaken or begging for food. We should be thankful if we have never needed to beg for money or food. Most of us don't even think about how blessed we are. It is so easy just to take all we have for granted. We are more likely to complain about what we do have to eat even though we have an abundance, such as most of the world knows nothing about. Does our thankfulness go beyond lip service to sharing with others what God has so graciously given us? Sometimes we forget that sharing with others is both a responsibility and a privilege.

- In what ways has God richly blessed me lately?
- Am I willing to share what I have with others as God leads me?
- *Lord, open my eyes to see how You have blessed me and make me willing to share those riches.*

Read: Revelation 2:1-7

Keep Your First Love

"To him that overcometh will I give to eat of the tree of life which is in the midst of the paradise of God."
- Revelation 2:7

Ephesus was the capital of Asia Minor, an influential city in the Roman Empire. Idol worship was widespread. The temple to the goddess Diana stood in Ephesus and the manufacture of idols of this goddess was a major industry. The people of the city were a wide mixture of nationalities, cultures, and beliefs. In the midst of this melting pot of humanity was a group of believers with whom John had spent much of his ministry.

Jesus introduced Himself in this letter as the One who "holdeth the seven stars in His right hand, who walketh in the midst of the seven golden candlesticks," (speaking of the seven churches), indicating that He alone is the head of the body of believers.

The church at Ephesus had stood strong over a long period of time. Jesus commends them for their hard work, their patience; for resisting sin, and for testing the claims of false apostles. They had suffered trials patiently and had labored for Christ tirelessly, responding as true believers should. This group of second-generation believers, however, had lost their zeal for God. They were a busy church, doing much good to benefit those around them, but the fires of their affection had died down, their enthusiasm had disappeared, and the true motive for worship and service was missing. *They had lost their first love.*

Jesus encouraged them to think back to the good days of their early faith, repent of their diminishing love, and return to their devoted service. He warned them that, unless they repented, He would "remove their candlestick." The church would cease to be an effective church, and their witness would die out. He then promised a blessed eternity with Him to believers who overcome the temptations of life and keep their love for Him alive and glowing.

Notice that this letter was the first of the seven letters. As Christians, our *first* work is to love the Lord who saved us! It is easy to be busy doing the Lord's work but not to take the time for Jesus Himself. He loves you, He values your relationship with Him, and He wants you to love Him. This is the first and great commandment. (Matthew 22:37, 38) If your love for Him has grown dim, repent! Revive it! Then your work in His service will be as effective as the shining light of a glowing candlestick to the world around you.

- What is the depth of my love for Jesus compared to the love I felt as a new Christian?
- Is my light growing dim? Does my enthusiasm need to be revived?
- *Lord, show me where I've lost my first love and restore in me a burning devotion to serve You effectively.*

Which Was Dead And Is Alive

"Be thou faithful unto death,
and I will give thee a crown of life."
- Revelation 2:10

Smyrna was an ancient, major seaport about thirty miles north of Ephesus. It had been destroyed so thoroughly by the Persians that no one even tried to restore it for 400 years, when it was finally rebuilt by the powerful Romans. Jesus introduced Himself to the people of Smyrna as the "*first and the last, which was dead, and is alive,*" speaking of His death and resurrection. Knowing the history of their city, that it had been dead for 400 years and now was made brand new, they could easily understand what he meant.

The church at Smyrna struggled against bitter attack by the Jews who had migrated to the city for financial gain, forsaking their Jewish laws and traditions and becoming loyal to Caesar. These Jews claimed to be God's chosen people, but their behavior was so wicked that Jesus called them "the synagogue of Satan." It was difficult, at that time, to buy or sell unless you joined yourself to these Jewish Romans and became loyal to them. As a result, the Christians at Smyrna lived in poverty and suffered much persecution.

Jesus assured these believers that He knew what they were going through and commended them for their faith in suffering. He reminded them that although they were poor in this world's goods, they were rich in Him. He encouraged them not to fear their present hardships or what was to come in the future. Their tribulation may be intense but it wouldn't last long and if they remained faithful they would be rewarded with "a crown of life."

This was another concept they could understand, as Smyrna was famous for its athletic games. Many of these games were fought to the death, and a victory wreath was the trophy for the champion of the game; the one who held out to the end.

Suffering is never easy, no matter what the cause. Whatever your condition in life, remember--you were dead and He gave you life! You were poor but now, as His child, you are rich! Know who you are in Christ. As He told the believers at Ephesus, "*love the Lord,*" and those at Smyrna, "*trust your salvation.*" Remember that God is in control and trust in His promises. Keep your eyes on Him, and you also have the promise of "*a crown of life.*"

- Am I going through, or living in, a situation that is trying my patience and stretching my faith?
- What decisions can I make today to remember God's promises more fully and to trust in Him more completely?
- *Lord, show me clearly that You are in control and help me to put my trust in You, knowing that, in You, I am rich.*

March 10

Read: Revelation 2:12-17

Stay Faithful

"To him that overcometh will I give to eat of the hidden manna..a white stone..and a new name."
- Revelation 2:17

Pergamos was a sophisticated center of Greek culture and education about 55 miles north of Smyrna. It was the gateway to trade in Asia from Europe. But it was also the home of several cults and much idol worship. It was the Asian headquarters for the cult of emperor worship. Caesar Augustus demanded worship of himself. To buy and sell in this town you had to have a number from Rome that was renewed each year by burning incense to Caesar.

Jesus presents Himself to them as having "the sharp sword with two edges." The believers at Pergamos were fully aware of how the Romans used their swords for authority and judgment and understood this representation of God's ultimate authority and judgment. Jesus assured them He knew they were living in the pit of sin, "even where Satan's seat is." He commended them for refusing to deny Him even when one of their members was martyred.

He goes on, however, to rebuke them for tolerating those who were leading people away from the church through the doctrines of Balaam and of the Nicolaitanes. Balaam sanctioned eating things sacrificed to idols and immorality. The Nicolaitanes are sometimes referred to as "make believe Christians," devout only when it is convenient, and teaching that those under grace were free to practice idolatry and immorality. Jesus urges them to repent and expel the evil teachers from their midst, or He would fight against them Himself.

He then promised several rewards "to him that overcometh." The hidden manna suggests spiritual nourishment coming from Jesus himself, the "Bread of Life." (I John 6:51) This heavenly food contrasts sharply with foods offered to idols and provides nourishment that satisfies the deepest hunger. The white stone may be symbolic of the Urim in the breastplate of the high priest, but it seems clear that it is a reward for the overcomer; engraved with a new name, evidence that an individual has been accepted by God and declared worthy of eternity with Him.

Like the believers at Pergamos, we are surrounded by sin on every side. It is easy to be sidetracked by Satan and lured off the path God has for us if we lose sight of His plan. The message for us today is the same as it was for the church at Pergamos. *Stay faithful!* Stay in tune with God by reading His Word daily and through regular times of prayer. Although it is not easy to live in "Pergamos," the rewards for the overcomer will be worth all the struggles here.

- Am I as faithful now as I was when I first became a Christian?
- In what ways can I change my life to stay more in tune with God's plan for me?
- *Lord, show me how I need to change to be faithful to You in all I do.*

Stay Focused

"And I will give him the morning Star."
- Revelation 2:28

Thyatira was a busy industrial town about fifty miles east of Pergamos, with many trade guilds much like today's labor unions. Folks wove wool into cloth, and from the surrounding countryside they gathered plants and berries to make medicines and dyes. They were known especially for their purple dye. Lydia, Paul's first convert at Philippi, was "a seller of purple" from Thyatira. (Acts 16:14) The city was basically secular, and to be successful you needed to join one of the trade guilds which involved honoring the god or goddess of the guild with lavish drinking parties and animal sacrifice. Some of the Christians were getting involved, joining them in eating the meat sacrificed to idols and even drinking the blood.

The Son of God is presented here as having "eyes of flame" and "feet of brass" speaking of piercing vision and threatened judgment. The church was commended for growing in good works, "the last to be more than the first." Their loving service and faithful patience were outstanding in the midst of such a sinful city. But God was not pleased with their tolerance of a woman who was teaching that immorality and eating meat sacrificed to idols were not serious matters for Christians. She was obviously more concerned about her own pleasure and freedom than about her fellow believers. She refused to repent, and God spoke His judgment upon her and any who followed in her way.

Then God spoke to the remnant of believers who had not accepted this doctrine or other false teachings. He urged them to hold fast to what they already had. He told them the victorious ones will reign with Him, as He rules over his enemies and judges evil. He promised them the morning star. A morning star appears in the sky just before dawn, when the night is coldest and darkest. Could it be that Christ will appear when the world is at its darkest point, exposing evil with His truth and bringing the promised reward?

Like the believers at Thyatira, your first "work" when you came to the Lord was with yourself--an ongoing personal commitment to staying in tune with God's will for you. Good works are born out of our love for our Savior, and they should increase as theirs did. But if are not careful, we can get so caught up in our good works that we lose our focus. We dare not allow things into our lives that should not be there. We must hold fast to that which we have. If we stay focused God will reward us in the end.

- Am I allowing anything in my life that displeases God?
- Am I staying focused on the most important part of my life---my relationship with Jesus?
- *Lord, show me anything in my life that doesn't please You and help me stay focused on You.*

 Read: Revelation 3:1-6

Be Watchful

"He that overcometh... shall be clothed in white raiment;
and...I will confess his name before my Father."
- Revelation 3:5

Sardis was a wealthy inland city about thirty-five miles south of Thyatira. It was the strategic stronghold of the Lydian empire and sat about fifteen hundred feet straight up the side of a mountain. At one time, the Persian army was camped at the foot of the mountain and could not find a way up to overtake the city. History says the Persian ruler, Darius, had offered freedom and great wealth to the soldier who could find a way to take Sardis. A soldier watching the city saw a Lydian soldier drop his helmet and climb down a crack in the mountainside to get it. So, at night, the Persian soldier took a band of men and climbed up the same crevice, taking the city as it slept. The men of Sardis thought their city was so secure that they didn't set a watch at night.

Spiritually, the church at Sardis had a reputation of being alive, but it was actually almost dead. The Christians there went through a formal, dull routine but they did not overflow with spiritual life. Jesus called them to a new zeal in strengthening what little remained as even that was showing signs of dying. He urged them to get back to the basic truths they had been taught. He warned them that unless they woke up and repented, He would come unexpectedly and deal with them in judgment.

Jesus knew there were a few in the church there who had not lost their Christian testimony. They were overcomers who would walk with Him in white. We are given this promise, too, if we are faithful overcomers. God tells us to ***be watchful***. How easily we lose sight of what is most important in this busy age of "doing." We can be so busy doing things *for* the Lord, that we lose our closeness *with* Him. Or, we can grow lifeless and cold, going through the routine of a daily Christian life, looking "alive" on the outside but, in truth, being nearly dead on the inside. Satan is crafty and deceptive. He is as diligent and determined as the Persian soldier watching the mountainside for a way *IN*. He knows how to get into our homes, our marriages, and our churches. If we don't set a watch of prayer around our lives, he will come through the smallest "crack" and wreak havoc. Be watchful! Strengthen the things that remain, and you will someday *walk with Him in white*, and He will *confess your name before His Father and before the angels!*

- Am I an "alive" Christian, or is Satan getting through the cracks and destroying my testimony?
- In what ways can I strengthen the watch around my life and the lives of those I love?
- *Lord, show me where my defense is weak and how to strengthen it in protection from the enemy.*

Keep An Open Door

*"Him that overcometh will I make a pillar
in the temple of my God."
- Revelation 3:12*

Philadelphia was an inland city twenty-five miles southeast of Sardis. When some minister friends of ours toured the area of the seven churches of Asia recently, they found the city in this area to be the friendliest city they visited. School children would wave, shout "hello" (practicing their English) and follow them to their tour bus.

The Lord had only words of praise for the believers here. He presents Himself as the "Key of David" with absolute power to open and close the door to His Kingdom. Then, He commends them for their works, for being strong, and keeping His Word. They had been faithful and had preserved the Truth by living it out in their lives. They had not denied His name. They had kept the doors of their hearts open to Him and to others. What a testimony!

Because of their faithfulness He was setting before them an *open door of opportunity* that no one would be able to shut. The professing Jews, who claimed to be God's people but were actually a synagogue of Satan, would have to admit that these Christians, whom they so despised, were actually God's chosen flock. They had the promise of God's presence and deliverance, and His encouragement to stand strong and be faithful, not allowing anyone to rob them of the victor's crown when it was so close at hand.

God is speaking this message to us today, also. As victorious believers, we will each be made a pillar in God's inner sanctuary. A pillar makes you think of strength, honor, and security. When The Moslems captured Turkey in the early 1400s, Philadelphia was the last Christian stronghold to fall. The church building there was old and massive, and the pillars were so solid and strong that the Moslems tore off the roof and left the pillars. When our friends were visiting this city, they saw those pillars still standing today! Four huge pillars of solid brick standing one and one-half stories high. God also tells us that we will have three names written on us, identifying us as citizens of the new Kingdom.

How do we measure up to the believers at Philadelphia? Some days that question could make me cringe! What a testimony to keep the doors of our hearts, minds, and churches open to fellow believers, neighbors, and friends. More importantly, though, to keep the doors open to Jesus; to love Him deeply, live faithfully, work zealously, and trust completely. Don't allow the devil or anyone else to rob you of the victor's crown waiting for you at the end of life.

- Does my life exhibit the qualities of the Christians at Philadelphia?
- What area of my life do I need to submit more fully to Jesus?
- *To keep the door of my heart open to You and others is my desire, Lord. Guide me in this right way.*

 Read: Revelation 3:14-22

A Heart On Fire

"To him that overcometh will I grant to sit with me in my throne."
- Revelation 3:21

Laodicea was thirty-five miles south of Philadelphia and was built to be a Roman soldier outpost. At that time there were no wells or other water sources there, so the Romans made cisterns to catch rain water for drinking and built an aqueduct to bring bathing water from nearby hot springs. By the time the water reached Laodicea, however, it was no longer hot nor was it refreshingly cool. It was unpleasantly lukewarm. The drinking water was always tepid.

Laodicea was the wealthiest of the seven cities, well known for its banking industry from which the United States actually got its first banking system. They dyed and manufactured woolen goods and had a medical school that produced eye salve. They abounded in this world's goods, and the church at Laodicea considered itself rich indeed.

The church at Laodicea had become disgustingly lukewarm with an indifferent idleness. God presents Himself to them as the supreme example of faithfulness and truth; the origin of all creation. He expresses His displeasure at their apathetic condition and tells them they were actually not rich but pathetically poor, wretched, miserable, blind, and naked. He threatened to spew them out of His mouth if they did not repent and turn from their indifference. He counseled them to buy gold tried in fire from Him, true spiritual treasures much more valuable than the world's goods. He urged them to purchase the white raiment of His righteousness and to use His eye salve so that they could see the Truth. Christ assured the Laodiceans that He loved them, or He wouldn't be chastening them. He gives the invitation to them which rings true for us today as well. "Behold, I stand at the door and knock…"

The Christians at Laodicea were so busy enjoying their worldly pleasures that they didn't notice His knock at their hearts. They felt secure in their wealth and didn't realize that letting Him in was their only true hope of lasting fulfillment. The city of Laodicea was too far from its source of water, and the people had strayed too far from their spiritual Source. The Christians were as lukewarm as the water they were drinking.

How about us today? Are you on fire for Jesus or have you drifted too far from the Source? Is Jesus knocking at your heart, longing for closer fellowship with you? He won't break and enter but is patient and persistent, promising us the reward of sitting with Him in His throne. Stay close to your Source now and enjoy the reward at the end!

- Is my heart alive for Him or have I become lukewarm in my devotion?
- Am I willing to confess my lukewarmness and to thoroughly repent of it?
- *Lord, Please replace my lukewarmness with a revival of your Spirit and your Word.*

Our Thought Life

*"Bringing into captivity every thought
to the obedience of Christ."
- II Corinthians 10:5*

As I was reading and meditating on a closer walk with God, He impressed me with the need to work on controlling my thought life. I've heard it said that all sin begins in the mind. Even entertaining thoughts that are from Satan is sin. In Philippians God has given us a list of characteristics by which to measure our thoughts.

He tells us to think on things that are *true*-- not false or unreliable but real; *honest*-- honorable and without pretense; *just*-- righteous both toward God and man; *pure*-- a life of high moral character; *lovely*-- admirable to think about; *of good report*-- worthy of being considered; *virtuous*-- moral excellence, above reproach; and *praiseworthy*-- deserving to be commended.

At first this list looked long and overwhelming. As I became more aware of my thoughts I was surprised, disturbed, and sometimes discouraged at how often my thoughts did not fit the list. Instead of comparing every thought to each word in the list, I found myself often thinking "*whoa, is this a lovely thing to think about?*" Lovely means to inspire love, and a bad thought in any way is not likely to be lovely.

Evil thoughts need to be replaced immediately, before they are followed by negative actions. We can't entertain wrong thoughts and thoughts of Jesus at the same time. The Lord will help us chase away evil thoughts, as we quote Scripture, sing a hymn, or meditate on Christ and what He has done for us. Satan will inject his evil into our minds over and over, sometimes in rapid succession. But if we flee from him each time, with God's help, we will gain victory over our thought life. God also promises to draw near to us as we draw near to Him. Just as our mouths speak from the abundance of our hearts, our thoughts spring from our hearts, also. Wholesome thoughts are formed in hearts of integrity.

- Do my actions reveal a well-controlled thought life?
- Is my heart conducive to producing wholesome thoughts?
- *Lord, help me to replace all evil thoughts with lovely thoughts from You today.*

An Awful Day

"Put on the whole armor of God, that ye may be able to stand against the wiles of the devil."
- Ephesians 6:11

My day was rapidly going from bad to worse, and my mood was going right with it. A discouraging phone call had left me wiped out emotionally. The children were fussy and three dozen eggs had been knocked to the carpeted floor in a sticky mess. To add to the confusion, the pressure was on to be ready for the evening revival meeting on time. I got the little girls ready to go, only to have them get dirty, needing to be changed. We were late to church after trying so hard. Then the baby abruptly threw up so I spent the rest of the evening in the van with her. And there were other darts from Satan, one after the other, until I finally dropped into bed, late that night, and cried.

"Why Lord?" I asked. "How could my peace be so completely shattered in one afternoon and evening?"

"Did you pray this morning?" I sensed Him asking.

Oh...I guess I didn't. I meant to. I read my devotional and Scripture for the day, but well...life just got in the way and I never did pray. I thought further. I had experienced two recent spiritual victories in my personal life. Satan doesn't like that, I know, and I had left myself exposed. I had not put on the full armor of God; therefore I was a prime target. Another reminder that we cannot afford not to pray! We don't have to remain unprotected. We have a choice. Beware of making the wrong one!

- Do I recognize the need to protect myself with prayer?
- Am I faithful in my praying regularly so as to stay in tune with my Protector?
- *Lord, life does get in the way, but help me to be faithful in prayer, trusting You for protection.*

Faith Without Visual Evidence

*"Now faith is the substance of things hoped for,
the evidence of things not seen."
- Hebrews 11:1*

"*I believe in God even though I can't see Him,/ Even when He is silent, I know He is there... I believe that the sun, even when I can't see it,/ Is there when the clouds keep it hidden from view...* Singing heartily, with full confidence that every word was the undeniable truth, Anna looked out the window and saw that it was snowing again. *Again!* Winters in Michigan can be long with lots of snow and little sunshine. For a brief moment she experienced disappointment, but then reminded herself once more that spring was indeed coming. The next day was sunny and thawing, every sound and smell speaking of spring. The following day, though, brought a frigid wind with blowing snow and they put more logs on the fire. However, even though winter just did not want to let go, Anna had faith that spring was on the way. The calendar said so, and the days were certainly getting longer. A little patience to go along with the faith would surely bring her the reward of a beautiful springtime!

When it comes to something like seasons, our faith stands firm in spite of any evidence to the contrary. That is precisely the sort of faith we want to have when we think about God. We can describe faith as confidence and certainty, two qualities which involve believing in God's character (He *is* who He says He is), and believing in God's promises (He *will do* what He says He will do). By believing that God will do as He has promised before we can even see it happening, we demonstrate true faith. (John 20:29) We may possibly never even see the fruit of our faith here on earth. We may become frustrated and impatient and want to quit. But take heart! God hears our prayers and is always working on our behalf. Remember, the best rewards we can hope for are waiting for us in Heaven!

- Do I truly and fully believe that God will keep all His promises to me?
- What challenges do I have that I could trust to God with more faith than I have been?
- *Lord, thank You for Your unfailing promises and help me to trust You with my whole heart.*

"I Believe in God" by Geraldine Koehm. Used with permission.

March 18

Read: Psalm 91

God's Promises In Times Of Trouble, Part I

"According to all that He promised: there hath not failed one word of all his good promise."
- I Kings 8:56

The world is full of promises that cannot be, or will not be, kept. Wedding vows are broken as often, or more often, than they are kept. Politicians make promises to gain supporters that we know they can't keep. Even the Presidents have made promises that were impossible to fulfill. Toothpaste ads promise romance if you just use *their* brand! Makers of creams and lotions promise beauty, sellers of herbs and vitamins promise youthfulness and good health. Children make rash promises to each other; which, as sincere as they are at the time, they may or may not be able to keep. We all know about these types of promises.

There is One, however, whose promises never fail. When we read God's promises in His Word, we can have full confidence that He will keep them. *He will never fail to come through on His promises*. His many promises are recorded all throughout the Scriptures. In the ninety-first Psalm God doesn't promise freedom from danger, but He does promise His help when we face danger. Many examples of this type of protection are recorded in the Scriptures, and these promises are available to us today.

Vv. 1, 2... The promise of protection is available to those who "dwell in the secret place of the most High." We can trust Him for safety, giving ourselves daily into His care, and abiding under the shadow of His protection. He will be a shelter to hide under during the storm, a strong fort that we can run to in danger. We can look ahead in confidence and say, "My refuge and my fortress: my God; in Him will I trust."

V. 3 refers to hidden dangers. A trapper will hide his trap, covering it carefully to catch the unwary animal. Satan's evil plot to trip us up is like a bird-trapper's hidden snare. He wraps his snares in all kinds of beautiful, safe-looking "bait." Staying in the shadow of God's protection will keep us from these traps and from evil, offensive influences and beliefs that are plentiful in our world today. It takes His protection and wisdom to discern what is of the Lord, and what is false teaching. We must stay within the shadow of His protection!

- Do I fully believe that God will keep His promises to protect me in every circumstance?
- How can I more completely avail myself of His protection today?
- *Lord, I thank You for your promise of shelter, and I ask You to put your shadow of protection over me today.*

God's Promises In Times Of Trouble, Part II

"For thou hast been a shelter for me,
and a strong tower from the enemy."
- Psalm 61:3

Verse 4 says we will be sheltered with His feathers and wings. Now feathers and wings are light and fluffy and might seem like flimsy protection. We'd likely prefer to be sheltered by thick walls or strong, trained warriors. I've heard a story, however, that would illustrate a different view.

A little prairie chicken that lived on the plains of Africa died in a roaring fire that swept across the land. A man who was out surveying the damage the next day came across the dead, charred chicken. He gave the burned body a slight kick with his boot and as the carcass rolled over, out tumbled a pile of baby chicks, alive and well. They had been completely protected by their mother's wings and feathers, and her commitment to shelter them to her death. This is the kind of protection God offers to us.

God's promises are sure. His Truth is a shield for us, a piece of armor, carried on the arm that is very effective in fending off the darts and blows of the enemy. Reciting memorized Scripture is an effective way to use this shield when Satan hurls his arrows of temptation our way. A buckler is a small shield worn on the forearm or held at arm's length for the same purpose of protecting its user.

All of us can probably remember times when we were afraid of the dark. An enemy attack at night is especially frightening because we cannot see the source of danger. Attacks during the day can be alarming too, because arrows fly fast. We may have very little time to decide how to defend ourselves. But if we have covered ourselves in prayer, and we have God's Word hidden in our hearts ready to quote, we will not need to be afraid. (v. 5) God has promised His protection against these attacks.

Evil and destruction can be present at night or in the middle of the day. Just as disease thrives in the absence of sunlight, so sin flourishes in the dark. (v. 6) But we know, plainly illustrated by acts of terrorism committed in broad daylight, that destruction is rampant even in the light of day.

The struggles of everyday life can seem as though we are in the midst of a raging battle with victory failing us on every side. (v. 7) In the end, however, victory will be ours. We will *see* the wicked punished, but we ourselves will be free from harm. We are safe in Him, *because we have made Him, who is our refuge…our habitation*. (vv. 8, 9)

- Do I recognize the danger all around me and those I love?
- How could I more effectively place my loved ones and myself under His protection today?
- *Lord, I praise You for Your unfailing protection, and I ask You to shelter my loved ones and me today.*

 Read: Psalm 91

God's Promises In Times Of Trouble, Part III

"He shall call upon me, and I will ...be with him in trouble; I will deliver him, and honour him."
- Psalm 91:15

God is present to help us through any situation. One of the roles of angels is to watch over believers. There are many examples of guardian angels in the Scriptures, and they are still protecting us today. Although we generally cannot see them, and may not recognize them when we do, it is comforting to know that they are there, even in times of great stress and fear. (vv. 11, 12) We can be assured of this protection as long as we are inside God's divine will. Satan quoted this passage when tempting Jesus to jump off the temple. (Luke 4:10, 11) For us to submit to Satan's proposals, however, even though he may quote Scripture, would be outside God's will and would not be covered by His protection.

In I Peter 5:8 Satan is portrayed as a lion that is terribly violent; stalking about looking for someone to destroy. In Revelation 12:9 he is described as a dragon and a snake, using sly and cunning schemes to deceive the whole world. We have the assurance here in Psalm 91:13 that with God's protection and help, *we will defeat the enemy* rather than Satan being triumphant over us.

In the last part of this chapter God gives six tremendous guarantees of His protection to the believer who is living under the shadow of His protection by staying within His divine will. He says clearly that if we set our love upon Him, *He will* deliver us; *He will* set us on high; *He will* answer our prayers; *He will* be with us in trouble; *He will* honor us; and *He will* satisfy us with full life and give us the gift of salvation.

These promises can actually be a bit confusing when we think of devoted Christians who have died of disease or in car accidents; or of missionaries who have been brutally murdered. We can end up with more questions than peace in our hearts. It is true, however, that there is safety for those who are living within the will of God. Believers walking with the Lord will not die until their work on earth is done. Jesus died young, at age thirty-three, but He knew that no one could touch Him until He had finished His work. So it is with us. Satan can't touch us without God's permission, but God allows trials to strengthen us and bring us closer to Him. We can trust Him to carry us through any time of testing.

- Am I staying within God's will for me, in all areas of daily life such as submission to my husband or employer?
- What situations can I think of when there may have been angels assisting me?
- *Lord, I believe that You will protect me and I ask You to help me stay within Your will for my life.*

It's All Yours!

"Whereby are given unto us exceeding great and precious promises."
- II Peter 1:4

I recently heard a story that went something like this. There was a man who had an extensive collection of art that was quite valuable. He had these pieces of art hanging on the walls in his home. The man's son was away fighting in a war, and one sad day he received the news that his son had been killed in battle. The boy's friend, who was on the battlefield with him, quickly sketched one last picture of his friend. He later gave this picture to the grieving father who hung it on the wall with the rest of his collection.

Time went on, years passed, and the old man became ill and died. His artwork was to be sold at a special auction, apart from his other possessions. The day arrived and art collectors gathered from far and near, excited and eager to purchase some of this man's well-known pieces. As the auctioneer began, the first piece he held up was the picture of the man's son. No one was interested. Failing to get a bid, he dropped the price again and again. Finally, when the price of the picture had become ridiculously low, someone in the back of the crowd raised his hand. "I'll take it," he said. "Sold!" the auctioneer called, "And the sale is over!" After a moment of stunned silence a murmur rose, and the confused collectors asked him what was going on.

Then the auctioneer explained. "The owner of these pieces left a notice in his will that whoever bought the picture of his son would receive the entire collection at no additional cost."

We can only imagine how that made them feel. Especially the one receiving the art. But God has an offer like this for us, too! Except there isn't an auction and there isn't just **one** "first item." Furthermore, that "item" is free of charge; a gift which we only have to accept. The gift is salvation, and it's available to everyone, already paid for by Jesus Himself through His death on the cross. Once we accept this gift, God's entire collection of promises is available to us. As we live out the life He has planned for us, seeking His will, serving Him where He plants us, loving Him with our whole hearts and sharing that love with others, we will be the recipients of these valuable promises that are available to us at "no extra charge." When we accept His gift of salvation, we can claim the promises that go with it.

- Am I familiar with all of the promises God has available for me?
- What promises could I claim now that would help me through the trials of the day?
- *Lord, I thank You for all of Your promises to me. Please remind me when I need to claim them today.*

 Read: Esther 4

God, Our Security

"He shall not be afraid of evil tidings:
his heart is fixed, trusting in the Lord."
- Psalm 112:7

In the story of Esther we read an amazing account of courage. We aren't told how old Esther was or how she felt about being brought to the king's palace. But it must have been a trial to leave the security of her familiar home and begin a whole new life in a strange place. God blessed her, however, and she "pleased Hegai, the keeper of the women."

After a full year of purification, Esther was called to the king's quarters. It had to be frightening to again leave the security of home and step into an unfamiliar situation. But God was still with her, "and the king loved Esther above all the women...and made her queen."

The biggest test, however, came when Haman contrived a plot to kill all the Jews, and Mordecai begged Esther to intervene. She knew it could mean her death, but she bravely risked her life for the sake of the Jewish people. Once again God protected her, the king accepted her request, and the Jews were saved.

While we may not be risking our lives, we all face difficult circumstances at times. Do you need to confront a friend about a touchy matter? Are you facing unpleasant medical tests or procedures? Perhaps you need to stand firm with a teenage child, knowing the reaction may be explosive. We would be foolish to think that we are secure in our own strength. Esther was the queen, sharing some of the king's power, but she still needed the security of God's protection and wisdom. We also can fully rely on Him to be our security, and He will bless us for it.

- Do I recognize the blessing of God's security in my life?
- What circumstances am I facing for which He can give me strength?
- *Lord, I praise you for protecting Esther long ago and for offering me that security today.*

A Piranha Personality

"For all the law is fulfilled in one word…
Thou shall love thy neighbor as thyself."
- Galatians 5:14

Have you ever had a chance to observe or study a piranha? They are actually quite small, about the size of a man's hand. Living in the rivers of South America, the Red-bellied piranha is the most well-known. It has very strong jaws and teeth sharp enough to bite through a steel fishing hook! They are voracious eaters and, traveling in a school, can devour prey much larger than themselves in a short time. They are attracted by the smell of blood but usually feed on what is left by others. Natives can swim in piranha-infested water without attacks as long as other food is plentiful for the fish. While the piranha's ferocious reputation may not be fully deserved, they are dangerous and not to be taken lightly.

We have an acquaintance who has a 35-gallon aquarium. In it there was just one fish you could see--a four inch piranha. Our friend explained that you can't very well keep even two piranhas in one tank. Sooner or later, one becomes lunch for the other. He went on to say that if the two were constantly supplied with an abundance of food, they might co-exist longer, but they would still take bites out of each other! Another interesting aspect of this aquarium is that there were two other small fish lying quietly in the bottom of the tank, blending into the landscape, who so far had not been bothered. The piranha didn't seem even to notice their existence.

Have you ever had a chance to *feel* like a piranha? Have you ever felt like taking a *bite* out of someone you know or even someone you love (at a moment when you're not *liking* them real well)? Maybe you become snappy, using words that bite and hurt, or you just self-righteously talk behind their back, focusing on their faults and weaknesses rather than building them up with kind words. Are you quick to criticize those who are noticeably serving the Lord with their talents, making mistakes here and there along the way; while you ignore those who stay in the background safely blending in with the landscape? Do you have a *piranha personality?*

I think we can all identify with this feeling. So, how do we avoid or give up this mindset? First of all, think about what you've been "eating." Are you voraciously feeding on God's Word, growing spiritually and in His likeness rather than feeding on the faults of those around us? God does not have a piranha personality! He instructs us to also love and serve each other, building each other up in the Lord.

- Am I showing a piranha personality to those around me?
- What am I feeding on right now? Do I need to be feeding more from God's Word to become more like Him?
- *Oh Lord, give me a keen appetite for Your Word; fill me with Your love and a desire to serve others for You.*

Read: Judges 16

The Strength Of Samson

*"For the Lord JEHOVAH is my strength and my song;
he also is become my salvation."
- Isaiah 12:2*

Samson was a man to whom God gave exceptional strength. He was a Nazarite, set apart from birth, to do a great work for the Lord. He was to begin to deliver the Israelites from the Philistines. (Judges 13:5) Even though Samson made some foolish choices and sometimes used his abilities unwisely, God still blessed him with His strength numerous times. But it isn't long until we read that Samson became proud and boasted only of his own strength. He began flirting with sin, thinking he was strong enough that it couldn't hurt him. But we all know what happened to Samson. His arrogance eventually stripped him of his physical strength. He was blinded and imprisoned by the gloating Philistines, and spent the rest of his life on a treadmill, grinding grain in the prison house, the object of scorn and mockery.

Was Samson a failure? If we think about it, just how different are we? How often do we think "I can handle it," and walk boldly into the face of temptation? Just like Samson, if we trust our own strength to sustain us in temptation, we can become blinded and enslaved. At the end of Samson's life, when he was humbled and had no strength of his own, God answered his prayer for the strength he needed for one final victory over the Philistines. Only when we realize our own weakness do we allow God to be our strength and salvation. With God all things are possible, without Him we are nothing.

- How often do I willfully entertain temptation instead of fleeing it?
- Is my confidence in God's strength or in my own?
- *Lord, help me remember that I cannot overcome sin or resist temptation in my own strength.*

Transformed

"Behold, I show you a mystery;
We shall not all sleep, but we shall all be changed."
- I Corinthians 15:51

The transformation that occurs during the life cycle of a Monarch butterfly is amazingly fascinating. Its life begins as a homely little striped caterpillar with funny antennae at each end. Its diet consists only of milkweed leaves, which are poisonous to many other creatures. It consumes huge amounts, growing so rapidly that it outgrows its skin every few days. At the right time the caterpillar will fasten its tail to a leaf or twig with a little silk and hang there very still. Soon it sheds its skin one last time, and forms a chrysalis, bright green with sparkling gold spots on it. What happens inside that chrysalis during the next phase is nothing short of a miracle. From a lowly worm comes a lovely butterfly. After emerging from the chrysalis the butterfly rests awhile, gently fanning its wings to expand and dry them. Then the butterfly is ready to soar away to begin its life in the air, stopping now and then to sip the sweet nectar from beautiful flowers. Who but God could perform such a miracle?!

As with the Monarch butterfly, God in His greatness is able to perform a miracle within us, too. A Monarch caterpillar's first food, the milkweed leaf, contains a milky-white substance. God tells us that we also should "As newborn babes desire the sincere milk of the Word that ye may grow thereby." (I Peter 2:2) As He changes the caterpillar in the chrysalis, God can perform miracles in our hearts and lives too. He is getting us ready for our own final flight to Glory, where we will dine on the pure sweet nectar of his love forever.

- Am I allowing God to transform me, making me into a new creature?
- How can I rearrange my day to make more time to feast on His Word, growing in Him?
- *Lord, work in this humble, awkward heart of mine, making me into a new creature.*

March 26 *Read: II Kings 5:20-27*

Honesty

*"Search me, O God, and know my heart:
try me, and know my thoughts."
- Psalm 139:23*

Reading the story of Gahazi gives us the impression that he was a greedy, dishonest man. Elisha had just instructed Naaman to wash in the Jordan River, and he had been cleansed of his leprosy. Naaman was very grateful and wanted to pay Elisha, but he refused to take any payment.

Gahazi, Elisha's servant, wasn't happy. He ran after Naaman and, telling him a false story, received double the payment that he requested. After hiding the money and clothes in his house, he lied to Elisha also, saying he hadn't gone anywhere. But Elisha knew exactly what he had done. Because of Gahazi's greed and dishonesty, Elisha put an instant curse of leprosy upon him and his descendants forever. It was an awful price that Gahazi paid to learn that "God is not mocked."

We do our best to teach our children that dishonesty doesn't pay. But what about us as Christian women? Are we always honest before God? Or do we sometimes gloss things over in our minds, trying to convince ourselves that we are being honest. Such as "I can go there without yielding to the temptations I know will beset me there," or "I can own something without thinking too highly of it." Or possibly keeping something from my husband that I know he wouldn't quite approve of.

Just as Elisha knew what his servant had done, so God knows the thoughts and intents of our hearts. And as Gahazi learned that dishonesty doesn't pay, so do we know that it is always best to be completely honest with ourselves, and with God. He will surely bless us for it.

- Is there something in my heart that I'm trying to hide from God, or even from myself?
- Am I willing to search my heart for hidden dishonesty?
- *Lord, help me always to be completely honest with myself and with you.*

Contentment

"He that loveth silver shall not be satisfied with silver; nor he that loveth abundance with increase: this is also vanity."
- Ecclesiastes 5:10

Achan could have avoided a lot of trouble and saved his life if he had been content with what he had. In Joshua 6 & 7, we read that God had told the Israelites not to take anything out of Jericho when they destroyed the city. All the wealth was to go into the treasury of the house of the Lord. But Achan coveted a beautiful Babylonian robe that he saw there. He took it, along with some silver and gold, and hid it all in the dirt floor of his tent. Because of his greed and deceit, the Israelites lost the next battle they fought. And the next day Achan and his family were stoned and burned, along with all of their possessions, including the stolen items.

I sigh to think of the times that I, like Achan, have coveted things I didn't have. More "silver or gold" to spend on my wants. A "Babylonian robe" that I didn't really need. More storage space, better dishes, another bathroom, nicer appliances, more conveniences. Or maybe, as a busy mother, just simply some leisure time! The list of wants can be endless and if we dwell on these our contentment will soon shatter. Satan will go to great lengths to rob us of our contented spirit, but Paul tells us in Hebrews 13:5 to be content with what we have. And I Timothy 6:6 says "godliness with contentment is great gain." We will find more enjoyment in the things that God has blessed us with, if we're content with what we have already.

- Would I be more contented with what God has already given me if I were to set my affection on things above instead of things on earth?
- Can I say with Paul that "I have learned in whatsoever state I am, therewith to be content?"
- *Lord, it's so easy to covet what I don't have. Open my eyes to the blessings all around me.*

 Read: Ruth 1

Loyalty

"But as for me and my house,
we will serve the Lord."
- Joshua 24:15

Reading the story of Ruth always tugs at my heart. It had to take courage and a true feeling of loyalty for Ruth to go with her mother-in-law to a strange land, with its strange people and customs. I don't blame Orpah for going back to her childhood home. But I admire Ruth for going on with Naomi. She loved Naomi dearly and had always been kind to her. (Ruth 1:8) Ruth continued to provide for her mother-in-law in Bethlehem by gleaning in the fields of Boaz. The story tells how she married Boaz, became the great-grandmother of David, and a direct ancestor of Jesus.

As a child living in Moab, Ruth must have grown up worshiping idols and being taught about the evil customs of their god, Chemosh. But through the influence of her mother-in-law she became a loyal and faithful follower of God. Ruth's commitment and loyalty are expressed in the following memorable response to her mother-in-law: "Thy people shall be my people and thy God my God."

And I wonder…am I, who had a Christian up-bringing, as loyal to God as Ruth was? Am I willing to sacrifice sleep or leisure activities to spend time in Bible study and prayer? Or to spend time helping others in need, as God prompts me? Or even to talk about how God is working in or blessing my life? My heart's desire is to be as faithful in my loyalty to God as Ruth was in her loyalty to Naomi.

- Am I as loyal to God as He wants me to be?
- Am I teaching this loyalty to my children by my words and actions?
- *Lord, help me to be loyal to You at all times.*

Courage

"Be of good courage, and He shall strengthen your heart, all ye that hope in the Lord."
- Psalm 31:24

In I Samuel 25, we read about the courage of Abigail. Her foolish husband, Nabal, had rudely refused to give any food to David and his army. This made David quite angry as Nabal was a wealthy man and David's men had protected Nabal's shepherds and sheep out in the desert. So David ordered his men to put on their swords, and they headed for Nabal's place, determined to get revenge.

As soon as Abigail heard what had happened, she loaded up food and wine and went to meet David. She was risking the wrath of her wicked husband and heading right into the path of an angry David. I can imagine that she must have experienced a myriad of emotions as she rode out to meet him. But David was impressed! He praised her for keeping him from shedding blood. And when Nabal died a short time later, David asked Abigail to be his wife.

David tells us in Psalms 31:24 to be of good courage, and God will strengthen our hearts. He certainly knew that it often takes courage to stand for the right. Whether we are hiding from those who are pursuing us, as David was, or walking into a room full of strangers, or facing other circumstances out of our comfort zone, God will give us the courage we need. He's ready to "strengthen our hearts" in any situation we may face in our daily walk with Him.

- Do I look to God for courage when my courage fails me?
- What circumstances am I facing today for which God wants to give me courage?
- *Lord, remind me to seek my strength from you, rather than relying on my own.*

Read: Acts 9:1-22

Obedience

"And the peace of God, which passeth all understanding, shall keep your hearts and minds through Christ Jesus."
- Philippians 4:7

As we read the story of Saul's conversion in Acts 9, we can only wonder how Ananias, a believer, must have felt when God spoke to him in a vision. God asked him to go find Saul and put his hand on him that he might see again. We know Ananias was worried, likely even afraid. He had heard about Saul and knew he was coming to Damascus to arrest Christians. Although Ananias doubted, he put his trust in God and went.

I am reminded of the times (more times than I care to think about) that God has convicted me of wronging someone. "Go," He would say in a still small voice, "And apologize. Make your wrong right."

"Oh, but God," I would argue. "Are you *sure?* I really don't think it's a big deal. She's probably forgotten all about it. I'm sure it didn't hurt her feelings," and so on--but, knowing I would have no peace until I obeyed, I finally relented and went.

It must have been a blessing to Ananias to witness Saul's sight being restored and to get to know him as a zealous new believer. I've been blessed too, with restored peace, and a stronger bond of friendship, as I was readily forgiven by God, and by the one whom I had wronged. Prompt obedience to the still, small voice of God is the only way to have that "peace which passeth all understanding."

- Am I keeping myself sensitive to that still, small voice through Bible study, prayer, and listening for Him?
- Am I willing to obey God's voice when He speaks to me?
- *Lord, make my spirit sensitive to your voice and make me willing to obey You.*

Perserverance

"Be thou faithful unto death, and
I will give thee a crown of life."
- Revelation 2:10

Reading the story of Naaman gives us a glimpse of how God rewards perseverance. Naaman took the advice of a little servant girl and traveled a long distance to see Elisha. He was expecting instant healing at the touch of Elisha's hand and was quite angry when he was told to go dip himself seven times in the Jordan River. But at the urging of his servants, he went to the river.

I wonder how he felt about the "seven times." Did he feel foolish as he came up six times still a leper? His servants were likely watching and after all, how could a dip in the Jordan possibly cure leprosy? But he didn't quit. He followed Elisha's directions to dip seven times, and God rewarded his perseverance by healing him.

There have been many times in my life when I have felt like quitting. When I have tried to overcome a bad habit and failed again and again. When I prayed and prayed about a particular situation and saw no results. And where more often than in training children? When it seems that no matter how hard you try, you're just not getting through. But wait. Do we really want to quit? It was only after the seventh dip that Naaman was healed. This may be the last time I fail with this bad habit. Today may be the day I see results from my prayers. Or it may be just a little longer until our training shows up in this child. God is working...don't give up! Persevere and He will bless you for it.

- Is there an area of my life that needs changing, that I've given up on?
- In the face of the seemingly impossible, am I willing to persevere, as a testimony to God's faithfulness?
- *Lord, give me the desire and strength to keep going in the ways that you would have me to go.*

April

Who's Listening

"Bringing into captivity every thought
to the obedience of Christ."
- II Corinthians 10:5

Our son and his wife had left their home in Montana and were driving toward Canada to spend the weekend visiting friends. Since he didn't have a lot of work the following week, they weren't in any big hurry to get back home. Before they reached the Canadian border, Mike called their friends and asked about the possibility of working a few days while they were there. They were told that there was, indeed, work for him if they wanted to stay awhile.

Some time later, they approached the border to discover that the Canadian authorities were waiting on them! Mike and Anna were escorted to the lobby of the border crossing station and questioned about their intentions for entering Canada. Unknown to them, it was illegal to go into Canada for work without a work permit! How did the authorities *know* that was their plan? Easy. Someone had overheard Mike's cell phone conversation (over their scanner most likely), had noted his full name and anonymously alerted the border patrol officials. Needless to say, Mike and Anna instantly changed their plans and assured the officials that they would not be working during their stay in Canada!

Several years ago a friend of mine told me how she had been hearing her neighbor's cordless phone conversations over her baby monitor. She let them know about it, and somehow they remedied the problem.

There are many stories of situations like this that can be rather humorous, but they can also be sobering and rather unsettling. We don't want others listening to us, especially when we don't *know* they're listening! That's understandable of course, but do we ever stop to think that there is One who hears (and sees) *everything* we say and do? We may go to great lengths to keep our words and actions hidden from others, but we are deceiving only ourselves if we think we can hide anything from God. The same God who created us and knows us intimately not only hears and sees everything we do, He also knows our very thoughts and intentions. One of Satan's tricks is to get us so focused on the worrisome fears of technology that we forget about our Father in Heaven. This world *is* getting more wicked all the time, but we need to remember that it is *God* whom we must answer to in the end, and there is nothing we can hide from Him.

- Am I constantly aware that my thoughts and actions are not hidden from God?
- What thoughts or actions am I struggling with today that God sees and wants to help me overcome?
- *Lord, help me to remember that You hear and see everything I do, even though I can hide from others.*

Read: Psalm 51

Are You Ready?

"Create in me a clean heart, O God;
and renew a right spirit within me"
- Psalm 51:10

A friend of mine was telling me about an inspiration God had given her recently. She had company coming and had thoroughly cleaned her house, including her bedroom where her guests would be sleeping. As she looked around at her clean, tidy room, she was struck with a thought that hadn't occurred to her before. While she kept the rest of the house tidy, she tended to let her bedroom go, because, after all, it was upstairs and no one else was going to see it. It's interesting that we seem to look at the house with new eyes when we expect someone else to be evaluating our housekeeping! And how easy it is to let things go when we do *not* expect other eyes to see the clutter and the cobwebs. With children of all ages, I know how quickly things can become untidy, and how difficult it can be even to try to keep things looking decent. And I know how relieved I am when a visitor stops in after we have cleaned up. And also how embarrassing it is when I have been just too tired even to care, and someone happens to come by and see our mess.

As we were discussing this, we talked about how it could relate to our Christian lives and not knowing when Jesus will return. When Jesus tells us to be ready, does He mean *always*, or just when we think someone will be evaluating our hearts? How easily we forget that He is always here, able to see how clean our hearts are! Jesus isn't critical when our "houses" are not perfectly clean. We cannot possibly keep a house spotless at all times without letting more important things go. It is also quite possible to function in a house with a good bit of hidden (or very visible) dirt and clutter. God is able to use us even though we have hidden "dirt and clutter" in our hearts. But it grieves Him, and just as it is easier to function in a tidy house, so we can be much more effective for Jesus if our hearts are clean…even the upstairs, out-of-the-way corners.

Inspecting our hearts closely can be rather painful just as it is sometimes appalling to really *see* all the dirt we have been ignoring in our house. We wonder uneasily just how many others have noticed. But, oh, how good it feels to clear out the clutter and polish the windows. Dust the furniture and vacuum the floors. Our spirits are lifted and our steps are lighter. We work with a new will. We are ready for any visitors who may stop by. We actually hope someone does! So it is when we clean up our hearts. We should not wait to examine our hearts and clean them up. We need to be ready when Jesus comes for His spotless bride!

- I know how clean my house is but what about my heart?
- Is my heart ready to serve Him in whatever way He leads?
- *Lord, help me to see into my heart and desire to clean it up so that I can be more effective for You.*

Saved By A Broken Stronghold

"For the Lord your God, He is God
in heaven above and in earth beneath."
- Joshua 2:11

It seems a bit odd that Joshua's spies would choose Rahab's house as a place to stay, but they could come and go from there without raising much suspicion. Her house was built into the wall so it was an excellent location for a quick escape, and God knew that Rahab's heart was open to Him. She lived a life of sin in a wicked city but she, too, had heard about Israel's God and how He had defeated their enemies. The people of Jericho were all afraid, but Rahab believed.

After hiding the spies under the flax on her roof, Rahab told them that she now believed their God was the true God. She fully believed that He would destroy the city of Jericho and begged the men to spare her and her family. They promised to repay her kindness by saving them all, as long as she marked her house with a red cord in the window and said nothing to anyone about why they had been there. The other stipulation was that all of them had to be in her house at the time of the invasion. They would not be responsible for anyone who had gone out into the streets.

This must have presented somewhat of a dilemma. I imagine Rahab gathered her family together as soon as possible, but they didn't know when or how this attack was going to take place. We don't know how many there were or how long they had to wait, but we do know that it was at least a week. Rahab and her family watched the Israelites' amazing daily march for six days before they finally invaded the city. It must have been an unnerving challenge to wait patiently with no way to get fresh provisions; but they would not have wanted to leave the house, either. There would be no escape for them until God had broken down the stronghold of Jericho and allowed their deliverers to save them.

Are you trapped in a "Jericho" that you need to allow God to break down, believing that He can, and will, deliver you from its grip? Have you confessed this stronghold as sin, and are you waiting patiently and prayerfully for deliverance in God's timing? Rahab went from a life of sin to living in Israel and becoming the great-grandmother of David, a direct link in the lineage of Jesus. Great blessings await those willing to let God break down strongholds of darkness in their lives. These blessings spill over to bless others in ways you would never dream possible. Ask God to reveal these strongholds to you and to deliver you from them.

- Do I know of any strongholds of wrong in my life or have I asked God to reveal them to me?
- Do I have complete faith that God is able and willing to break down these "Jerichos" for me?
- *Lord, I long to be free from all strongholds of wrong in my life. Show me what they are and how to be free.*

April 4

Read: John 13

Discipleship

"By this shall all men know that ye are my disciples, if ye have love one to another."
- John 13:35

Sometimes, as disciples of Jesus, we can begin to feel as though we are not worthy to be called His disciples. We want to be worthy--good and pure, having our thoughts centered on Him. We want to dedicate our lives to His service without hesitation or complaining. But we are human, and the daily grind of life wears us down.

But we are not alone! Not only do our fellow believers struggle with the same things, even Christ's disciples did. They lived and walked with Him, surely they wouldn't struggle with being worthy would they? But let's think for a moment... about the upper room, where twelve men were eating supper with Jesus before His death. Judas was ready to betray his Lord. (Do we ever betray Him with our words or actions?) Thomas was a doubter. (How often do we doubt His power to help us?) And Peter was soon to swear and deny that he ever knew the man. (Do we ever grieve Him with wrong talk or deny Him our time, skipping devotions or rushing through them?) In short, all twelve men sitting around that table were ready to desert Jesus before morning. This was no secret to Him. He knew it all and could have thrown up His hands and given up on them as hopeless. But He didn't. Instead, He got on His knees and lovingly washed their feet. And He gave them a new commandment that they should love one another as he loved them. What an amazing love!

Would He do any less for us? I don't think so. He knows and understands everything we are feeling. He will lovingly cleanse our hearts and minds of unworthy thoughts and feelings. And He still desires that we would love one another as He loves us. By this shall all men know that we are His disciples.

- Am I showing a life of true discipleship by my love for Jesus and others?
- Jesus forgave and served those who wronged Him. Do I?
- *Lord, forgive me when I deny You in any way, and give me the courage to always be true to You.*

Fight The Good Fight

"Fight the good fight of faith, lay hold on eternal life, whereunto thou art also called."
- I Timothy 6:12

Reading historical novels can be an interesting way to get a feel for history. Friends of ours had been reading several books about the Middle Ages and knighthood. One recurring theme had to do with young men "earning their spurs." This required them to do some valiant deed, especially in battle, to impress the authorities with their ability and skill so they could be knighted. The hero in one particular story was the son of a wealthy land-owner who had more interest in his own research than in going to war. Also, since England was actually at peace at that time, it looked as though this young man would have to attach himself to a powerful knight and maybe even become a professional soldier in another country's war to be able to distinguish himself. He would actually be seeking out danger and discomfort, risking capture, pain, and death, to prove to himself and to the world that he was worthy of honor. He spent long hours in training so that he could attack his fellow man with sword, lance, or pike and hopefully avoid having someone else use those same terrible weapons on him.

Can we relate to this young man as a "soldier?" As Christians, we are definitely engaged in warfare. We don't, however, have to seek out battles, as we have an enemy who is determined to destroy us even though he has already lost the war. How do we approach these battles in our lives? This man welcomed them, trained for them, and went into them bravely, knowing he was well prepared for the fight. We can also face the battles of life bravely, knowing that our Commander goes before us and that we are well equipped with the full armor of God. With the Spirit to guide us, prayer to give us confidence, memorized Scripture to ward off Satan, and our fellow "soldiers" for strength and encouragement, we can march into battle with just as much faith and courage as any young man going to war.

- Am I adequately prepared for the battles in my life?
- What areas of my life need more training if I am to bravely face these battles?
- *Lord, life is full of battles, and I need Your armor to protect me, and Your strength to keep me going.*

 Read: Exodus 15:22-16:3; 17:1-6

The Coming Out Of Israel

"By strength of hand the Lord brought us out from Egypt, from the house of bondage."
- Exodus 13:14

The Israelites had lived in bondage to the Egyptians for four hundred and thirty years (Exodus 12:40) and had cried to the Lord for deliverance from their distress. Anything, they thought, would be better than where they were. Eagerly they prepared for the journey to the Promised Land and started out confidently and in good spirits. God led them by a pillar of cloud during the day and a pillar of fire at night. He miraculously parted the Red Sea for them and destroyed their enemies. They had nothing to fear for God was with them!

It wasn't long, however, until they began to realize that this coming out was not as easy as they had thought it would be. In fact, it was just plain hard. Only three days after they had left the Red Sea, they were in the wilderness without water. Rather than waiting patiently to see how God would supply their need, they murmured against Moses. They were thirsty, and their children and animals were thirsty. God did provide sweet water for them and they went on.

Two and a half months after they left Egypt, they were ready to go back. They were hungry and angry with Moses and Aaron. "We should have stayed in Egypt!" they complained. "We were slaves, yes, but we had it made there. We had plenty of food and could eat our fill, and now you have brought us out here in the wilderness to kill us with hunger!" God then provided manna for them to eat, and they were satisfied. That is, until they needed water again. Then they harassed Moses, demanding water and murmuring against him, accusing him of trying to kill them. So soon they forgot all the ways God had provided for them.

It may seem strange to us that after all the years of cruel slavery, the Israelites would actually think that their old life had been better than the new. But really, how different are we? Time after time we witness the Lord's grace and deliverance in our lives and the lives of others, but when the going gets tough we grumble. A child gets sick when we had plans to go somewhere. We feel the sting of criticism from a sister when we thought we could trust her with our feelings. We watch in dismay while our plans for the future crumble around us, and we wonder "Why, Lord?" But just as God provided for them in the wilderness, so He will provide for us today. When we are tempted to murmur, we may choose to trust Him instead!

- Do I see in myself the same murmuring spirit that I see in the Israelites of long ago?
- In what situations do I need to trust God, rather than worry or complain?
- *Lord, I know You took care of the Israelites in their need, and I choose to trust You to meet my needs today.*

The Coming Out Of Lazarus

"Loose him, and let him go."
- John 11:44

It was not an easy thing for Lazarus to come out of the grave! He had been in there four days. In those days, the Jews believed that for three days after a person died, the soul would try to return to the body. If, after those three days, it could not get back in, the person was truly dead. Since Jesus waited four days to come to the grave, there was no question in anyone's mind that Lazarus was dead. After four days his body also would be in the process of decaying and would certainly not be smelling good. Another hindrance was the wrapping enclosing his body. His head was bound up in a napkin and his body in linen cloths. It was the custom also to wrap spices in with the cloth; up to *75 pounds* of spices may have been used for Lazarus. Then there was the barrier of the sealed tomb. A large stone had been rolled in front of the tomb as protection from animals or other intruders. To the mourners gathered at the tomb with Jesus, raising Lazarus from the dead looked like a complete impossibility.

Jesus, however, is never limited by the impossible. He allowed all of these things to happen so that the people with him would truly know that what He was about to do was a miracle. After telling them to move the stone, He thanked God for hearing Him and for showing the people the unity between God and Himself. Then he called out for Lazarus to come forth. And out hobbled Lazarus, still wrapped up in his grave clothes and probably weighed down with spices. Jesus told the astonished onlookers to "Loose him and let him go," which they must have done with great joy.

You are not dead and lying in a cave, but you may be in a "pressure cooker" with stresses pressing down on you from all sides. You may be bound up in the "cloths" of your past, causing you to hobble through life rather than to stride confidently through the challenges. You may be weighed down with situations you can't control and that seem to be controlling you. Coming out of your "pressure cooker" may look completely impossible. But remember, Jesus isn't limited by the impossible. He can bring you out of your "pressure cooker," cause the "grave cloths" to fall away and the burdens to roll out of your heart. Your situation may not change, and life may continue on as usual, but your heart will be free. Jesus is able and ready to bring you out. Pour out your heart to Him and let Him do it!

- Do I believe in my heart that Jesus can bring me out of my pressure cooker?
- What burdens does He want me to roll off onto Him?
- *Lord, help me to trust You to free my heart from the heaviness of my life.*

Read: John 20:1-8

My Coming Out

"And ye shall know the truth,
and the truth shall make you free."
- John 8:32

Jesus, like Lazarus, came out of the grave. He had also been wrapped in the grave clothes with spices and laid in a tomb. (John 19:40) A large stone was rolled in front of the entrance to seal it shut. Jesus, however, had no difficulty coming out of the tomb. The stone was not rolled away so that He could get out; it was rolled away so that others could see in. When Peter and John came to the tomb early in the morning, Jesus was gone, but the grave clothes were still in the tomb, as if Jesus had passed right through them.

Do you see the difference here? Lazarus came hobbling forth still bound in the grave clothes, unable to function until he was loosed and let go. He couldn't see, probably couldn't hear well, and could hardly move his arms or legs. He was dependent on those around him to remove the bonds that held him captive. When Jesus came forth, He left the grave clothes behind. He came out free and unhindered, ready to do His Father's will.

Does it ever seem to you that even though you have "come out of the grave" you're still bound by the grave clothes? Are you depending on those around you to remove the trappings? Are you waiting until you are free from your bonds so that you can function as a servant for the Lord? It is not easy to come out from deadness into life. But we don't *have* to drag those grave clothes out of the tomb with us! The bad habits of criticism, swearing, overeating, worry, or unbelief that have held us captive can be folded up and left behind. Our negative, fleshly reactions can be changed to gentle responses that glorify the Lord. The ungodly thoughts that plague us daily can be godly thoughts that bless our lives and spill out to bless others. The bonds of sin have a callusing effect on the heart and life, dulling the conscience and covering the guilt. Don't let Satan or the world convince you that you are still bound in these grave clothes of death. Ask God to help you understand and accept the truth that will make you free. Satan is the father of lies and a deceiver who loves to keep us bound and trapped. But in Jesus we can live in newness of life, coming forth in freedom to do His will. Let Him speak to you through Scripture, your experiences, or godly counsel, and enjoy the blessings that come with freedom!

- Do I truly understand the freedom that is mine in Christ?
- What sin am I allowing in my life that is keeping me from experiencing this freedom?
- *Lord, show me where I'm trapped in sin, and help me to accept the freedom You have for me.*

A Tale Of Two Kings

"And Jesus...was moved with compassion toward them, because they were as sheep not having a shepherd."
- Mark 6:34

n this passage we read the stories of two very different men. Each man was a king. Each king was the host at a banquet. Beyond this, however, the stories portray an immense difference in the attitude of the two kings.

Herod was a selfish man. He had thrown John the Baptist, whom he actually respected as a holy man, into prison to satisfy his angry wife. Now he was in a fix. At his birthday banquet his wife's daughter had entertained his guests and him by dancing for them. She pleased them all so greatly that Herod recklessly promised her anything she wanted. When she asked her mother, Herodias was ready. "Ask for the head of John the Baptist on a platter." Herod was trapped. Because of his oath and all the people there watching him, he felt he had to grant her request. Satan had used a birthday party; a selfish, immoral man; and an evil woman to destroy a fearless witness of Jesus.

The next story tells about another King who was as compassionate as Herod was selfish. Jesus and His disciples were tired and sad. They had been so busy they had not even had time to eat. They must also have still been grieving the death of John. Jesus invited His disciples to come with Him, and they left quietly in a boat to go into a desert place for some much needed rest. When they reached their destination, however, a crowd of people was waiting for them. We can only imagine how the weary disciples must have felt about the crowd on the shore. But Jesus did not send them away. He was moved with compassion to see them there, looking as lost as a flock of sheep without a shepherd. He healed the sick (Matthew 14:14) and taught them many things. He did not even send them away in the evening, when it was time to eat, and everyone was hungry. Instead, He hosted a "banquet," feeding over 5,000 people with a little boy's lunch of five loaves of bread and two fish. Only after everyone had been taken care of did Jesus send the disciples away in a boat. Finally, Jesus could be alone for awhile.

What a contrast between these two Kings! What a wonderful privilege we have to be serving a King who is so compassionate that He cares about every detail of our lives. He doesn't get irritated when we are in a situation, *again,* that looks hopeless to us. He doesn't make rash promises that He later regrets. He doesn't "dispose of us" when we act in a way that is not pleasing to Him. Jesus, the King over all creation, is compassionate, ready and longing for us to bring our cares to Him. He will supply all our needs in His way and in His time.

- Do I rejoice in serving the King of Kings?
- How well do I understand the compassion of Jesus?
- *Lord, my desire is to serve You, as the King of my life. Thank You for being compassionate.*

 Read: John 19:1-16

Behold Your King

"When Pilate...brought Jesus forth...
he saith unto the Jews, Behold your King!"
- John 19:13, 14

It's hard to know just what Pilate was thinking and feeling when he brought Jesus out to face the angry mob. He surely must have felt trapped, torn between allowing an innocent man to be executed and fear of losing his position or even his life. He may have been seeing Jesus as the True King or, in his own frustration, he may have just wanted to annoy and further irritate the Jews. For whatever reason, Pilate presented Jesus to the crowd as their King.

At His birth, the humble shepherds were among the first to see Jesus. It must have been a holy time as they stood there gazing upon the infant and talking with Mary and Joseph. They were not seeing just another sweet baby, they were seeing their King. Afterward they returned to their work, spreading the good news with joy. (Luke 2:8-20)

Mary and Joseph took Baby Jesus to the temple when He was eight days old. Simeon came into the temple and immediately recognized Jesus as the Messiah. Joyfully holding their Baby in his arms he blessed them and prophesied that Jesus would be a light to all the world. Anna, a widow who lived in the temple, also knew that she was looking at a King, not just another baby boy. She was overjoyed and spoke of Him to many people. (Luke 2:25-38)

Acts 7:54-60 tells us that when Stephen was being stoned as the first Christian martyr, he looked up into heaven and saw Jesus. We can be sure that Stephen was not just seeing a man standing there; he was seeing his Savior, the King.

Some, as Zacchaeus, started out seeing a man but became believers, seeing Jesus as their King. When Zacchaeus, from his perch in the tree, saw Jesus coming, he may have just curiously watched a famous man walking toward him. But by the end of the day, after having served Him as his guest, Zacchaeus believed. (Luke 19:1-10)

When the woman of Samaria came to the well and saw Jesus sitting there, she saw Him as a man. (John 4:1-42) But after He "told me all things that ever I did," (v. 29) she believed that He was the Christ. Hearing her testimony, many of the people from the city came out to hear Him. "And many more believed because of His own word." (v. 41)

How do you see Jesus? Do you *see* Him as the King when you are reading your Bible? Do you *recognize* Him when you see Him? Do you *know* His voice when He speaks? We must *know* Him before we can *share* Him. The day will come when every knee will bow before Him and we will *all* see Him as our King.

- When I read about the life of Christ in the Bible, am I just reading the words or do I see the King through the words?
- Do I share my testimony of this King with others as these Biblical people did?
- *Lord, Help me to always see You as my King and to be eager to share Your goodness with others.*

What Seekest Thou?

"If ye then be risen with Christ, seek those things which are above, where Christ sitteth on the right hand of God."
- Colossians 3:1

As we read through the accounts of the resurrection, we see folks who were seeking. The women who went to the tomb early in the morning were seeking their Master. They didn't realize that they were seeking the *wrong man* in the *wrong place*. They sought a dead man in a grave. They were puzzled with the empty tomb. The angels standing there asked them, "Why seek ye the living among the dead?" They reminded the women of what Jesus had told them about His being crucified and rising again on the third day. The women remembered His words and hurried to tell the others. (Luke 24:5-9) Jesus was not dead! He was alive and could not be found in a man-made place.

The two believers walking on the road to Emmaus were seeking something too. They may have been seeking an answer for what had happened to the Man they thought would rescue them from their political enemies. Not only were they walking in the wrong direction--away from the believers in Jerusalem--they were so focused on the *dead Jesus* that they didn't recognize the *Living Jesus* who was walking right beside them! (Luke 24:13-35) When their eyes were opened they were amazed and went back to Jerusalem with the message that "The Lord is risen indeed." (v. 33, 34)

What are you seeking? Everyone is seeking something. Young men seek young women. Young women seek young men. Children seek to grow up and adults seek--well--lots of things! We look for *fulfillment* in our work, *hope* in our dreams for the future, and *pleasure* in recreation. We seek *deliverance* from bad habits or from difficult situations. Often times we never find what we're looking for and sometimes when we do, it turns out to be quite different from what we expected, and we're disappointed. The Israelites had spent years searching for a Messiah and thought they had found Him in Jesus. What a bitter disappointment when He was killed just as an ordinary criminal.

Jesus wasn't what His followers thought He was...He was a whole lot more. He rose again and is the WAY, the TRUTH, and the (Resurrected) LIFE. (John 14:6) What are you seeking? Paul tells us in Colossians 3 to seek those things which are above. We are to seek to serve, to give, and forgive. Is what you are looking for pleasing to the Lord? Nothing will satisfy your soul like Jesus. He overcame death, sin, and Satan. He is a VICTORIOUS Savior! As we minister and fellowship together, let's point each other back to Jesus who is living and real in our lives today.

- What am I seeking in my life today?
- Are my thoughts centered on Jesus and how I can serve Him by serving those around me?
- *Lord, show me where I'm seeking the wrong things in the wrong places and lead me back to You.*

 Read: John 20

A Heart Of Devotion

"But Mary stood without at the sepulchre weeping... and looked...and seeth two angels."
- John 20:11, 12

Mary had a heart full of devotion for her Lord. Earlier, Jesus had cast *seven* devils out of her. Freed from a miserable life of demon possession, Mary's gratitude and love were deep and heart-felt. Her courage and determination were evident as she hurried down the path toward Jesus' tomb on resurrection morning. Heavy hearted and knowing the tomb was sealed, she still carried spices, hoping to properly prepare His body for burial. It was still dark and likely not even safe for women to be out alone with all the people in Jerusalem for the Passover. Most of the disciples were actually hiding behind locked doors in fear of the Jews. But Mary bravely went forth. Shocked at seeing the opened grave, she ran to tell Peter and John. After coming to see for themselves, Peter and John returned home.

But Mary stayed, weeping. Looking again into the tomb, she saw what the disciples had not, the angels! She spoke with them, then turning around, she saw Jesus standing there. In her grief, however, and her focus on finding Him somewhere else, she completely missed Him. Thinking He was the gardener, she begged Him to tell her where He had put Jesus' body. She was determined to find Him, bring Him back, and care for Him. It wasn't until He spoke her name, however, that she recognized Him. After a sweet, blessed reunion, she ran back, overjoyed, to tell the disciples what had happened.

Mary loved Jesus *first*. Whom do you love first? Why do you go to church on Sunday morning? Are you there with a heartfelt desire to worship Jesus in love and praise for all He has done for you? Are you eager to learn more of Him and to grow in Christ-likeness? Maybe it's just a habit, something you're "supposed to do," or perhaps just a chance to see your friends and catch up on what's happening in the community. Why do you do kind deeds for others, such as taking a meal to a new mother, taking Grandmother to the grocery, or kissing the bump on a small child's head? Is it for the glory it will bring to you, just because you love the person you're serving, or is it because of your love for, and devotion to Jesus? Of course, Jesus wants us to love our families, church families, neighbors, and friends, but He wants us to *love Him first and foremost*. There is no substitute for Jesus as #1 in your life!

- Do I love Jesus more than anything or anybody else in my life?
- What is my true reason for going to church and doing kind things for others?
- *Lord, help me to focus more on You, increasing my love and devotion to You.*

The Fact Of The Resurrection

"Why should it be thought a thing incredible with you, that God should raise the dead?"
- Acts 26:8

A minister stood in front of the private school students sharing the resurrection story. "How many of you have ever seen someone rise from the dead?" he asked. Of course, none of them raised his hand. "How many of you believe that Jesus rose from the dead?" Every hand went up in response. "Now, how many of you believe that, someday, all in the graves will rise?" All hands went up again. These children had been well taught and they *believed*.

Mary Magdalene didn't believe Jesus would rise again. That's understandable as she likely hadn't seen anyone come back from the dead, either. She loved her Lord deeply, as she had known a life without Him and then, life *with* Him as her Savior. His death was very hard on her. As she went sadly to the tomb that morning, she fully expected to find Jesus in the grave. She was going to embalm His body, doing everything she could still do for Him, giving Him every respect. She was shocked and distressed to find the tomb empty and her Lord gone. When she realized, a little later, that the man she was speaking to was not the gardener, but Jesus Himself, she *believed*. (I John 20:10-18)

The Roman Soldiers who were assigned to guard the tomb did not believe that Jesus would rise from the dead, either. They were likely quite relaxed, thinking their job was pretty easy. After all, who was going to bother the grave with them standing there *and* a huge stone sealing the door of the tomb? They got a real shock, however, when the earth began to quake and an angel appeared to roll the stone away from the tomb! It frightened them so badly that they "became as dead men." (Matthew 28:4) If they survived the fright, they must also have *believed*.

The same day, Jesus appeared to two believers walking along the road to Emmaus. Not recognizing Him, they told Him about all that had happened. They were skeptical about Jesus being alive again. As they shared a meal with Jesus, "their eyes were opened, and they knew Him." (Luke 24:13-35) They *believed* and hurried to tell the others.

What about you? Do you believe, without a doubt, that Jesus did, indeed, rise from the dead on the third day? Or, is the story of the empty tomb a disappointment to you? If you *believe*, let this resurrection season be a reminder to rejoice; to worship and praise God for raising Jesus up again to be our Living Savior. If you are still skeptical, read through the resurrection story again and let the Truth soak into your heart and mind until you, too, *believe*.

- How strong is my faith in believing that Jesus died and rose again *for my sake?*
- Do I have a true spirit of praise, worship, and love for Jesus because of what He did for me?
- *Lord, if I am at all unsure of this resurrection story, show me just what I need to see to fully believe it in my heart.*

The Hope Of The Resurrection

"For I know that my Redeemer liveth, and that He shall stand at the latter day upon the earth."
- Job 19:25

Job was miserable. He had endured trials that tested his faith to the breaking point. He had lost all of his children, his wealth, and his health. He was so discouraged, he wished he had never been born or at least had died at birth. His wife had suggested that he just curse God and die. Now his friends were gathered around him, supposedly to comfort him, but instead, Job listened to them talk on and on, criticizing him and pointing out his faults and sins. At that point he was feeling like even God was against him. But in spite of all this, Job was able to tell his friends with confidence, "*I know that my redeemer liveth and that he shall stand at the latter day upon the earth.*" Although at that time Israel did not have a clear concept of the resurrection, Job fully believed that God and he together would triumph in the end.

Our trials may not be nearly as severe as Job's were, but we can have the same hope he had. After Adam and Eve had disobeyed God in the Garden of Eden, God said that the woman's Seed (the Messiah) would crush the head of the serpent (the devil), completely defeating him. (Genesis 3:15) This happened at Calvary where, with His death and *resurrection*, Jesus decisively triumphed over Satan, giving us a hope of eternal life with Him in Heaven.

As Christian women, this hope reaches right into our daily lives. The same power that raised Jesus from the dead can raise us up daily as we battle the enemy's attempts to destroy us. No matter how large or how small the temptation, the "woman's seed" will crush the "serpent's head" if we just *believe* that God is able, *ask* Him for help, and *claim* His promise to defeat the devil.

Teach this hope to your children by pointing out to them the ways in which God is working in your life. Build and strengthen their faith while they are young and equip them with armor for life. Don't be afraid to share your victories with others, glorifying God and reinforcing their hope also. This is what the Christian life is all about. If it were not for this hope, concluding with the blessed hope of life eternal with Jesus in Heaven, we would be "of all (women) most miserable." (I Corinthians 15:19) *Believe it! Claim it! Teach it! Share it!*

- Do I truly believe the hope of the resurrection is for me personally?
- How could I be more diligent in claiming this hope, teaching it to my children, and sharing it with others?
- *Lord, strengthen my belief in this awesome hope and guide me in teaching it and sharing it with others.*

The Unsinkable Ship

"For whosoever exalteth himself shall be abased; and he that humbleth himself shall be exalted."
- Luke 14:11

Ruth Becker was just twelve and very excited when she boarded the Titanic with her family to sail to America on its maiden voyage. The boat was huge and beautiful, treating its passengers to unsurpassed comfort and luxury. On a lower deck were a swimming pool, racket courts, and Turkish baths. They could play miniature golf and use the gymnasium on another deck. Plush cabins catered to millionaires, and family quarters were roomy and comfortable. As Ruth happily explored, she found a fancy restaurant and dining rooms. She checked out the well-stocked library, the sitting room, and the grand staircase, the likes of which she had never seen before. Elaborate elevators transported those not wanting to take the stairs. And, best of all, this ship was *safe*. It had been built by a premium ship building company to be virtually unsinkable. The few required lifeboats hanging around the outside of the deck were a mere formality. One seaman was even heard to say matter-of-factly, "God Himself could not sink this ship."

But we know the story. In the early morning hours of Monday, April 15, 1912, the Titanic went down. They had hit an iceberg damaging the "unsinkable ship" severely enough to sink her. Now the shortage of lifeboats became a tragic problem. Women and children were put into the boats first, with many families becoming separated. Many refused to leave the ship, not believing it would actually sink. Young Ruth Becker sat stunned in the lifeboat, listening to the lonely but beautiful strains of "Nearer My God to Thee" as the eight-man band continued to play until they were thrown from the sinking ship. Only 700 people were saved and over 1500 lost their lives that terrible night, including Captain E. J. Smith who went down with his ship. The tremendous amount of pride in that amazing ship did nothing to save them from heart-breaking death in the middle of the Atlantic Ocean.

Pride is just a little word with disastrous consequences. According to the dictionary, pride is "A high opinion of oneself or something one owns, arrogance, haughtiness." God views pride as a form of idolatry which is defined as "an extreme devotion to, or worship of something or someone." In other words, anything that hinders or comes between you and your relationship with the Lord has become an idol. Search your heart. If there are any idols in your life, you would do well to remove them before they become great enough to sink you.

- What activities in my life are becoming too important to me, hindering my time with the Lord?
- What can I do to remove the danger of them becoming a tragedy in my spiritual life?
- *Lord, help me to see these dangers and give me the courage to remove them.*

Read: John 9

Something New For You

"Ye have put off the old man...and have put on the new man...after the image of Him that created (you)."
- Colossians 3:9,10

As Jesus was leaving the temple one Sabbath day, He passed a beggar who had been blind since he was born. The disciples who were with Him wondered who had sinned, the man or his parents that he had been born blind. That this kind of suffering resulted from sin was common thinking in Jewish culture. But Jesus told them that no one had sinned; this man was born blind so that God could be glorified through him. Jesus then made mud by mixing His saliva with the dirt on the ground, smeared it on the man's eyes, and told him to go wash in the pool of Siloam. This blind man, who likely had been mocked and ridiculed all of his life, obeyed Jesus. He groped his way to the pool, mud on his face, probably the object of even more scorn and laughter. But... "He went his way therefore, and washed, and *came seeing*." This man had willingly allowed Jesus to have His way with him (mud on his face), had blindly obeyed Him (washing at Siloam), and had received the blessing that followed (he could see). Jesus had *done something new* in this man's life.

Jesus wants to do something new in your life too! Do you ever feel that you have "mud" in your life? As the challenges press upon us, discouragement sets in, and we begin to feel like the blind beggar--worthless. But is not God more often revealed to us in our misery and weakness, rather than in our strengths? When we come to the end of our strength saying "I can't do this," Jesus will step in and do it for us. The challenges that bring us to this point become an "anointing" in our lives. (John 9: 6) When we willingly allow Jesus to work with us, and trustingly obey His commands, we will receive the blessings that follow. Go to the "pool of Siloam." If you are not a Believer, wash yourself in the blood of the Lamb. If you are a Believer, immerse yourself in the Word of God, letting it flow over you, cleansing your heart and mind. Let the Spirit of God fill you, and make you a new person, rejoicing and praising Him. (v. 38) Jesus *wants* to do something new in your life. He *can* do something new for you, and He *will* do just that!

- Do I believe that God wants to do something new in my life and do I want Him to?
- What challenges or discouragements might be an "anointing" rather than "mud" in my life?
- *Lord, remind me that in these hard times You can be revealed through me as I obey You.*

A Driving Desire

"For the children of this world are in their generation wiser than the children of light."
- Luke 16:8

Diane cringed as the scenario she was reading aloud to the family came alive in their minds. The author of the book had finally convinced a native of the area to show him a family cave. In the scene, two men were descending a 150 foot cliff that plunged into the sea. Their supports were narrow ledges and precarious hand-holds. The final bit of descent involved a carefully choreographed turn-around before sliding feet first over the edge and finally easing down to the last ledge which was still high over the sea. Then began the process of crawling on their bellies through a lava tunnel into a dark cave! When they were finished exploring, they had the return trip back up the cliff...after nightfall, carrying sacks of stone images collected from the cave.

What could have possibly motivated this man to do something that terrified even him at the time? What had motivated him at other times to cross thousands of miles of the Pacific on a balsa-wood raft, and to sail the Atlantic on a reed boat? He had a driving desire to learn all he could about this interest and set about to fulfill that desire.

After Jesus had learned about the death of John, He and His disciples crossed the Sea of Galilee to a desert place for some privacy and rest. But many of the people saw them go and followed them; longing to hear more of what Jesus had to tell them. They must have had to cross the lake or walk all the way around. They weren't concerned about food or where they were going to stay that night. They had a driving desire to learn all they could from this Teacher.

Do we have that kind of consuming desire to know about things that will last? Do we devote that kind of time and energy to learn about our God and King through study, fellowship, and daily service? It is easy to become so preoccupied with the daily affairs of life that we don't even think about learning more, and we certainly wouldn't deny ourselves common comforts to satisfy such a desire! Oh, that we would follow the example of these devoted, curious people and pursue a deeper knowledge of Jesus ourselves.

- Does my desire to learn about Jesus even compare to the driving desire of these people?
- When was the last time I went without food or sleep for the single purpose of learning more about Him?
- *Lord, increase my desire to learn to know You in a deeper, more intimate way.*

April 18

Read: II Chronicles 34; 35:20-24

Am I Missing Something?

"Forbear thee from meddling with God,
who is with me, that He destroy thee not."
- II Chronicles 35: 21

Josiah began his reign as king at the very young age of eight years old. He was a good king, doing "that which was right in the sight of the Lord." (v. 2) When he was 26 years old, he arranged for the house of the Lord to be repaired. In the process of these repairs, Hilkiah found a book of the law that Moses had written--possibly Deuteronomy--which had been lost during the reigns of the evil kings. Hearing it read to him, Josiah realized just how far his people had strayed from God's commandments. He was so grieved that he tore his clothing and sent a group of men to a prophetess to find out more about these words. They returned with the news that God would pour out His wrath upon them, but Josiah would be spared because of his tender heart of repentance and grief.

King Josiah gathered the people together to hear the book read and to make a covenant with them *"to walk after the Lord, and to keep His commandments, and His testimonies, and His statutes, with all (their) heart, and with all (their) soul, to perform the words of the covenant which are written in this book."* (v. 31) He began a major reform throughout the land immediately. (II Kings 23) He tore down and burned idols and places of idol worship. He killed idolatrous priests. He "put away" wizards, images, and all other abominations. He completely "cleaned up" the land.

Unfortunately, "*After all this...*" (35:20) Josiah completely missed a commandment from God. The King of Egypt was marching his army north through Judah on their way to a battle at Charchemish. Josiah did not appreciate this, set out with his army to stop them, and was warned by Egyptian King Necho. "What have I to do with thee, thou king of Judah? I come not against thee this day but against the house wherewith I have war: for God commanded me to make haste: forbear thee from meddling with God, who is with me, that he destroy thee not." Josiah paid no attention, put on a disguise, and went out to fight. It wasn't worth it. He lost his life to an archer's arrow.

We shouldn't be too critical of Josiah. After all, Necho was king of a heathen nation and would not be part of God's larger plan, would he? Would God speak through a heathen king? Josiah's mistaken belief cost him his life.

God's messages can come in unexpected ways. We can miss them easily through prejudice or false assumptions. Sometimes God uses ungodly people to carry out His plans. We must stay in tune with Him lest we miss His messages!

- Is it possible that I am missing a message from the Lord today?
- What could God be trying to tell me that I don't want to hear?
- *Lord, open my ears to hear Your words, regardless of how they come to me.*

Waiting... Patiently Or Anxiously?

"Rest in the Lord, and wait patiently for him"
- Psalm 37:7

Often we are called to wait patiently on God's timing. This waiting is not easier now than it was many years ago. The Bible records many examples of women who went through times of waiting that must have caused a great deal of anxiety. We can read about the results of their patience or the unfortunate results of their anxiety.

For ninety years ***SARAH*** waited to have a child. Her patience undoubtedly waxed and waned just as it would for any woman today. At one point, however, her impatience got the best of her. She jumped ahead of God's plan and ended up making a mess of things. Fourteen years later, her patient waiting was rewarded when Sarah gave birth to a son, Isaac. (Genesis 16, 21:1-8) Others suffered greatly, however, for Sarah's impatience.

We can only imagine the feelings of ***JOCHEBED*** as she placed her newborn son, Moses, into a little basket and hid him among the reeds at the river. As she went back home and waited, her anxiety must have been overwhelming, but her joy inexpressible when she received him back to nurse. Then the real waiting began when Moses was taken to the house of Pharaoh to be raised and trained. Many years passed before Moses became the leader of the Israelites, but his mother's prayers through that time of waiting surely had a great influence on his life. (Exodus 1-10)

ESTHER went through trying times of waiting as the queen of Persia. Her patience and sweetness pleased the keeper of the women as she spent a year in preparation to go in to the king. After she was made queen, she began an intense time of waiting after receiving the message that all of the Jews were to be killed. This period of waiting was particularly difficult because she knew that she could be killed for approaching the king with a plea for her people. We are inspired by her patient, confident waiting on the Lord which resulted in the miraculous deliverance of her people. (Esther 2-9)

To wait patiently on God's answer during trying times in our lives takes a faith that something *will* happen. We need to stay focused on that truth, knowing that all things work together in *God's timing* and that our interference will likely just hinder what God wants to do. If we are willing to wait prayerfully and patiently, we can trust God to work out everything to His glory.

- Do the anxieties of waiting periods threaten to overcome me at times?
- What steps can I take to make these times of waiting restful instead of becoming so anxious?
- *Lord, the waiting isn't always easy, but I want to be patient, knowing You will work things out in Your time.*

April 20

Read: Psalm 91

The Marks Of Christ

"Let no man trouble me: for I bear in my body the marks of the Lord Jesus."
- Galatians 6:17

Recently I read a touching testimony of a Mennonite missionary family in Guatemala. Before returning to the States, they decided to spend a day at the Pacific Ocean. As they were walking along the shore, back to their vehicle, two men rode past them on bicycles, then abruptly turned and grabbed the cell phone from the father's belt. In a blur of moments, his daughter screamed, while his wife exclaimed "He has a gun!" and began praying. The man waved the gun around, and pointed it at the girls' heads. Then without asking for their cameras or money, the men began backing away. But, for some reason, the one with the gun turned back and shot, hitting the father in the thigh. With the bullet still lodged beside the bone, the father made his painful way back to the parking lot and then home for help.

The humiliation of being a victim and the command of Christ to forgive the assailants was a struggle. Later, home from the hospital, an elderly visitor reminded him that the Apostle Paul was a persecutor before his conversion. Perhaps God would use his forgiveness to bring about a change of heart in these men. An encouraging thought! Thinking of Job's testimony, "Though He slay me, yet will I trust Him," inspired this father to remember that God allows trials to strengthen those who are walking close to Him. Inasmuch as he was bearing the marks of the Lord Jesus in his body, he realized that God had spared his life for a reason. Knowing that the harvest truly is great, but the laborers are few, increases his desire that God be glorified and the reader humbled through his testimony.

- Am I willing to bear the marks of the Lord Jesus as I commit my life to Him?
- Do I freely forgive wrong-doers and accept the trials God sends my way?
- *Lord, my desire is to be fully committed to you, regardless of the cost.*

A Tiny Tormentor

"I will both lay me down in peace, and sleep: for thou, Lord, only makest me dwell in safety."
- Psalm 4:8

A mosquito is a very small critter compared to the trouble it can cause. Anyone who has tried to sleep with a mosquito buzzing around his head knows how annoying it can be! That high pitched whine is enough to keep you awake, swatting, and increasingly irritated, for a long time.

A friend of mine finally killed the mosquito that was keeping her awake one night only to discover that it had not been alone. After several hours of frustrated attempts to sleep, it occurred to her that if she just got a fan and aimed it toward the bed, it would blow the mosquitoes away from her! It worked, and she was finally able to get some much needed rest.

The next morning as she was thinking about the bothersome mosquitoes, she began to realize that there was a deeper lesson here. How many times do we go to bed (or through our days) with petty little annoyances keeping us from the peace that God intends for us to have? An unkind word carelessly spoken by a friend, a husband focused on the newspaper when we wanted his attention, or an employer that seems inconsiderate of our time and needs. Children have a way of innocently causing little (and big!) stresses all through the day that can pile up and seem overwhelming. Neighbors are bothered by our pets or children who are not acting as they think they should. Lying down to sleep, these aggravations can swirl through our minds like angry mosquitoes buzzing around our ears. We roll them over and over in our minds, tossing and turning, unable to sleep. Finally, we fall into a fitful sleep and wake up exhausted and not ready to face the day.

But wait…There is another solution! God is always there ready to intervene, more effectively than any fan. And we don't have to worry about Him being asleep when we need help. While a fan may help us deal with mosquitoes, God is able and willing to rid us of all the little (and big) irritations that are keeping us awake.

- What irritations am I allowing to rob me of a peaceful sleep?
- Do I take the time to turn all my grievances over to the Lord before I go to bed?
- *Lord, this may seem like a small thing, but I know You are always there to take my burdens, great or small.*

Read: Hebrews 11:1-6

A Better Country

"These all...were strangers and pilgrims on the earth...
but...desire a better country, that is, an heavenly."
- Hebrews 11:13, 16

As a young girl, "Rhoda" went on a tour of the Southwest with her parents. One of their stops was at a Navajo trading post. Rhoda went inside but as she looked around at all of the unfamiliar articles, she felt very uncomfortable. Everything was strange, she was no longer in her "world," and she certainly didn't feel as though she belonged there.

More recently, a friend of Rhoda's returned from a year of living in the Far East region of Macau in China. She had been there as a missionary teacher. In sharing with others about her time in a foreign country it was clear that, even after a year of living there, this missionary still felt like a foreigner. She never felt completely comfortable, especially when people would stare at her or laugh at her mistakes when she tried to speak the language. However, after a year away, she didn't really feel at home here in the States, either. In Macau, the language, the food, the customs, and the mode of dress all contributed to her feeling of not fitting in. Back in the States, a year of absence had changed the way things looked and felt to her. She pointed out that, as Christians, it ought to be that way for us no matter where we are. We are pilgrims and strangers here on earth, citizens of a heavenly country.

How is it for us? It's pretty easy to settle in here and be comfortable. The language isn't strange. Or is it? If you are in a group of unbelievers, it often is not long until you feel quite uncomfortable with the language. The food, customs, and mode of dress (or undress) can all seem pretty foreign, too. We can become accustomed to unfamiliar surroundings if we experience them on a regular basis. But as Rhoda's friend didn't feel at home after a year in Macau, neither should we become completely comfortable with life here on earth. Our thoughts and desires should be for a "*better country, that is, an heavenly: wherefore God... hath prepared for (us) a city.*"

- Do I think of my home here as temporary?
- How comfortable do I feel as I interact with the world in my daily life?
- *Lord, my desire is to keep my mind on my Heavenly home, and not get too comfortable here.*

Restore unto Me The Joy

"Restore unto me the joy of thy salvation;
and uphold me with thy free spirit."
- Psalm 51:12

A friend shared with me her testimony of a frightening but enlightening dream she once had. I want to share it with you in her own words:

"I dreamed I walked into a room where lay a young cousin, that I love, sound asleep. With no emotion whatever, I picked up a heavy object, hit her in the head and killed her. A sense of the enormity of the deed quickly began to envelop me, and I remember feeling utterly trapped and terrified. I could only imagine the grief of the parents when they found her. Then, too, was the inevitable investigation; even if I was not pinpointed, how could I live with this horrible secret? Yet how could I ever confess and be forever branded a murderer? The swirl of emotion and regret was suffocating. I couldn't change what I had done and felt choked by my powerlessness.

Then----I woke up. I hope I never forget the incredible blessing and joy that flooded my soul as I realized that I was ***Not Guilty!*** I have felt guilty countless times, but never have I experienced a dream like this, or seen so clearly who I am without Jesus. Words cannot describe the joy of being free from the bondage of condemnation."

"We feel this joy when we give our lives to the Lord and experience the freedom and peace of His love, but as time passes, it becomes too easy to lose the joy we once had in the marvelous truth that we have been declared *Not Guilty*. David also felt this lack as he went to the very source of joy and prayed, 'Restore unto me the joy of Thy salvation." (Psalm 51:12) He continues, '*Then* will I teach transgressors Thy ways and sinners shall be converted unto Thee.' (v. 13) Surely our light is dimmed by our lack of joy. If our faith does nothing for us - why should anyone else want it? There is something magnetic about joy that makes us enjoy being close to joyful people. The Psalmist also said, 'In Thy Presence is fullness of joy.' (Psalm 16:11) Perhaps lack of joy in our lives is a warning that we have lost some contact with Him and do not spend enough time alone in His presence just loving Him and enjoying His love. May we come continually before Him in repentance and know once more the joy of being declared *Not Guilty!*"

- Do I fully understand the enormity of God's grace in forgiving my sins?
- What situation in my life do I need to repent of, confessing it to Him, to experience the joy of forgiveness once again?
- *Lord, words can't describe what You have done for me. Help me to rejoice always in Your love and mercy.*

April 24

Read: Ezekiel 47:1-12

There's A Fountain Free

"And whosoever will, let him take the water of life freely."
- Revelation 22:17

Many of today's cities were designed with a beautiful fountain in the center of town. These fountains cost a lot of money and have no actual purpose but to add beauty to the city and provide enjoyment for those who live or work there. People spend thousands of dollars on landscaping to put fountains in their own back yards, and businesses put them in their reception areas. A fountain of water showering down into a pool is beautiful, peaceful, and relaxing.

We read about another fountain in Genesis seven that was not beautiful or peaceful. When the "great fountains of the deep" broke up in the Great Flood, terror, panic, and chaos were rampant as people ran for their lives, climbing the hills and pounding on the door of the ark. They were too late, however, as the rapidly rising water covered everything, even the mountains, cleansing the earth of sinful man.

Go now, in your mind, for a moment, to the cross. It is an indescribably horrible scene which nevertheless produces a beautiful fountain. The fountain of Jesus' blood which, flowing from His side, washes us clean of our ugly sins as Jesus pays the price of death for all of us. As the Great Flood cleansed the world of the sinners, Jesus' blood cleanses the sinner of the world. Though man paid the price of his own sin in the flood, Jesus paid the price of our sins with His blood.

There is yet another fountain, provided for us by Jesus, that is beautiful and refreshing. It's the Water of Life that He invites us to partake of freely. (Revelation 22:17) It is available to all at no cost, and just like the fountains in the cities, it never runs dry. These are the waters of salvation, and blessings will flow through our lives as we drink of them and share them with others. They are healing waters, as the river in Ezekiel 47, safe and gentle, expanding as they flow. You may drink of it without hesitation, allowing it to fill you, bless you, and flow out to bless others. Sip on Scriptures throughout the day, enjoy communication with Him through prayer, and soak in fellowship with other believers. It is a choice we all have. Jesus does not force it on us, but He has paid for it in full and invites us to come and drink.

- Am I partaking of these Waters of Life Jesus is offering me?
- In what way could I share these blessings with others?
- *Lord, fill me with Your Living Waters and show me how to share the blessings with those around me.*

Trusting Through Trials

*"The eyes of the Lord are upon the righteous,
and his ears are open unto their cry."
- Psalm 34:15*

We were having another unpleasant morning with our 14-year-old son, and I was gloomily rolling it over in my mind as I dressed the baby. I was still deeply upset and frustrated with him when he came in from the barn. Frankly, I was in no mood to see him, much less listen to what he had to say.

"Mom, I have something for your journal," he informed me.

"It has to end up good to make it into my journal," I answered shortly.

"It is good, Mom," he went on. "I just went out to the barn to apologize to Dad." My head jerked up in surprise. "And Mom, when I went into the barn it was raining. Then, when I came out the sun was shining. I felt that meant I'd made a good choice."

"Oh Son, you did make a good choice," I said as I hugged him tight with tears in my eyes.

Sometimes as we pray for our children, we get impatient and wonder where God is or what He is doing. We know what we are doing. We are pacing and fretting and chewing our nails. But God loves our children even more than we do. He hears our prayers, and our job is to trust Him. Not to tell Him how to fix things or to question His timing. Our job is to pray…and wait. Prayer releases our tension and changes our outlook. We can praise God for His faithfulness, knowing that He is working, even in this situation, even when we can't see anything happening. True peace is not dependent on the problem being resolved—there will always be more problems! True peace comes from knowing that God is working out all things for our good and for His glory.

- Am I at peace during hard times, knowing that God is working?
- How can I rearrange my schedule so as to have more time to spend in prayer?
- *Lord, life can be so difficult. Help me to wait patiently and trust You as you answer our prayers.*

April 26

Read: John 4

Waterpots

"The water that I shall give him shall be in him a well of water springing up."
- John 4:14

Jesus was on His way from Judea to Galilee, taking a direct route through Samaria. He was resting at a well when a Samaritan woman came to draw water. She was surprised when Jesus spoke to her, a woman of Samaria. After talking with Jesus for awhile, she was so amazed that she "left her waterpot and went her way into the city" to tell others about Him.

We don't know just how valuable that waterpot was, but it must have been worth a good bit, since waterpots were essential for carrying life-giving water. But the Samaritan woman had found something far more precious than her waterpot, and she either forgot it or didn't mind leaving it to take her news back to the village.

Jesus had spoken to the woman about the living water He could give her, that would be in her "a well of water springing up into everlasting life." This is a precious, refreshing, life-sustaining gift that comes only from Jesus, and He still offers it to us today. As we empty ourselves of self and drink this living water, it will fill our hearts and overflow into the lives of others.

What about the waterpots in our lives? Are we permitting our possessions, our friends, our work, our finances, our goals, or even our families to become more important to us than doing God's will and showing His love to others?

- Am I drinking the Living Water that Jesus provides?
- What "waterpots" do I have in my life that may be coming between God and me?
- *Lord, fill me with living water and show me any "waterpots" that may be too important to me.*

Canaanites In The Land

"Who shall go up for us against the Canaanites first, to fight against them?"
- Judges 1:1

The Canaanites were a wicked people. Their religion consisted of many evil practices. They were cruel, immoral, and selfish. God had ordered the Israelites to utterly destroy the Canaanites. (Deuteronomy 7:2) Joshua had faithfully obeyed the Lord, leading the Israelites in military victories. But after he died, the tribes began failing to drive the evil Canaanites from their land. They were likely tired of fighting and lacked the discipline and energy to reach their goal. Perhaps they were afraid, thinking the enemy was too strong. Or maybe they thought they could be more prosperous by doing business with them and could handle the temptations there.

Just as the Israelite tribes each had an area of land; God has given each of us an allotted space...our life. Are we actively driving the "Canaanites" out of our space? We encounter many Canaanitish influences and values around us. Negative attitudes can influence us almost without us realizing it.

Some of the people of those lands were giants, just as the influences around us can seem gigantic. The Israelites knew what to do but failed to do it. This failure to obey brought them many problems and miseries. When we know what to do but fail to follow through, our relationship with God deteriorates, and we grow tired and weak. We will fail as the Israelites did if we try to conquer any temptation in our own strength. Staying strong through prayer and Bible study will allow God to fight your daily battles for you, as He did for them.

- Do I recognize negative influences in my life that hinder my walk with God?
- Am I willing to give up anything that is influencing me in wrong ways?
- *Dear Lord, show me anything in my life that needs to change, and make me willing to change it.*

Read: Mark 11

The Fig Tree

"But the fruit of the Spirit is love, joy, peace, long-suffering, gentleness, goodness, faith, meekness, temperance: against such there is no law."
- Galatians 5:22, 23

On the morning after Jesus' triumphal entry into Jerusalem, He and His disciples were heading back into Jerusalem from Bethany. Jesus was hungry, so He walked over to a fig tree that was leafed out. A fig tree will bear fruit twice a year, in the late spring and in the early fall. Once the tree has leaves in the spring the early figs have usually appeared, too. But this particular fig tree had no fruit. It looked promising but was barren. And Jesus cursed the tree saying, "No man eat fruit of thee hereafter forever." The next morning, the fig tree was dried up from the roots.

How do our lives compare to the fig tree? Does God see an abundant crop of ripe fruit there? Or does He find mostly leaves with little or no fruit? Since God looks on the heart and examines our motives, what does He find? Does He detect that we act a certain way just because our church tells us to? Do we perform acts of service for others in order to bring glory to ourselves? Perhaps we sacrifice a few minutes for devotions just to keep guilt at bay. These actions are leaves, not fruit. Good actions, done for the wrong reason, are not even healthy leaves. Is the fig tree of your life drying up from lack of faith? A faith filled life has great potential for Kingdom building. Ask God to show how you can bear fruit that will bless others and bring Him glory.

- Do I manifest a true faith that seeks to please God, and not self?
- How can I keep the fig tree of my life alive and healthy so that it will bear good fruit for the Lord?
- *Lord, show me how to serve you for your glory and help me to be willing to sacrifice for you.*

Going The Extra Miles, Part I

"Be ye therefore followers of God."
- Ephesians 5:1

God had called my husband and me to visit a young hurting family who lived a few states away from us. Later, when we were in the area seeing family, we drove the extra miles to see them before we returned home. We were both rather nervous as we didn't know "Silas" and "Rebekah" well at all.

We had mixed feelings when we arrived and no one was home. (We were so nervous that we had not even called ahead!) We were disappointed…we really did want to answer God's call. We were puzzled...why did He lead us all the way here only to meet with failure? We were also, admittedly, a bit relieved. "Whew, we're off the hook! At least we tried. Maybe another time…" Leaving a note on the door, it was pretty easy to slip back into our comfort zone and head toward home. I had visions of a long evening in a nice motel. A leisurely meal out with my husband. The book and bubble bath I had tucked into my suitcase and had not yet had time to enjoy.

Imagine our surprise when we just happened to meet up with Rebekah in a small town one-half-hour from her home! As we made plans to follow her back home and have supper with them, my visions for the evening popped like a bubble.

What followed, however, was so much more satisfying than my plans would have been: a long evening of sweet fellowship, heart to heart sharing, and prayer. Spirits lifted, and a precious bond of friendship formed. We parted in the wee hours of the morning, each feeling that we had received much more than we had given. We were so glad we had gone and were once again reminded that God richly blesses those who are willing to go the extra miles.

- Am I willing to "go the extra miles" when God calls?
- What may God be calling me to do today that I am resisting?
- *Lord, following Your call often takes me out of my comfort zone, but my desire is to go wherever You call.*

Read: I Thessalonians 5:12-28

Going The Extra Miles, Part II

"Faithful is he that calleth you,
who also will do it."
- I Thessalonians 5:24

As we visited with Silas and Rebekah, we shared with them what had happened before we made connections. We laughed about our nervousness and marveled over how God had worked things out.

We learned that Silas would not have seen the note we had left if God had not prompted us to move it from the front door, where we had first put it, to the side door, which is the one they use. We were amazed at our unexpected meeting in town. We had left the note saying to call our cell phone if they got home within an hour or so. We then spent around three hours (longer than we had planned) visiting in the area, drove 1/2 hour, and stopped for gas. Silas, in the meantime, had found the note, called Rebekah, and she called us, thinking we'd be long gone (Silas did not even know who we were!) Rebekah had been with a friend, shopping in a larger city and was on her way home. She was about a mile from the gas station where we were and pulled in a short time later! Coincidence? I don't think so. And it fit right in that she'd just picked up a large pizza, plenty for two more people for supper!

We also felt that we were being tested. Like maybe God was wondering just how far we were willing to go in order to encourage someone for Him. After all, we were headed towards home and had to backtrack about thirty miles. We were also ready for a relaxing evening and early bedtime! We could have spoken our regrets and made vague plans to "get together another time." But, thankfully, we decided to go back.

When we respond to a call to do God's work, we can rest assured that He will work out the details. Even if it seems confusing at times, that it is not working out the way we think it should. If He calls us, it will work out just the way He wants it to, even if we never know just why it turns out the way it does. And the blessings we receive from obeying the call can be long-lasting, even eternal.

- Do I trust God to work out the details when He calls me to do something for Him?
- What is He calling me to today?
- *Here I am, Lord, use me in any way You choose for Your glory.*

May

Christian Courtesy

"That ye may be blameless…in the midst of a crooked… nation, among whom ye shine as lights in the world."
- Philippians 2:15

It was springtime, and "Ruth" was enjoying rototilling part of her family's large garden. The machine was large and awkward and she could barely maneuver it, but she had learned a technique that made it possible to turn around at the end of each row. Unfortunately, this time, as she was approaching the barn, her technique failed, and the tiller ended up hitting the barn wall with a bang. End of job; the tiller was dead. The only option now was to take it to the repair shop thirty miles away.

The part they needed to fix the tiller had to be ordered. As the repair time stretched out into a month, they were in contact with the shop several times to keep up with the status of the repair. A month! In the Spring. In a climate with a short growing season. They needed that tiller! Impatience and frustration threatened but were not revealed as they spoke with shop personnel. Finally, they received the call that the repair was complete and gratefully went to pick up their machine. It was later, through someone else, that they learned just how much they had impressed the shop owners with their patience. Ruth was amazed. Apparently, by just treating those people courteously when they communicated with them, they had unknowingly left a good testimony.

We may bear witness to Christ more often than we know in just this way. Not by setting out consciously to "work for the Lord," but by simply going about our necessary work and letting Him work through us without our even realizing it. He does not always allow us to see the results, but we can appreciate it when He does, and be encouraged by it to go on living a Christian life "in the midst of a crooked and perverse nation."

- Do I show common courtesy when dealing with unbelievers in daily life?
- Where are my weak areas in being courteous to strangers?
- *Lord, I know I represent You at all times. Help me remember to treat others as You would treat them.*

 Read: Numbers 11

Danger! Disappointed With God

"Thou shalt see now whether my word shall come to pass unto thee or not."
- Numbers 11:23

Our human nature is not prone to always enjoy the situations God brings or allows into our lives. And sometimes we might even get angry at Him and be disappointed that He would "do such a thing to us." The Israelites got tired of the manna God had provided and wished they were back in Egypt with the fish and the melons, never mind the slavery that went with it. Being disappointed with God is an age-old matter.

My sister is single, lives by herself, and works out of her home. After she bought her mobile home on a small piece of land, she struggled for awhile with the debt load. But finally the time came when she made the last payment on one of her loans. She could now see that in a few months she would be debt free except for the house payment.

It soon became evident, however, that God had other plans. A long siege of illness left her unable to work for about five weeks. In the course of a few months, instead of being almost debt free, she was more deeply in debt than she had been two years before. It was a huge disappointment, but for several months she tried valiantly to smooth it over and cheerfully make the payments. After all, a Christian shouldn't get upset with what God brings into one's life...*right*?

But one day it all crashed in on her. She clearly saw that she was just plain furious with the debt load. To think...if she hadn't gotten sick she would be almost debt free. It was quite humbling to realize that in reality she was angry at *God,* as He was the One who had allowed this sickness in her life! Once she repented and acknowledged her anger, however, she was able to work through it and move on. She knows God has a far greater plan for her than she can see with her mortal eyes. Realizing that joy comes from within and not from present circumstances has helped speed her on the way to joyfully making her payments and thanking God for the means to pay them.

Being disappointed with God is as prevalent now as it was in Moses' time. The problem is not that God does not know what is best for us. The problem comes when our focus shifts from what we have to what we *don't have*. The Israelites forgot about all the miracles God had done for them, and they thought only about the good food they had left behind. But let's not be too hard on them. Are we grateful for what God has given us, or do we think too much about what we want and don't have? We dare not let our unfulfilled desires crowd out our gratitude for all of God's gifts to us!

- Am I thankful for what God has done for me, or do I constantly wish for more?
- What has God given me that I haven't been fully thankful for?
- *Lord, You do so much for me and I tend to forget. Forgive me and accept my praise for your faithfulness.*

Doorways

*"Behold I have set before thee an open door,
and no man can shut it."
- Revelation 3:8*

I have heard it said that life can be viewed as a hallway with doorways on either side. Some of these doorways are open with opportunities beckoning us. Some are closed, and some God closes as we attempt to go through.

For nine years my husband worked on a dairy farm that processed and marketed its own milk. When the owner decided to sell one of his out-lying farms, we were interested, sensing it as an open door. God led us through the door and smoothed the way. In a few months we had signed the papers and moved to the farm. God has blessed our years on the farm, even though it means being tied down and making other sacrifices that go with dairy farming.

After about ten years, for various reasons, we were seriously considering selling the farm and moving on. We checked into another line of work, and it looked good. In our minds, we had released the farm and were enthused about the switch. Just before we listed our place with a realtor, however, God showed us clearly that this was not the right thing to do. He closed the door and turned us around. As we switched gears again, back to dairy life, we felt a mixture of disappointment and relief. Looking back now, we can see more clearly God's wisdom, and we are thankful we were in tune enough to sense His leading.

As we walk down the corridor of life, we do not need to fear the doorways or worry about whether to walk through them if we diligently seek God's guidance. He can easily open and close doors, and we must not try to push them open or refuse to walk through the ones He opens for us.

- Am I daily seeking God's will as I consider the doorways in my life?
- Is there a particular doorway that I need to be praying about today?
- *Lord, help me to keep in mind that You will open and close the doors in my life and keep me from needless worry.*

 Read: Galatians 1

So Soon Removed

"I marvel that ye are so soon removed from Him that called you into the grace of Christ."
- Galatians 1:6

Our minister had just preached a sermon on the first chapter of Galatians. Paul was talking to the Christians at Galatia who had turned away from the true message and believed another. He was shocked that they were so soon removed from what he had taught them.

Now we can begin to feel pretty smug that we have not believed a false message as those early believers did. However, as my husband was bearing testimony, he shared with us his experience that morning. As he was reading through Galatians 1, verse 6 stood out to him and he felt that he was doing pretty well at not being "removed from Him." But when he went to the barn later and found that things were not going well, he was appalled to find out just how fast he could be "removed from Him." The peace was gone, and he struggled to get it back.

After services, a sister shared with me how she had lost her peace that morning, also. Another family member had frustrated her to exasperation, and she had reacted angrily. And my conscience smote me. I had not done so well myself. Things had gone fine until the one-year-old pulled the three-year-old's bowl of cereal and milk onto the floor. My reaction, I'm sure, would fit the description of being "so soon removed from Him."

We don't have to turn away from God's message to be "removed from Him." But He is always ready to restore us into His grace and peace if we just ask.

- Do I frequently react in a way that causes me to be "removed from Him" and lose my peace?
- In what way have I been removed from that peace lately?
- *Lord, reveal to me my actions that cause me to be removed from You and give me the strength to change them.*

Instilling Values

"The word of the Lord was unto them precept upon precept...line upon line...here a little, and there a little."
- Isaiah 28:13

Our children are going to need a deep-rooted set of spiritual values, which we as parents are responsible to instill.

We find excellent Biblical examples of godly values in Joseph and Daniel. Both young men were in captivity far from home. Both purposed in their hearts to live for God. Daniel refused to eat the king's meat. And Joseph refused to do wrong with Potipher's wife. They didn't make these choices because of what their parents would think or say. Or because of their church rules. Their parents and church were far away! They chose God's way because of the deep values they carried with them into captivity.

We instill these values in our children "precept upon precept, line upon line, here a little, there a little." By including them in family devotions; by reading Bible stories to them; and by singing and memorizing Scripture with them. Even very young children will begin to learn songs and verses. Perhaps the most important way we teach them our values is by our actions. The saying "actions speak louder than words" proves true, as our children quietly observe the way we deal with life. We might try to enforce the "do as I say, not as I do" theory, but what they pick up from our actions will influence them the rest of their lives. For me, as a mother, this is a sobering, sometimes frightening thought. The only way to instill these values in our children is to have them deeply rooted in my own heart first. Our values must be nourished by daily quiet time and communication with our heavenly Father, so that they can be passed on to others.

This concept can be true for any children in our lives, not just our own. A teacher, babysitter, grandmother, or anyone else who interacts frequently with children can have a big influence on a young life. A little bit here and a little bit there can add up to a big difference in the lives of children as they grow to adulthood.

- In what ways am I actively instilling wholesome values into the hearts of the children in my life?
- Do I have godly values deeply rooted in my heart?
- *Lord, help me to be faithful in passing on godly values to the children I influence.*

Read: I Samuel 17

Facing The Giant

"I come to thee in the name of the Lord of hosts."
- I Samuel 17:45

When the Israelite army needed a man to go up against Goliath, the logical choice must have been Saul, who was a very tall man himself. But Saul didn't volunteer. Neither did any of the other soldiers who were with him. But who can blame them? Goliath was *huge!* He was almost 10 feet tall. His coat of armor alone weighed 125 pounds! The head of his spear weighed 15 pounds. He was fully protected and heavily armed. As added protection he had a man with a shield go before him. And he was *bold*. For *forty days* he appeared morning and evening, taunting the army with his daring challenge.

Then came David, a young shepherd bringing food for his brothers. He was appalled at Goliath's challenge. What was to be done about this man who dared to defy the living God? After speaking with some of the soldiers and ignoring his brother's criticism, David offered to go up against Goliath himself. There is nothing to indicate that David was even thinking about the reward--great riches, a wife, and freeing his father's house. David was fighting for his God and God's people.

Although David was only a young man, he possessed attributes that God could use in a mighty way. Because of his past experiences, David had ***confidence*** that he was able, with God's help, to slay the giant. He had ***faith*** that God would help him destroy this reproach to Israel. This confidence and faith gave him the ***courage*** to face this giant with only his staff, his sling, and five smooth stones. And at exactly the right time, God gave David the ***strength*** to hurl that stone so precisely that it hit the only unprotected spot on Goliath's body--his forehead. David had conquered the enemy.

David's military training did not take place on the battlefield in the heat of combat. It was on the quiet hillsides with the sheep that David had learned to trust God and to bravely face fierce opponents. So it is with us today. It is during the quiet times of study and communication with God that we gain the armor needed to face the daily battles of life. We can slay giants too! Armed with confidence, faith, and courage, God will give us the guidance and strength we need to live victoriously.

- Am I properly arming myself for the battles I face daily?
- Do I, like David, put my full trust in the Lord to fight my battles for me?
- *Lord, the enemy is big and the battles are fierce, but I choose to put my trust in You today.*

The Worst Prison

"For if ye forgive men their trespasses, your heavenly Father will also forgive you."
- Matthew 6:14

"Where is the worst prison in the world?" The minister had asked, and I was a bit puzzled. I did not know enough about prisons to even guess. But after listening a bit longer, I realized that I have indeed, experienced the worst prison on earth. That is, the minister explained, the prison of unforgiveness.

Unforgiveness affects a person in different ways. If we spend much time thinking bitterly about someone who has wronged us, plotting revenge (not that we would actually do it of course), we are truly in bondage. If we find ourselves going to great lengths to avoid someone we are having a hard time forgiving, we isolate ourselves in our own personal prison. Unforgiveness takes a lot of energy and leaves us weak and defenseless.

Unforgiveness affects us emotionally and spiritually. We struggle with anger and resentment until "a root of bitterness springing up troubles us." (Hebrews 12:15)

Our relationship with family, church family, and others suffers as we become irritable and withdraw into a shell of bitterness. The relationship is still there, but the fellowship is gone.

Harboring unforgiveness alienates us from God. It hinders our prayer life and opens the door for Satan. God seems far away and our peace is lost.

Choosing to forgive someone who has wronged you will free you even if the person you have forgiven refuses to accept your forgiveness. By confessing our feelings to God and accepting the pain that was inflicted on us, we can choose to forgive, even though we don't feel like it. When we truly forgive, we cancel the debt and release the offender. The peace of restored fellowship with God and others is priceless. We dare not harbor unforgiveness in our hearts. *When we choose to forgive, we also set ourselves free.* You don't need to wait until you *feel like forgiving. If you choose to forgive*, the feelings will follow.

- Is there anyone in my life that I am having a hard time forgiving?
- Am I willing to accept the pain the offender has caused me and forgive him?
- *Lord, reveal any unforgiveness in my heart and give me the desire and courage to forgive.*

 Read: Luke 6:27-49

The Fragrance Of Forgiveness

"Forgive, and ye shall be forgiven."
- Luke 6:37

Forgiveness is an essential attribute in a Christian's life, absolutely necessary in restoring relationships. The definition of forgiveness is: "giving up resentment against, or the desire to punish." When we truly forgive, we release the offender. It can be difficult to forgive when we are hurting and possibly angry or bitter. But any relationship will suffer if we refuse to forgive when offenses come.

With God...although we ultimately want God's will for our lives, things can happen that cause us to lose that focus. We can blame God for the pain and confusion in our lives. Until we repent and ask Him to forgive us for blaming Him, our fellowship with Him will be broken.

With family...offenses may occur often in a family setting. Forgiveness, for even minor offenses, is the oil that keeps the family unit running smoothly.

With brethren...as we work together with our church family, much charity and grace is needed. God made each of us unique, and as humans there will always be differences of opinion and conviction. Forbearance, which is closely related to forgiveness, will keep many small issues from becoming large ones.

With mankind...We may meet with offenses as we mingle with non-Christians. Forgiveness is necessary to our Christian witness, as well as to the relationships we have with neighbors and friends.

There must be forgiveness, and acceptance of that forgiveness, before there can be reconciliation between two individuals or groups. We can, however, choose to forgive even if that forgiveness is refused. It will free us to go on and grow to be more like Jesus in our hearts. Forgiveness does not make the other person right, but it sets us free. *Forgiveness is the fragrance of a crushed flower on the heel that crushed it. Harboring an unforgiving spirit leaves one crippled.* When you choose to forgive, you free both the person who offended you and yourself.

- As I examine my heart, do I see any traces of unforgiveness?
- Is there anyone in my life that I need to forgive?
- *Lord, I thank you for your example of forgiveness, and I ask for that same desire to forgive.*

Boomerang Blessings

"Blessed be the God and Father of our Lord Jesus Christ, who hath blessed us with all spiritual blessings."
- Ephesians 1:3

On our way home from Indiana late one night, I went, alone, into a convenience store for some snacks and a drink. The lone clerk behind the desk was very large and had quite an unusual hair style. At that point I was not actually sure if "he" was a man or a woman! As I gathered my selections, I felt the Spirit's prompting. "You know you sometimes wish you were braver in saying 'The Lord bless you' to people. You have a prime opportunity here."

"Ooh, but God." I cringed. "Didn't you see how *big* he is? What if he doesn't take kindly to something like that?" I fleetingly wondered if I could get out the door before he came over the counter. (Oh, the excuses Satan will hurl through our minds!)

God did not answer that (although He may have been smiling), so I apprehensively took my things up to the counter. The clerk was actually a friendly man, and we made small talk as he rang up my bill and I paid him. He even asked me some questions about the way I was dressed and expressed appreciation for it.

Then I gathered up my purchases (and my courage), smiled, and said "Thank you… and the Lord bless your night!" (as I was turning toward the door for a fast get-away.)

But I stopped when his face lit up with surprise and delight. He put his hands into the air and exclaimed: "Whah, *thank* you! And da *Lawd* do da *same* fo you!"

I smiled bigger, thanked him again and went on my way chuckling, but feeling deeply that I had been blessed, too! And also wondering how many times I had failed to lift someone up because I had ignored that prompting or perhaps I just was not listening, or did not have the courage. It was a good reminder that in passing on God's blessings, we are blessed in return. We should never be too busy to hold out the lamp of Christ to weary people.

- Do I take advantage of opportunities to pass on a blessing to others?
- In what ways could I bless others through word or deed, even just in small ways?
- *Lord, I'm timid sometimes, but my desire is to bless you by blessing others.*

Read: Matthew 18:1-6

Our Valuable Possessions

"But bring them up in the nurture and admonition of the Lord."
- Ephesians 6:4

We all have possessions which we consider assets. Some are obviously more valuable than others. Our homes and our vehicles may be worth quite a bit. The telephone, vacuum, stove, and refrigerator are not worth as much, but they are definitely assets. Some of our assets may be valuable to us because of a sentimental attachment we have to them. Our children, however, are by far our most valuable assets.

Just as we maintain our other possessions, we need to put time and effort into our children. Our home needs to be established on godly principles, not the standards of the world. Establishing a regular family worship time is very important. As parents we must have a vision of our children serving the Lord and make choices with that goal in mind.

Communication is a vital tool in our homes. We must take the time to listen to and talk with our children, whether they are small or teenagers. We need to show them, and tell them, that we love them. We all need to be loved and accepted. Love begets love.

And most of all, as Christian mothers, we need to pray for our children daily. I have been almost surprised at times to see how much it means to our children to know that their mother is praying for them. Even when my prayers are hindering their independence or rebellion, my prayers are a security that they want and need. When I asked our son, who was struggling at one point, if he wished I would just quit praying for him, he responded with an emphatic "No, Mom!"

The time we invest in our children now is time well spent that will pay dividends in eternity.

- Are there changes we could make in our home to better care for our children?
- Do I truly see our children as the most valuable possessions in our home?
- *Lord, I thank You for these children and pray that You would show us how better to train them to serve You.*

Jochebed's Vison

"Where there is no vision,
the people perish."
- Proverbs 29:18

Jochebed had a vision. She couldn't have known what Moses' future held or how God would use him, but she did know that taking his life would be very wrong. So she hid him for three months. We don't know what all led up to her decision to put him in a little basket and place it in the river. It must have been a terribly hard thing to do. But Jochebed had faith that God would take care of her son. And He did. How happy she must have been to be reunited with her baby! How clever of Miriam to suggest finding a Hebrew nurse for the child. It must have been just as hard, though, when Moses was weaned, to take him to the palace and hand him over to the princess to raise. But once again, Jochebed's faith carried her through. She gave her son into God's care and trusted Him. She had a vision of a godly son serving the Lord wherever he was, and we can believe she spent time in prayer for Moses every day. We are not told anything about his growing-up years or if he ever saw his family, but I imagine he adjusted as children do and was happy in the luxurious life as an Egyptian prince.

Moses showed that his heart was still with his people, however, when he impulsively killed an Egyptian who was beating a Hebrew man. Later, when the Pharaoh wanted Moses killed for his actions, he fled to Midian and became a sheepherder. What a contrast in lifestyles! But we can see that God was preparing Moses for the enormous job of leading the Israelites out of Egypt. After many years of living the life of a shepherd and a nomad, Moses was ready. God spoke to him from a burning bush and, though Moses felt so inadequate that he tried to excuse himself, he was God's choice as a leader. Moses spent the rest of his life in the great journey of leading the Israelites from bondage to the promised land.

Do we have the vision for our children that Jochebed had for hers? Do we shelter them from the evils of the world as she sheltered Moses? Are we willing to fully and completely entrust them into God's care? How much time do we spend in daily prayer for our children? We don't know how long Jochebed lived or if she witnessed the leadership of Moses. But we do know that her faith not only served her well, but also the whole tribe of Israel. God will bless us, too, as we give our families to Him in complete faith.

- Have I truly given our children and other loved ones into God's care?
- Am I praying for our children daily and trusting Him to answer my prayers in His time?
- *Lord, give me a faith as deep as Jochebed's and help me to live it out in a way that honors You.*

May 12 *Read: Psalm 121*

Carried By Our Saviour

"And even to your old age I am he…
even I will carry, and will deliver you."
- Isaiah 46:4

Waiting in the car while his wife went into a local department store, our friend was interestedly watching the people coming and going in the parking lot. Soon his attention was drawn to a young mother who came striding along, carrying a child. Not a large woman, she was actually quite small, and the child was several years old. To make things more difficult, the little one was sound asleep with her head on her mother's shoulder. Arms and legs dangling, she was a dead weight and looked like quite a burden. This woman, however, did not appear to be heavily burdened but walked briskly all the way to the end of the row, tucked her daughter into her car seat, and drove away.

Watching this little scene unfold, he thought about how much like Jesus it was. Like the familiar story of the footprints in the sand. At times in our lives we are spiritually awake, walking along through life with Jesus at our side, leaving two sets of prints in the sands of time. But there are times for all of us when we become sleepy, tired of the trials and the pain and the difficulty of putting one foot in front of the other. We become weak, tempted to sin, and powerless to overcome. We are ready to sit down and quit. It is at times like these that God picks us up and carries us. We may feel like a dead weight, but He is quite able to carry us through. Our part at these times is just to rest in Him, allowing Him to carry us until once again we can walk beside Him. The sleeping child put up no fuss; she just rode along in her mother's arms. It will be much easier for Him to carry us if we're not resisting but willingly allowing Him to bear our burdens.

- Do I trust God to carry me through in times of distress?
- What situation am I dealing with now that I could allow Him to carry me through?
- *Lord, I thank You for being willing to carry the burdens that are too big for me. I ask You to do that for me today.*

Pray And Release

"For this child I prayed; and the Lord hath given me my petition which I asked of Him."
- I Samuel 1:27

Hannah had not been able to have a child and, in Old Testament times, she was considered a failure. It was a social embarrassment for her and her husband. Elkanah would even have been permitted to divorce her as a barren wife. To make it even worse, Elkanah had a second wife, Peninnah, who had children and mocked Hannah unmercifully. Elkanah loved Hannah and tried to console her, but Hannah was too distressed to be comforted.

Hannah had every reason to be bitter and to lash out at Peninnah, but instead she took her heartbreak to the Lord. Elkanah's family had made their yearly journey to Shiloh to worship at the temple. Hannah went to the temple to pray, upset by Penninah's taunting. She wept as she cried out to the Lord to give her a little boy. Her longing was so great that she made an amazing vow. She promised that if God would give her a child, she would give the child back to serve Him in the temple all of his life. It's hard to imagine a longing so great that she would actually promise to allow Eli to raise her son. Eli didn't exactly have a good track record as a dad. His sons were wicked men who were called the "sons of Belial." (2:12) But Hannah made the vow and she kept it. Eli noticed her praying there in the temple and at first thought she was drunk but, realizing how deep her longing was, he assured her that her prayers would be answered.

We can only imagine the joy Hannah must have felt as she returned home, and even more joy when her baby boy was born. He was probably around three years old when she took Samuel to the temple to willingly, (and heart-brokenly), surrender him to Eli to serve the God who had answered her prayers. Samuel grew up to be a great man of God.

Hannah prayed for Samuel before he was conceived. Her prayers were *sincere* cries from her heart. She *believed* Eli's assurance that God would answer her heart's desire, and she *released* her prayer as she went on her way rejoicing. Hannah was a praying mother who undoubtedly continued praying for Samuel as long as she lived.

It is not easy to release a heart-cry. It is easier to hang on to it, fretting and thinking we need to help God figure out the answer. We have the same assurance today, however, that God will answer our prayers. Are they *sincere*? Do you *believe* God answers prayers? Then you can *release* your prayer and know that He will answer in His own time and way.

- What desires am I praying about today that I need to fully release to the Lord?
- Do I truly believe that God can and will answer as He sees best?
- *Lord, this releasing is not easy. Help me to trust Your love for me and to know that Your answer will be the right one.*

Read: III John

Seeds Of Faith

"I have no greater joy than to hear that my children walk in truth"
- III John: 4

We were hearing a sermon on Faith. The minister was speaking about the "seeds of faith" and how they're sown. Some are planted into the hearts of young children through Bible stories read to them by their mothers. An unbelieving adult may receive these seeds through a conversation with a believing friend. Perhaps simply the wonders of God's creation will cause seeds of faith to take root. God then expects us to nurture those seeds and grow in faith.

As my heart was agreeing with these thoughts, my mind was going to an all-too-familiar scene in my life.

"Mommy, can you read me a 'tory? Can you, pease? Can you read me a 'tory, Mommy?"

"Hmm?" would be my distracted answer.

"Can you read me a 'tory, pease?"

"Not now honey, Mommy's busy and I really need to get this done. Maybe later." I would feel a twinge of guilt as my little daughter walked away with disappointment on her face.

Seeds of faith cannot grow if they are never planted. Our children's hearts are a fertile ground, just waiting for those seeds. It's never a waste of time to snuggle your little ones close and read those beautiful old Bible stories to them. What about others that we work with or neighbors that we visit with from time to time? Are we afraid to speak of Jesus for fear of what they will think or how they will react?

Planted seeds need to be nurtured. We can water them with words of encouragement and fertilize them with continued teaching and conversation. We should avoid drowning them by being demanding or pushing too hard for growth. Rather, we should gently nourish as God gives us opportunities. A healthy, fruit-bearing plant is satisfying for a gardener to see. A spiritually healthy person--child or adult--must be a beautiful sight in the eyes of God. We mothers have opportunities to sow and nurture seeds of faith in the lives of those around us today.

- What could I do to plant seeds of faith in my children?
- Who else in my life would benefit from my nurturing today?
- *These seeds of faith are so important, Lord. Show me ways in which I can be Your gardener today.*

A Puddle... Or An Ocean?

"Ye are the salt of the earth."
- Matthew 5:13

There is a vast difference between a water puddle and an ocean. A puddle is stagnant, dirty, and supports no life. It is shallow and soon dries up and disappears. Animals will drink from puddles, and children, drawn like magnets, delight in walking through rather than around them. Puddles, however, are basically dead and have very little worth.

Oceans, on the other hand, are a world of their own. Oceans are deep, salty, and productive.

Seawater is rich in minerals and metals. Sand, gravel, and oyster shells used in construction are found on the ocean floor. Offshore wells produce oil and gas for petroleum production. Oceans hold potential as an alternate source of energy and are teeming with life. There is nothing dead about an ocean!

Oceans are *deep*. The average depth of the world's oceans is 16,000 ft. with mountains, ridges, and canyons all under water. Ocean trenches can reach depths of more than five miles. There is nothing shallow about an ocean!

Oceans are *salty*. The Great Salt Lake is more than 150 parts salt to 1000 parts water. The oceans of the world average around 35 parts salt to 1000 parts water. Visiting the Gulf of Mexico off the coast of Florida one winter, we were quite surprised at how salty the ocean really is. There is nothing bland about an ocean!

How is your spiritual life? Does it resemble a puddle -- kind of stagnant with bits of dirty debris floating in it? Do you feel spiritually dead, unproductive, and shallow? Would you not rather be an ocean?

In the Sermon on the Mount, Jesus teaches that we are the salt of the earth. (Matthew 5:13) We, as Christians, are to season the world around us. We cannot be a seasoning if we have lost our flavor! If we become like the world, we are shallow, unproductive, and worthless in His Kingdom. As salt brings out the best flavor in food, we need to affect those around us in a positive manner.

Jesus wants our relationship with Him to be deep and meaningful. He longs to spend time with us, showing us His will for our lives through Scripture and communicating with us through prayer. We bless Him as well as others when we are productive for Him. The needs around us are overwhelming, but with His guidance and support, we can affect the lives of others more deeply than we may ever know. Let's be as an ocean...deep, salty, and productive!

- What is the condition of my spiritual life today?
- How can I improve on the depth and productivity of my life?
- *Lord, my life has lost some of its savor. Lead me to a greater depth and worth in my service to You.*

God's Checking Account

*"If ye shall ask any thing in my name,
I will do it."
- John 14:14*

My friend has her name on the signature card for several bank accounts, and only one of them is actually hers. Recently she put her signature on another card. She has no part in her son's construction business, but he wanted to have his business account accessible to someone else, just in case he was unable to withdraw money himself for some reason. He obviously trusts her. He knows that, while she might use his account to pay his lumber bill, she won't go out and buy a new car for herself unless he specifically tells her to.

When God says, "Ask, and it shall be given you," (Matthew 7:7) or "If ye shall ask anything in my name, I will do it," (John 14:14) He is saying, in effect, that He has put our signature on His account. He owns everything. He can do anything. In prayerfully asking Him for something, we "write a check" to obtain whatever we need. Do we believe that? Then why do we hesitate? While our personal checking accounts have a definite limit, God's account is limitless. Philippians 4:19 says, "But my God shall supply all your need according to his riches in glory by Christ Jesus." His riches will never run out, and He longs to share them with us. They are ours by writing a check through prayer.

If God does not seem to be "cashing our checks," perhaps we should examine what we have written that "check" for. His store is boundless, but He always spends it wisely and expects us to do the same. We can believe that, along with the authority He has given us to approach Him confidently in prayer, He can also give us the ability to know what we need to ask for. We have His written Word and the Holy Spirit to guide us. If we are asking within His will, there is nothing He will not supply. He sees our lives from beginning to end and knows exactly what is best for us while we see "through a glass darkly," (I Corinthians 13:12) and sometimes just *think* we know what is best. When we seek His will for our lives, we can write our checks in faith, knowing He will cash them at just the right time for us.

- Do I have faith that God can and will meet my every need if I just ask?
- What needs do I have today that I could write a check for?
- *Thank you Lord, for Your wonderful store of riches, and Your desire to share them with me.*

Intercessory Prayer

"I exhort therefore, that...supplications, prayers, intercessions... be made for all men."
- II Timothy 2:1

In Ezekiel 22:30 we read that God was searching for a man among the people of Jerusalem to "stand in the gap," interceding for the land. But He found none, causing Him to pour out His wrath upon them. He needed only one man and found none.

When Abraham prayed for the city of Sodom, God agreed to save the city for ten godly people. (Genesis 18:20-33) Although fewer than ten godly people were found, God honored Abraham's prayer. One person's intercessory prayer had made a difference.

King Hezekiah interceded reverently but boldly for the people of Judah to be delivered from the king of Assyria. (II Kings 19:14-19) In answer to his prayer, God sent an angel to the camp of the Assyrians that killed 185,000 men in one night. The prayers of one man had saved the nation from a seemingly hopeless situation.

In Acts 12 we read of Peter's deliverance from prison. King Herod had imprisoned him and intended to put him to death. But verse 5 says "prayer was made without ceasing of the church unto God for Him." The earnest intercession of the church changed the outcome of Herod's plan. Peter was miraculously delivered from prison and from Herod by an angel.

Supplication and intercession in prayer take time and self-discipline. But one person interceding for an individual, a church, a nation, or other situation can make a remarkable difference. Our problems are God's opportunities, so we can bring them to God with confidence. He may be depending on you or me to "stand in the gap."

- Do I truly believe that my intercessory prayers make a difference?
- What situations can I think of in my life and others' that need my prayers today?
- *Lord, give me a heart that loves and feels for others and that prays unceasingly for them.*

Humility

"Serving the Lord with all humility of mind."
- Acts 20:19

King Hezekiah was a godly ruler who "did that which was right in the sight of the Lord." In dramatic contrast to his wicked father King Ahaz, Hezekiah boldly cleaned house. He destroyed altars, idols, and pagan temples. He even broke in pieces the bronze serpent that Moses had made because the people had made it an idol. He reopened the temple in Jerusalem and reinstated the Passover. He brought revival to Judah. He also won many battles and became a wealthy man. II Chronicles 31:21 says that "every work that he began in the service of the house of God.... to seek his God...he did it with all his heart, and prospered." We can see from Hezekiah's life that complete dependence on God yields amazing results.

Past obedience, however, does not remove the possibility of present disobedience. This is evident in the life of King Hezekiah also. It seems that his wealth and honor had made him proud. When ambassadors from Babylon came to visit, he rashly showed them all of his wealth, leaving none of his treasures unseen. He chose to impress the foreigners rather than giving God the credit for all his blessings. His choice caused Judah a lot of future trouble.

As Christian women, we desire to serve God as Hezekiah did, "with all our hearts... and prosper." As God blesses us for our service to Him, we need to guard against feelings of pride--in our obedient children, our marriage relationship, or the work God has led us into. Unconfesssed pride will eventually be revealed and may negatively affect many people besides ourselves.

- Do I recognize the blessings I enjoy as being from God?
- In what ways might I be proud of those blessings?
- *Lord, I thank you for blessing me so richly and ask that You reveal any pride in my heart.*

Inner Beauty

"But we have this treasure in earthen vessels, that the excellency of the power may be of God and not of us."
- II Corinthians 4:7

A geode! Walking along the beach, my friend's sons had just found a dull, rough rock about the size of a tennis ball. Granted, it was not one of those spectacular specimens you see in museums and rock shops where someone has carefully sliced the rock in two. Those gems are displayed at their best with the cut surface polished to a beautiful shine. Really, the geode was nothing you would look at twice, except that there was a hole on one side that gave a glimpse of some fragile, clear crystals around a hollow cavity. Still, it was a special find that had apparently been uncovered recently as the sand was washed away by the waves on the shore of Lake Superior.

An intact geode lying on the ground doesn't look like anything special. Yet, when broken open, a rare beauty is exposed. This inner treasure becomes visible only if the geode is broken. What a beautiful picture of the Scriptural figure of "treasure in earthen vessels." Paul speaks of that treasure in today's reading. We are frail, perishable, human containers with priceless contents. God's Message and His power dwelling in us are even more rare and beautiful than the lovely crystals inside an ordinary geode.

Though we are weak creatures, God uses us to spread His Good News, and He gives us the power to do His work. Remembering that our power comes from Him motivates us to stay in contact with our Power Source. As we serve the Lord in humility, others will be able to see Jesus through us. Any excellency we may have will soon wither away as the grass and be gone. But the excellency of God's power is eternal.

Too often, we are not broken enough for His beauty to show forth. Geodes must be broken or cut in order to discover their inner beauty. As we go through hardships and painful trials, we gain a patience, understanding, and compassion that does not come any other way. As our ministry to others becomes more effective, the excellency of God's power is revealed through us.

- Am I willing to be broken enough to reveal Christ's beauty through me?
- Am I allowing the trials of life to produce Christ's beauty in me, or am I becoming bitter and angry at God?
- *Lord, I long to have Your beauty shining through my life. Help me to be willing to allow that to happen.*

 Read: Romans 12:9-21

Overcoming Evil With Good

"Be not overcome of evil, but overcome evil with good."
- Romans 12:21

In his book The War of the Worlds, H.G. Wells tells vividly a story of a world doomed by the invasion of Martians. You can feel the desperation of those hunted by an invincible foe as the Martians went around catching people and killing them. And just as the situation seems entirely hopeless, the enemy is defeated. Defeated by disease, caused by bacteria from human blood, something that had not even been considered by the attacking forces.

Although the book is a Science Fiction story and is not written from a Christian perspective, we can see a parallel to the Christian life. Our world has, in fact, been invaded by a seemingly invincible foe. That enemy is evil. How often do we feel overwhelmed by the evil around us? We can feel insignificant and incapable of stemming the flood. Like the victims in the story, we may feel desperate and helpless.

But we do have weapons at our disposal. "The weapons of our warfare are not carnal, but mighty through God..." (II Corinthians 10:4) We can, with God's help, overcome evil with good. *Prayer* is a mighty weapon that is always ready for battle. *Fasting* can add power to our prayers. We can possibly change someone's negative thoughts or actions with just a *smile* or a word of *encouragement*. Or lift a family member's spirit of discouragement with a heart-felt hug or a candle on the table for no special reason. Just lending a *listening* ear can make a difference to a weary mother, a struggling teacher, or a confused teenager. God can do mighty things with our simple "weapons" if we just put forth the effort to use them.

- Do I have a deep burden for those in the heat of life's battles?
- What weapons could I use today to help overcome evil with good in someone's life?
- *I praise You, Lord, for supplying the weapons and ask that You show me how to use them.*

Waymarks And High Heaps

"Set thee up waymarks, make thee high heaps: set thine heart toward the highway."
- Jeremiah 31:21

In Jeremiah 31, God tells His people that they will return to Israel from all over the world. He tells them to set up waymarks and high heaps to mark the way they took as they left their homeland. In those days it was common to pile up heaps of rocks for landmarks. These signposts and landmarks were to clearly identify the way of their return to Israel.

As Christian women, we are leaving signposts along the paths of our lives. These markers will be seen and read by our children, our neighbors, our co-workers, or other people whose lives we touch along the way. What kind of signposts are we leaving? Are they directing others to Jesus and to a Heavenly Home? We can leave good signs by singing hymns of praise with our children or reading Bible stories to them. We can teach them to pray and to recognize God's answers when they come. Sharing testimonies of God's blessings and answers to our prayers can also inspire others to press on. We can leave landmarks by gathering together for family devotions regularly, by lovingly serving others in a time of need, or by praying with the sick, elderly, or downcast.

Have you planted any signposts that you need to go back and take down? Bad examples or habits that are stumbling blocks rather than landmarks? Keeping the signposts of our lives leading others in the right direction will bring blessings that will benefit not only us, but also those around us.

- Are my attitudes and actions signposts for others to follow?
- What signposts in my life should I remove?
- *Lord, give me wisdom in planting these signposts and show me any that need to be removed.*

Read: Matthew 24:36-25:13

Ready Or Not

"Therefore be ye also ready: for in such an hour as ye think not the Son of man cometh."
- Matthew 24:44

Many times in life we need to make preparations to be ready. Just preparing a meal for Sunday dinner guests takes thought, time, and effort. By the time you plan the menu, shop for groceries, prepare the food, set the table, and serve your guests, you may feel like you have put in a week's work. But what would your guests think if you put a platter of raw meat on the table? Or if the dishes were dirty or the bread stale? Yes, it takes work to be ready, but we are willing to do our best for our guests.

On another day we may set out to sew a dress. If we have not prepared properly, we may experience a frustrating disaster. If we must spend time hunting fabric, matching thread, zippers, buttons, scissors, pins, or anything else we need but may not have on hand, we won't have a very profitable day.

How about traveling? Have you ever gone on a trip without everything you need? I know from experience what a headache that can be. You need enough money, maps, clothes (clean and mended) and all other necessities. At times you may need to make reservations for lodging and prepare food to take along. You may even begin to wonder if it is worth it. But a trip can be very worthwhile and a blessing for everyone--if you are properly prepared.

There is another event coming that far outweighs any of these scenarios. It is one in which we will *all* participate. It is unique in that we don't know *when* it will happen, but it is urgent that we all make the proper preparations and that we are ready at all times. Jesus has promised that He is coming again for His faithful servants. If we are not watchful, we can too easily go about our daily lives without ever thinking that *this could be the day!!* We get careless and "forget the oil for our lamps." We do wrong and neglect to ask forgiveness from God and those we hurt.

Spiritual readiness is not something like lamp oil, that can be borrowed or bought at the last minute. We are each responsible for our own spiritual condition. Is my relationship with Jesus what He wants it to be? We won't live here forever. Either we will meet God in death, or we will face Him when He comes again. Either we will enjoy eternity in His glorious presence, or we will suffer eternally in the lake of fire. Jesus wants everyone in Heaven with Him! ***Are you ready?***

- Have I truly surrendered my will to Jesus as Lord and Saviour of my life?
- Am I living in "newness of life," maintaining a close relationship with Him, and seeking His will for my life?
- *Lord, I long to be ready to meet You, but I get so distracted. Draw me to Yourself so that I may be ready when you call.*

Stubborn... Or Determined

"But without faith it is impossible to please Him."
- Hebrews 11:6

How would you describe your faith? Stubborn? Determined? Would your faith sustain you through anything? Penelope Stout was a woman with an incredible faith. She was born in 1622, married a Dutchman, and went with him by boat to the settlement of New Amsterdam (now New York City). The trip, however, didn't turn out as they had planned. They had almost arrived when their ship was wrecked on the Jersey coastline. They survived the shipwreck only to be attacked by hostile Indians on land. Her husband was killed and she was horribly wounded. According to the story, she was scalped. Her left arm was injured so badly that she couldn't use it, and her abdomen was laid open so that she had to use her right hand to hold herself together. Miraculously, Penelope survived. After being left for dead, she managed to crawl into a hollow log where she lay for several days, until she was discovered by another group of Indians. These folks, thinking to cash in on some ransom money, took her back to their camp and stitched up her wounds with fishbone needles and vegetable fiber. The poor woman lived on and was eventually ransomed by the Dutch colonial officials. She later married Richard Stout and had ten children. Penelope lived to the ripe old age of 110 and has many descendants.

Our minister's mother was a delightful elderly woman who was accused by a family member of being stubborn. With a twinkle in her eye she replied: "I'm not stubborn, I'm determined!" I'm thinking these two women had a rich character trait in common. An immovable, steadfast faith.

While lying in the hollow log, Penelope had no provisions with which to maintain or strengthen her faith. Nothing but some moss to eat, her incredible pain, and her thoughts. We cannot know what she must have thought about as she lay there waiting to die. She surely had some deep thoughts about death and God.

In contrast to her meager resources, most of us have Bibles to read and study, as well as many Bible study helps. Other believers with their faith-building testimonies can influence us to be faithful. We have no excuse. A determined faith will see you through the most difficult of trials. Be a Penelope!

- In what condition is my faith today?
- Am I using the resources available to me to strengthen and maintain my faith?
- *Lord, it can be scary to ask for a stronger faith, but that is what my heart desires today.*

Read: Matthew 11:20-30

Spiritual Alzheimer's

"Take my yoke upon you, and learn of me...
and ye shall find rest unto your souls."
- Matthew 11:29

David, a friend of ours, works as a nursing assistant in a nearby nursing home. One of the ladies he helps take care of suffers from Alzheimer's. When he started working there two years ago, this woman was very combative when anyone tried to help her. She would get very angry, and there were days when it was impossible to give her the care she needed. One day David was visiting with this woman's daughter, who told him that her mother had always enjoyed singing the old hymns. That evening when another aide asked for help with this lady, David decided to try something different. Sitting on the edge of this unhappy lady's bed, he began to sing one of the old well-known hymns. As he started to sing the second verse, the old lady began to hum along. Soon she was sitting on the edge of her bed and within fifteen minutes they had her in the bathroom, cleaned up, and ready for the evening. As they left her room she was smiling and singing.

Spiritual Alzheimer's is even worse than this lady's condition. Physical Alzheimer's begins with a hardening process that blocks the flow of information to the brain. It destroys the ability to know and remember. As the disease progresses, the person loses the knowledge of his condition. Spiritual Alzheimer's begins with a hardening of the heart. When a person chooses to reject the Truth, believing Satan's lies and saying "no" to the voice of God, his heart begins to harden. As the "disease" progresses, spiritual blindness sets in and the person loses the ability to even know his true condition.

I don't know what sort of person this lady was as a younger woman, but I doubt that she is even aware of her present condition. There is no known cure for her disease, but there is a cure for Spiritual Alzheimer's that is readily available, free, and in abundant supply. Jesus says, "*Come unto me, all ye that labour and are heavy laden, and I will give you rest.*" (Matthew 11:28) As David was able to reach the lady with song, so Jesus wants to reach us with His love, healing the hardened areas of our hearts. You can keep your heart soft by believing the Truth, loving the Truth, and living the Truth in all areas of your life.

- If I honestly examine my heart, what condition is it in today?
- Am I allowing Satan's lies to begin a hardening process in my heart?
- *Lord, only You know the true condition of my heart. Please reveal to me any areas of hardness there.*

The "Y" In The Road

"Enter not into the path of the wicked,
and go not in the way of evil men."
- Proverbs 4:14

My sister was driving from her home in Virginia to Indiana for a visit. Passing through West Virginia, she was traveling west on Highway 64. At Charleston, Highway 64 connects with Highway 77. For about a mile before the road splits again, the four-lane highway is divided down the center by a cement barrier, with drivers on one side ending up on 77 going north, and drivers on the other side ending up on 64 going west.

Driving along the barrier, she thought about how easy it would be to end up on the wrong side of that divider, headed in the wrong direction. Just a subtle shift to the right or left, before the first cement section, and you would be stuck, flowing with the traffic down the wrong road.

And then she thought about how much our lives can be like that. We can be traveling along through life on the right road, serving the Lord and enjoying fellowship with our fellow travelers. We may hardly notice a shift, taking us to the wrong side of the barrier. Still traveling alongside the right path, we may be surprised to find ourselves separated from God and heading down a strange, unfamiliar road.

But there is a way back. Although it can be inconvenient and frustrating to drive to the next exit and find our way back to the right road, it can be done. And it is also possible, through repentance and confession to return to God's way. By using the Bible as our road map and Jesus as our guide, we can avoid those shifts to the wrong road and end up at our desired destination --Heaven!

- Am I traveling on the right side of the barrier today?
- Am I looking to Jesus and the Scriptures for guidance on the highway of holiness?
- *Lord, I thank You for being a willing Guide, and I ask for wisdom to stay on the right path.*

 Read: Revelation 3:14-22

Purified By Trials

"It is good for me that I have been afflicted; that I might learn thy statutes."
- Psalm 119:71

One day a friend of mine was preparing to cook a large pot of macaroni. As she lit the gas range to boil the water, it struck her--*you can't boil water without a flame.* Well, obviously! But wait; maybe there is more here than meets the eye. How many profound things do we overlook just because they are so commonplace?

What came to her mind next was Revelation 3:15. How do we change from cold or lukewarm to hot? What is the flame that makes the difference? The counsel given to the Laodiceans here is "to buy of me gold tried in the fire..." In I Peter 1:7, we read again of gold being tried with fire. Our faith is purified through trials. That is not a very pleasant thought, but James 1:2-4 speaks of being joyful when our faith is tried. In Romans 5:3-5, Paul also speaks of glorying in trials, because he had learned to anticipate the good things they produce in him.

As my friend lit the stove she was seeing not just the process of heating water; she was also anticipating a good dish of macaroni and cheese. Just so, when God gives or allows trials, He knows what they can accomplish. Although we cannot know what He knows, we can, with His help, focus on the assurance that whatever happens is in His hands and will be to our benefit. While we are feeling the flame, we want to remember that it is the remedy for the lukewarmness the Lord hates, and He is making us into the people He wants us to be.

- Do I recognize trials as opportunities to strengthen my faith?
- Can I look back and see trials God has allowed in my life to help me grow in faith?
- *Lord, it's a challenge to glory in trials so help me to trust You for the benefits of the fire in my life.*

Joy In Suffering

"That your rejoicing may be more abundant in Jesus Christ." - Philippians 1:26

We do not fully understand the concept of rejoicing in suffering. But we have some good examples in the life of the Apostle Paul. He often suffered for promoting the Gospel. Being chained to a Roman prison guard twenty-four hours a day could not have been pleasant, yet he rejoiced in the opportunity to preach the Gospel message to the Jews.

Writing to the Philippians from prison, Paul rejoiced that even though his circumstances were undesirable, the Gospel was being furthered as the guards and others in the palace learned he was there for serving Christ. Other believers, also, were becoming bolder in speaking of Jesus.

While Paul was in chains, some other men were preaching out of jealousy, trying to make a name for themselves or causing trouble for Paul. But rather than becoming upset, Paul rejoiced that the message was being preached, regardless of the reason!

How do we respond to unpleasant circumstances? As I was discussing this with my sisters at church, one shared that she has learned to be joyful even though her house is "falling down around her"...literally! Although the situation does not make her happy, she rejoices that her family has a roof over their heads, a blessing that many in the world do not have. Another sister has experienced joy in the midst of grieving. Though losing a loved one to death is a hard trial, feeling God's presence intimately can bring joy. Joy surpasses happiness, and we experience it as we yield our lives fully to God's plan for us, even when it means suffering for Him. Suffering joyfully strengthens our faith and encourages fellow sufferers.

- Am I familiar with the joy that comes through tribulation?
- What circumstances in my life today could I fully submit to God, thereby experiencing that joy?
- *Lord, this is a hard thing, but I desire to know the joy that comes from fully submitting to You.*

Read: II Samuel 9

Confident Christianity

"Having predestinated us unto the adoption of children by Jesus Christ to himself."
- Ephesians 1:5

King David was remembering the covenant he had made with his friend Jonathan to show kindness to all of his descendants. (I Samuel 20:14-17) He then learned that there was, indeed, one left of the house of Saul. Mephibosheth was King Saul's grandson, but he was "lame on both his feet" from a fall he had taken when he was five years old. (II Samuel 4:4)

Imagine his surprise and fear when he was called to see King David. Most kings in David's day tried to wipe out the families of their rivals to prevent descendants from seeking the throne. Mephibosheth must have thought his life was over. A helpless, crippled enemy with an appointment to meet the King. Imagine then, his further amazement when King David told him not to be afraid and explained why he had called him. He kindly restored all of the family property to Mephibosheth and arranged for him to eat at the royal table from then on. A helpless, crippled outcast adopted into the royal family!

What a beautiful picture of our adoption into God's family. Like Mephibosheth, we were helpless and our condition was hopeless. Mephibosheth was from Lo-debar which means "a barren land" and even his name means "a shameful thing." He had absolutely no claim to any inheritance, and was too lame even to come to the king to beg for mercy. By grace, Mephibosheth was *sought out* by King David, even as we by grace are *sought out* by God. Once found, King David restored to Mephibosheth great riches and a place of fellowship at the king's table. While Mephibosheth deserved nothing, he received a magnificent inheritance. Although we are totally undeserving, by God's grace we are adopted into His divine favor. We are elevated to a place in the family of God and made joint-heirs with Jesus Christ Himself. Our welcome to His table is even warmer than the welcome King David gave Mephibosheth.

Are you living a life of *confident Christianity?* Knowing and embracing the truth of our adoption into the family of God should give you a confidence and a full assurance of your status as *His daughter.* You have been *sought out* and declared righteous with all the benefits and privileges of an heir. Believe it! Embrace it! And live in the fullness of your God-given position.

- Do I understand and believe that I have been adopted into God's family as a joint-heir with Jesus?
- In what ways am I living out that position?
- *Lord…"Love so amazing, so divine, demands my soul, my life, my all!" (Isaac Watts)*

From Home To Rome

"For He hath said, I will never leave thee, nor forsake thee."
- Hebrews 13:5

Paul was on a journey from his home in a Caesarean prison to Rome for sentencing. After many days and much trouble, a shipwreck landed the crew and passengers on the island of Melita where they were greeted by the local inhabitants. These residents are described as barbarous--uncivilized savages--who nonetheless welcomed the prisoners and treated them kindly.

After spending three winter months on the island, the centurion and his prisoners departed for Rome. They left in an Alexandrian ship that had been wintered there. This ship had a figurehead of Castor & Pollux carved into its bow.

In Greek mythology, Castor & Pollux are twin brothers worshipped as gods. Heathen sailors believed they helped shipwrecked sailors and brought favorable winds to those who made sacrifices to them. At this point, Paul's group was sailing under the sign of Castor & Pollux. Apparently they had no more trouble and soon arrived in Rome.

Our journey is not from *home to Rome* but rather, from *Rome to Home*. While Paul sailed under a heathen sign, we sail under the Kingship of our Lord Jesus Christ. We also suffer through shipwrecks along our way. These storms can be devastating and frightening. But just as God assured Paul that there would be no loss of life in that storm (Acts 27:22), He promises us, too, that He will never leave nor forsake us." As we sail along, we also meet unbelievers, some who treat us kindly and some who do not. Paul surely must have felt uneasy when first meeting the local residents. And again when they decided he was a murderer! And possibly even when they changed their minds and called him a god. He certainly did not have a spiritual kinship with them and yet he treated them with respect. He prayed for them and healed many of their sick. This earned a high respect from them, also.

How do we treat those who do not believe as we do? Kindness and respect have a powerful effect in drawing unbelievers to Christ. Paul's ministry had a huge effect on many people during his trip from home to Rome.

As you look back on your journey thus far, what do you see? Do you see only shipwrecks and snakebites and prison cells? Or do you see people strengthened and encouraged as you ministered to them? If Paul could continue his ministry as a *prisoner* on his way to be tried in Rome, surely we can minister for Jesus on our journey, too. If we keep our eyes on Jesus instead of fearing the dangers, we can bring glory to Him on our trip from Rome to Home!

- How am I doing on my trip Home?
- Can I see Jesus as I go through the storms and trials? Am I ministering to those He brings into my life?
- *Lord, I thank You for Your guidance and protection. Show me how I can serve You on this journey.*

Read: Romans 8

Kill Or Be Killed

"My heart is fixed, O God, my heart is fixed:
I will sing and give praise."
- Psalm 57:7

I think it is safe to say that most women are not into killing. Unless it's a pesky mosquito or other annoying insect, of course. We prefer that someone else kill the mice in the house. The awful "thump, thump, thump" under the car when we hit an animal on the road is a sickening sound. And for some of us, it is hard to even *imagine* killing a beautiful deer or a magnificent elk or bear. We will leave that to the men!

But there is something in each one of our lives that needs to be killed. *SIN*. It can seem as small as a bothersome mosquito or as huge as a hungry bear. Satan, our adversary, is very much alive and "as a roaring lion, walking about, seeking whom he may devour." (I Peter 5:8) He is an experienced, cunning hunter who will lay any kind of trap needed to kill us. But the Bible tells us to resist him in steadfast faith. (I Peter 5:9)

So, just how do we kill this beast called *Sin?* What weapons are most effective? First of all we must *recognize the presence of sin* and confess it. (We can't kill it if we don't know it's there.) We can then keep it at bay by *fixing our hearts upon God*. Singing, praising Him, and thinking on spiritual things will keep our minds unavailable to the enemy. *Meditate on the Word of God*. "Thy word have I hid in mine heart, that I might not sin against thee." (Psalm 119:11) *Commune regularly with Him in prayer.* "The effectual fervent prayer of a righteous (woman) availeth much." (James 5:16) And finally... *practice obedience*. Jesus said, "If a man love me, he will keep my words." Love for Him enables us to obey.

When we have been crucified with Christ, we are to "reckon ourselves to be dead indeed unto sin, but alive unto God through Jesus Christ our Lord." (Romans 6:11) As we walk with the Lord in the awareness of His victory over sin, He enables us to mortify (put to death) the deeds of the body and triumph over sin.

Fix your heart upon God. Ask Him to reveal and destroy any sin in your life. Pray for the courage to stand up against the enemy and to avoid his traps. We are to put on the whole armour of God that we may be able to stand against the wiles of the devil (Ephesians. 6:11)

- Am I equipped with every part of God's armor?
- Which of these weapons do I need to use on a more regular basis?
- *Lord, reveal to me any sin I am allowing in my life and show me how to kill it before it kills me.*

A Flickering Light

"That ye may...
shine as lights in the world."
- Philippians 2:15

Gazing into the heavens on a dark, clear night you will see an amazing sight. The darker it gets, the brighter the moon and the stars shine. As you watch, the moon sometimes seems to take on a happy face, and the stars twinkle as they silently and cheerfully fulfill the roles for which God created them. If the clouds roll in, however, the lights dim. The moon's luster fades, and the stars lose their twinkle.

As Christian women, we are to "shine as lights in the world." Do you ever feel as though your light has gone out? Do you ever feel as if the clouds of life have rolled in so heavily no one can even tell that you *have* a light, much less a *twinkle?*

One of Satan's favorite ways to try to snuff the light out of our lives is to get us to compare ourselves with others whose lights seem to shine so much brighter than ours. Sometimes I look around and see other women who seem to have it all together. They get up early and spend time with Jesus. Their marriages are blossoming, their children are well behaved, their houses are in order, and they have plenty of time and energy to help others. Or, if they are single they may be teaching school, nursing, or serving Him in other ways that are not even options for me. *They* are shining lights for Him! Anyway it *seems* that way. Then I look at myself. I drag myself out of bed just in time to rush the children to school, come home to face my untidy house, and listen to my younger children bickering over whatever they can find to argue about. I don't even have the energy to make an encouraging phone call, much less witness to my neighbor or spend time with elderly patients at the nursing home. I don't even *have* a light to shine. As Satan ruthlessly hurls his flame quenchers, my light dims and flickers, threatening dangerously to go out completely.

Think about it, though. God did not make us all alike. He expects each one of us to fill a unique role. Not everyone is a sun. Some of us are stars! You would not put a 200 watt bulb in your closet, and you wouldn't put a 60 watt bulb in your barn. Is the sun better than the stars? Is a 200 watt bulb better than a 60 watt bulb? No! They are each perfect for their particular place, and you are perfect for the role God has called you to fill. If God didn't make you a 200 watt bulb, be a 60 watt bulb and keep shining! If He didn't create you to be a sun, be a star and keep twinkling!

- Do I struggle with wishing to be a different person than I am or serving in a different role than where God has me?
- How does my thinking or attitude need to change in order to accept who and where I am in God's Kingdom?
- *Lord, my desire is to cheerfully serve You wherever You have placed me. Help me to be content right where I am.*

June

To Whom Do You Belong?

"I am crucified with Christ: nevertheless I live;
yet not I, but Christ liveth in me."
- Galatians 2:20

In verse 17 of Galatians 6, Paul talks about the marks of the Lord Jesus that he bears in his body. We would assume these marks to be the scars which he received at the hands of his persecutors. He certainly would have had plenty of them. He was whipped severely, beaten with rods, stoned and left for dead, shipwrecked several times, and thrown into jail. (II Corinthians 11:24-25) These marks were visible reminders of who Paul belonged to.

While we may not bear visible scars, there are other marks that we should bear.

LOVE should be a visible mark to remind us that Jesus' love was unchanging while He was here on earth and is unwavering today. He loves us as His own children and commands us to love Him with all our heart, soul, mind, and strength. (Mark 12:30) That love will then spill out to bless those around us.

KINDNESS is another mark. Jesus lived a life of compassion as He comforted the broken hearted and healed the sick and lame. While the old law ordered "an eye for an eye and a tooth for a tooth," (Matthew 5:38) Jesus taught that we should not resist evil but return good for any wrongs. Do not plan revenge…pray for the wrongdoer!

FORGIVENESS can be tough, but think about how Jesus forgave even the soldiers who nailed Him to the cross. Even as they were gambling for His robe He said, "Father forgive them; for they know not what they do." (Luke 23:34) Can we be as forgiving to those who do far less to us? We do not need an apology; we can just choose to forgive.

SUBMISSION…The greatest act of submission in history took place in Gethsemane, as Jesus in His humanity struggled intensely to fully give up His will to His Father's will. (Luke 22:42-44) Although it was an extremely hard thing to do, Jesus was willing to go to the cross. Am I willing to fully submit to God's will for my life, though it may be hard at times?

SACRIFICE…Jesus made the ultimate sacrifice when He gave His life for us. Is there anything that's "too much" for us to sacrifice for Him? He wants us to "deny ourselves, take up our cross, and follow Him." (Mark 8:34) The blessings He has for us are unlimited, as we turn every area of our lives over to Him and His will for us.

As we bear these and other marks of Jesus in our lives, we can truly say with the Apostle Paul: "I am crucified with Christ: nevertheless I live; yet not I, but Christ liveth in me." (Galatians 2:20)

- Do I bear in my body the marks of the Lord Jesus?
- How do my attitudes, thoughts, and actions need to change to more visibly bear these marks?
- *Lord, help me to show through my life that I truly belong to You.*

June 2

Read: Philippians 2:1-11

Let's Go With A Winner

"Wherefore God also hath…given Him a name which is above every name."
- Philippians 2:9

Not long ago my husband and I went with a widowed sister to an appliance store to help her pick out a new washer and stove. We looked at many different ones, comparing features and prices. One of the most important things we considered, however, was the brand name. They had many; some well known with good reputations, some well known with tarnished reputations, and some completely unknown to us. In the end, she picked out a washer and stove having brand names with which she was familiar and comfortable. The salesman was encouraging about the reliability of these brands and their guarantees. Our friend is now enjoying them, confident that she made a good choice.

Our own washer story is a bit discouraging. Several years ago we purchased a top-brand washer with a top-notch reputation, thinking it would serve us well for a long time. Unfortunately, we did not know that this particular model had not been on the market long enough to have the bugs worked out of it. Over the next several years we encountered three major problems that required service calls, repairmen, new parts, and plenty of money. We were surprised and disappointed that this reliable brand name had let us down.

A good name is sought in many areas of life. If you are thinking of building a house, you are going to look for a reputable builder with a good name. A well-known brand of car sells better than one with a reputation of problems. Lawyers, doctors, accountants, and architects all do far better if they have achieved a good name for themselves.

Good names, however, don't always remain good. Today's top names may not be tomorrow's top names. Especially in the areas of entertainment, sports, government, or religion. People come and go in popularity. Some last a long time and for some the fame is fleeting.

There is a name, though, that will never let you down! Jesus is the Name of all Names, reliable to the end, with no warranties or contracts needed. While other names come and go, "Jesus Christ (is) the same yesterday, and today, and for ever." (Hebrews 13:8) While some good names bless us with help and convenience in our daily lives, the blessings we receive from Jesus are eternal. Divine love, forgiveness, courage, strength, and wisdom are just some of the ways we are blessed when we put our confidence in Him. Jesus never fails. Let's go with a winner!

- Have I been let down in the past by a brand name I trusted?
- In what ways has Jesus blessed me even when I didn't expect it?
- *Lord, I thank You for Your faithfulness and ask for eyes to recognize what you do in Your love for me.*

"Give Me This Mountain!"

"If so be the Lord will be with me, then I shall be able to drive (the giants) out, as the Lord said."
- Joshua 14:12

The land of Canaan was being divided between the tribes of Israel. When it was the tribe of Judah's turn, Caleb went to Joshua with a request. He wanted the land of Hebron. "Now therefore give me this mountain," he said. Now, this was not just a beautiful mountain; this was the land of the Anakim who were giants! These were the people who had made the spies feel like grasshoppers when they first went in to spy out the land. (Numbers 13:33) And Caleb was not a young man. He was 85 years old, but he reminded Joshua that he was just as strong as he had been at 40. He was ready for another conquest and so, he was given the city of Hebron and the surrounding area.

Caleb was remembering the promise God had made to him forty-five years earlier, of a personal inheritance of the land, because of his complete trust that God would help them drive the enemy from the Promised Land. (Numbers 14:24) He also remembered his commitment to God when the other spies backed out in fear. Most of all, he remembered God's faithfulness to him as He spared his life through a plague that had killed the unbelieving spies; through years of wilderness wanderings; and several years of war in Canaan. He had full confidence that God would help him drive out the Anakim. Being giants wasn't a big challenge. They were as grasshoppers in the sight of God! Caleb's faith, courage, and strength were undiminished as he went on to drive out the giants and take over the land God had given him.

Are you facing mountains and giants that make you feel the size of a grasshopper? Do you, like most of the spies, shake with fear and defeat, wishing you could run back to an earlier stage in your life? Health problems; relationship struggles; work overload; tenacious strongholds; or broken dreams can make life look like a mountain and daily responsibilities like giants. But we do not have to be defeated. We can stand up like Caleb saying, "Give me this mountain!" We can also rest in God's promise to us: "Whatsoever ye shall ask the father in my name, He will give it you." (John 16:23) We can remember our commitment to Him at other times in our lives, and most of all we can remember His faithfulness to us as He has shown Himself strong for us in the past. Go forth as Caleb, confident that God can and will fight your battles for you as you trust Him, searching the Scriptures and praying for guidance and strength. He is just as faithful now as He was in Caleb's time!

- What mountains and giants am I facing today?
- Am I as confident as Caleb was, facing the obstacles before him?
- *Lord, the mountains are too tall and the giants too big for me to handle alone, but I trust You to help me through.*

 Read: Isaiah 26

Focus... Or Crash!

"Thou wilt keep (her) in perfect peace, whose mind is stayed on thee: because (she) trusteth in thee."
- Isaiah 26:3

Our son is taking Driver's Training. Anyone who has been through this stage knows what it's like to literally put your life into the hands of a teenager who has way too much confidence and way too little experience. ("I'm taking Driver's Training, Mom, I know how to drive! Besides, I'm way younger than you are, and my reflexes are much quicker. If I need to hit the brake, I will!"...and so forth.) But when he drifts across the center line because he is watching a deer standing in the field; or he pulls out (too slowly!) into oncoming traffic, it is very hard not to react with "Watch what you're doing, Son!" Without a proper focus he could easily crash the car, hurting not only himself, but others too.

Teenage drivers are not the only ones who need to focus. All day long we risk crashes as our focus wavers from the situation at hand. A plate slips from our grasp and shatters on the kitchen floor while we are talking on the phone. A friend feels hurt when we are too preoccupied with our sewing to listen or help when she needs it. The toddler empties the full waste basket as we doze on the couch. Supper burns as we catch a "quick" moment to read a chapter in a good book. Husbands get a bit irritated when we are too busy to focus on them. Without a proper focus, our crashes can also hurt, not only ourselves, but others, too.

There is a focus, however, that is much more important than the multitude of little daily focuses that make up our lives. A focus on the Lord is essential to keeping everything else in perspective. Matthew Henry says "The main duty of a Christian lies in the right management of his mind." How do we manage our minds in the right way? By staying in touch with the One who created them. If we roll out of bed late and rush through the day trying to catch up, we are likely to experience any number of crashes. If we get up early enough for a relaxed, uplifting quiet time with the Lord, we will not be as frazzled through the day, even if we do have a crash or two. Unfortunately, crashes are part of an otherwise normal day, but we can remain focused on God even when our circumstances make it seem as though we're not. Pray for patience and attentiveness to the needs of others as you concentrate on your daily duties. Memorize Scripture as you work. Keep your focus clear. He will keep you in perfect peace as your mind is stayed on Him. What a beautiful promise. Don't miss out on it!

- Just how much is my mind "stayed on Him" during my day?
- How could I turn my focus more to godly thinking as I go about my duties?
- *Lord, my days are so full that it's easy to crowd You right out. Help me to stay focused on You for that perfect peace.*

Pressing Toward The Mark

"I press toward the mark for the prize of the high calling of God in Christ Jesus."
- Philippians 3:14

Phil, a local community man, well known by some in our church family, had a hearty enthusiasm for life. He was in his mid-sixties, healthy, robust, and operating in one speed -- full throttle. He worked hard and he played hard. Most importantly, he was a man of God, dedicated in service to his Lord, and his life reflected that outlook. He spent his days "pressing on toward the finish line." Last Friday afternoon Phil and his neighbor were moving a piece of farm equipment when he collapsed with a massive heart attack and was gone. He left this life with the same pace that he had lived it...full speed ahead.

We can only speculate what his last thoughts were as he lay on the ground with the crushing weight of pain coursing through his chest and his distressed neighbor bending over him. Was he thinking "This is it; I'm going to meet the Lord today?" Was he thankful that he could die on the farm where he had spent so many happy years? Was he thinking of his wife and children? Possibly he was wondering who would take care of the extensive line-up of John Deere tractors he and his son had collected. We can be pretty sure, however, that he was thankful for every moment he had spent "pressing toward the mark."

Phil left a good example for the rest of us. His goal, like Paul's in Philippians 3, was to know Christ, to be like Christ, and to be all Christ wanted him to be. If we could talk to Phil now, I think he would strongly encourage us to keep "pressing toward the mark." "Keep your eyes on Jesus!" I can hear him saying. "It's too easy to go astray if you lose your focus." And he would add: "Live faithfully! Use the Scriptures you have and know, and be faithful to Him and each other. Pursue godliness! Think of the examples you have had all through your life, of godly people whom the Lord has brought into your life at just the right times. Press on to answer His call! God calls you to repentance, salvation, and a total dedication to Him. He wants a quick response when He calls you to perform a service for Him or to minister to others in His name. Cooperate with God's work to mold and conform you to be like Jesus!"

Press on! Last week, Phil met his finish line unexpectedly. Give it your all! Phil did and now he is enjoying "the reward of them that diligently seek Him."(Hebrews 11:6) I can hear him saying enthusiastically, "It's worth it all!"

- Is my life one of "pressing on toward the mark?"
- What areas in my life need to change to become more enthusiastic for Jesus?
- *Lord, help me to allow Phil's example to have a good influence on my life. Help me to keep my eyes on You.*

Read: Hebrews 4

Stepping In The Light

"Let us labour therefore to enter into that rest,
lest any man fall."
- Hebrews 4:11

"One...two...three...four...five...six steps down to the landing; seven more to the bottom." A friend was sharing a lesson with me that God had impressed upon her. You would think that after using the same set of stairs for twenty-five years, it wouldn't be necessary to count them--just go! Some things become automatic, and feet have a remarkable ability to judge height of steps. Unfortunately, some of us never learn to just rest in that.

"When I use stairs," my friend said, "I need to see each step. And sometimes, even then, my eyes will give a false message and I'll find myself clutching the railing in panic as if I had just avoided a misstep. If I close my eyes, however, my feet are free to operate automatically."

Thinking that some things just do not make sense, she had to wonder also how often our spiritual walk is like that. If we're always "watching the path," life can seem pretty complicated and difficult. It is easy to panic, and things just don't make sense. If, however, we "close our eyes," rest in the Lord, and just trust Him to lead, life becomes much easier. Completely trusting God through the rough times in life brings us the peace of knowing that He will get us through without a nasty fall.

- Do I find myself "watching the path," trying to judge the future myself?
- What situations in my life today do I need to completely trust God for?
- *I praise You, Lord, that I can fully trust in You and ask that You guide my life today.*

Look Up And Be Radiant

"They looked unto Him,
and were lightened."
- Psalm 34:5

David wrote this Psalm to praise the Lord for his goodness in delivering him from Abimelech, the king of Gath. Fearing for his life, David had pretended to be insane, and the king, not needing any more madmen in his life, had dismissed David.

In the Psalm, David recognizes the tremendous value in the gift of salvation and has an overwhelming desire to "bless the Lord at all times." Having praise for Him "in our mouths" at all times will bless us too, and in no way can we ever over-thank Him for this gift to us. David also knows that our "boast," or glory, should be in God, not in ourselves or our achievements. Everything we do should be to bring praise to our Lord, rather than to draw attention to ourselves. Without Him, we can do nothing. The glory belongs to Him.

As our souls fill with thanksgiving and praise to God, we also have an overwhelming desire to share with others the wonder of His goodness. "O magnify the Lord with me and let us exalt His name together!" We want to share with others how God has heard our cries and delivered us from our fears or troubles. As we look unto Christ in faith, trusting Him to guide us through life we become "lightened," or radiant. David had some rough times in his life, but as he looked unto the Lord continually, his amazing faith carried him through, making him a "man after God's own heart."

We all desire, in any situation, to "look unto Him and be radiant." How is this possible? When I'm looking around me, which is such a human thing to do, can I at the same time look up and be radiant? I can't be looking up when I am trying to live up to my own expectations or what I think others expect of me. Depending on the support of others, rather than leaning on Jesus, results from looking around. At times, we Christians will let each other down. Only Jesus will love us and accept us unconditionally, and we can believe that fact with joy! If we keep our focus on Him, His image will be reflected in us. We will become radiant and bear much fruit as He desires us to do, but we must look up, not around or at ourselves.

- Do I look up to Jesus in the midst of a trial or a heartache, or do I try to fix things myself?
- Do I recognize God's glory when my problems are solved?
- *Lord, I know You are there, waiting to help me. Fill me with Your radiance as I look to You for strength and courage.*

 Read: Matthew 15:21-28

Lord Help Me

"But without faith it is impossible to please Him: for he that cometh to God must believe that He is, and that He is a rewarder of them that diligently seek him."
- Hebrews 11:6

Jesus was in the region of Tyre and Sidon on the Mediterranean coast when a Canaanite woman came to Him begging for help. Her daughter was being tormented by a devil, and she was desperate. The disciples were disgusted. This woman was a Canaanite! She was a Gentile, an alien who had no business approaching Jesus that way. She even addressed Him as the Lord, the Son of David, a title that the Jews used for Him. The disciples urged Jesus to send her away, she was just being a bother.

But Jesus saw beyond her race and position to a woman with faith and knew that His grace could shine through her. Testing her, He reminded her that His first ministry was to the Jews, not the Gentiles. She bravely accepted that and worshipped Him, saying, "Lord, help me." As the disciples stood there waiting for Him to dismiss her, Jesus proved her faith by testing her further. He told the woman that it was not good for Him to stop tending to the Jews in order to tend to her, reflecting the Jews' attitude toward the Gentiles.

This gracious woman did not argue or turn and slink away, she simply agreed with Him. "Truth Lord," she said. She agreed that she was not worthy of His blessing and would be satisfied with just the "crumbs which fall from the Master's table."

Jesus then commended her for her great faith and immediately healed her daughter.

This woman had a heart of faith and a diligence in seeking the Lord that we would do well to pattern our lives after. She knew that Jesus could heal her daughter, and her love for the girl gave her the courage and persistence that she needed to seek Him out and beg for His help. We don't have to seek Him out in a crowd and beg for "crumbs." He invites us to "come and dine" on all of the blessings that He has to offer to us. We don't deserve it any more than the Canaanite woman did, but He is waiting and wants to reward our faith and diligence with His blessings. Take your cares to Him, believing that He is and that He will reward you for your faith and diligence in seeking Him.

- What is my true attitude when asking the Lord to help me with my problems?
- Do I ask in faith that He will answer my prayer in the way that is best for me?
- *Lord, strengthen my faith and keep me diligent in seeking your will for my life.*

A Blessing And A Wounding

"And He blessed him there."
- Genesis 32:29

Jacob was a strong, wealthy, and powerful man. He had built up an impressive herd of animals while working for his father-in-law, Laban. Now he was on his way back home to face his brother, Esau. The last time he had seen Esau, his brother was so angry at him that he wanted to kill Jacob! Jacob was naturally fearful about seeing Esau again. He sent some of his servants ahead with gifts of animals and servants for Esau, hoping to gain his favor. He was still terrified, knowing that Esau was on his way to meet him with an army of 400 men!

The night before the brothers met, Jacob camped by the Jordan River. During the night he got up and sent his family and possessions over to the other side of the river and stayed there alone to pray. An angel came and wrestled with Jacob for the rest of the night, until finally, seeing that he was not going to overcome Jacob, he struck Jacob's hip and knocked it out of joint. He told Jacob to let him go, but Jacob refused to let go until he had received a blessing. The angel then changed his name to Israel and said he would have power with God and would prevail with men.

Jacob received his blessing and went on the next day to a joyful reunion with his brother. But in the process of obtaining this blessing, he also received a wounding. From that night on, he walked with a limp.

God wants to bless us, too. Sometimes it takes pretty serious circumstances, such as Jacob faced, to bring us to the point of wrestling with God. And in the wrestling we are wounded. Maybe you are facing the death of a loved one, or you have big dreams that are shattering into a million pieces at your feet. Or possibly your plans were working out just fine, and now your life is changing direction so fast you can not even keep up with it. These circumstances are completely out of your control. And you wrestle with God. You pour out your heart to Him and search the Scriptures for direction and comfort. You listen for His voice and cling to His promises. And, in the end, you are blessed. The wounding happens, too. The loved one passes away. The dreams stay shattered and your life continues to follow the new path. But you are blessed with the peace that passes understanding, a fresh sense that God is in control and wants only the best for you. You have a new empathy for those who are facing similar circumstances. You are a stronger person and more effective in God's Kingdom. Claim His promise of blessing. The wounding is worth it!

- Do I believe that God wants to bless me through the hard times and that the wounding is worth it?
- Do I claim God's blessing and wrestle through prayer and Bible study until I receive that blessing?
- *Lord, give me the courage and strength that I need to receive a blessing and accept the wounding that goes with it.*

Read: James 3:1-12

Idle Words

"Every idle word that men shall speak,
they shall give account thereof."
- Matthew 12:36

One day as a friend of ours was parting ways with his small daughter, he said to her jokingly, "May your feet itch!" He then went on with his day, and the comment was forgotten.

Not long after, however, the little girl came to her parents, complaining that her feet itched. Examining her feet, they saw that she had hives. A little observation over the following days revealed that she had suddenly developed an allergy to cool, wet grass! No more going barefoot on dewy, summer mornings.

Imagine how the father felt when he remembered what he had said. He was appalled! Feeling that he had put a curse on his little daughter, he repented, and prayed that the affliction be removed from her. His daughter was healed, but not until several months had gone by. In the meantime, her father had a lot of time to think about the consequences of idle words, and of the power there apparently can be in the spoken word.

How many times we say things without thinking. How many times are there consequences that we do not even see? Jesus compares our tongues to a raging fire. Idle words can spread destruction rapidly, and the results cannot be stopped once they're spoken. Before you speak, remember that words are like fire. You cannot control or reverse the damage they may do. As we strive to improve in this area, the Holy Spirit will give us power to control what we say.

- Am I in the habit of speaking without thinking?
- How can I more closely monitor what I think before I speak?
- *Lord, help me to speak only words that uplift and edify, speaking peace to those around me.*

Celebrating Your Uniqueness

"For who maketh thee to differ from another? And what hast thou that thou didst not receive?"
- I Corinthians 4:7

I have a friend who is an avid gardener and likes to try out new ideas. In the spring at planting time, or before, she will stand in her garden plot and ponder. "Should I try raising pole beans on a teepee style support instead of the usual bush beans? I wonder if it would work to divide the space into squares with old lumber as the dividers. The lumber would do double duty as paths. It seems like that would be very attractive, but what would happen when the plants get larger? Would it even work on my hill the way it does on someone else's flat ground?" While another gardener's ideas can be very appealing, they won't necessarily work in her garden. Every garden is unique and all the different aspects of each spot must be taken into account while planning and planting the garden.

Each person, each situation is also unique. Our Father knows us as individuals, and He has a place for us and a work for us that will fit the way He made us. None of us will fit into anyone else's mold, so we need not fret because our devotional time is not just like someone else's, or that we can't pray as eloquently as some do. My style of mothering isn't exactly like anyone else's, and we all differ in how we do our cooking, cleaning, and laundry. We can be comfortable with the way God "wired us" to do things, and realize that in many areas, there is no right or wrong way to do the job. If I observe another woman whose "style" of doing things is different from mine, I must refrain from judging or scoffing at her approach. What just would not work for me may be just right for her. Though she is not "wired" just as I am, we can learn from each other. Someone may have just the right answer for a problem I have, and we can both be blessed as we accept each other's differences and share ideas. As we learn to heed the Scriptural admonition not to compare ourselves with others, we can more easily accept ourselves as we are and be ready to receive help from others.

- Do I understand that God made me unique and that He has a plan just right for me?
- Am I willing to accept others as they are and share ideas back and forth with them?
- *Lord, help me to celebrate the uniqueness that You created in me, and to accept that same uniqueness in others.*

Read: Ephesians 2

A Dwelling Place For Jesus

"In whom ye also are builded together for a habitation of God through the Spirit."
- Ephesians 2:22

Imagine with me that Jesus and some of His angels are taking a walk through the earth. The angels are looking for the house in which Jesus lives. They are picking out some magnificent places, thinking that each one looks like it might be suitable for a king. "Is that your home?" they ask, pointing to a beautiful castle overlooking the sea. Or maybe they are studying a mansion in the woods and wondering if Jesus lives there. On they go, choosing the biggest, loveliest places as possible homes for Jesus. But to all their choices Jesus answers, "No, I do not live there." Finally, coming to a small, humble shack, Jesus points to it and says, to the angels' amazement, "There is my home."

We know that as believers, Jesus lives within us. But do you ever feel like a shack in bad need of some renovating? Do you have some windows that need to be repaired (foggy, confused thoughts that you need to pray about), or some wallpaper peeling off (a good habit that is slipping away)? Maybe you have a leaky faucet (unkind words or gossip leaking past your lips), worn floors (a weary body and mind with little time or energy for devotions), and shabby furniture (an unwillingness to follow God's promptings in ministering to others). Perhaps your ceiling has some ugly water stains (bad habits that are showing up and causing trouble in your life).

We may think we need to do extensive remodeling before Jesus can move in, be comfortable, and work through us. But this is not true! Jesus meets us right where we are and loves us just as we are. We need to invite Him in, welcome Him, and let Him do the renovating in our "houses." He is so much better at it than we are! We are not worthy of Him, but Jesus chooses to dwell within us. We are His. He has paid a high price for us, so why should we not allow Him to take care of our earthly tabernacles? When we welcome Him into our hearts and homes, we will be amazed at the remodeling job He does in our lives.

- Do I believe, with full assurance, that as a believer, Jesus is dwelling within me?
- Am I allowing Jesus to repair the areas of my tabernacle that need to be fixed or replaced?
- *Come, Lord Jesus, live in me, work through me, and do Your remodeling in all the needy areas of my life.*

A Green Light Faith

"Fear ye not, stand still,
and see the salvation of the Lord."
- Exodus 14:13

Oh, for a faith that will not shrink;
Though pressed by many a foe;
That will not tremble on the brink;
Of any earthly woe.

This aspect of faith could be called a walking faith or a running faith. It is a faith that allows us to walk, or even run, into the future without hesitation. It is a faith that moves ahead, knowing God will provide everything we need to go forward into His will, even when it looks impossible.

The children of Israel thought for sure they were doomed. They were trapped between the Red Sea and the fast-approaching Egyptian army sweeping in for the kill. They had just experienced God's powerful hand delivering them from Egypt, but this was too much. They railed on Moses in fear and despair, saying they should have just stayed in Egypt. Moses however, calmly told them not to fear, but to be still and watch the wonderful way God would rescue them. Moses was not trembling! The Israelites were certainly being "pressed by every foe" and this could definitely be called an "earthly woe," but Moses' faith was not shrinking as he watched the war chariots coming closer and closer.

The situation looked absolutely impossible, but as Moses prayed in faith, God plainly told him it was time to stop praying and get moving! And Moses moved. As he stretched out his hand over the sea, God parted the water to form a dry path through the sea. You can be sure the Israelites did not just stand there marveling at the miracle, or trembling in fear that the waters might close again. They went into the midst of the sea (probably ran!) and crossed to safety on the other side. Then, as they fearfully watched their enemy racing across after them, God released the waters and completely destroyed the entire pursuing army.

What a lesson in faith! We have never been in this particular situation, but sometimes we do find ourselves in tough circumstances in which we see no way out. Prayer is vital at times like this, but there is also a time to get moving. If you know what God wants you to do, get going! Do not continue to pray as an excuse to keep from moving ahead. Walk or run into the future with an absolute faith that God will lead you where He has called you.

- Am I in a situation today that looks impossible?
- Should I be praying about this situation, or is God already telling me what to do? If He is, am I obediently stepping out?
- *Lord, give me such a faith as this, to do Your will without trembling and shrinking from it.*

 Read: Job 13

A Trusting Faith

"Though he slay me,
yet will I trust in him."
- Job 13:15

That will not murmur nor complain;
Beneath the chas'ning rod;
But in the hour of grief or pain;
Can lean upon its God.

Job was a prosperous farmer in the land of Uz, with thousands of camels, sheep, and other livestock. He had a large family of ten children and many servants. Job was an upright man with a good life, when Satan accused him of trusting God only because his life was going so well. Receiving permission from God to test Job, Satan made his attack.

In a mind-boggling series of events, Job loses all his possessions, all his children, and even his good health in a very short time. As he sits in the dirt, covered with painful boils, he regrets the day he was born. His wife actually tells him to "curse God, and die." (Job 2:9) When his friends come to grieve with him, they just make things worse by telling him he is to blame for everything that has happened. Then another young man appears who tells him God is punishing him for becoming too proud. Job knew he was innocent, but he couldn't convince his "friends" that they were wrong. If ever anyone felt the "chastening rod" it was Job. His "hour of grief and pain" was indescribably agonizing. (2:13) It seems Job would have been tempted to blame God and become dreadfully bitter, wondering why all this was happening and what he had ever done to deserve it. He could have become angry at his friends and ordered them to get off his property and never come back. He could have followed his wife's advice and cursed God. But the Bible says that "in all this Job sinned not, nor charged God foolishly." (1:22)

It's sobering to think about how my faith compares to Job's. When circumstances are not exactly to my liking and I murmur and complain saying, "What's the problem here, Lord? It would be so easy for you to..." Then I think of Job. Unbelievable trials, yet he says: "Though He slay me, yet will I trust in Him..." My struggles are a far cry from what Job endured and I know God wants the best for me, and His timing is always perfect. My choice, then, is whether or not I'm going to "lean upon my God." It is not always easy, and often the outcome looks impossible, but it's always worth it. God blessed Job's trusting faith with more than he had before. (42:12-17) He'll bless yours too!

- What trials am I going through now for which I need to patiently trust God?
- Am I willing to allow God to work His perfect will through the hard times of my life?
- *Lord, my faith is weak some days, but my desire is for Your perfect will to be worked out in my life.*

A Courageous Faith

"Our God whom we serve is able to deliver us...and He will deliver us out of thine hand, O king."
- Daniel 3:17

A faith that shines more bright and clear,
When tempests rage without,
That when in danger knows no fear,
In darkness feels no doubt.

Defying a King who was threatening terrifying consequences would take courage, indeed. King Nebuchadnezzar had ordered a huge gold statue, ninety feet tall. He set it up in the plain and called all of the nation's leaders together for a dedication ceremony. The musicians were ready to begin playing at his command. At the sound of the music, the people were to fall to the ground and worship the golden image. As an incentive, there was a "burning fiery furnace" standing ready to receive anyone who dared to disobey. Now, this was not a small cooking oven, nor was it an ordinary home-heating wood stove. It was a huge industrial furnace that may have been used for making bricks or melting metals. The flames could probably be seen roaring from the top and the heat so intense that one could not get close to it.

Shadrach, Meshach, and Abed-nego made the choice to honor God's command: "Thou shalt have no other gods before me." (Exodus 20:3) They remained standing as everyone else bowed to the ground and worshiped. The King was furious but gave them a second chance. These young men told the King that even if their God chose not to deliver them, they would not worship any other god or image. Nebuchadnezzar was so angry that he commanded the furnace to be made seven times hotter and the young men to be tied up and thrown in. We do not know just how these three friends were feeling, but the fearless courage they showed in the face of danger was heroic. They did not doubt their decision; they just trusted God with a faith that shone out bright and clear. They were tossed into the furnace and, a moment later, the King was astonished to see four men clearly alive in the flames, one of them obviously not human! The king called them out and saw that the only thing that had been touched by the fire was the ropes that had bound them. He immediately blessed God and decreed that no one should speak any word against the God of Israel.

The same power that gave these men their courage is available to us today. We can trust God in every situation, no matter how impossible it looks. We don't always know the reasons for trials, but God does. We can be thankful that our lives are in His control.

- Am I willing to face a "fiery furnace?"
- Am I allowing God to bless me with the courage He gave Shadrach, Meshach, and Abed-nego?
- *Lord, life gets hard sometimes, but I know You are able to fill me with a courageous faith just as You did for them.*

Read: Daniel 6

A Focused Faith

"He delivereth and rescueth…who hath delivered Daniel from the power of the lions."
- Daniel 6:27

That bears unmoved the world's dread frown;
Nor heeds its scornful smile
That seas of trouble cannot drown;
Nor Satan's arts beguile.

King Darius's presidents and princes were jealous. Although Daniel was a foreigner, he was such a responsible and diligent worker that the King respected him above all of them. The King's plan to set Daniel over the entire realm was too much for the officials to bear. They looked and looked for something by which to condemn Daniel, but they could find nothing. So they decided to attack his religion in an attempt to destroy him.

King Darius was a good King, but he had a major flaw -- pride. When his officials had their conspiracy fine tuned, they talked him right into making himself a god for thirty days. Then they watched Daniel. And, sure enough, they caught him. Daniel's faith was focused on the Lord, not on man. Acting as though the law had never been made, Daniel continued to kneel before his open window and pray to his God three times a day. Talk about "the world's dread frown" and "scornful smiles!" Daniel was in a "sea of trouble." The officials gleefully hurried to the King to tattle on him.

When King Darius realized he had been tricked, he was "sore displeased with himself." He had no choice but to order Daniel thrown to the lions. First, he assured Daniel, however, that his God would deliver him. After a sleepless night, the king hurried to the den early in the morning and was "exceeding glad" to find Daniel alive! To make amends, the king in his anger had the accusers and their families thrown into the den. Then he went home and issued another decree to "all people, nations, and languages," honoring Daniel's God.

A faith that is focused on God rather than on things of the earth can have a real and lasting influence on those around us. Remembering that God is in control, fighting our battles for us, can help us respond as we should to someone who is attacking us with criticism or in other hurtful ways. Daniel knew that prayer is essential to a close walk with God. Our prayers are not usually interrupted by threats as Daniel's were, but by the pressures of schedules and daily life. We need to stay focused and pray regularly. Daily prayer is as essential for us today as it was for Daniel in his day. If we keep our focus on the Lord, Satan's arts cannot beguile (deceive) us.

- Have I allowed the pressures of life to take my focus off God?
- Is my prayer life what it should be or do the daily cares interrupt and crowd out my time with the Lord?
- *Lord, my focus strays too often. Help me to be like Daniel and never let anything intrude on my relationship with You.*

A Pure And Lasting Faith

"Behold the handmaid of the Lord;
be it unto me according to thy word."
- Luke 1:38

A faith that keeps the narrow way;
till life's last hour is fled,
And with a pure and heavenly ray;
lights up a dying bed.
- William Bathurst, 1831

I can't think of a better example of a pure and lasting faith than Mary. Luke didn't go into great detail about her visit from the angel, but it certainly was not an everyday experience. It likely was startling, even frightening. We know she was troubled and wondered what the angel was doing there. And when he had gently given her the message from God, she was understandably puzzled. How could she, a virgin, possibly have a baby? And why her? She was young, poor, and unmarried. We can only imagine the thoughts that filled her mind. A young unmarried girl expecting a baby risked disaster. Who would believe her? People would think she was crazy. She would be rejected by her friends and possibly even her family. She could be forced into a life of begging or even prostitution to support herself. At best, she would probably remain unmarried all her life. And what of Joseph…her beloved, who was planning to marry her?

Mary couldn't possibly have known the extent of the pain her future held, as she humbly submitted to what the angel was telling her. When the angel reminded her that "with God nothing shall be impossible," she responded with an humble, sweet spirit. "Behold the handmaid of the Lord; be it unto me according to thy word." What an example of pure faith.

Mary's faith carried her through trial after trial. Joseph's near rejection (Matthew 1:18-21)…the long, miserable trip to Bethlehem and giving birth in a stable (Luke 2:4-7)…fleeing to Egypt to escape Herod's wrath (Matthew 2:13-15)… losing Jesus for three days in Jerusalem when He was twelve years old (Luke 2:42-49)…and the eventual heartbreaking abuse, rejection, and murder of her Son. We do not read anywhere that Mary resented her circumstances. She relied on God to carry her through whatever He might have in store for her. What a beautiful, lasting faith.

As a young woman, Mary had faith to allow God to use her in a mighty way for His glory, even though she felt completely unqualified. Such faith supports God's plan and enhances His glory.

- What is the condition of my faith today?
- Am I willing to be used in whatever way God chooses to further His Kingdom?
- *Lord, it's scary to fully submit myself to Your will, but that is the spirit I long to have. Please strengthen my faith.*

Read: Romans 6

Newness Of Life

"We are buried with Him…
that like as Christ was raised up from the dead…
even so we also should walk in newness of life."
- Romans 6:4

After a monarch caterpillar sheds its skin for the last time, it forms a chrysalis, inside of which incredible changes take place. Within hours, the entire body of the caterpillar has changed into a gel-like substance that has no resemblance to the original creature. The only part that is even identifiable is the heart. As a week passes, an entirely new creature forms around the heart, so different from the caterpillar that one can hardly see any relationship at all.

So it is with our transformation in Christ. When He brings us to the point of conversion, old things are done away with and, beginning with the heart, a completely new being is formed. The new creation, like a new butterfly, has far-seeing eyes where as the caterpillar could see nothing except what was right in front of it. The new creature can soar, whereas the old could do nothing but creep. In newness of life, we have completely different appetites, preferring the pure nectar of God's Word and spiritual fellowship over the rough "food" we ate before. And even when we do try to "eat leaves," our "digestive systems" no longer accept them, because we are utterly changed! We have become new beings, with different habits and different purposes. The blessings hidden in this new life are bountiful and deeply fulfilling. They cannot be fully explained, but must be experienced to be understood. Praise God, the marvelous Creator, that He can turn this lowly caterpillar into a beautiful butterfly, and these worthless self-centered lives of ours into more abundant lives of service to Him.

- Is this newness being expressed in my daily life?
- What areas of my life need to be yielded to Christ to more clearly reflect the transformation He has wrought in my heart?
- *Lord, perform in my heart the miraculous changes that will allow me to experience this newness of life.*

Broken Cisterns

"For my people have committed two evils; they have forsaken me the fountain of living waters, and hewed them out cisterns, broken cisterns, that can hold no water."
- Jeremiah 2:13

A cistern is a pit dug into the soil or rock to collect rainwater. Cisterns were necessities for the long, dry summers in Israel. Empty cisterns were sometimes used as prisons, such as what Joseph was thrown into by his brothers. Not a pleasant place to be. Even in a good, full cistern, the water surely must have gotten stale and dirty, quite undesirable compared to a crystal clear stream of flowing water.

In Jeremiah 2, the Israelites had once again turned away from God and were worshipping idols. God told them they had committed two evils. Not only had they forsaken Him, the fountain of living waters, but they had dug cisterns, broken cisterns that did not even hold water. Why would anyone choose a dry, broken cistern over a sparkling stream of fresh water?

Could I possibly have any empty cisterns in my life? Do I spend too much time in useless activities, when I could be helping someone in need? Am I reading books with no value, rather than wholesome, up-building material? Do I spend money wisely or squander it on wants? Are my friendships encouraging me in my Christian walk or are they dragging me down? Each area of our lives that is dedicated to the Lord is like a refreshing stream of flowing water. Any area that fails to glorify Him is like an empty cistern that yields no lasting pleasure.

- Do I recognize any area of my life as a dry, broken cistern?
- How could I replace these areas with activities that glorify God?
- *Lord, fill my cisterns to overflowing with your Living Water that will make me fruitful and refresh those around me.*

Oh, What A Savior, Part I

"For by grace are ye saved through faith...
it is the gift of God."
- Ephesians 2:8

During the time Jesus hung on the cross, He made seven statements that are precious to the believer. They demonstrate that He was both a man and God. These statements illustrate the last hours of all that Christ went through so that we could have our sins forgiven and spend eternity with Him.

"Father, forgive them; for they know not what they do." (Luke 23:34) It is easy to be angry at the men who did the terrible deed of putting Jesus on that cross. But Romans 3:23 tells us that we have ALL sinned. We are guilty, too. We are just as much in need of forgiveness and reconciliation as those men were. And just as Jesus prayed for God to forgive those wicked men, so will He plead on our behalf before this Holy God. **Oh, what a Savior!**

"Verily I say unto thee, Today shalt thou be with me in paradise." (Luke 23:43) This dying thief was repentant and received words of comfort and hope from Jesus. In his last moments of life, the man acknowledged his sin and the justness of his punishment. He confessed Jesus as Lord. He confessed his faith in the eventual triumph of Christ's Kingdom. He begged for mercy and forgiveness. (Luke 23:40-42) Jesus rewarded him for his amazing faith with the promise of eternity in Paradise with Him. This assurance and confidence is available to us too! We can know that, with repentance, He will grant us forgiveness of our sins and an eternal future with Him. **Oh, what a Savior!**

"Woman, behold thy Son!" "Behold thy mother!" (John 19:26, 27) With these words, Jesus created a new family. John became a son to Mary and he took her into his own home. With His work on the cross, Jesus has provided the gift of a new family for us too. With this family relationship we also have the responsibility to care for one another, out of love for Jesus, as John cared for Mary. When we accept His gift of salvation, we become a part of His family with God the Father as our Father, too. Oh, what a family! **Oh, what a Savior!**

- Do I have a good understanding of the work Jesus did for me on the cross?
- How would I explain this amazing "work" to someone who had never heard it or didn't understand?
- *Lord, give me the understanding I need to fully accept your precious gift to me.*

Oh, What A Savior, Part II

"Who his own self bare our sins in his own body... that we... should live unto righteousness."
- I Peter 2:24

"Eli, Eli, lama sabachthani?" That is to say "My God, my God: why hast thou forsaken me?" (Matthew 27:46) During His trial and crucifixion, Jesus suffered the full range of human rejection—hatred, abuse, and deception. Jesus understands our feelings of isolation, loneliness, abandonment, and suffering. Through Him, we can experience complete reconciliation, acceptance, and forgiveness from the Father. **Oh, what a Savior!**

Jesus knowing that all things were now accomplished...saith, "I thirst." (John 19:28) Jesus voluntarily and willingly endured the cross—thirsting terribly so that you and I can drink freely from the Father's fountain of living water. (Revelation 21:6) He now offers us eternal satisfaction that we never need thirst for any other fulfillment. **Oh, what a Savior!**

When Jesus therefore had received the vinegar, he said, "It is finished." (John 19:30) Paid in full. Nothing can ever be added to or taken from Christ's work on the cross. The complex sacrificial system of that day ended when Jesus became the perfect sacrifice for sin by offering Himself for us. We need to see His accomplished work for the Father and for our benefit as perfect and lacking nothing. We can have total forgiveness and total fellowship with the God of Heaven. Now, believing in the death and resurrection of Jesus, we can come to God freely, escape the penalty for our sins, and live eternally with Him. **Oh, what a Savior!**

"Father, into thy hands I commend my spirit" and: having said thus, he gave up the ghost. (Luke 23:46) Jesus, knowing that He had faithfully finished His mission, could deliver Himself into His Father's hands. Jesus is more than just a Savior, He is also a Deliverer. He is able to deliver you from any form of bondage, or any stronghold or stranglehold that life, sin, or Satan may have on you. Through this same Savior—our only Redeemer—we can also surrender, with confidence and peace, our lives into the Father's hands. **Oh, what a Savior!**

- Am I at peace with surrendering my entire life to God's plan for me?
- How can I further show my gratefulness for what Jesus did for me?
- *Lord, I thank You for being willing to endure so much for me. I truly want my life to reflect Your love to others.*

Read: Ezekiel 37:1-14

Dry Bones

*"Behold, I will cause breath to enter into you,
and ye shall live."
- Ezekiel 37:5*

Ezekiel had a vision. God showed him a valley full of old, dry bones. He asked Ezekiel if he thought the bones could live again, but Ezekiel didn't know. Then God told him to say to the bones, "O ye dry bones, hear the word of the Lord." God also promised the bones that He would give them back their flesh and skin, and breathe into them and they would live again. As Ezekiel watched, the bones came together and became bodies. But it was only after God had Ezekiel tell the wind to breath upon the bodies that they became alive.

Even though you and I strive to live a consistent Christian life, do we sometimes find ourselves feeling like those lifeless bodies in the valley? We may look good on the outside. Wearing the right clothes, doing the right things, going to the places we're expected to go, and speaking the right words. But on the inside, we are more like a heap of dry bones. But take heart! If God can put life into old bones, He can surely breathe new life into living bodies. We need first to "hear the Word of the Lord." And we need the breath of God flowing over us, breathing His power into our lives. As we listen closely while reading His Word and spending time in prayer, He will impart new life to us. Confessing our barrenness may well be the beginning of the refreshing work of God's Spirit in our hearts.

- Am I going through a "dry bones" time in my life?
- What areas of my life need new life flowing through them?
- *Lord, please breathe your power into my life and show Your love through me.*

Heaven's Light

"We then, as workers together with Him."
- II Corinthians 6:1

How do we respond to heaven's light? Saul, a well-known persecutor of Christians, was on his way to Damascus with some pretty awful plans. Plans he intended to carry out with a vengeance. But before he got there, a dazzling light flashed down from heaven, and Saul dropped to the ground. Jesus spoke to him, and immediately Saul's mission in life changed completely. Even his name changed from Saul to Paul. He now had new priorities and a new purpose. Instead of fighting against Jesus and His followers, he became a zealous, stalwart witness for Jesus Christ. Nothing stopped him as he traveled about, preaching, encouraging, and starting new churches.

We should be able to identify with Paul's "light from heaven" experience, although our experience was likely less dramatic! When God spoke to us, we too decided to live a changed life. We acquired new purpose and new priorities. Are we still as zealous now as when we began our Christian walk? Heaven's light is still available to shine through us, to light up the lives of those around us. As we keep our souls illuminated through daily Bible study and prayer, listening for God's voice in quiet meditation, we, like Paul, will continue to be enthused, willing workers for Him.

- Is heaven's light shining through my life?
- Is this light visible to those around me?
- *Lord, fill me with your light and let it radiate to others in my daily life.*

 Read: Ephesians 4:17-32

Compassion

"And be ye kind one to another, tenderhearted, forgiving one another."
- Ephesians 4:32

Our minister friend and his wife offered a ride to a young Jewish girl one day. During their conversation, he asked the girl who Jesus is to her. She answered that He was the greatest Jew that ever lived. Then she gave him her opinion of Christians. In her mind, Christians are not compassionate people!

That is rather disturbing for a Christian whose desire is to be compassionate. As the minister meditated on this sentiment, he concluded that there are three good times to test yourself as to just how compassionate you really are.

When you go to church to worship… Matthew 5:23, 24 says I need to be reconciled to anyone who has a grievance with me before I come to worship. Broken relationships hinder our relationship with God. We cannot truly love God while hating others. Our relationship with God is actually reflected in our attitudes toward others.

When you pray… In Mark 11:25, 26 Jesus tells us we need to forgive others as we pray. He says plainly that if we refuse to forgive others, our Heavenly father will not forgive us. Who of us does not need the Father's forgiveness? We all do; and forgiving those who have wronged us is mandatory, in order to experience the blessing of His forgiveness.

Before you sleep at night… Ephesians 4:26,27 says that we should never let the sun go down on our wrath. Bottling up anger inside causes us to become bitter, and will destroy us within, hardening our hearts and giving place to the devil. If there is someone with whom you are angry, begin today to mend that relationship.

This is a pretty revealing test! I felt convicted as I heard it preached, and I'm feeling convicted as I write it. Satan is tempting me to throw this one out. After all, unforgiveness is a rather easy sin to hide. We can go to church every Sunday with a smile and go through all the motions of worship without revealing our true feelings. We can pray often with bitter hearts. We can even go to sleep night after night, angry or sad with no attempt to fix a relationship. But sooner or later, our feelings become thoughts and our thoughts become words and our true attitude comes out. Is this how we want to come across to others…as uncompassionate Christians? Of course not. God knows exactly what is in our hearts and what we need to do about it. He's just waiting to help us restore that relationship and enjoy peace in our hearts again.

- Is there a relationship in my life today that I need to take steps to reconcile?
- Do I truly believe God will give me the courage to do this, and that He will bless me for it?
- *Lord, I long to be compassionate to others as You are to me. Please express your compassion for others through me.*

The Fullness Of The Blessing

"And to know the love of Christ...that ye might be filled with all the fullness of God."
- Ephesians 3:19

*Are you looking for the fullness of the blessing of the Lord?** We sing the question, but do we really think about its meaning? The widow we read of in II Kings 4, had a distressing financial problem with drastic consequences. She needed help desperately. This woman went to the man of God who asked her what she had in the house. She had nothing but a pot of oil. Through the Prophet Elisha, God told her to go borrow vessels from her neighbors.

God blesses us through others also--perhaps to keep us humble and dependent on others; squelching that self reliance again. When the woman had the vessels, she was to go into her house and shut the door; probably to keep out the birds, bugs, animals, and quite likely some very curious neighbors. When we spend time with the Lord in prayer and meditation, we need to shut the door, also, on the distractions of life. We need to close out the worries, the hurts, and the cares of our lives. God will have surprises for us too when we learn to take the lid off the vessels of our hearts and allow ourselves to be filled with the fullness of God's blessings. We notice that the oil stopped flowing as soon as the widow's empty vessels were all filled. In a similar manner, the abundance of the blessings in our lives are in direct relation to our emptiness of self, and our willingness to be filled with God's Spirit.

- As I search my heart honestly, just how empty of self am I?
- How can I allow God's Spirit to fill me more completely today?
- *Lord, help me to purge my life of self, so I can experience the fullness of Your blessings.*

**Mrs. C.H. Morris; 1912*

Read: Ephesians 3

Are You looking?

*"And of His fulness have all we received,
and grace for grace."
- I John 1:16*

---

*Are you looking for the fullness of the blessing of the Lord,
In your heart and life today?
- Mrs. C. H. Morris*

We can read about the fullness of the blessing of the Lord, but just how do we go about looking for it? The saying "you get out of life what you put into it" could apply here. How far are you willing to go to experience this fullness?

Some of us want to be close to the Lord, but not too close! After all, He might ask me to do something I really don't want to do, or take me somewhere I really don't want to go. Besides, I often find myself short on time and self-discipline, and it takes both to stay close. But, the closer we stay, the fuller the blessing!

Sometimes we want to be spiritual, but we would rather go a little easy on being Biblical. Some of these Bible truths go against our flesh. It is not always comfortable to live out God's Word daily, and we fail often. Is it worth it? Yes, the closer we follow, the fuller the blessing!

Maybe we want to be part of a congregation, but we are reluctant to being fully committed. Floating to church and back home again each Sunday is certainly easier than being committed to building up and supporting the church family. But think of all the blessings we miss out on when we are just floating. Participating in a congregational work project rejuvenates you, even though you may have been tempted to excuse yourself for being too busy or too tired to help. You are blessed as you listen attentively to a message and apply it to your life. Taking time to fellowship with others rather than hurrying off right after the service has a way of increasing your appreciation for God's manifold blessings. Yes, it all takes effort, but the greater the effort, the fuller the blessing!

If you sense a need to be filled, and are truly looking for the fullness of His blessing, "He will fill your heart today to overflowing!"

- Do I sincerely desire the fullness of God's blessing?
- How can I better serve God and others?
- *Lord, I claim Your promise to fill my heart today as I serve You where You have placed me.*

Treasures On Earth

*"Lay not up for yourselves treasures upon earth...
but... treasures in heaven."
- Matthew 6:19,20*

I have a set of Currier & Ives dinnerware that I have been adding to ever since we have been married. Not available new, we have found most of them at antique stores. Recently I was thrilled to find glasses to match the set. Since they are quite expensive, we bought just a few, hoping to add to them later.

Now, as I stood at an auction sale, looking down at a small set of these same glasses, I was smitten. There were four tumblers, and five cute little juice glasses, and I wanted them. I wanted them badly. So for two and one half hours, I kept an eagle eye on that set. As other folks would walk through and pick up a glass, looking at it with interest, I bristled and thought, "You can't have those, they're mine!" I knew some of the people were antique dealers, and I actually got disgusted with them before the glasses were even sold. I just knew they would bid them way up, and I would not even have a chance.

Finally, knowing I was being unreasonable, I just prayed (reluctantly, I admit), "Lord, I like these glasses way too much. If You want me to have them, great. If not, that's fine too. I'll just take it as a lesson in not laying up treasures on earth."

When the set finally came up for bid, I was quite surprised when the bidding went much more quickly than I expected and delighted to get the glasses for a fraction of what they were worth. But I was also rather alarmed at (and ashamed of) the feelings I had harbored toward the folks who evidently weren't nearly as interested as I thought they were. Jesus tells us to lay up our treasures in heaven. Whether our treasures are things, relationships, money, or perhaps even church membership, things of the earth, though they are good things, will not last through eternity. In contrast to earthly treasures, our relationship with Jesus and His kingdom is what will endure.

So the glasses now sit in my china cabinet; a useful addition, but also a visible reminder that earthly treasures are not the important things in life!

- Do I have treasures in my life that mean too much to me?
- Would I be willing to give up these treasures if God asked me to?
- *Lord, help me to keep my earthly treasures from being more important than my service to You.*

Read: I Corinthians 13

Swine Style

"And walk in love, as Christ also hath loved us, and hath given himself for us."
- Ephesians 5:2

A minister was telling us a story about his hogs. Some of them had broken down a partition and had gotten mixed in with another group. With no sure way of identification, separating them again was only by guess. The next morning he realized that he had guessed wrong on at least a few. Hogs do recognize each other and do not accept strangers in their midst. One of the intruders was dead. Another was in bad shape. As he stood there dismayed, anger rising in him, the tormentors just gazed at him with innocent expressions. One of them walked over to the injured hog and "lovingly" nuzzled its face and neck. In the next instant, she opened her mouth and viciously chomped down on the injured hog's ear. Seeing that, he had a strong urge to pick up a big stick and thump those hogs hard!

And then he wondered...does God ever look at us Christians that way? Does He see us treating each other lovingly at times, but at other times making critical, biting remarks, either to someone, or behind their back? Does He see us wounding each other with our words and actions? Have we possibly even killed someone's desire to dwell with us as believers, driving them away from the church or even from serving God? How often, he wondered, does God have an urge to pick up a big stick and thump us good?

Jesus tells us to love one another as He loves us. Love produces far more desirable results than criticism and backbiting. If we have the love of Jesus within us, our true desire will be to love others as He loves us.

- Do I understand the pain that can be caused by thoughtless comments or actions?
- In what ways could I be more loving to my family, friends, and others?
- *Thank you, Father, for your love for me and help me to serve others in Your love.*

Bride Pride, Part I

"The letter killeth, but the spirit giveth life.."
- II Corinthians 3:6

Recently, a friend shared with me that she had heard someone speak of a danger that could possibly be present in our love for, and devotion to, our own church fellowship. The speaker called this "Bride pride." As she thought about that and tried to imagine the bride of Christ in love with herself, she decided to take a hypothetical visit to two brides with absent grooms. The following is an allegory she wrote about her "visit."

"The first bride obviously loved being a bride and focused on being a good one. There were bridal magazines lying around, and she sang many beautiful songs about brides. She showed me a book of letters the bridegroom had written to her. 'I don't really understand very well what he means,' she confided, 'But I've made a list of everything I think he wants me to do, and I am going to do all of it. Some brides do not follow their list as closely as I.' It seemed the groom was quite fortunate to have her. At the same time she worried about not being good enough. 'Do I look all right?' She asked fearfully. 'I hope I'm doing enough. I try to do a lot of good things and I keep busier than most brides. He said to stay occupied 'till he comes.' This bride excitedly told me about her future home. 'He's prepared a mansion for me and he said the streets will be gold and the gates pearl. My loved ones will be there and I love to sing songs about it. It's what I'm working for and I can hardly wait.'

Walking away I realized how little I had heard about the bridegroom."

This bride was an excited bride--and sincere about pleasing her bridegroom. She was living an abundant life and she seemed happy. But do you sense, with me, something missing in her life? She was focused on herself. She was missing the intimate relationship with her bridegroom. Instead of focusing on how she looked and what she was doing for him, she could have been getting to know him. By focusing on him; talking with him, and studying his letters, she would have become more intimately acquainted with him. There was no need for fear. She would have known how to please him, and she would have been assured of his unconditional love for her.

God wants us to love and support His church, but He doesn't want us to become so focused on how we look and act that we miss out on a more abundant life, experienced by a personal relationship with Jesus!

- Do I have that deep, abiding relationship with Jesus that casts out all fear?
- In what way could I be spending more time getting to know Him as my personal Savior?
- *Lord, show me the way to a more abundant life of knowing You and Your love for me.*

Read: Colossians 2:6-23

Bride Pride, Part II

*"As ye have therefore received Christ Jesus
the Lord, so walk ye in him."
- Colossians 2:6*

"As I settled in for a visit with the second bride, I could soon tell that this bride was longing for her beloved. She loved him deeply and was very thankful for the daily contact she had with him.

'He's given me a number to call -- Jeremiah 33:3' she said with shining eyes. 'I can call him anytime and as often as I choose. He's written a book of letters to me and when I don't understand something I can always ask him to help me. He's so good to me that I've had fears of being unworthy of him. We talked about it, and He told me His love has made me worthy, and that perfect love casts out fear. He will help me if I misunderstand his will (Philippians 3:15), and He promised if I keep looking to Him I'll become more like him! (II Corinthians 3:18) He cares so much about my well-being that I have a deep desire to be obedient to all He asks of me. It breaks my heart to think of disappointing Him.'

I asked where they would live and her face lit up again. 'You know, It is rather a mystery to me. He has told me some lovely things about it, but it doesn't really matter as long as He is there. Did you know he saved my life? I was dying an agonizing death and he gave his own blood to save me. Now he wants me as his bride and is planning a feast for us. His wonderful care is so complete he is even supplying my wedding dress. (Isaiah 61:10) It's not important to me where we live; I just want to be where he is.' As I left, I could hear her singing a beautiful song about him."

As I read this narrative written by my friend, I had to think further. We all struggle with keeping our eyes focused on Jesus, but I wonder… Our daughter is engaged and will soon be very busy with wedding preparations. Her beloved knows this, but how would he feel if she became so wrapped up in how she looks and what she is doing that she neglected him? I don't think he would rebuke her or force her to focus on him--he's a very kind young man--but he would surely be disappointed and sad that she did not have time for him. He loves her deeply and is looking forward to the day when she will come to live with him. In the meantime, he enjoys spending time together on a regular basis.

As Christians we are part of the Bride of Christ. Jesus is lovingly preparing a Home for us. In the meantime, until he takes us to live with Him, He longs for our love and devotion. He won't force us to spend time with Him, but He surely is sad and disappointed when we rush about so focused on ourselves that we neglect Him.

- If I look deeply and honestly into my heart, where is my main focus?
- How can I more fully focus on Jesus?
- *Lord, help me to know You and to desire to keep my focus on You.*

July

Rest In His Love

"The Lord thy God in the midst of thee is mighty;
He will save...He will rest in His love."
- Zephaniah 3:17

Lazarus was sick. He was getting worse instead of better, and his sisters were quite concerned about him. Being good friends with Jesus, these sisters knew He could heal Lazarus and everything would be okay. So they sent someone to Jesus with the message that their brother was sick. Although the messengers pled with Jesus to come quickly to heal Lazarus, Jesus stayed where He was for two more days.

Mary and Martha must have been devastated. They knew Jesus loved Lazarus and could have come right away, but He chose to wait. When they finally saw Him coming, it was too late. Their brother was dead. Martha ran down the path to meet Jesus. She expressed her disappointment in Jesus, but her faith shone through. Even in her pain, she believed that Jesus was "the Christ, the Son of God, which should come into the world." (v. 27) Then Mary, who must have been too heart-broken to come out at first, came to Jesus, weeping. Jesus was touched by the sorrow of these sisters and wept with them. Then, he went to the grave, raised Lazarus from the dead, and many believed.

As I write this, our family is coming to grips with a deep disappointment. For several years we've been trusting God to work out a situation to His glory. (In the way we desired, of course.) Now, it looks as though He has forgotten us. Our dreams and hopes are dead and we are struggling to bury them. Why did He let this happen? We know He loves us, but does He really care? But wait...God is bringing to my mind the story of Lazarus. Jesus could have healed Lazarus and glorified God, but he waited until Lazarus was dead and buried. Then He restored the situation and brought even more glory to God. And I know... He can, and will do the same for us. It may not be in the way we were hoping. It may be in a completely different way that would surpass even our greatest expectations. We don't know. At this time, we are still hurting, still healing. But through it all, we are content to... rest in His love.

Are you struggling to accept a painful situation? Can you rest in His love, knowing He loves you and He cares? In His great love for us, He will "rest" in some situations, allowing them to unfold to His glory and for our good. And because of this, we can rest in His love, too.

- What situation(s) am I struggling to accept?
- Do I believe God is working them out to His glory and to my good?
- *Lord, I long to "rest in Your love," while You are working out the problems in my life. I give them all to You.*

Read: Hebrews 12

Staying In The Currents

"Let us lay aside every weight,
and the sin which doth so easily beset us."
- Hebrews 12:1

A hot air balloon is a beautiful sight as it floats peacefully through the sky. It doesn't start out at those heights, however. It starts out flat on the ground, of no use to anyone, and going nowhere. It's either tied to anchors with ropes or weighted down with sandbags to keep it from lifting off too soon. As the hot air rushes into the balloon, it begins to rise and expand. The fuller it gets, the harder it tugs at the restrictive weights, straining to get free. As long as the weights or ropes are in place, the balloon is helpless, unable to rise or move. When the riders are safely in the basket, the ropes are untied or the sandbags are thrown off and up it goes--higher and higher. Once in the air, the balloon can be raised or lowered by regulating the hot air going up into it, but it has no navigational devices to steer it or even to make it drift. It is fully dependent on the air currents to move it and the strength of the breeze to determine how far it will go. When the riders are ready to come down, they have to decide where to land based on where they are at the time. Even then, they may end up in a spot different from what they intended. Every ride is going to be different from another, depending on the weather.

As Christians, our lives are a lot like a hot air balloon. We can become so weighted down with all kinds of sandbags that we are grounded. We are of no use to the Lord and going nowhere. Many of those sandbags are things we have allowed to take root and grow into major weights. They can be things or habits or hobbies or even our families or jobs. Anything that comes between us and God will keep us from serving Him as He desires. As we deal with the sin and other weights in our lives, we are freed to rise above them into the currents of the Holy Spirit. We need to get rid of our own navigational devices and allow Him to lead us in the way He would have us to go. Just as every hot air balloon ride is different from another, so is each life as the Spirit leads and we follow. If we foolishly take on more unnecessary sandbags, we'll find ourselves sinking lower and lower under the weight until we crash or sink right back down to the ground, helpless once again. We don't need to let the sandbags of life weigh us down! We can stay up in the breezes where God can use us for His purpose and glory.

- What weights am I allowing to keep me grounded today?
- Am I willing to allow the Spirit to help me throw off every weight?
- *Lord, I want to be rid of these weights and to be free to serve You. Help me to throw them off today.*

Our Declaration Of Freedom

"Where the Spirit of the Lord is,
there is liberty."
- II Corinthians 3:17

On January 6, 1941, President Franklin D. Roosevelt addressed Congress on the state of the war that was going on in Europe. At the close of his address, he spoke of a world founded on four freedoms. They were: Freedom of Speech...Freedom of Worship...Freedom from Want...and Freedom from Fear.

Romans 8 can be called "The Christian's Declaration of Freedom." As believers we can truly say:

Since Christ be in you...you are free from guilt. (vv. 1-4) Verse one says "there is therefore now no condemnation to them which are in Christ Jesus." That doesn't mean we never fail. Satan tries hard to trip us up at every opportunity, and he knows our weak spots. And it doesn't mean we don't need to confess our sin and ask forgiveness. But it does mean we are not condemned; we are forgiven!

Since Christ be in you...you are free from defeat. (vv. 5-17) As Christians, we have not been released from being tempted to sin, but we have been released from the power of our flesh. The Holy Spirit frees us from the desire to sin and enables us to triumph over our self-life. We are victorious daughters of God, adopted into His family and joint-heirs with Christ.

Since Christ be in you...you are free from discouragement. (vv. 18-30) We know that life can get quite discouraging, even to the point of despair. Those are human feelings and responses to human problems. But through it all, God assures us that the glory which awaits us is not comparable to what we are suffering now. We know that all things work together for good to them that love God. We know that God is in control of all the details of our lives, and we can have peace in the midst of the storm.

Since Christ be in you...you are free from fear. (vv. 31-39) Do you ever fear that God will not save you because you are not good enough? Do you fear that He will no longer even love you because you have let Him down? Do you fear other people, situations, or the future? "God has not given us the spirit of fear, but of power, and of love, and of a sound mind." (II Timothy 1:7) With Christ in us, we have no need to fear. Through faith, we are more than conquerors; we are overcomers! Will you believe it and claim it for yourself?

- Can I declare myself free in these four areas?
- In which area will I need the most help?
- *Lord, I acknowledge your promise of freedom in these areas and desire your help in claiming them all.*

Read: James 5:13-18

An Answered Prayer

"Be careful for nothing; but in everything by prayer and supplication with thanksgiving let your requests be made known unto God."
- Philippians 4:6

Too often we try to fix things on our own. We worry and ponder and fret and pace. And finally, we think to pray.

Our two-year-old daughter had just had her tonsils out. We took her home the same day, with strict orders to get plenty of liquids into her or she would have to go back to the hospital for IV fluids. We were now finding out just how impossible it is to force a two-year-old to eat or drink when her throat hurts! You can't exactly reason with a child that age, either.

Early the next morning, I called the doctor and talked to him. He stressed again the importance of fluids within a certain amount of time. With the deadline only a half hour away, I was exhausted and near tears at the thought of going back to the hospital. But she was not cooperating. In desperation, I called our prayer chain with an urgent prayer request. "Please pray," I said. "We have only one-half hour to get her to eat or drink something, or we have to go back."

"Okay," she said immediately. "I'll send it on."

We continued to plead with our daughter and, about ten minutes later, she abruptly opened her mouth and took a bite of popsicle! One whole popsicle, some ice-cream, and several swallows of water later, we said "Thank you, Lord!" And "Thank you prayer warriors!"

Prayer should not have been a last resort. I was so busy and stressed trying to fix the situation on my own, that I didn't even think to stop and pray. Sometimes God is just waiting for us to ask, and our prayers are answered immediately.

- Am I facing a situation for which I need to pray about right now?
- Do I really believe that God can and will answer my prayers?
- *Lord, remind me to pray before life gets rough and give me the faith to trust You for Your answers.*

A Soil Analysis

"For God maketh my heart soft."
- Job 23:16

In the parable of the sower and the seed, Jesus likened the seed to the Word of God as it falls on our hearts. He named four places that the seed fell.

By the way side...with no soil in which to sprout, the birds soon ate up the seed. A heart that is hardened with sin will not understand God's Word or allow it to sink in and grow. The ears hear, but the heart is not receptive, and Satan snatches away the seeds.

Upon stony places...Since there was a little soil there, the seeds sprouted and quickly sprang up into little plants. But in the sun, they withered away because they had no root systems. These hearts receive the word joyfully and live thereby for awhile, but since their roots are not deep, a little trouble will quickly discourage them and they fall away.

Among thorns...which grew up and choked them. Some people take the Word into their hearts and have good intentions of applying it to their lives, but the cares of the world choke it out, and it brings forth no fruit.

Onto good ground...These seeds sprouted, grew, and brought forth good fruit. This life hears the Word, understands it, and lives it in a way that produces much good fruit.

Maybe it's time for a soil analysis of my heart. Do I listen attentively to sermons, asking God's help to understand and apply His truth to my life? Do the cares of life choke out the time I need to devote to Him for devotions, prayer, acts of service, child-training, or other selfless deeds? If we ask God to analyze our soil, He will help us improve it where necessary, enabling us to bear more abundant fruit!

- Is the soil of my heart soft, ready to receive the Word of God?
- Do I accept the seeds that fall and do my best to help them grow?
- *Lord, show me any area of my heart that needs to be softened in order for the seeds to grow.*

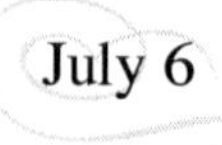

Read: Luke 5:1-8; 7:36-50; 8:41-56

At The Feet Of Jesus

"And he fell down at Jesus' feet, and besought Him that He would come into his house."
- Luke 8:41

In Luke 5:1-9 we read of Jesus' disciples fishing all night and catching nothing. Discouraged, they were cleaning their nets when Jesus asked to use their boat to teach the people. Later, when Jesus asked Simon Peter to try again for fish, Peter was skeptical. But he chose to obey, and they were blessed with so many fish that they filled two boats. Peter was so awestruck at this miracle that he fell down at the feet of Jesus and expressed his sinfulness in comparison to Jesus' holiness. He truly saw Jesus as more than a man, able to meet all of his needs.

The woman in Luke 7:36-50 was a prostitute; a sinner who was certainly not invited to the Pharisee's dinner party. She had heard that Jesus was to be there and had entered the house uninvited, to see Him. She was aware of her sinfulness and deeply grateful for the forgiveness she had experienced through Jesus. As Jesus reclined at the table, she stood at His feet, washing them with her tears, drying them with her hair, and anointing them with her ointment. She clearly saw Jesus as her Savior, filling her need of forgiveness and giving her a clean slate in life.

Jairus had a need, too. (Luke 8:41-56) His only daughter was dying. He needed someone who could restore her life, and he went to Jesus, falling at His feet and begging Him to come to his house. It was rather unusual for a respected synagogue ruler to do something like that, but he saw Jesus as a Man who could give life, and Jesus honored his faith. His daughter, although she had died before Jesus arrived, was restored to life and good health.

On the way to Jairus' house, a woman who had had an issue of blood for twelve years, pushed her way through the crowd, reached toward the feet of Jesus and touched the hem of His garment. She had seen Jesus as her healer, and her faith was rewarded with immediate healing.

Do you have a need today? Are you casting out your nets only to have them come up empty? Is there sin in your life that needs forgiveness? Do you have a relationship that needs to be resolved? Is someone sick or dying? Simon Peter gave his nets to Jesus, and they were filled. The sinful woman gave her loyalty to Jesus and was forgiven. The synagogue ruler gave his daughter to Jesus, and she was restored to life. The diseased woman gave her faith to Jesus and was healed. Jesus will meet your every need, in the way that is best for you, if you just come to His feet in faith and ask.

- What situations in your life are taking you to the feet of Jesus?
- Do you truly see Jesus as the One who cares about the details of your life and can meet your every need?
- *Lord, I come to Your feet in thankfulness and ask You to meet the needs You see in my life today.*

The Credible Witness

"Blessed are they that have not seen,
and yet have believed."
- John 20:29

"Mom! The people living on the next road over have a camel!" Two of my friend's children had just returned from a two-mile walk full of this exciting news. Mom, needless to say, was skeptical. They had seen llamas in the neighborhood, but a camel in Michigan seemed quite unlikely! Her daughter insisted, however, that there was, indeed, a camel in the neighbor's pasture, a dromedary to be exact.

The next day Mom went with those same two children on a walk, but there was no camel to be seen, just two curious horses that had also been there on the first walk. Two weeks later, the young folks returned from the same route to report that there was still no camel, but that there were stripes on one of the horses! They couldn't agree, though, on the direction of the stripes. Maybe the evening light was playing tricks on them.

When the spring weather turned warm again a couple weeks after that, Mom joined the two eye-witnesses for an outing. As they walked past the neighbor's pasture, they saw no camel. But wait. The short stocky horse had very vivid black and brown stripes. It was a "zorse!" Quite curious by now, they saw the neighbor in his yard and asked him, "Do you by any chance have a camel?"

"Yes, I do," he answered with a smile. "Her name is Millie. Would you like to meet her?"

Following Jesus' resurrection, Thomas had trouble believing that the other disciples had seen the Lord. (John 20:24-31) Since he had not been present when Jesus had appeared to them, he was purely skeptical, stating that he would have to see to believe. Later, the Lord appeared to Thomas too, and he then believed.

How about us? The Scriptures were written so that we can believe that Jesus is the Christ, and so that we can have life through Him. (v. 31) We can believe this Credible Witness. We can be among those who believe, though we have not seen. As we believe, we can experience that more abundant life that Jesus came to give us. (John 10:10)

- Do I truly believe that Jesus is alive today, and am I living that more abundant life which He offers to all?
- In what ways has Jesus appeared to me, showing me that He is real and cares about me personally?
- *Lord, forgive my unbelief, and help me see that You are real and that You are here for me at all times.*

 Read: James 1

The Engrafted Word

"Receive with meekness the engrafted word... (and)..be ye doers of the word, and not hearers only."
- James 1:21, 22

Grafting is commonly used in growing fruit trees. It's a way to combine positive characteristics of two different trees. For example, branches or buds of a tree that produces excellent quality fruit are grafted onto a tree that produces inferior fruit but has a stronger trunk. Friends of ours recently purchased and planted some dwarf fruit trees. About four to six inches above the bare roots there was a knot with a branch grafted into it. The instructions that came with the trees stated that it was important to keep the knot above the soil in planting as well as while they were growing. As long as the graft stayed out of the dirt and in the light, the tree would grow as it should and they would have a dwarf tree. If the graft became covered with soil, however, it would put down its own roots and start growing into its original size and shape. James tells us we are to rid our lives of all that's wrong and receive "the engrafted word"--the salvation message, which is the only way to save our souls. As the fruit tree is grafted into a strong root base, so we are grafted into our root base, Jesus Christ. It's just as important for us to stay out of the dirt (sin) and in the Light, as it is for the growing tree. When we allow sin to take root in our lives, we soon start to go our own way, growing further and further from what God would have us to be. It takes plenty of the Light of God's Word to produce the healthy fruit of the Spirit.

We know from experience that we will frequently find dirt in our lives. That's as normal as rain splashing dirt on a tree graft. But it's important that we don't leave it there and allow roots to grow. We can wash that dirt out of our life by confession and repentance. As we stay in the Light by reading and studying the Word, we develop a healthy root system. As we grow in Christ, His strength will flow through us, producing healthy fruit that blesses the lives of others around us.

- Am I keeping the dirt out of my life on a daily basis?
- How much effort am I putting into staying in the Light?
- *Lord, show me where I need to improve in producing the fruit that glorifies You.*

Are You A Pilgrim?

"Dearly beloved, I beseech you as strangers and pilgrims." - I Peter 2:11

The minister was telling us of an incident that happened once while he and his wife were on a trip. After a spilled coffee mishap at a restaurant, they went to a laundromat to wash some clothes. Another woman was there also with a little girl. The girl was fascinated by the minister's wife's dress and prayer covering. After walking past the minister's wife three times, looking her over, she finally summoned up all her courage and asked, "Are you a pilgrim?"

"No," his wife replied with a smile, "I'm not a pilgrim!"

Thinking it over later, however, they wondered just how correct that answer was. It satisfied the little girl, but God says we are to be pilgrims. The definition of a pilgrim is "an alien, sojourner, person who travels about, without a home."

At a time when the Waldensians were settling in Switzerland, the nearby Catholic priests resented them. The Catholics were losing members to the Waldensians, and finally gave them three days to come back to the mother church. Some returned, but others fled with the Waldensians across the mountains in the middle of winter. They buried babies, grandparents, and other loved ones in the snow along the way. These folks were pilgrims, heading for a better home.

This world is not our home. We are traveling through this life with Heaven as our destination. But how easily we become too focused on our daily life with its struggles, challenges, and goals. Life can become pretty comfortable and we become too content with our home here. But is this what we really want? Or do we long for a better home? Are we truly pilgrims?

- Am I keeping my main focus on my journey to Heaven rather than life here on earth?
- What areas in my life may be hindering that focus?
- *Lord, reveal to me anything in my life that is keeping my focus off of You.*

Read: Romans 8

The Death Rattle

"For to be carnally minded is death;
but to be spiritually minded is life and peace."
- Romans 8:6

We stood in a small, solemn group around the bed of a dear elderly friend who was dying. Cancer had taken its toll, and he was on the threshold of eternity. In what seemed like a holy moment, he very peacefully took his last breath, his soul taking flight as his wife and daughter tenderly held his hands. Wiping away tears, I realized that the gurgling we had heard earlier in his breathing was what they call the death rattle, signifying that the end is near.

In a sermon we heard recently, the minister compared the physical death rattle with the spiritual death rattle. Physically, the rattle is a sign that the lungs are filling up, and life is being snuffed out. If the lungs are not cleared, the body soon dies. Spiritually, the death rattle means that one's life is filling up...snuffing out the time, or even the desire for the things of God. Symptoms include cutting out personal devotions and prayer, losing the vision for family worship or the desire to attend church services. Lonely, elderly people wait patiently for visitors that don't come. The pangs of guilt grow dimmer and dimmer as we ignore God's promptings to serve others in various ways. And if our lives aren't revived, our spiritual life suffers, growing weaker and weaker, until finally life is snuffed out.

Does your life reflect the grace of God? Or do you hear the death rattle? Clear away the things that keep you too busy for the Lord. Spend time in Bible reading and prayer. Listen for God's voice and obey the promptings He sends. The death rattle will disappear, and you'll enjoy the blessings of a healthy spiritual life.

- Are there areas of my life that need to be cleared for better spiritual health?
- What activities are snuffing out the time I should be spending with the Lord?
- *Lord, give me the desire for a healthy life that reflects You.*

Thou Art Loosed

"Jesus... said unto her, Woman,
thou art loosed from thine infirmity."
- Luke 13:12

It was the Sabbath Day, and Jesus was teaching in one of the Jewish synagogues. As He spoke, He noticed a crippled woman in the audience. This woman had been bent over, unable to straighten up at all, for eighteen years! Think about what a terrible handicap that would be. It would be difficult to live your daily life, much less go anywhere, but she was there, in the synagogue to hear Jesus speak. When Jesus saw her, he called her to Him, not waiting for her to ask for help. He spoke to her, telling her that her days of suffering were over. Then He reached out with His hands and touched her, healing her crippled body. Imagine how she must have felt as she stood up straight for the first time in eighteen years! She "glorified God" as she rejoiced in her new freedom.

While this is a heart-warming story, it doesn't stop here. Jesus is still a compassionate Friend, wanting to heal people of their pain. Many people saw the crippled woman at the synagogue, but Jesus saw her pain. There may be many people in your life who are oblivious to the burden you are carrying, whether it is physical, mental, emotional, or spiritual. But Jesus sees your pain. He relates to the burden, and He cares. He is calling you to come to Him. Jesus broke the tradition of the day by healing on the Sabbath. But this woman was more important to Him than man-made traditions, and so are you. Are you, my dear sister, "bowed together" with a burden too heavy for you? Jesus invites you to come to Him. Let Him speak His comfort and assurance to you as you pour out your heart to Him in prayer. Let Him reach out and touch you, perhaps through the hands or heart of another caring person. Let Him heal your pain. You are precious, and He cares.

- Am I bowed with an "infirmity" that Jesus would heal for me?
- Am I willing to allow Him to speak to me, maybe through someone else?
- *Lord, make me sensitive to Your voice calling me to You, and I thank you for Your loving touch.*

Read: Luke 8:4-15

Pretty But Poisonous

"And they...are choked with ...pleasures of this life, and bring no fruit to perfection."
- Luke 8:14

A friend of mine was traveling through a neighboring state. Having a fascination for nature and an eye for detail, she enjoyed watching the scenery as they drove. She noticed the flowers on the roadsides, in the ditches, and in the hedgerows. Suddenly she was struck with the abundance of tall plants wearing lacy white tops, but different from the usual Queen Anne's lace. No one she inquired of seemed to know what they were; few had even noticed them. One friend told her that they had appeared only in the last few years. Finally, locating a field guide, she decided that the plants were most likely Poison Hemlock! A beautiful plant to be avoided.

Could there be a parallel here? she wondered. How many things do we have in our lives that are too obvious to miss, yet we miss them? Attractions that have a lovely appearance and yet are deadly. They creep in unawares and thrive without us noticing. Maybe, she thought, it could be an addiction to a favorite, unhealthy beverage. Or spending time on personal hobbies rather than writing an encouraging letter to a friend. Or even a focus on entertainment. Unnecessary shopping, buying things we want but don't really need. Or reading romance novels, rather than the Bible or other wholesome materials.

As the Poison Hemlock is pleasing to the eye but deadly to the body, so many things in life can be pleasing to the flesh, yet harmful to our spiritual life. Since the wages of sin (rejection of God's will) is death, it is urgent that we ask God to eradicate all poison from our lives.

- What things may be creeping into my life that could be poison to my soul?
- Am I willing to allow God to help me weed out of my life deadly habits or activities?
- *Lord, I thank You for the beauty of nature, and I desire to apply the lessons from it to my life.*

Forms

"And be not conformed to this world: but be ye transformed by the renewing of your mind."
- Romans 12:2

God has a problem with man. (And woman!) That problem is the heart. Back in the beginning, in the midst of the beauty of the Garden of Eden, God formed a man and a woman. He put within each of them a perfect heart, unmarred by sin or shame. He gave the man a heart to provide and the woman a heart to nurture.

It wasn't long, however, until Eve met up with Satan and was deceived into disobeying God's Word. Satan delighted in deforming the heart that God had given to Eve, and he delights just as much today in deforming our hearts, even quoting Scripture, as he did with Eve.

Although Satan delights in deforming our hearts, God delights in transforming us. Just as Jesus cast out many demons during His time on earth, He still can and wants to cleanse our hearts of sin, transforming our lives into His image and letting the Son shine through us, spilling over to all with whom we come into contact.

He wants to reform our lives by removing the faults He sees in us. As the children of Israel had to get rid of the idols they were worshiping to receive God's blessings, so we need to purge our lives of the "idols" that may be coming between us and God.

As we allow God to reform us, He wants to inform us of His will through His Word. We will get to know Him and His Son intimately as we spend time in His Word daily, feasting on His love and guidance. In order to conform to the image of God, rather than to the world, we must know who God is. And Bible study, prayer, teaching, and fellowship with other believers is the way to get to know Him. As we conform to His image, we will enter into a spiritual uniformity with other believers around the world, united by the Spirit of God working in us and through us.

Don't miss out on this! Let God *transform* you, *reform* you, *inform* you and enjoy the rich blessings of being in unity with His people as you become *conformed* to His image.

- Am I harboring some sin that Satan is using to deform my heart?
- How can I get to know God better, conforming my life to His will?
- *Lord, show me the defects in my heart and give me a longing to be conformed into Your image.*

Seasons Of The Soul

"To everything there is a season, and a time to every purpose under the heaven."
- Ecclesiastes 3:1

In our part of the country, a big, beautiful oak tree is a good reflection of the changing seasons. In the spring it awakens from its winter slumber and changes begin to happen. We observe them as the sap rises in the trunk and the buds burst open into fresh green leaves. As spring turns to summer and the weather gets warmer, the leaves grow and deepen in color. They provide cool, refreshing shade and serene beauty, giving off oxygen needed by animals and man. When fall arrives, the tree is a feast for the eyes, as the leaves become brilliant reds, golds, and browns. In other areas of the country, some trees yield fruit or nuts that are harvested and shared with people around the globe. Then, as the temperatures drop, so do the leaves. The branches contrast starkly with the winter landscape. The tree appears dead. But it is far from dead! The tree is not fighting God's plan for it but simply resting, waiting patiently for the spring to come again, as the Master has promised it would.

Let's compare this with the seasons of the soul. Sometimes we are in a spiritual springtime, coming out of winter. We feel fresh and renewed with changes happening within. The fire glows within us, melting the snow and ice as we move into summer, cultivating this new growth, feeding on His Word, and serving Him as He leads us. The sun shines brightly as we enjoy the fall, reaping the harvest of blessings and sharing encouraging and exciting testimonies with others. But at times we find ourselves in a season of winter. Life seems barren and cold as icy winds blow across our souls. We feel dead and useless. But this is not a time to despair or fight against God's plan. It is a time to rest, remembering God's faithfulness, re-thinking our life's goals, and recapturing the excitement of the good things He has done for us. As we wait patiently, the sun will shine again. Remember, spring will come--it may be just around the corner!

- Am I in a winter season in my spiritual life?
- What can I do to grow in Him during this time of waiting patiently for spring?
- *Lord, I thank You for the promise of spring and ask You to work in my heart during the winter months.*

The Devil's Tackle Box

"But every man is tempted, when he is drawn away of his own lust, and enticed."
- James 1:14

As I gaze into my husband's fishing tackle box, I see objects of all sorts, designed specifically to entice fish. Lures are available to tempt any kind of fish you can imagine. Big lures and small lures. Bright, multi-colored, and shiny gold or silver. Some are simple and some complex with feathery tails or other gadgets. Most of them have their name stamped on the bottom. I find them a fascinating study. If you look closely, however, you will see that on each lure is a sharp, wicked-looking hook that is not meant to be noticed. It's small, plain, and, if possible, at least partially hidden by the fancy lure. Each hook has a barb, hard to remove once it is set. These hooks are made to hold. Then I see some extra fishing line. It's almost clear, making it hard to see in the water. Its thin fragile look is deceptive. It's hard to see and may stretch but it seldom breaks, even fighting a determined fish. I see extra reels, bobbers, pliers for removing hooks, and other miscellaneous items.

As I observe and study, I think of Satan and his tackle box of enticing allurements. He knows just which lure to use for each person and has a ready supply of all types. Many types of enticing worldly lures are designed to attract Christians, but if you examine them closely, you may find them labeled pride, negative thoughts, or gossip. While they may look good, they are hiding deadly hooks. Satan's line is almost invisible as he reels in his catch, little by little. The further we get from the safe waters, the harder it is to wiggle free from his hold.

But we have a Savior whose vigilance protects us from Satan's barbed hooks. If we do become hooked, He is able and always ready to release us into the safe waters of His care again. With diligent study of God's Word, and earnest prayer for protection, we can avoid capture, "for we are not ignorant of Satan's devices." (II Corinthians 2:11)

- Am I staying close to the Master of the harbor in the safe waters?
- What dangerous lure is Satan trying to tempt me with today?
- *Lord, I know the temptations are many, and I ask You to cover me with Your protection today.*

 Read: Philippians 2:1-18

A Reverential Fear

"Work out your own salvation
with fear and trembling."
- Philippians 2:12

When we spend a day at the zoo, we usually don't leave without visiting the lions. Why are we drawn to these animals? Probably because they are the fiercest and most feared predators of the wild. However, when we stand in front of their cage and stare at them in wonder of their power and beauty, we have no reason to be afraid of them. The zoo staff has taken adequate steps to insure our safety by installing thick glass walls around them or by digging deep wide moats and building fences around their pens.

We are not afraid of the lions, but we have a healthy respect for them because of what we know they could do. If we were to break the zoo's rules and jump over the fence; or if we were to meet up with one of these majestic beasts known as the "king of the jungle" in the forests of Africa, we would have reason to tremble. Seeing a lion charging at us if we were unprotected would understandably overwhelm us with pure fear, as he would likely have *"dinner!"* on his mind! Standing the same distance from them in a zoo produces only feelings of awe.

In much the same way, we were all once on the wrong side of the fence, living in disobedience to God's Law. "For all have sinned and come short of the glory of God." (Romans 3:23) And the consequences of our rebellion were bearing down on us swiftly. But God, in His mercy, instead of allowing the judgment we deserved, chose to stop and spare us, giving us another chance to follow Him. If we love and obey Him, God promises that we will have nothing to fear. "There is therefore now no condemnation to them which are in Christ Jesus, who walk not after the flesh, but after the Spirit." (Romans 8:1) If we disobey Him, however, He has every right to discipline us. Just as the fence protects us from the lions without hindering our freedom, God's Law protects us from His judgment without enslaving us.

While God does not want us to be afraid of Him, He does inspire a reverential fear. We should all tremble at what could have been, what should have been, and seek to honor God by learning to know Him better, to love Him more, and to obey His commandments. We should be awestruck because of His unfailing love evidenced by His death on the cross for us, and His continuous grace and mercy toward us.

- When I think of being in God's presence, do I feel afraid or do I feel a reverential awe?
- Do I allow Him to place a wall of protection between me and the evil one?
- *Lord, thank You for Your mercy and help me to trust in the safety of Your protection.*

A Father's Love - The Lost Sheep

"Yea, I have loved thee
with an everlasting love."
- Jeremiah 31:3

In Luke 14:25-35, we read of a crowd that had been following Jesus for various reasons. Some may have been curious about the miracles He had been performing, others may have been hoping for a free meal after hearing about Jesus feeding the five thousand, and some may have simply been jealous and looking for a chance to criticize this man who was becoming popular. It seems, at this point, that by teaching what it would cost to be a disciple of His, Jesus thinned down the crowd to those who were genuinely interested in what He had to say--the publicans and the sinners. (15:1)

This didn't set well with the Pharisees and scribes who grumbled because Jesus was speaking to these low class people. So Jesus told them three parables to demonstrate His great love for the outcast, despised, and unlovely.

In the parable of the lost sheep, we see a shepherd's love for his flock. Each sheep is highly valuable to its shepherd and worth searching for diligently. Sometimes a sheep will slowly wander away from the fold, one mouthful of grass after another, until it is completely lost. But instead of trying to find its way back to the fold, it will just lie down and wait. Knowing this, the shepherd in this story didn't wait back at the fold for the sheep to come home; he went looking for it. When he found the lost sheep, he didn't drive the animal home, like you would cattle, but he tenderly picked the sheep up, put it across his shoulders, and carried it home. Then, he was so happy about finding the lost sheep that he called his friends and neighbors together for a rejoicing party.

Jesus has this kind of surpassing love for us, too. When we were sinners, He didn't just wait for us to come to Him, He came seeking us. And even now, at times when we wander away from Him, lured by Satan's temptations and weakened by a lack of Scripture reading and prayer, Jesus doesn't just wait for us to come back to Him. He comes seeking us until He has our attention, then He tenderly forgives us, picks us up, and carries us back into the safety of His fold. The love of our Father for us surpasses any love we know here on earth. He loves each of us with an everlasting love, and Heaven rejoices over each repenting sinner that returns to the fold.

- Do I feel the Father's extraordinary love and know that I am valuable to Him?
- Am I wandering away from Him and ignoring His search for me?
- *Lord, I want to be secure in Your protection, and I thank You for Your great love for me.*

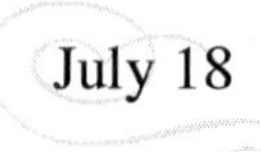

Read: Luke 15:8-10

A Father's Love - The Lost Coin

"Who shall separate us
from the love of Christ?"
- Romans 8:35

When a woman in this culture was married, she received ten silver coins as a wedding gift. These coins were very valuable to her. Besides the security the money provided her, they were also high in sentimental value, much like a wedding ring is to many people today. This woman had lost one of her coins and she was distraught. Her house was likely small with a dirt floor and dimly lit. She lit a lamp and swept her dirt floor carefully, looking for a glint of silver, searching... searching until she found her coin. And then, like the shepherd who found his lost sheep, she called in her friends and neighbors to celebrate with her.

We may find ourselves outside of God's fellowship for different reasons. Like the sheep, we can wander away without even realizing that we are losing touch with God. Or maybe, like the coin, we are pushed away by the influence of others. Sometimes, we may even choose to walk away from what we know is right, as the prodigal son in the next parable did. We have all been that lost sheep, that lost coin, or that lost son at one time or another. God sees all of our faults, our failures, and our tendency to wander away from Him. We have been the unlovable. Others may see us as ugly or despised, one to be avoided, as the Pharisees looked at the publicans and sinners. But God still loves us with a surpassing love that doesn't just wait for us to come to Him, but seeks us out, searching...searching until He finds us. We are each precious to God! He grieves over each lost soul and rejoices each time one is found and received into His kingdom. And all Heaven rejoices with Him!

What about the lost coins around us? Do we seek them out and do what we can to help them? Are we praying for those who are lost and uncared for? Do we encourage them with a smile, a kind word, or deed? Do we see them as precious to God and worth searching for? If we keep our eyes open and our hearts ready to serve, God will reward our search.

- Am I now in the position of a lost coin? Or should I be looking for other lost coins?
- Do I feel the Father searching for me, and am I willing to be found?
- *Lord, make my heart willing to be found or help me to find other lost souls who need a caring touch.*

A Father's Love - The Lost Son

"For God so loved (you) that He gave His only begotten Son that (you) should..have everlasting life."
- John 3:16

In the third parable that Jesus told the Scribes and Pharisees, the younger son showed complete disrespect for his father's authority by asking for his share of the inheritance. After receiving the inheritance, he took off, probably thinking he had it made, with freedom and plenty of money. He had no way of knowing that he had just begun a downward spiral that would take him to the depths of despair and bring him back home begging for a job. He just knew he was on his own, and he had a wonderful time "wasting his substance with riotous living." Eventually, however, his money ran out, and on top of that, "there arose a mighty famine in that land." Now life wasn't so much fun. With no money to buy food, he became so desperate that he did something terribly degrading to a Jew. He took a job with a pig farmer. He even had to feed the swine. Hogs were unclean to the Jews. Even touching a hog would defile them. Then, sinking even lower, he got so hungry that he would have gladly eaten the pigs' food.

Finally, this young man repented in his heart and, with his repentance, took action. He went home. It must have been a very long walk, likely with little food or drink. Imagine his feelings when, long before he got there, he saw his father coming. Running! With a bear hug and a kiss. As they walked home, the son apologized, but before he could even ask for employment as a servant, his father was making plans for a party. The broken young son was being treated like royalty, not like a rebellious young man coming back to work as a servant. Our Heavenly Father's love for each of us is indescribable. He is waiting and watching, ready to meet us on the road when we come to our senses and return to Him.

The older brother was not happy when he came in from the field and heard the music and dancing. He considered himself a faithful son, but no one had ever had a party in his honor! He was so upset that he wouldn't even go in to see his brother. When his father heard that his older son was angry, he didn't just ignore him and go on celebrating; he took the time to go out and talk with him. He expressed appreciation for his elder son and explained that it was appropriate to rejoice because his brother had been lost and was found.

Our heavenly Father loves us, too, even when we are acting in an un-Christian manner. He will come to meet us right where we are and forgive us immediately when we repent.

- What action could I take that would bring me into closer fellowship with my Father?
- Am I harboring a self-righteous attitude such as the older brother, that prevents full fellowship with my heavenly Father?
- *Lord, I thank You for accepting me as I take steps back to You.*

Read: Esther 4

Who Knows?

"Who knoweth whether thou art come to the kingdom for such a time as this?"
- Esther 4:14

Haman had tricked the king into making a decree that all the Jews should be killed. This decree had been sealed by an imprint of the king's ring and could not be reversed. Esther had not revealed her Jewish heritage, and the king had no idea that his own ring was signing her death sentence.

When Mordecai read the decree and realized what had happened, he was extremely upset. He tore his clothes and put on sackcloth and ashes, a sign of mourning, and sat by the king's gate. Esther was not aware of Haman's evil plans and hearing what Mordecai was doing, she sent her personal servant, Hatach, to talk to him. Mordecai showed Hatach the decree and through him, begged Esther to go to the king and plead for their lives. When Esther protested, knowing she would be risking her life, he reminded her that she was a Jew too, and would not escape death just because she was the queen. Then he ended his plea with a thought-provoking question, "Who knoweth whether thou art come to the kingdom for such a time as this?"

Esther was convinced. She sent a message back to Mordecai with instructions for prayer and fasting, and she said, "I will go in unto the king, which is not according to the law, and if I perish, I perish."

We know the end of the story. The king accepted Esther's request and was very angry when he found that he'd been tricked. Haman was hanged, and a second decree was issued to allow the Jews to defend themselves. God's people were saved because Esther put aside her own fear and courageously risked her life to intercede for the Jews.

Are you facing a difficult or dangerous situation? Are you trembling at the thought of confronting a friend on a tough subject, taking on a task that looks like a mountain, or just facing another day with babies, toddlers, cooking, cleaning, laundry, school, and the mountains of other work waiting on you? Would you rather just avoid your responsibilities with excuses as Esther was tempted to do? We all need God's strength and protection, which He is longing to give. The longer we dread and put off difficult assignments, the more difficult they seem. Today, God works through people just like Esther, you, and me. We can take responsibility with the confidence that God knows just why He planned for us to fill a certain role at this time in history. "Who knoweth whether thou art come to the Kingdom for such a time as this?"

- What situation am I facing now that takes more courage and strength than I have to offer?
- Do I fully believe that God will protect and provide for me the way He did for Esther?
- *Lord, though my faith is faltering, I long to have the courage of Esther and I choose to trust You in this difficult time.*

Our Anchor Of Hope

"Which hope we have as an anchor of the soul,
both sure and steadfast."
- Hebrews 6:19

My husband has a fishing boat and is familiar with lake and river fishing. On the river, an anchor is necessary to keep the boat from drifting. To suddenly realize your anchor has pulled loose, and you have drifted into an area of weeds or rocks can be rather startling. If this happens, you must pull up that anchor quickly and move before the situation gets worse. And then you must make sure the anchor is firmly embedded into solid ground so the anchor doesn't dislodge again. The cable is also important. An anchor with a broken cable is no good. It should be inspected regularly and kept in good repair.

Our lives can be like that. We need to be firmly anchored in Jesus Christ, diligently seeking Him through Bible study and prayer. This should include listening for His voice and following His leading. All of us at times will find ourselves adrift, with old habits and negative thoughts popping back up. The irritations and stresses of daily life threaten to overwhelm us, and we wonder if it's all worth it. At that point, we had better exit those dangerous waters and replant our anchor of hope into Jesus...our solid rock. And we should check our cable of faith and ask God to help us repair any frayed or torn areas. If our anchor is firmly planted in Jesus, and our cable of faith is strong, even though the cable may stretch, it will hold us steady in any storm that comes our way.

- Is my anchor of hope firmly planted in Jesus, or am I drifting into dangerous waters?
- Have I been carefully maintaining my cable, or am I just assuming it will be there when I need it?
- *Lord, some days my boat drifts and my cable stretches. Show me the danger and help me return to safe waters.*

Read: Philippians 2

Take A Closer Look

"Look not every (woman) on (her) own things, but every (woman) also on the things of others."
- Philippians 2:4

As an avid gardener, my friend enjoys touring other people's gardens. Usually she finds it best to just ignore any weeds, but sometimes one will catch her eye because it's unusual. At that point, she just may take a closer look at it. Recently, she saw one that was new to her. She had never had that particular weed in her garden. (For which she was thankful, as she has plenty of other varieties!) Stooping to study the tiny flowers on the weed, she was fascinated. They were white with green lines and it actually took a magnifying glass to see the detail. What intricate beauty! On a weed. Who but God could beautify a weed? We often miss that kind of beauty by destroying the weed long before it has a chance to bloom.

Later as she was talking with her daughter, describing this weed, they discussed the benefits of taking a closer look--at anything. How often do we overlook something wonderful because it seems too small to be bothered with? Obviously, we can't always be examining the details, but we can always be sensitive to the Spirit's prompting to "take a closer look." Looking closely at the natural beauty around us can give us a better understanding and appreciation of the greatness of God. When we hear a friend make a wistful comment, we can use that cue to help us as we seek ways of ministering to her. Perhaps we can encourage her in a struggle she's experiencing.

As busy mothers, we need to pause frequently to take a closer look at the lives of our children, not only to observe their beauty, but also to detect areas where they need extra guidance or support. We can better support our husbands by taking a closer look at their work, their concerns, or other interests they may have. Asking God to help us see through the magnifying glass of His wisdom will show us details we might otherwise miss. A closer look will disclose the beauty and splendor of our Creator in unexpected places--even in weeds! Let's pause in our busyness to take a closer look so we don't miss what God has for us.

- Am I too busy to take time for a closer look at the small things in life?
- What should I take a closer look at today?
- *Lord, remind me in the midst of my busy schedule to stop and take a closer look whenever You prompt me to do so.*

Snakes

"And it came to pass, that if a serpent had bitten any man, when he beheld the serpent of brass, he lived."
- Numbers 21:9

Picture, if you will, walking through a land of poisonous snakes. There is no escape! You must keep moving, and you know that if you are bitten, you will die. What an unpleasant picture. This is just the dilemma the Children of Israel found themselves in after grumbling in the wilderness. Many died, and the natural reaction of others would have been to kill those snakes. But God had another plan for them. Those who had been bitten could be saved by looking upon the brass serpent on the pole.

Likewise, we are walking through a land of snakes. Snakes with names like Pride, Bitterness, Moral Failure, and Anger. Even snakes called Gossip, Slander, Dishonesty, and Unkindness. All of these serpents are of the same species: SIN. Now, our natural reaction is to kill these snakes. Chop their heads off before they bite us! But it's too late for us, too. We have already been bitten. Even before we were born. Psalm 51:5 says, "I was shapen in iniquity and in sin did my mother conceive me."

Like the Israelites, our only hope of salvation is to look up. To allow the blood of Jesus to cover these snakes and render them harmless. It doesn't work to try to chop their heads off ourselves. The bites are rendered harmless only as we repent of our sins, confess them, and allow the Holy Spirit to work in our lives to conform us into the image of Jesus.

- Are there any "snakes" in my life today that I need to surrender to Jesus?
- Do I believe that through Jesus I can defeat these "snakes?"
- *Lord, I know I've been bitten by these snakes, and I ask You to help me to victory over these bites of sin.*

Living On A Sliver

"And (since) Christ be in you, the body is dead because of sin; but the Spirit is life because of righteousness."
- Romans 8:10

I once heard the story of a man who wanted to cross the ocean to visit a foreign country. He saved a long time and finally had enough money to buy passage on an ocean liner. The ticket, however, took all of his money, and he could afford nothing but bread and cheese for the journey. Each day as the other passengers went to the luxurious dining room to feast on sumptuous fare from the bountiful banquet tables, this man sat in a corner and ate his bread and cheese. Each night as others enjoyed their beautiful comfortable rooms, he slept in a corner of the sitting room. On the last day of the voyage, a curious man asked him, "Friend, why do you always eat just bread and cheese, and sleep here on the floor?" Upon hearing his reply, the man said in astonishment, "But sir, the room and food were included in the price of your ticket!" This poor man really missed out. He experienced only a sliver of what he could have enjoyed on his long trip across the ocean. If he had only known! How could he have been so ignorant? we wonder.

But really, are we so different? We tend to live life on a sliver, too. Since Christ be in you, you have access to all of God's promises, all of His provisions, all of His power. Do you feast on all He has for you, or do you exist on "bread and cheese?" Jesus promises life abundant to all who follow Him. God provides everything we need to live a life of service to Him. Through His power we can be more than conquerors, glorifying Him through our obedience to His will and our love for each other.

If you're living on a sliver, your life could be much richer. Since Christ be in you, you are welcomed at the King's banquet table. Feast on the promises in His Word and let them nourish your soul. Since Christ be in you, you can enjoy the peaceful rest of knowing He will provide all that you need for your journey. Since Christ be in you, you can journey confidently knowing that His power will sustain you until you reach your Destination.

Don't miss out on this richness! Don't exist on "bread and cheese" when you could be feasting! Don't "sleep on the floor" when you could be sweetly resting in Him. We all go through times of "living on a sliver" but we don't have to stay there. Read His Word, pray without ceasing, follow His leading, and you will experience that richness that only life in Him can give. You'll also have a testimony that you won't have if you're living life on a sliver.

- Am I living my life on a sliver of what God wants to provide for me?
- How could I begin today to enjoy a richer life?
- *Lord, I know You have more for me and I ask You to show me what I am missing.*

The Touch Of Jesus

"Believe ye that I am able to do this?"
- Matthew 9:28

The word touch comes from two root words that mean "to fasten" and "to kindle, or set on fire." From this we can know that when Jesus reaches out and gently "fastens Himself to you" it will kindle something inside that becomes a living fire burning in your heart and lighting up your life to touch others.

Matthew 8:1-4. This passage tells of a leper who knew that Jesus had a *healing* touch. This man had the faith and courage to approach Jesus and to ask Him for help. And Jesus--even though the man's skin was covered with a dreaded, incurable disease--reached out and touched him, curing him instantly. The man then went to the priests, (as the law had prescribed), and showed them firsthand the miracle he had experienced.

Matthew 8:14-15. Peter's mother-in-law was sick and feverish, certainly not feeling like being a hostess, when Jesus arrived at her home. She not only experienced the healing touch of Jesus, as He reached out and touched her hand, but she also felt His *calming* touch and immediately got up and began to serve Jesus and His disciples. What a beautiful response to the soothing touch of the Master!

Matthew 9:27-31. The *revealing* touch. These blind men not only had faith and courage, they were persistent. They followed Jesus along the way and right into the house begging for mercy. After testing their faith, Jesus touched their eyes and they could see. When the men left, they spread the news about their healing all over that country.

Mark 7:31-37. As Jesus opened the ears of this man and healed his speech disorder, He gave him the *freeing* touch. He was now free to hear the Gospel and to tell others about what he had experienced.

Matthew 17:1-8. When Peter, James, and John heard God's voice on the Mount of Transfiguration, they fell on their faces, terrified. Jesus came to them and touched them, telling them to get up and not to be afraid. Receiving His *focusing* touch, they looked up and "saw no man, save Jesus only." We also need the touch of Jesus to be able to focus on Him--the most important aspect of our day-to-day life.

While we receive many different touches in our lives, the gentle Touch of the Master is an intimate, precious connection that can bring about many blessings in the building of His Kingdom.

- Do I recognize the touch of Jesus in my life?
- In what ways can I reach out to others with the touch I have received from Him?
- *Lord, help me to observe the ways You touch my life and to be willing and ready to touch others with Your love.*

Treasures Of Darkness

"And I will give thee the treasures of darkness."
- Isaiah 45:3

Cyrus is the only Gentile ruler in the Bible who is said to have been anointed. God had a special plan for him. He ruled an expansive kingdom and under his rule, things were going to change dramatically. In the beginning of Isaiah 45, God tells Cyrus just how much He is going to help him to subdue nations. The treasures of darkness may represent the huge amounts of valuable spoils the Babylonian armies had brought back from previous battles. These spoils were hidden, locked away in vaults and other secret places. God promised Cyrus that He would break down the brass gates of the city, cutting through the reinforcing iron bars, even giving him access to the hidden riches.

As we battle dark times of grief, loneliness, or crushing disappointments, God is faithful in blessing us with the "treasures of darkness" also. A sermon or devotional may touch us in a deeper way than it would have at another time. A hymn may speak words of comfort, or friends may offer encouragement and support. Scripture takes on new meaning as we read it with tears in our eyes and discouragement in our hearts. Other treasures may be recognized only in the light of day, after the darkness has passed. We treasure what we have learned about compassion, obedience, and trust. We treasure the intimate relationship with Jesus that we have gained through the battle. While we enjoy the good days with which God blesses us, we should not resist those dark times. As you maintain faith in God, He will lovingly reveal priceless riches to you as He walks beside you through every step of the battle.

- What battles am I fighting today with which God will help me?
- Am I recognizing the hidden treasures along the way?
- *Lord, I thank You for the love You show through these "treasures of darkness."*

Little Things

"And whosoever shall give to drink unto one of these little ones a cup of cold water... he shall in no wise lose his reward."
- Matthew 10:42

Little things can make a big difference in our days. Pleasant little things make life brighter, and unpleasant little things can make a smooth day turn rough.

Consider how quickly a baby's smile warms your heart. A tiny, purple crocus pushing up through the snow gives us a glimpse of spring. A little puppy's enthusiastic greeting can make us feel loved and needed. These are blessings God has given us to enjoy.

You and I can brighten others' days also. A friendly smile may light up the day of an elderly person you meet in town. An impromptu hug can make a child feel loved and secure. A pat on the back or a sincere compliment may lift the drooping spirit of a teenager. A plate of cookies for the teacher, a casserole for a busy mother. A back rub for your weary husband, a bouquet for a neighbor. The list is endless!

Of course, we want to avoid the unpleasant little things. Petty criticisms, gossip, short answers, and angry looks are just a few of the "little foxes that spoil the vine." (Song of Solomon 2:15)

Even little things can have a big effect on the lives of the people around us. To be a doer of the good little things in life, we must stay connected to the Master--the giver of all good. This connection will also prevent the negative things from getting us down. That connection is vital!

- Am I making a difference in the lives of other people with pleasant little things?
- How could I make someone feel special today by a simple, little action?
- *Lord, prompt me to make a difference in someone's life by the little things I can do today.*

Read: Philippians 2

Willing To Be Willing

*"For it is God which worketh in you both to will
and to do of His good pleasure."*
- Philippians 2:13

Hanging laundry in a strong wind had to be one of those things that irritated my friend more than anything else. It made her thankful she doesn't live in a place where wind is a constant factor. But other than that, it made her downright grouchy, neither feeling nor displaying the joy of the Lord.

One day as she was fighting with sheets, trying to convince them to stay put while she pinned them to the line, Philippians 2:13 came to her mind. "For it is God which worketh in you both to will and do of His good pleasure." The next verse says, "Do all things without murmurings…" Other translations would be "complaining," or "grumbling." Uh-oh. "Okay God," she thought, "make me willing to enjoy your wind, even though I really don't want to be willing!" Could He make her willing to be willing? She could almost feel a physical resistance to giving up that grumbling! Of herself, she certainly didn't have much to offer. God, however, can work with the smallest yielding that we can muster. He can turn faith as small as a grain of mustard seed into something great. God did take her tentative and reluctant willingness and made her willing to give up her dislike of wind. Then He took the edge off that dislike. She still does not rejoice in having to hang out laundry on a windy day, and she is still thankful not to live in a windy area. Now, however, even when the wind is blowing, she can hang out her laundry cheerfully. When we have a hard time being willing to do something God is asking of us, He will honor our willingness to become willing.

- Is there an area in my life that I need to be willing to change?
- If I'm not willing, am I at least willing to be willing?
- *Lord, I desire to allow Your perfect will to replace my stubborn will.*

Gifts

"Having then gifts differing according to the grace that is given to us."
- Romans 12:6

When we buy a gift, we don't purchase it for our own use. We present it to the person it was intended for, and we expect them to use it. We would be a bit hurt if they just stashed it in a closet and ignored it. A fruit tree does not produce fruit for its own use. Neither does a grape arbor produce its beautiful clusters of grapes for itself. God provides many gifts of nature for us to use and enjoy.

Likewise, God gives each of us gifts that He expects us to use. He must be disappointed if we choose to ignore His gifts because we're too busy. Perhaps we tend to hide our talents for fear of appearing proud of our abilities. Or we have no confidence in our abilities, thinking we're not nearly good enough to share our gifts with others. Something is wrong with this thinking. God didn't give us these gifts to be stashed in the closet!

Your gift of hospitality can refresh fellow-pilgrims. Your gift of singing or writing could brighten the day of an elderly shut-in. God may want to use your talent for cooking, or your special way with children to bless others outside your home. Many busy mothers would appreciate your gifts. Your gift of compassion could bless someone's life with your caring words. Don't be afraid to use your gifts for God's glory. You can bless the lives of many by using your God-given gifts, and you will be richly blessed in return.

- What gifts do I have that would bring glory to God today?
- Am I willing to step out bravely and share those gifts with others?
- *Lord, You gave me the gifts I have. Give me the courage to use them to bless the lives of others.*

Read: I Peter 4:7-19

Waiting And Watching... Or Just Waiting?

"But watch thou in all things...do the work of an evangelist, make full proof of thy ministry."
- II Timothy 4:5

I am not a deer hunter, but I know several women who do enjoy hunting. They take a gun to the woods and find a spot to sit, either on the ground or in a deer blind. They may be up in a tree stand or in a box-type blind that someone has built on stilts with windows on each side. Some deer blinds are pretty deluxe with battery-powered heaters, coffee makers, and microwave ovens. The best time to hunt deer is early morning or evening, at sunrise or sunset. A good deer hunter will be in his chosen hunting spot before the sun is up, braving the cold and darkness to get a chance at the big one he is hoping to see.

But not every hunter sees a deer. Just sitting and waiting is not always enough. Some hunters fall asleep after leaving their warm beds at such an early hour. Some scare the deer away by making too much noise sipping coffee from a thermos or trying to get comfortable on a seat of leaves. Others may be distracted by the conveniences in their deer blinds. Still others may simply be lost in their own thoughts.

The hunters who are alert while they wait get to see the deer. They are looking for signs that deer have been there and listening for any noise indicating that deer are present. Their guns are loaded and ready for use. They are watching for the deer rather than just waiting for one to come into view. When their chance comes, they don't miss it. They are the ones who are rewarded for their patience and diligent observance.

Living life in the Lord's service can be a lot like that. Instead of passively waiting for a service opportunity to fall into our laps, we need to be actively watching for an opportunity to help someone in need. It can be so easy to just sit back and wait for God to bless us in a big way rather than to watch for ways that He is blessing us every day. We get tired and fall asleep spiritually. We get too "noisy" to hear His voice. We are too easily distracted by all the duties and cares of daily life. For some of us, most of our opportunities for service occur right in our own homes. Wherever we spend our days, we don't need to just plug along, waiting for those opportunities to present themselves squarely in front of us. We can be watching for whatever God has for us to do and whatever He has to teach us.

- How diligent am I in watching for opportunities to serve Him?
- Do I recognize those opportunities in the mundane activities of my daily life?
- *Lord, remind me to watch for chances to serve You and open my eyes to see them.*

Read: Hebrews 9:11-28 July 31

Guilt And Shame

"How much more shall the blood of Christ...purge your conscience...to serve the living God?"
- Hebrews 9:14

My dictionary defines guilt as being responsible for an offense or wrongdoing. Guilt feelings are a remorseful awareness of having done something wrong, and shame is defined as a painful feeling of guilt for improper behavior.

We are all familiar with these terms and how they relate to life. We are all human and we sin. Sin is accompanied by guilt and followed by guilt feelings. We feel shame as we realize we have grieved our Heavenly Father, and as we wonder what others will think of us if they find out what we have done.

Guilt and shame will paralyze a Christian. Guilt cuts off the believer's motivation for serving the Lord. When guilt and shame take over, the flow of love is blocked from the heart. To serve as an effective witness, we must have a clear conscience before God.

How does one deal with guilt and shame? How does God deal with guilt and shame? In Old Testament times, you would have had to take an animal--with no defects--to the temple to be offered as atonement for your sins. You would have had to lay your hand on the head of the animal as it was slain by the priest, symbolically transferring your sins to the animal. The animal's blood would have been sprinkled on the altar and the carcass burned. (Leviticus 1) This burnt offering would have covered your sins, but would not actually have forgiven your sins. It did not remove the guilt or guilt feelings.

No longer do we have to offer these cumbersome sacrifices. Jesus paid the ultimate sacrifice when He died on the cross for us. His blood has cleansed us from our sins and from the resulting guilt and shame. We are human and we still stumble into sin at times. We can, however, be forgiven and restored if we confess and forsake our sin. I John 1:9 says: "If we confess our sins, he is faithful and just to forgive us our sins, and to cleanse us from all unrighteousness." He has set us free to serve Him with a clear conscience. What a privilege!

- Have I been released from the guilt and shame of all wrongdoing?
- What do I have on my conscience that is keeping me from serving the Lord effectively?
- *Lord, I believe Your blood is able to purge my conscience from guilt so that I can serve you joyfully.*

August

His Blood Provides

"I will put my laws into their hearts,
and in their minds will I write them."
- Hebrews 10:16

The blood of Jesus not only saves us from our sins, it also offers other provisions for our lives if we are only willing to accept them. His blood provides:

ATONEMENT: While the blood of Old Testament sacrifices covered sins, Jesus' blood removes sins. "Being justified freely by his grace through the redemption that is in Christ Jesus." (Romans 3:24)

REMISSION OF SINS: "And almost all things are by the law purged with blood; and without shedding of blood is no remission." (Hebrews 9:22)

REDEMPTION: "Neither by the blood of goats and calves, but by his own blood he entered in once into the holy place, having obtained eternal redemption for us." (Hebrews 9:12)

JUSTIFICATION: "Much more then, being now justified by his blood, we shall be saved from wrath through him." (Romans 5:9)

ACCESS TO THE THRONE ROOM OF GOD: "But now in Christ Jesus ye who sometimes were far off are made nigh by the blood of Christ. For through him we both have access by one Spirit unto the Father." (Ephesians 2:13,18)

A PURE CONSCIENCE: "How much more shall the blood of Christ...purge your conscience from dead works to serve the living God." (Hebrews 9:14)

CLEANSING: "And the blood of Jesus Christ his Son cleanseth us from all sin." (I John 1:7)

SANCTIFICATION: "By the which will we are sanctified through the offering of the body of Jesus Christ once for all." (Hebrews 10:10)

A NEW COVENANT: "This is the covenant that I will make with them after those days, saith the Lord, I will put my laws into their hearts, and in their minds will I write them; and their sins and iniquities will I remember no more." (Hebrews 10:16, 17)

Don't miss out on these life-giving provisions that Jesus provides through His blood!

- Do I truly accept these wonderful provisions of Jesus?
- How can I live that would more clearly show my thankfulness for these gifts?
- *Thank You, Jesus for the wonderful gifts You have given us through the shedding of Your blood.*

A New Life Transplant

"But this man...
offered one sacrifice for sins forever."
- Hebrews 10:12

Our good friend, Wilbur, has had a kidney transplant. Before that time, however, his health had deteriorated to the point of needing kidney dialysis. For six months, he went to the Dialysis Center three days a week to be hooked up to the artificial kidney for a minimum of five hours each time. As he watched his blood circulate through the tubes he marveled at the life and warmth that is in the blood. The machine did its work, removing the poisons from Wilbur's body, and he would leave the Center feeling well. He knew, however, that in two days he would be back, no longer feeling so well. He was in need of a transplant.

The Israelites needed a transplant, too. They had to make frequent trips to the temple, taking their animals to be offered up in their stead. They could go home, knowing their sins were covered by the blood of their sacrifice for now, but that they would soon be back to repeat the process.

These procedures kept folks going. Without them, death--either physical or spiritual--was likely to occur. These procedures were reminders. As Wilbur was reminded of his physical condition each time he entered the Dialysis Center, so were the Israelites reminded of their sinfulness each time they offered a sacrifice for sin. These procedures required a substantial payment. For Wilbur, it was a cost of $1,800 per treatment. For the Israelites, it was an animal without blemish, which was expensive to purchase or was a costly sacrifice from their own flock.

Someone willingly "paid the price," donating his own kidney to Wilbur, who no longer needs to have dialysis and is now experiencing a new life of physical health and freedom. Jesus has willingly paid the price of His own life, so that we no longer have to go to the temple with our sacrifices. We can enjoy a new life of spiritual health and freedom by accepting the "transplant" of His perfect sacrifice.

- Have I accepted that "new life transplant" that Jesus died to give me?
- Am I willing to give my life in service to the One who gave me this transplant?
- *Thank You, Lord, for being willing to go to the cross to give me that perfect transplant.*

Crossing The Jordan

"Faithful is He that calleth you,
who also will do it."
- I Thessalonians 5:24

When it was time for the children of Israel to cross the Jordan River into the Promised Land, God instructed the priests to go first, carrying the Ark of the Covenant. Now, this was no small matter. The river was at flood stage, and it must have taken a lot of courage for the priests to just walk right up to the edge and put their feet into the deep surging waters as they were told to do. Can you picture the people holding their breath in suspense, waiting to see what would happen? Bravely, the priests touched the water with their feet, and no water replaced that which flowed away down the river. The river bottom had become a road!

What if the priests had not been willing to obey the instructions they had received? They could have said, "Walk across the river? You can't be serious. It's flooded!" That would certainly have been a natural response. But think of the blessings they would have missed, and denied future generations, if they had refused to follow God's instructions.

How does this apply to us Christian women? When God asks us to treat others as we would want to be treated, do we obediently try our best to do that? If someone is rude to me, do I treat her kindly in return? If someone steals something from me, will I freely let her have it? What if someone would hit me? Would I literally turn the other cheek? Or would I be more likely to think, "You can't be serious, that's not necessary!" Does Jesus really mean it when He tells us that this is the way we should act? Did God really mean it when He told the Israelites to cross the swollen Jordan River?

Yes, He meant it then and He means it today. We can read this story and know that all we really need to do is "get to the edge, and put our feet into the water," and then let God do His part. We may still get hurt. We may still lose our possessions. There may be many blessings, though, that we can't see from this side of the river. How am I going to respond? God is still looking for followers willing to go to the edge and put their feet into the water.

- Do I truly believe that God means for me to treat everyone kindly, regardless of how they treat me?
- Are you and I willing to listen for God's voice, and then respond to His will?
- *Lord, show me where I'm failing, then give me the desire and the courage to make things right.*

Let Jesus Drive

"It is not in man that walketh to direct his steps."
- Jeremiah10:23

Larry and Becky, our minister friend and his wife, were on their way from Ohio to Michigan to help at a singles retreat, hosted by our congregation. Not too far down the road they approached a busy intersection where a semi began making a left turn directly across their path. Larry, seeing an interesting challenge, immediately began calculating in his mind just how much time he had to miss the truck without slowing down, based on the rate of speed of each vehicle. He figured he might have to swerve to the right a little to miss the back corner but they'd make it. Becky, however, would have done things a bit differently. "Watch out! That SEMI! SLOW DOWN!" she gasped. They made it safely past the semi, however, and traveled on.

After stopping for lunch, Becky took over the driving so Larry could rest and meditate on his messages for the weekend. "I think we'll take Route 30 over to 31 North for a change," she decided. Larry, however, would have done things a bit differently. He agreed verbally, but in his mind he was thinking, "Now if I were driving, we'd take Highway 69 to 96. We'd make better time that way--faster speed limits, fewer towns..."

As Christians, we truly desire to have Jesus in the driver's seat. How often, though, do our plans conflict? How often do we gasp and say, "Watch out, Lord! There's danger ahead!" (As though He couldn't see it.) We wish desperately that we were in a Driver's Training car with a brake on our side. (We'd likely stomp on it often and hard.) We want to reach over and grab the wheel to steer life our way. (Sometimes we actually do.) At other times, we feel like saying, "Move over, Lord, I'll take it from here." At the least, we'd certainly like to plan our own route! It would surely be easier, faster, and more scenic.

What happens inevitably, though, when we take the wheel? Does life go as smoothly as we thought it would? Do we know the route better than Jesus does? Too soon we find ourselves on a road full of potholes, spinning out of control, and heading for a crashing halt. We shouldn't just want to take Jesus with us wherever we go. We ask Him to drive. Our job is to sit in the passenger's seat and be quiet. It may be scary at times, but peaceful, as we allow Him to choose the route and get us there safely.

- Am I inclined to take the wheel of my life?
- Do I truly believe God is able to direct my life better than I am?
- *Lord, it's scary to let You have complete control, but I choose to let You plan my route and drive for this entire trip.*

My Grace Is Sufficient

"My grace is sufficient for thee:
for my strength is made perfect in weakness."
- II Corinthians 12:9

The Apostle Paul had a "thorn in the flesh" that was severe enough to hinder his ministry. We don't know what this problem was, only that he pleaded with God three times to heal him. God's answer to him was only that His grace was sufficient, and that He would sustain him through the tough times.

Rather than to sink into depression or just give up, Paul made a remarkable decision. He purposed in his heart to, "gladly...glory in his infirmities that the power of Christ may rest upon him." He went on preaching through his misery, commending folks for receiving him in spite of it. (Galatians 4:13, 14) He believed the power of Christ would fill him and be his strength. He actually took pleasure in these hindrances:

Infirmities: illness, frailness, disability, and disease. *Reproaches*: criticism, slander, gossip, insults, verbal abuse, scorn, blame. *Necessities*: needful burdens; responsibilities; drudgery. *Persecutions*: A persecutor will stalk a victim, harassing and intimidating, causing trouble in any way possible, causing unfair suffering and torment. *Distresses*: pressure, a difficult narrow way to walk through, danger, suffering, grief, or disaster.

Paul was able to rejoice in these trials because he knew and believed that Christ would be his strength. He knew that his weakness was no hindrance to God. He believed God was bigger than anything he would face. He lived the truth that his life and ministry were God's work and battle, not his. He knew God was watching over him in infinite love and compassion. He believed God had purposes for his life that were far bigger than what was happening to him or that he could understand. He chose to praise God for this humbling disability and for his ministry.

The grace of God available to Paul is just as available to each one of us today. Although it's not easy to glory in our trials, we can be thankful that God is waiting to show himself strong through our trials.

- Do you and I truly believe God wants to show Himself strong in our lives?
- What hindrances am I facing today for which I could accept His strength?
- *Lord, the hindrances are many and I am weak. Thank You for the strength and grace You have promised.*

A Mountaintop View

"My brethren, count it all joy when ye fall
into divers temptations; Knowing this,
that the trying of your faith worketh patience."
- James 1:1, 2

During a time when our family was "in the valley," a friend shared with us some encouraging thoughts about mountains. Climbing a mountain is an exhilarating experience. The air is clear and pure and when you reach the top you are breathless, not only from the climb but also from the beauty. The vista stretches before you, thrilling you with its splendor.

Our spiritual mountaintops are similar...so close to God, we have a vision of the future stretching before us, and our spirits soar. But have you ever examined the top of a high mountain? What is there? Rock! No trees... very little grass...almost nothing grows there. It is a wonderful place to visit, but it does not sustain abundant life.

The valley, on the other hand, is lush with growing vegetation. Though we cannot see as far there, growth is happening all around us.

Our spiritual valleys are somewhat the same. Though we may feel closed in, even discouraged, that is where we grow. We can learn to appreciate the valleys, too, for they are what make the mountaintops special. An occasional trip to the mountaintop renews our vision, clears our minds, and gives us energy to go on. But it's in the valleys that we grow. Jesus is the Lily of the Valley, not the mountaintop. He is on the mountaintop, too, but He knows we need something beautiful in the valley to cling to.

- Can I look at times in the valley as times for growth, rather than becoming downcast and bitter?
- In what ways should I change my thinking about going through times of trial?
- *Lord, help me to see those rough times as opportunities to grow in my relationship with You.*

Temptation

"Blessed is the man that endureth temptation...
he shall receive the crown of life."
- James 1:12

Temptation is Satan's way of seducing us to do wrong. Just as he tempted Eve in the Garden of Eden so long ago, he is still busy today, tempting God's people to sin. He uses many different ways to trip us up, hitting us most often where we're the most vulnerable.

Our senses are an effective avenue for temptation. We probably all have looked with longing at an advertisement that came in the mail. Or we are tempted to overeat, because the food all smells and tastes so delicious. We hear a friend talk about the benefits and wonders of a certain appliance and find ourselves wanting one too, even though we don't really need it. We're tempted to spend money on something we know will make us feel good, whether we can afford it or not.

There are many reasons we give in to temptation. It may be to satisfy a craving for a certain food or beverage, an attempt to escape the pain of loneliness or rejection, or to cover up feelings of bitterness or anger. Or perhaps we're just plain bored.

Previous yielding to a particular temptation will make that temptation even stronger the next time. A friend once told us that when Satan puts a tempting thought into your mind, you have four seconds to get rid of it. After that the temptation is harder to resist. With God's help we can resist these temptations, becoming stronger until finally we no longer have to struggle so hard against them. As a song writer expressed it, "Each victory will help us some other to win*." Endurance to the end will be rewarded with "the crown of life" when we meet Jesus face to face!

- Do I have a sincere desire to steadfastly resist all the temptations that Satan hurls at me?
- What areas of temptation do I specifically need to guard against?
- *Lord, I know temptations are inevitable, and I ask for Your strength to resist Satan today.*

**Horatio R. Palmer 1868*

Stewardship

"Even so minister the same one to another as good stewards of the manifold grace of God."
- I Peter 4:10

We can learn a lot about stewardship by studying the life of Joseph. A steward is put in charge of another's possessions or finances.

Joseph was made a steward over Potiphar's entire house. Genesis 39:6 says Potiphar didn't even know what he owned except for the food he ate! Joseph was a faithful steward, and "the Lord blessed the Egyptians' house for Joseph's sake." (Genesis 39:5) We are all to be God's stewards, also. We serve a rich God, and it is our responsibility to be faithful in our stewardship. (I Corinthians 4:2)

We are not required to be popular, successful, famous, or even accepted. But we are required to be faithful. We need to be good stewards of our *time*... not wasting it with activities that don't glorify God. Of our *money*...asking God's direction for our spending and giving. Of our *possessions*...taking good care of what we have and being willing to give as opportunities arise. Even our *relationships*...putting time and effort into them, building up and encouraging others on a regular basis. Faithful stewards have no need to worry when they are called to give account of their stewardship.

- Does my life reflect faithful stewardship of what God has blessed me with?
- In what ways could I be a better steward of these riches?
- *I thank You, Lord, for that which You have blessed me with, and I desire to be a good steward for You.*

Goose Bump Moments

*"In all thy ways acknowledge him,
and he shall direct thy paths."
- Proverbs 3:6*

Several years ago, against our better judgment, our strong-willed, teenage son became the owner of a brand new, high powered snowmobile. He was thrilled, of course, but we realized almost immediately that we had made a major mistake in allowing him to have it. Not long after, as I was focusing on our son during my prayer time, I keenly felt the Spirit's instruction to "get rid of that snowmobile." As my husband was feeling the same leading, we approached our son, fully expecting explosions of protest and possibly outright refusal. He listened to our explanations, thought a bit, and said "Well, if it was that clear, I'll get rid of it." A goose bump moment! He advertised the snowmobile and soon had it sold.

More recently, my single sister was feeling a bit adrift in life, wondering just where it was that God wanted her to serve Him. Her current job wasn't fully utilizing the talents and skills that God had blessed her with. After a time of desiring something different, she just prayed, "OK Lord, I don't know where you want me, but I'm yours to use wherever." Two days later, she received a totally unexpected phone call from a man who was recruiting help for a Christian curriculum publishing company. A goose bump moment! In an amazingly short time, she had moved across the country and was settling into her new home and job.

Being in tune to God's will and following His leading produces faith building "goose bump moments" as He works in our lives, sometimes in amazing ways. We can always trust Him to do what is best for us as we completely lean on Him.

- Do I recognize the "goose bump moments" in my life as indications of God's intervention and thank Him for them?
- Am I allowing God to direct the unknown aspects of my life?
- *I know You are working in my life in amazing ways, Lord. Help me to see them and be thankful.*

August 10 *Read: Psalm 46*

A Whole Heart Trust

"God is our refuge and strength,
a very present help in trouble."
- Psalm 46:1

"How much of your heart does Jesus have? How much of your heart and life are you willing to give Him?"

The minister was speaking one Sunday morning, and I was feeling pretty good about myself and my heart condition. After all, I don't have any trouble trusting God with my life.

"Do we tithe our hearts?" The minister went on. "Give ten percent to the Lord and keep the rest under our control? Of course not. How about a fifty-fifty deal with God. "You can control half of my life, but I feel more comfortable hanging on to the other half myself." Or maybe we do better than that. "Ninety percent, Lord, but there is this other ten percent..."

Uh-oh. My spirit began to squirm, and suddenly I wasn't quite so comfortable. My husband and I had been struggling with one of the children and knowing how to handle certain situations. I tended to worry, sometimes feeling helpless and despairing. I thought long and hard about how to fix things. I knew I wasn't fully trusting God to answer our prayers and fix things in His own time and way.

As I began to humbly, and sometimes painfully, relinquish that area to God, I not only saw Him working, but I also felt a peace that I had not felt before. Failing to allow Him to control every area of our hearts and lives is unintentionally inviting Satan to take over. At the least opportunity, he plots to bring about all kinds of trouble and heartache. We can let it go! God is fully trustworthy and waiting to display His power in our lives.

- Is there an area of my life in which I am not fully trusting God?
- Am I willing to completely give up my will and trust God to work in His own time and way?
- *Lord, it isn't always easy, but my desire is to trust You fully in all areas of my life.*

Hugs For The Heart

"Be kindly affectioned one to another with brotherly love;
in honor preferring one another."
- Romans 12:10

One of the things a home-schooling friend of mine really enjoys is the need to stay ahead of her students, which gives her a good excuse to study and learn. She'd really been enjoying the study of some math that she hadn't seen since high school. She discovered, however, that a study of conic sections was one thing she would be glad to finish. Somehow, though, as she worked through the section, her mind kept coming back to the ellipses and hyperbolas until finally there was a flash of light! It occurred to her that the only difference between the two is a simple sign. Two terms connected by a "+" sign makes an ellipse (a kind of oval or circle). The same two terms connected by a "-" sign makes a hyperbola, like this:)(. The positive connector makes a sort of embrace; the negative connector makes a symbol for rejection! Such a small difference that makes such a big difference.

We can clearly see the same connection in our lives. As we touch the lives of those around us; our families, neighbors, friends, and church families, our actions make a big difference. We can have positive connections, such as a simple smile or "hello," a handshake or a hug, a card or letter, a friendly conversation or a heart-to-heart talk over a cup of coffee. These types of connections create a circle of warm friendship or fellowship, a kind of "hug for the heart." We can also make negative connections. It hurts others when we ignore them or the painful circumstances they may be going through. Unkind thoughts or words about another will create walls of rejection in our hearts and possibly theirs, too. Outright rejection causes pain that ripples out into our families and church families. All kinds of problems stem from these negative connections, many of which could be avoided by just changing them to positive connections. Such a small difference can make such a big difference! It is our choice. Which will we choose?

- As I check my connections to the others in my life, are they positive or negative?
- What connections do I need to change today rather than leaving them for someone else to fix?
- *Lord, show me clearly the connections that I need to change, and give me the wisdom and courage to change them.*

August 12 *Read: Colossians 1*

Consider The Raindrop

"Which hath made us meet to be partakers of the inheritance of the saints in light."
- Colossians 1:12

Consider the raindrop. Each tiny raindrop acts as a prism, refracting and reflecting the rays of sunlight into the colors of the spectrum. As the sun's rays shine on many raindrops coming together, each a tiny prism, a rainbow is formed. To our naked eyes, this may look like a simple thing--beautiful--but simple. A colorful arch in the sky that lasts but a short time. A raindrop seems like a simple object, also. All tiny raindrops look alike to us. If we were to examine them more closely, however, we would find that each raindrop has its own unique size and shape. Each holds its own unique position in the sky. Each has its own distinct place to fill in the making of a lovely rainbow.

Consider mankind. Ideally, in God's plan, we are each to refract and reflect the light of the Son. A group of believers working and worshiping together in His Light can reflect a testimony to those looking on that is as beautiful as a rainbow. As God-created human beings, we all look basically alike. And, in our humanness, we may desire to be just like those around us, blending in to be accepted. But God has created each of us with our own unique nature and abilities. We each have our own position to fill in life. We each have our own God-given ways of reflecting the Light. While a raindrop plays its role without complaint, we tend to fuss and resist our position or responsibility in God's plan. We grieve the Father and deprive those we come into contact with when we fail to willingly fill our own unique role in the spectrum of God's plan.

A raindrop, when its work here is finished, ascends back into the heavens in a process called evaporation. My soul, when its work here on earth is finished, will ascend into heaven at God's call, to live eternally with Him in Paradise. A raindrop is capable of being a great blessing to the earth and to mankind, but it also has the capacity for serious destruction. My life, like the raindrop, has the potential to be a great blessing to God and to those around me. My careless words and actions, however, can have harmful results.

- Is my life reflecting the love of Jesus to those around me?
- In what ways could my actions be more of a blessing to those I interact with today?
- *Lord, make me as willing as the raindrop to simply perform the job You have for me, to Your glory.*

A Tale Of Courage

"Howbeit, as the disciples stood round about him, he rose up, and came into the city."
- Acts 14:20

I find the story of Paul's missionary journeys fascinating. Especially the time he and Barnabas were preaching in Lystra. The time some Jews came down from Antioch and Iconium and turned the people there against Paul. They ended up stoning him, dragging him out of the city, and leaving him in a heap, dead. Or so they thought. But Paul wasn't dead. With his disciples standing around, "He rose up and came into the city." Talk about courage and fortitude! I think I know what I would have done. I would have high-tailed it back to Jerusalem to lick my wounds and whimper to my friends about how I had been treated. I don't know if Paul was tempted to do that or not, but he didn't. He got up and went back into the city.

This lesson became very real to me during our years of homeschooling. I had students who needed extra help, and who at times were quite unmotivated. I also needed to care for our little ones and all the work that goes with a large family on a dairy farm. With pressures on every side, I would sometimes find myself in our bedroom, in tears, crying out to God for strength. He would gently remind me of Paul and strengthen me to get up and go back into the classroom.

When the pressures of life threaten to overwhelm you, ask God to give you the courage of Paul. God is faithful to give us the strength we need to "get up and go back into the city."

- Am I facing situations today that could use some extra courage?
- Do I believe God can give me the strength and courage of Paul in any situation?
- *Lord, remind me in times of need that You will give me the resources I need to go on.*

Read: Psalm 8

Hands

"Whatsoever thy hand findeth to do,
do it with thy might."
- Ecclesiastes 9:10

When was the last time you thought about your hands? Really thought about the wonderful way they are made and thanked God for them? Each of your hands is made up of 27 bones. Each hand has two sets of muscles and two sets of tendons. A normal, healthy hand has an amazing range of motion, allowing us to do an incredible variety of tasks with it. We can get quite weary of performing all the tasks we have to do with our hands, some of them day after day after day, but what would life be like without them?

How would you feel if you could not make your own bed in the morning? Could not brush your own teeth or turn the pages in your Bible? If you could not set the table or fry the eggs for breakfast? If you could not dress your children or pick up a fork to feed yourself? What if you were unable to write out a check, drive the car, or open a letter from a friend? What if you could not wash the dishes, sweep the floor, or mend the clothes? What would you be missing if you were unable to pick up your baby when she's crying, take your toddler's hand for a walk, pat your teenager on the back for a job well done, or massage your weary husband's shoulders? What if??

As you go about your duties today, think about your hands. Consider them an extension of Jesus' hands and use them for His glory. Think about how beautifully they are fashioned and thank Him for them. "I will praise Him for I am fearfully and wonderfully made!" (Psalm 139:14)

- Do I fully appreciate the way God has made my hands and do I use them for His glory?
- In what ways could I better glorify God with my hands?
- *Lord, I thank You for hands and the ability to use them. Show me how to serve You better in the use of my hands.*

Worship

*"God is a Spirit: and they that worship
Him must worship Him in spirit and in truth."
- John 4:24*

Worship is essential to the spiritual life of a Christian. But how can we be qualified to worship the Lord in holiness? First of all, we need to have a desire to worship. Worship services must not become a mundane habit, but a time of refreshment that we look forward to with anticipation. We also need to have a heart of confession, freely confessing our failures to God, allowing Him to cleanse our hearts of ugly weeds, making room for good seed to take root and grow. We can ask Him to show us all He wants us to see. And we need to put aside the cares of the past. How was your week? Can you put aside the worries about the child who is failing in school work, or the concerns for a daughter who is rebelling against your authority? How about the bills that were put back into the file marked "unpaid" because the paycheck didn't cover them? Can you rise above the exhaustion that comes with a newborn or an aging parent keeping you up at night? Maybe you have continuous pain from a physical infirmity.

Satan would be delighted to keep you focused on the distresses, calamities, or just plain busyness of the past week; or the worries of next week. Don't let him rob you of the riches God has for you in the blessing of worship.

- How can I prepare my heart to worship the Lord in holiness?
- What circumstances are keeping me from the joy of worship?
- *Lord, give me a deep desire to worship You in the beauty of holiness.*

 Read: Luke 11:1-13

Lord, I Need Patience... Quick!

"And I say unto you,
Ask, and it shall be given you."
- Luke 11:9

It was Friday. The day had only begun and I was already tired. Company was coming the next evening, and I needed to be gone for a part of each day. Everywhere I looked there was work waiting; cooking...cleaning...laundry...and children to tend. It felt impossible. The phone rang and it was a close friend, so I shared with her how I was feeling. She promised to pray for some extra energy for me, and I went back to fixing breakfast, grateful for her caring spirit.

Soon the phone rang again and I went to answer it, leaving my almost-two-year-old sitting on the counter. (Mistake #1) When I returned several minutes later, she had broken an egg and smeared it all over her legs. Her hands, her dress, and the counter were a mess. Quite aggravated, I jerked her off the counter (mistake #2), and knocked a bowl of grapes onto the floor, sending them rolling everywhere. Squishing grapes underfoot all the way to the laundry room sink, I wailed, "Oh God, we prayed for energy but I forgot the patience! I need some...quick!"

Later that evening, as I surveyed the clean house, the prepared food, and the piles of folded laundry, I realized that our prayers had been answered. God had supplied energy through a good nap, and patience through showing me the humor in the morning's messy mishap. Another reminder that He is always available. He doesn't sleep or go on vacation. When we call on Him, He hears and supplies just what we need, even when we need it...quick!

- Has it become natural for me to share my daily stresses and frustrations with God?
- Do I remember that God cares about the small things of daily life, and wants to help me through?
- *Lord, remind me when I'm struggling that You are present and ready to supply what I need.*

The Eye Of The Hurricane

"For thou hast been a strength to the poor…
a refuge from the storm."
- Isaiah 25:4

During the time our son was visiting friends in Florida, two hurricanes came blowing through. Folks all around prepared for the approaching storms. Windows were boarded up, extra food and water were purchased and stored. Traffic heading north clogged the main highways as many people headed for safer areas. And they had good reason to take precautions. Hurricanes are powerful, slow-moving storms that can be many miles wide with very strong winds and flooding rains.

After the hurricanes, our friends and son spent several days helping clean up the devastation in a town several miles east of them. He called home at one point and said, "Mom, this is terrible. It looks like a bomb was dropped here." (Months later, the destruction was still evident along the gulf shores.)

There is a place in these violent storms, however, that is calm and peaceful. The very center, called "the eye of the hurricane," is a good place to be during the storm. With vicious winds whirling around in a circle, one doesn't need to stray far from the center to feel the turmoil.

Sometimes life can seem like a hurricane. With the "winds of adversity" whirling all around you, the safest place to be is in the center of God's will. Straying in any direction will soon disturb the peace in your heart and destroy the "calm in the storm." Ask God to reveal His perfect will for you. Read His Word and spend time in prayer. When the "winds get wild," threatening to destroy the very foundations of your life, stay in the "eye of the hurricane" to experience the peace that only Jesus can give.

- Is a storm raging in my life today?
- Am I able to abide safely in the "eye," the center, of God's will for me?
- *Lord, I thank You for providing a safe refuge. Help me to stay in that refuge.*

Read: Psalms 119:65-80

Thorns In My Bed

"It is good for me that I have been afflicted; that I might learn thy statutes."
- Psalm 119:71

The clerk behind the desk at a motel will often ask you, as you are checking in, if you would like a wake-up call in the morning. If you say you would, she will program your room number and the time you want the call into the main telephone. At just the right time the next morning, the phone in your room will ring (and keep ringing) until you wake up and "answer" by lifting up the receiver.

God has a wake-up service too, and it's not always as "pleasant" as a ringing telephone. Sometimes it takes a lot more than an annoying phone call to wake us out of spiritual sleep. And so He has a "thorns in your bed" system that, while uncomfortable and even quite painful, can be an effective wake-up call.

While most wake-up calls in a motel are the same, God's wake-up calls are as unique as the people He created. A friend of mine is facing a move in the near future and she doesn't know where their family of eight is going to go. Another friend has no working vehicle right now that's large enough for all nine of them to go anywhere together. Still another's husband has been out of work for an extended time, causing severe financial struggles. Getting our new business up and going is an exercise in faith such as we've never experienced before, at times becoming a crushing load. A sick child or parent...a difficult co-worker...broken relationships...loneliness...pain of any kind...unnoticed or unappreciated efforts. The list of "thorns" is endless, but they can all serve the same purpose--to wake us up from spiritual slumber.

When you respond to your motel room wake-up call by answering your phone, no one answers. The automated call was intended only to waken you, and then you are on your own. When God sends you a wake-up call, however, you are not on your own. He is always there to help you out of your "thorny bed," to soothe the wounds, and to lead you back to a productive life. We just need to recognize those "thorns" as a wake-up call, quit tossing and turning on them, and allow Him to assist us with the Light of His Word, the companionship of the Holy Spirit, and the soothing oil of His love.

- What "thorns" do I have in my "bed" right now?
- Do I recognize them as a wake-up call, and am I willing to wake up and trust God to restore me to spiritual vitality?
- *Lord, it can be much easier to stay asleep, but I long to be out of this thorny bed and in the comfort of Your will.*

A Dry, Thirsty Land

*"I stretch forth my hands unto thee;
my soul thirsteth after thee, as a thirsty land."
- Psalm 143:6*

There's probably no better example of a dry, thirsty land than the "dust bowl states" in the 1930s. Farmers in that area had plowed the grasslands deeply and planted it to wheat. During the years of plentiful rain, the land produced bountifully. But the early 1930s brought droughts that caused the land to become unproductive. As the farmers continued to plow and plant, the ground cover that held the soil in place was destroyed. The winds that swept over the plains whipped up towering clouds of dirt, called black blizzards, that rolled across the land, darkening the skies and leaving a thick layer of dirt everywhere. At times it drifted like snow, burying farm equipment and small buildings.

Imagine being a housekeeper at that time! When you saw a dust storm approaching, you would all run to the house and frantically stuff wet rags around the doors and windows, trying to keep out as much of the dirt as possible. Then you would tie cloths around your nose and mouth to keep from breathing in any more dust than you'd have to. When the storm had passed, you would open the doors and windows and help shovel and sweep the dirt out of the house and off the porch. Then you'd wearily clean house--again; anticipating a meal of gritty food and another long, exhausting laundry day. And, with the lack of water, you wouldn't just have everyone take a shower!

In Psalm 143, David's life was a dry, thirsty land. He was being pursued relentlessly and forced to run for his life. Caught in a whirlwind of depression and paralyzing fear, he was desperate before the Lord. His soul longed for God as the parched ground of the dust bowl longed for the rain. He was begging for mercy.

As Christians, we typically do more talking about our struggles than we do praying about them. We want a closer walk with the Lord, but we're too busy to talk with Him. Our lives become a dust bowl because we haven't properly prepared the soil. The winds of adversity blow across our days darkening our skies. We struggle to keep out the "dirt" and wearily clean up the mess after the storm. Then we live in dread of the next round.

It doesn't have to be this way! Prayer is the rain that soaks into our parched hearts as we ask God for deliverance and guidance. Unlike rain in the dust bowl, God's mercy is available to us for the asking. We don't have to wait around, hoping for a few drops to fall on us. When we come to Him in fervent prayer, He will hear and answer.

- Is my life a dust bowl longing for the rain of God's mercy?
- How much time am I spending in His presence, praying and listening?
- *Lord, give me the strength to spend time each day with You, soaking up the living moisture of Your mercy and truth.*

 Read: II Timothy 2:1-13

Walking The Plank

*"Thou therefore endure hardness,
as a good soldier of Jesus Christ."
- II Timothy 2:3*

She almost missed it. Some friends were camping on a lake in Michigan's Upper Peninsula, and had invited her to spend some time there with them. Now she had an opportunity to view the night-time sky through a telescope. While that sounded fascinating, she wasn't so sure about what she had to go through to get to the telescope. It was cold and very dark, and the flashlight she had really wasn't bright enough for her to be comfortable walking the uneven ground. Then she had to "walk the plank" to get to the telescope which was on a pontoon boat at the end of a narrow pier. Not wanting to miss this opportunity though, she breathed a prayer for courage and went. The view through the telescope was glorious! Stars are the most visible on a very dark night, and the colder it is, the clearer the air seems to be. Viewing God's beautiful handiwork through an amazing man-made instrument, she knew that any discomfort she had endured getting there was worth it.

Do we sometimes almost miss an opportunity to see the glory of the Lord? How much discomfort are we willing to endure in His service? There are times God has asked me to do something I really didn't want to do. I knew the end result would be good, possibly even "glorious," but I also knew, at least partly, what it was going to involve getting to that end result. Fear or reluctance, however, doesn't alter God's call into service for Him. He will provide the courage and the resources we need to stumble through the cold dark night and walk the plank. Then, when we have willingly completed this service for Him, we will clearly see His glory shining, whether it is in the form of a beautiful new friendship, a closer relationship with Him, or even some material possession with which He has blessed us. Next time God calls you to do something for Him, go! Not just for the blessing at the end, but because He has called, and you know that prompt obedience to the Lord is the only right response.

- Do I see these opportunities as being worth the discomfort they may cause me?
- Am I willing to confess my lack of courage when God calls me to a task requiring it?
- *Lord, show me Your way clearly, so that I don't miss any opportunities to glorify You.*

Inconvenienced Again

"And we know that all things work together
for good to them that love God."
- Romans 8:28

Perry and Susan, friends of ours from Florida, were on a much anticipated trip to Alaska. Flying from Sarasota, they arrived at the Atlanta airport only to discover that their flight to Utah had been delayed 24 hours.

Now, this just can't be, Perry thought. I have places to go and people to see! Walking up to the ticket counter, he explained to the clerk that this arrangement really wasn't workable, as they needed to meet some folks at a certain time in Alaska. The clerk helpfully found them another flight, through Seattle, and they were soon on their way again.

At this point Perry was not really interested in reaching out to other people and he was hoping for a nice quiet flight with just his wife as company. But they were joined by a Muslim man, Tahir (Ta-heer), who soon started a conversation. For the next 3 ½ hours they visited about Jesus and who He was to each of them. Tahir shared that to him, Jesus was the Messiah, (in Muslim the "Mu-SEE-ah") meaning "the cure of all ills." Perry was quite surprised at that explanation and immediately used the opportunity to connect it with Jesus curing our worst ill, our sin and separation from Him. He spoke quite frankly and earnestly, not knowing just how this new acquaintance would respond. But Tahir was very open to consider new truths, and he responded with questions and thoughts of his own. When they parted in Seattle, Tahir gave Perry a warm handshake and a smile saying, "You are my friend. I'm glad to listen to you."

Although Tahir didn't make any commitments during their conversation on the plane, Perry knew the seed had been planted. He may never know what becomes of Tahir, but He does know that God can take a tiny seed of belief, water it with His wisdom and grace, and make it grow into a mighty, working faith in Him.

Perry and Susan arrived at their destination later than planned but still with plenty of time before their scheduled meeting. They marveled, once again, how our inconveniences can be God's opportunities, and how He works everything out for His glory. Perry prays often for Tahir, that he will open his heart to God's love and be saved.

We need to pray that God will open our eyes and hearts to times like these, also, and give us the courage to speak out for Him. It may be as simple as a smile for an elderly person in the grocery store, or it could be a chance to actually share the love of Jesus with a stranger. As we keep our hearts open, we may be amazed at how God uses our simple efforts to draw others to Himself.

- Is my heart open to share Jesus with others?
- How can I be more alert to opportunities God wants to give me?
- *Lord, this can be a scary thing, but keep my heart open and brave for You!*

 Read: Titus 2:3-5

Being A "Titus 2" Woman, Part I

"That they may teach
the young women."
- Titus 2:4

Recently, we attended a wedding out of state and stayed overnight with a young church family whom we had never met. We enjoyed our visit, getting to know them and their five young children. Before we left for home the next day, I was visiting with our hostess and she hesitantly (but bravely) asked me a personal question about family planning, a sensitive subject she had been struggling with. As I began answering (a bit hesitantly also, I admit), she sensed that she had found a safe friend, one who understood what she was going through. This young mother, who barely even knew me, poured out her heart, sharing her difficulties and pleading for help to sort through them.

What followed was a heart-to-heart conversation that I never dreamed I would be having with this young woman. As I had observed the family, it looked to me as though she had it all together. She is a beautiful young woman with a lovely home; polite, well-behaved children, a kind, helpful husband; and a sweet serving spirit. But, underneath it all, she was struggling. She needed to talk with someone who would understand. I would not have known that if she had not had the courage to share her need, trusting me with her thoughts and feelings. And, I cringe to think of her pain had I crushed her spirit by rejecting her concerns or making light of her burdens.

Now, I don't consider myself old, but I am a good bit older than she is—with seven children—and many more years of experience. As we talked about our time of sharing then, and in a later phone call, we realized that God had clearly led us to each other at that time. She was surprised to learn that our conversation had blessed me too. You see, this is a two-way street. God instructs the older, more experienced women to willingly teach and encourage the younger women. The younger women, in order to learn from their older friends, must be willing to observe, ask, and listen. This can be scary on both sides! But if we are willing to follow God's leading and to be open and honest, the rewards, as my friend and I discovered, are well worth it. This type of sharing can forge a lifelong bond of friendship that is a rich blessing to both women. Sometimes even a one-time encounter becomes a sweet lingering memory. Ask God to make you a "Titus 2" woman and to make you sensitive to His leading whether He is asking you to teach or to be teachable.

- Is there someone whom God is leading me to minister to, or to trust as a mentor?
- Am I willing to be that mentor, or to trust her with my heart?
- *Lord, this is not an easy thing you ask of us. Make me sensitive to Your leading in this area of my life.*

Being A "Titus 2" Woman, Part II

"That the word of God
be not blasphemed."
- Titus 2:5

In order to fulfill God's command in this passage, as older women, our lives must represent the virtues we are trying to teach and encourage. Now, this does not mean that we have to be perfect! It means we are committed to a life that influences younger believers to live in a way that honors Him. Our conduct should be reverent, rather than giddy and frivolous. Never should we engage in malicious gossip. Nor should we be addicted to strong drink or other beverages, food, or even hobbies. Rather, we are to be teachers of good things---things that please God.

Years of experience and study of God's Word make older women an important source of counsel and encouragement as younger women learn what it really means to be sober, to love their husbands, and to care for their children. This is unconditional love, not based on how worthy your family is. They fail, too. This love is shown by a true respect for your husband's headship, and by being supportive when things aren't going well for him. Being content with his income and consulting him before making major decisions honors his position as your leader. As wives, we must confess promptly, forgive freely, and accept his weaknesses, but focus on his strengths. We must be open with communication and never, ever, criticize (or ridicule, rudely interrupt, or correct) our husband in the presence of others. We love our children by spending time with them, teaching them the things of God, and praying with them. Disciplining fairly and firmly will help mold them into service for the Lord, rather than for the world.

Being discreet means to have a sense of what is appropriate for a Christian woman, avoiding extremes and using good judgment. A chaste woman is faithful to her husband, keeping herself from impure thoughts and actions. Keeping a godly home is the Christian woman's responsibility, a divine service to fulfill for God's glory. Through the example of older godly women, we can learn to be "good," living for others by being gracious, generous, and hospitable rather than self-centered and possessive. We can learn to be obedient to our husbands, acknowledging and encouraging their headship and supporting their decisions.

The purpose of living a holy life is to keep God's Word from being dishonored. This passage can be a bit overwhelming but, with God's help, we can commit ourselves to learning, living, and teaching the ways of a Titus Two Woman. Don't let fear or discouragement keep you from experiencing the blessings God has for you!

- What areas of my life need improvement in this subject of holy living?
- Am I willing to commit to learning, living, and teaching the ways of a "Titus Two Woman?"
- *Lord, help me fulfill Your will for my life, so that Your Word be not dishonored.*

Seven Keys To Victorious Living:
1. Expanding My Horizons

"Looking unto Jesus the author and finisher of our faith."
- Hebrews 12:2

As believers, we all want to live in victory. As humans, we know there will be bumps in the road, discouragements to trip us up, and trials that threaten to knock us flat. But we can emerge from these storms triumphantly. There are many keys to living a victorious life.

One key is to expand your horizons. Look past the problems of today, tomorrow, or next week. Look past the fussing children, past the piles of laundry and dirty dishes, past the bulging "bills to be paid" file, and past the unresolved issue with your husband, child, or friend. Look past the perplexing church problems, the neighbors who seem to think it's their job to make your life difficult, and the teenager who is breaking your heart with words and actions so contrary to what you've tried to teach him. Look past the child who can't seem to learn no matter how much time you spend teaching her, the child who just doesn't respond to discipline, or past the pain of childlessness.

Look even further...past where you are in life today. Very possibly there is some way in which you are not where you would like to be. Maybe it's where you live or work, your weight loss or habit breaking goals, relationships with your husband, children, or another person. Possibly you want to be more submissive or helpful as a wife or more supportive as a friend. Quite likely it's true in your spiritual walk. Most of us wish we were more mature spiritually, and we think we should be for as long as we have been serving the Lord.

But right now, look beyond all that and reach out for all God has for you! When you pause for a refreshing moment (sometimes you only have a moment) in the Word or in prayer, quiet your whirling mind and troubled heart to hear God's still, soft voice speaking to you words of encouragement and love. If He convicts you of some wrong to make right, accept His grace to mend matters with love and humility. When you're headed for church services on Sunday morning, take a few minutes to earnestly pray for God to open your heart and mind to what He has especially for you in today's message. Bask in the blessing of childish sweetness and a teenager's awkward hug. Release the cares of trials too big for you and watch the Lord work them out for you. Share your struggles with a trusted sister and feel them diminish as she listens and cares. Look beyond the cares and struggles of today and experience the "more" that God has for you!

- What struggles do I have that are keeping me from seeing the better things God has for me?
- What can I do today to help me comprehend what God wants to share with me?
- *Lord, there are so many obstacles in my way. Help me to see past them, allowing You to broaden my horizons.*

Seven Keys To Victorious Living: 2. Seeing Myself As God Sees Me

"Therefore if any (woman) be in Christ,
(she) is a new creature...all things are become new."
- II Corinthians 5:17

How do you see yourself as a woman? Let me guess. As women, we tend to view ourselves negatively. Women have been looked down upon ever since Eve was deceived in the Garden of Eden. Around the world women are degraded, scorned, and violated. Heartbreaking crimes extend even to little girls. While we personally may not face extreme persecution as women, we do have our own issues. We may be too bold...too loud...too shy... not pretty enough...or not smart enough. We see ourselves failing as wives and mothers or ineffective in our roles as single women, not good enough to attract a husband. We're too much or not enough, and we definitely need to lose weight! "Life would be so much easier if I were just a better person. Then I would deserve to be loved. All these bad things would not be happening if I were doing things right. It wouldn't be my fault and I wouldn't feel so guilty."

Why do we really feel this way? Is it because of our circumstances? Is it the result of experiences we had as little girls? Is it because we really aren't good enough? No. It's because Satan especially hates women. Think about it. Whom did Satan target in the Garden? He went after Eve. He knew that she was the "mother of all living." (Genesis 3:20) And that women forever would be the ones to give birth and nourish life. Women are a major threat and Satan's evil heart can't stand it. He attacks us in every way possible and many of us are living with the guilt that somehow it's our fault and we deserve the bad things that happen to us.

But how, exactly, does God see you? Does He see you as not being good enough? No! First of all, He created you in His own image. "So God created man in His own image... male and female created He them." (Genesis 1:27) He loves you unconditionally. "I have loved thee with an everlasting love." (Jeremiah 31:3) And just as we long to be loved and desired, God longs for us to love Him and to seek Him with our whole hearts. "And thou shalt love the Lord thy God with all thy heart..."(Mark 12:30) As we seek Him, accepting His love for us, and growing in His likeness, we become "new creatures" in Him. When God looks at us, He doesn't see someone who isn't good enough; He sees Himself! He sees all of our faults and blemishes to be sure, but He looks past all of that and sees us the way He made us, in His own image. You are His child and He loves you passionately.

- How do I personally see myself as a woman?
- Do I believe in my heart that God sees me as a child of His, made in His image, and precious to Him?
- *Lord, I thank You for Your love. Help me to accept that love and to live victoriously in You.*

August 26 *Read: Genesis 37:18-36; 39:7-23; 40:7-23; 45:1-11*

Seven Keys To Victorious Living: 3. Letting Go Of The Past Through Forgiveness

"Let us lay aside every weight, and the sin which doth so easily beset us."
- Hebrews 12:2

If ever there was a person who had a reason to hang on to the past and let it affect his life, it would be Joseph. He had been betrayed by his brothers, the ones who should have loved, encouraged, and supported him. Although he had done no wrong, Pharaoh had thrown him into the dungeon and left him to rot. Then, to add insult to injury, the butler, after he had been restored to his position, forgot all about Joseph, still in prison. We can imagine him struggling with bitterness and feelings of despair. He could have spent his time plotting revenge and comforting himself with thoughts of killing his brothers if he ever got out of prison. But he didn't! Think about it. If he had actually been bent on vengeance, would God have let him out of prison? Probably not, because he wouldn't just have been killing his brothers, he would have been killing the leaders of ten of the twelve tribes of Israel including Judah, from whose lineage Jesus came. Joseph would likely have languished in prison the rest of his life.

God was with Joseph through all of his trials, even in prison. (39:21-23) The prison keeper liked Joseph and gave him oversight of the prisoners. The prisoners must have trusted him as two of them came to him with dreams they could not interpret. And finally, the time came when God gave Joseph the meaning of Pharaoh's dream. From the depths of the dungeon, Joseph was promoted to second-in-command in Egypt. At this point he could have had his brothers killed or killed them himself. Because of his political position, Pharaoh would not have opposed him. But Joseph's heart was not set on revenge. Joseph forgave all his brothers and brought them and his father to Egypt to live in plenty during the rest of the famine. He even told his brothers not to feel badly about what they had done to him. He assured them that it was not they who had sent him to Egypt, but God who had sent him to save their lives during the famine.

What an amazing example of forgiveness! What a wonderful example of what God can, and will, do with a forgiving spirit. Satan hates us and delights in controlling our minds by using offenses from the past. The only way to live in victory is to let go of past offenses. Ask God to show you any areas of unforgiveness in your heart. Confess grudging as sin and trust God to cleanse and free you to live a life that is more victorious than you ever dreamed possible.

- Am I hanging on to any offenses, blaming others or refusing to let go of the pain?
- What would God have me do today to begin the healing process in my heart?
- *Lord, please help me release those who have wronged me and to forgive them even as God has forgiven me.*

Seven Keys To Victorious Living: 4. Reprogramming My Thinking

"Thou understandest my thought afar off."
- Psalm 139:2

Many of us are plagued with thoughts that are more negative than positive. Our feelings follow these thought patterns and we not only think negatively, we feel negative. We worry about circumstances beyond our control, feeling uneasy or afraid. We think about how worthless and inferior we are and feel rejection, self-pity, and hopelessness. Seeing no solutions to our many problems, we easily become discouraged and depressed. When we focus on the pain others have caused us, we flounder in anger and bitterness. Wishing for more material things rather than being thankful for what we have already produces covetousness, greed, and envy. A focus on past failures, forgiven or unconfesssed, triggers guilt and discouragement. A preoccupation with the faults of our spouse or with our perceived unmet needs can lead to immoral thinking and desires that violate God's will for our bodies. Centering my thoughts on my own rights and needs to the exclusion of others is selfish and just makes me unhappy. These negative thoughts can result from who we are or from the pain of rejection that we have felt from others. Thoughts lead to feelings and feelings lead to actions. We are what we think. "For as he thinketh in his heart, so is he." (Proverbs 23:7)

What an overwhelming subject. What an effective way for Satan to steal the victory from our lives. But Satan does not have to control our thoughts! God knows and understands everything that comes into our minds. "For I know the things that come into your mind, every one of them." (Ezekiel 11:5) God has provided a way to overcome these negative thought patterns. We can bring every negative thought (lies from Satan) into the light of Scripture and replace it with God's truth. Writing down negative thoughts with which we struggle, then asking God to show us His truth in Scripture, is a sound strategy for reprogramming our thinking. Meditating on God's truths enables us to recognize and reject Satan's lies. Satan desperately wants to defeat us by influencing our thoughts. But God will lead us to victory as we submit our thought life fully to Him. How comforting it is to know that God is aware of our struggles and is compassionate toward our feelings. Negative thought patterns are destructive and defeating, but we will experience freedom from them as we learn to yield every thought to the control of Jesus.

- Am I willing to put into practice now what Jesus wants me to do?
- Do I truly believe that Jesus is able to heal my pain and lead me to victory over wrong thoughts?
- *Lord, show me where I need to change my thought patterns and give me the strength and courage I'll need.*

Seven Keys To Victorious Living:
5. Speaking A Blessing To Myself And Others

"Out of same mouth proceedeth blessing and cursing."
- James 3:10

There are times when, as we gather at the supper table, the mood is anything but pleasant. With seven children, it's not unusual for one to be mad at another. If a couple are mad and someone else (could be me) is sulking about the unfairness of life, and someone else is demanding his own way right now, it's not exactly a storybook picture.

"OK" we say. "This is not a healthy way to eat a meal together. Before we pray, we're going to go around the table and each person is going to tell the one to his right something he appreciates about that person." Ooh. That brings on the painful grimaces, rolling eyes, and slouched bodies. But we wait and eventually, one by one, the compliments are given; to avoid forfeiting supper if nothing else. They have to be genuine and said nicely, and it's amazing the change that comes over the atmosphere in the room. By the time we are finished, the children are usually giggling instead of snarling. And of course, we all enjoy it when it's our turn to receive the compliment.

The Book of James says our tongues, (even if they're used in blessing most of the time), can in moments of unguarded anger, spew out a curse on another. We all know how true that is and how damaging it can be to relationships. We also have all experienced the pain of receiving that curse and how defeated it can make us feel. Being careful of what we say is not enough; what we don't say is just as important. An uncontrolled tongue is like a raging fire founded in hell. (v. 6) We can speak a blessing on someone whether he is in our presence or not. We can build up, encourage, comfort, reassure, and cheer others face to face, in prayer, or in conversation. Before we speak, we should ask ourselves, *"Is this true? Is it necessary? Is it kind?"* How would I feel if the one I am getting ready to talk about would hear what I want to say? (He just might hear it in a round-about way.)

You can speak a blessing to yourself by reading or reciting Scripture out loud that speaks to your soul, encouraging, reassuring, or cheering you on your way. You can also speak a blessing to yourself by blessing the Lord through song, worshipping and praising Him as you go about your work.

Our speech may puzzle us at times, pouring forth both blessing and cursing, as Satan wants us to destroy each other. But as the Spirit purifies our hearts, He gives us self control to enjoy the victory that comes with pure speech.

- Have I surrendered my heart and tongue to the control of the Holy Spirit?
- How can I remember that God asks me to limit my speaking to that which is beneficial to others' spiritual progress?
- *Lord, I fail so often in this, and I know how damaging evil speaking is. Help me to speak blessings to others today.*

Seven Keys To Victorious Living: 6. Being A Deed Sower

"For we are His workmanship, created in Christ Jesus unto good works." - Ephesians 2:10

Dorcas was a deed-sower who made a big impact on her community. She was well-known for making clothes for the poor. The widows she had sewn for were devastated when their much-loved friend died. They called for Peter to come quickly, and they stood around her bed weeping and showing him the garments she had made for them. Sadly, they left the room at Peter's request. They must have been overjoyed when Dorcas was restored to life and joined her Christian friends once more. Although Dorcas was not a preacher or teacher like Peter or Paul, God used her willing heart and her gift of kindness to bless the lives of others. He can use you, too, to make a difference for Him. Rather than wishing you had someone else's talents, make good use of the talents He has given you.

Paul makes it clear in Ephesians 2 that good works do not save us, but rather they are the result of salvation. There is nothing we can do to earn our way to heaven, but we are saved by God's grace through faith in Jesus. (v. 8) The result of our salvation is that we are His workmanship, masterpieces of God, created for good works. (v. 10) Salvation is not for our benefit only, but also so that we will serve Him and build up His church. When we understand the amazing grace behind God's mercy and the enormity of Jesus' work on the cross to save us, we want to do everything we can for Him. Our gratitude should know no bounds! We should have a deep desire to be a deed-sower for Him.

As Christian women, what kind of good deeds are we expected to do? Should we think ahead and plan out our days, sticking in a good deed here and there so that we are sure to fill our quota for the week? No. Paul says in verse 10 that God has already prepared these good works for us, and we just need to walk in His plan. He has a blueprint for our lives and invites us to seek His plan for us each day. This will bring about the greatest amount of glory to Him, blessing to others, and rewards for each of us.

How do we discover His "good deeds plan" for us? First of all, we must confess and forsake sin in our lives, as we become aware of it. Study God's Word, communicate with Him in prayer, and be completely and continually yielded to Him. As we take advantage of available service opportunities, God will bless our lives of deed-sowing.

- How do I cultivate a deed-sower mentality in my life?
- How could I make myself more aware of God's plan for my life today?
- *Lord, I want to bless you by being a deed-sower for You. Show me what You have for me to do today.*

August 30 *Read: Judges 6:11-23*

Seven Keys To Victorious Living: 7. Finding God's Strength Through My Weakness

"My grace is sufficient for thee:
for my strength is made perfect in weakness."
- II Corinthians 12:9

Gideon was clearly puzzled and reluctant in this conversation. This man, whom Gideon didn't recognize as an angel at first, was telling him that God was going to use him to deliver Israel from the Midianites. In the first place, Gideon was afraid of the Midianites! He was in the middle of threshing his grain in a winepress; a low spot that was hidden from the Midianites. (Normally, threshing was done on a hill so the wind could blow the chaff away.) He protested that his family was poor (weak), and he was the least (important) person in the family. He certainly didn't seem a likely candidate to defeat the invading army. But God assured him that He would be with him and that defeating the enemy would be like killing one man. We can read the rest of the story in chapter seven. With just three hundred men, burning torches in clay jars, and blowing trumpets, they surrounded the enemy campsite after night, scaring the Midianite army so badly that they began killing each other! They chased the survivors far away and killed their leaders. Gideon didn't have to do a thing but stand and watch.

We are a lot like Gideon in that we often make excuses when God asks us to do something that looks overwhelming. It could be a major change like serving Him on the mission field in a unfamiliar foreign country, or it could be something smaller like changing a bad habit into a good one. Either way it's a stretch, and we don't think we're up to it. We're afraid, we're weak, we're unimportant, and surely someone else could do a better job. Or, this habit that I'm stuck in really isn't that bad. Or whatever it is that He is asking us to do. But think about it this way. Every weakness that surfaces in us is an opportunity for the Lord's power to be revealed. And He promises that His grace will be enough for us. It's through our weaknesses that His strength is made perfect. Self-sufficiency can be our enemy when it makes us think we can do all things in our own strength. The only confidence we have in victory is through the power of God. He understands our fear and reluctance, but when we are willing to step out in faith, He will supply the courage to move ahead. The way He fights our battles may be just as amazing as the way he fought for Gideon. As we seek His guidance through prayer and Bible study, and as we obey when He calls, we can trust His strength to be made perfect in our weakness.

- What battle am I facing today?
- Do I truly believe God is able and willing, and actually wants to fight this battle for me?
- *Lord, I believe. I give this battle into your hands and I trust You to be my strength and my victory.*

Love Is...

"Therefore shall a man leave his father and his mother,
and shall cleave unto his wife."
- Genesis 2:24

As we read through chapter 8 of Solomon's Song, we can identify seven aspects of married love. Well worth thinking about, love is:

Planned by God (v. 5) God's plan of marriage began in the Garden of Eden. He also has a plan for each couple He brings together in marriage today.

Possessive (v. 6) As a wife, I need to respect the God-given jealousy of my husband as good and right, not doing anything that would make him uneasy.

Permanent (v. 6) Death is permanent, and God also meant for marriage to be "until death do us part."

Persevering (v. 7) Love isn't always easy! But the rewards are great if we choose to keep on loving, even when we don't feel like it.

Precious (v. 7) While love in any relationship is precious, there is nothing that compares to the love between a husband and wife in a godly marriage.

Priceless (v. 7) Love is a gift. It cannot be bought for any price.

Providential (vv. 8-14) God has instilled a natural desire in women to marry. He has a plan for each of us, whether or not it includes marriage. Running ahead of God's plan for us brings heartache rather than the blessings we receive by staying within the will of God.

- If I am single, do I trust God to bring about His best in my life?
- If I am married, do I recognize and respect God's plan for a healthy, happy marriage?
- *Lord, increase my desire to accept your plan for my life.*

September

A Clean Heart

"Create in me a clean heart, O God."
- Psalm 51:10

After God led me to pick up a book about prayer at the local Christian book store, I was ready to begin a fervent prayer quest to fix my husband. After all, it's a very important duty of a wife to pray for her husband and to keep him on the right path, isn't it? However, as I began to read the book, I realized that the very first area in which I was to pray for my husband was... his wife!

"Now just a minute," I thought, a bit offended. "I'm okay. It's my husband we need to fix!" But as I quieted myself before the Lord, He gently showed me that I did, indeed, have an area of my heart that needed to change. An area dark with unforgiveness that I was harboring toward my husband. It was humbling but cleansing to confess that area to God and to my husband and to receive ready forgiveness from both.

Our prayers for others are much more effective if our own hearts are clean. We can't expect our prayers to be effective if we tolerate sin our own lives. It's very important that we clean up our own hearts before we try to influence someone else's life through prayer.

- Is there an area of my heart that needs cleansing?
- Am I willing to confess, and allow Jesus to make me free from all sin?
- *Lord, show me where I need Your cleansing to make my prayers effective.*

Fuel For Your Fire

"Quench not the Spirit."
- I Thessalonians 5:19

We have a fire ring in our back yard that is circled with large stones. We enjoy sitting around a cozy fire, visiting or singing with friends. That fire, however, won't stay warm and cozy without fuel to burn. And it cannot supply that fuel itself. It takes a certain amount of skill to start a fire and keep it going. We begin with newspapers or other trash that burns easily. Slowly adding wood kindling, and maybe blowing on it now and then, we coax the flame to grow. When we are sure the fire is going to survive, we add larger pieces of wood, and later, as the fire gets low, someone will throw on another log or two. Watching the yellow and orange flames dance and swirl can be fascinating and relaxing as the sky darkens and life settles down for the night.

While paper and wood will keep a fire burning, it takes something entirely different to quench that fire when we are finished with it. We can douse it with water or smother it with sand. Either one will quickly and completely snuff out the flames that we worked so hard to get going.

The Holy Spirit came upon the apostles like tongues of fire and filled them. (Acts 2:3,4) In I Thessalonians 5:19, Paul tells us not to "Quench the Spirit." As believers, we are filled with this same Holy Spirit, and we are responsible for keeping it glowing. God has provided the fuel we need to keep the fire of the Spirit burning within us. We can start by reading His Word to learn more about this Spirit and get the flame ignited. Then we carefully add an attitude of prayer as we spend time with the Lord in our prayer closets and communicate with Him as we go about our daily work. Fellowship with other believers, sharing their testimonies of struggles and triumphs strengthens our confidence in the Spirit's power and faithfulness. If our fire is burning low, we can add a chunk or two of worship in song, lifting our hearts in praise and thanksgiving. If we take time to faithfully tend our fire, it will burn clear and bright within us!

Unfortunately, there are plenty of Spirit quenchers in life. Sin can quickly and completely snuff out the Spirit's fire in us. Satan desperately wants to quench that fire and he will try to do it in any way he can. Love of the world, close associations with ungodly people, the temptations of life, or simple neglect can extinguish our fire. Guard your fire closely and keep it fueled!

- Does God want me to relinquish anything to permit the Holy Spirit to burn more brightly within me?
- Which fuels do I need to replenish to keep my fire burning brightly?
- *Lord, I truly desire to have the Spirit's flame burning in my heart. Help me to keep it properly fueled and burning.*

The Bond of Brotherhood

"So we, being many, are one body in Christ,
and every one members one of another."
- Romans 12:5

A family we know had a friend who was involved in the war that was going on in Iraq. A deep bond developed between the young men who were there serving along with him. These men were far from home and their families. They didn't enjoy even some of the most basic comforts we take for granted every day. These men faced some miserable conditions, and they lived with the daily threat of injury or death. This friend discovered just how deep his relationship with his fellow marines had become when a buddy of his was killed. His deep grief gave him a new understanding of what brotherhood meant. These young men had trained together, eaten together, slept in the same tent in a foreign land, and, in a way, had become part of one another. The bond of brotherhood was deeply forged as these soldiers shared loneliness, discomfort, and adjusting to hostile, foreign surroundings.

As Christians, we are also members of a brotherhood, the Body of Christ. How well do we relate to that? Do we feel the bond of brotherhood and really worship and share together, or are we just in the same building worshiping in our own little world? How much do we know about what is actually going on in each others' lives? Do we know enough to be able to help and be helped, to share joys and sorrows, and to pray effectively for each other? Although our lives may not be as closely entwined as the lives of the marines in Iraq, we can be open with each other in sharing our struggles, joys, and sorrows. As Christian women, with feelings and emotions sometimes (or often!) running rampant, this "sisterhood" bond can be a wonderful encouragement and can give us strength to keep on in our roles of godly women. We can, in fact, become part of one another.

- Do I feel a true bond of "sisterhood" in my relationship with my sisters in Christ?
- How could I change to make this bond stronger?
- *Lord, show me just what it is that I could do to enjoy a deeper bond of fellowship with my fellow Christians.*

Be Strong And Courageous

"Be strong and of good courage...for the Lord thy God is with thee whithersoever thou goest."
- Joshua 1:9

At one-hundred-twenty years of age, Moses knew he was soon going to die. He called Joshua, and before all the people, Moses turned over his leadership position to Joshua. After encouraging the people to be strong and courageous, Moses also encouraged Joshua to "be strong and of a good courage." (Deuteronomy 31: 6, 7) Moses knew it was not going to be easy to conquer the land of Canaan that God had given the Israelites, but God would be with them.

The Lord then spoke to Moses and Joshua, revealing to them the coming disobedience of the Israelites. He encouraged Joshua to be strong and courageous (Deuteronomy 31:23), with the promise that He would be with him. We read in Joshua 1:5-9, that God again encouraged Joshua by promising to be with him, to safely guide him, and to be a sustaining power for him.

Later, as Joshua was preparing the people to enter Canaan, they assured him they would support his plan for conquering the land and they would obey him. They also encouraged him to be strong and of a good courage. (Joshua 1:18) Joshua received encouragement from Moses, from God, and from the people. He was facing a very difficult and challenging time, but he could go into it fully supported and encouraged.

As Christian women, we can certainly claim these promises for ourselves. God wants us to be strong and courageous, serving Him in whatever way he calls us. But what about our fathers, brothers, husbands, and sons? God wants them to be strong leaders, or to be growing into men who will be strong and courageous for Him. Encourage them! Let them know you are praying for them. Support them in word and action. If Joshua had been criticized and discouraged, he surely would not have had the courage to go up against all those enemies in Canaan. The men in our lives need our encouragement to reach the potential God is calling them to, also. Joshua reminded the people in his last message that God had been faithful to them. "Not one thing hath failed of all the good things which the Lord your God spake concerning you..." (Joshua 23:14) These promises are for us, too. Keep them close in your heart!

- In what areas do I need to ask God to supply me with the courage I need?
- How can I encourage the men in my life to be all they can be for the Lord?
- *Lord, as I face the difficult and challenging times in my life, I ask that You supply the courage I need.*

The Gift of Pain

*"And whether one member suffer,
all the members suffer with it."
- I Corinthians 12:26*

Pain is certainly something we all want to avoid, but Paul Brand, a distinguished doctor who started out to study leprosy, found that pain is one of the most valuable gifts we have from our Creator. Leprosy destroys nerves and the sensation of pain, with the result that lepers damage themselves without even knowing it. They can walk on an injured foot until the foot literally wears away! They get to the point where they really don't care. If they can't feel the body part, neither do they feel related to it or responsible for its well-being. He became aware of a child who felt no pain and would defiantly bite off part of her fingers simply to get her own way in one matter or another. She felt no connection to parts of her body that she could not feel, and she was too young to be concerned about a future with such deformities. If a person with leprosy was concerned about his feet, it was possible to buy special shoes that were designed to protect feet by distributing pressure in different ways. People with no feeling of pain in their hands could learn to pay close attention to the feeling of pressure or heat and avoid many injuries.

Dr. Brand relates this to our relationship with other members of Jesus' Body here on earth. If we do not feel one another's pain, we do not feel connected to one another. As we continue to interact with our church family, unaware of the pain in another's heart, we can unknowingly deepen their hurt or discouragement by careless words or actions. We need to become involved in each other's lives to the extent that we feel related--like a family; and therefore we feel a caring responsibility for each other's welfare. When one goes through a rough time, the rest of us should be there to help relieve the pressure and stress through understanding and support. By sharing our experiences, we can also learn from each other to recognize the pressure and heat that come from getting too close to Satan's fire and to flee from it. As we share and encourage, we become more adept at recognizing the signs of stress in the lives of our "family members." The whole family is blessed when we support and are supported as opportunities arise.

- Do I feel a family relationship to my fellow believers?
- How quickly do I recognize the pain in others' lives? Do I let them know I care?
- *Lord, give me sensitivity to others and the willingness to be a supportive sister.*

Read: Psalms 119: 1-16, 89-112

A Walk Through The Word

"Thy word is a lamp unto my feet,
and a light unto my path."
- Psalm 119:105

Several different approaches could be used in conducting a study of a woods or forest. You could fly over the woods in an airplane. Looking down from above, you would see the size and shape of the whole stand of trees. You could see thin spots and clearings, thick areas, and possibly damaged areas where disease or fire had swept through.

Another method of study might involve walking around the outside of the woods. It would be easier to see the height of the trees, the density of the forest floor, and even a few of the kinds of trees and plants along the outside edge. At that point we can feel a pull to "come inside the cool, quiet woods and rest awhile."

You could conduct a more thorough study by walking through the woods. In this way, you could examine the bark and leaves on the trees closely, and the flowers that grow in the peaceful shade. By keeping quiet, you could watch the birds, squirrels, and chipmunks come out to play. By looking carefully, you might find a variety of tiny insects. Even a small area of woods contains a wealth of information if you are right inside it, studying what you see.

Compare this to our study of the Bible. We can get a "fly-over view" of a Book of the Bible by reading through it and recording the high points in each chapter. We learn to know the writer of the book, and the reason he wrote it. We become acquainted with the people he is writing about, and we have a basic knowledge of the contents of the Book.

Getting a little closer, we can walk around the Book and get a glimpse of the problems and triumphs the writer is talking about. As we come a little closer to the lives of the people we are reading about, and the culture of the day, we begin to feel a pull to come inside the Living Word of God and learn of Jesus.

In a more intimate study, we spend more time in each chapter, studying, and praying that the Lord will show us what He has for us in this particular passage. Then as we learn from our studies, we work to apply that knowledge to our lives, in whatever way God leads us. Each method of study will bless us in our Christian growth. Don't neglect it!

- Am I spending time in God's Word each day?
- Which method of study helps me the most to learn about God and His will for me?
- *Lord, my desire is to know You and Your will for me. Help me to be disciplined in my Bible study.*

Sowing And Reaping

"For he that soweth to his flesh shall of the flesh reap corruption; but he that soweth to the Spirit shall of the Spirit reap life everlasting."
- Galatians 6:8

A well-kept garden is a place of beauty and a real satisfaction to the one who tends it. As we observe the straight, healthy rows of corn, beans, strawberries, and flowers, we don't even wonder what kind of seeds or plants were planted there. We would be mighty surprised if we planted peas in the soil and pumpkins came up!

It's a fact of life, both physically and spiritually, that we reap what we sow. If we spend time gossiping about people, we will likely find that we have few friends. We will probably hear our children criticizing others if they have heard us being critical. If we waste time in unnecessary activities, we will find ourselves feeling discouraged because we are behind in the work we should be doing. However, if we plant good, we will reap good. A healthy life style will result in a healthier body. Kind words and deeds will strengthen relationships and cause love to grow deeper. Diligent training and loving will produce well-adjusted children.

Tending a garden that is nonproductive due to drought, disease, or other misfortunes is disheartening. Likewise, it can be quite discouraging to see little or no results from your efforts to do good or to get no thanks for what you do. But Paul tells us in Galatians 6:9 that we should not be weary in well doing, for we will reap a harvest of blessings in due season, if we plant to please God.

- What seeds am I planting in the soil of my life that will last into eternity?
- Are there seeds I need to dig up and destroy before they sprout and grow?
- *Lord, help me to find my strength in you so that I don't become weary in well doing.*

The Hall of Faith

*"Now faith is the substance of things hoped for,
the evidence of things not seen."
- Hebrews 11:1*

Faith is more easily described than defined. It is the confidence and the certainty that God will keep His promises. It is the conviction that we will experience the blessings God has for us. It is holding on to His promises in spite of the impossibility of our situation.

As we read through this chapter, sometimes called "The Hall of Faith," we see that the people listed here were just ordinary individuals with a deep faith in God. However, if we look a little closer, we see that they had several things in common.

First of all, these people all knew that GOD IS. They didn't flounder in uncertainty wondering whether or not God existed. They knew with assurance that He IS. Believing in God's character, that He is who He says He is, is a key point of our faith.

Second, they knew that GOD IS FAITHFUL TO HIS WORD. When God makes promises, He does not forget or change His mind. He is faithful to fulfill His promises. These people did not receive all the promises themselves before they died, yet they believed. They never lost sight of heaven. It's easy to become impatient and wonder why our expectations are not met immediately. We feel defeated and want to quit. But we can take courage from these heroes of faith and keep our eyes on the goal!

Third, they were courageous, steadfast folks who PERSEVERED. You may have heard the story of the marathon runner who took a bad fall and came staggering across the finish line long after the other runners had come in. When asked why he didn't just quit when he was injured he said, "I didn't come here to start the race, I came to finish it!" That seems to have been the life-long outlook of the men and women in the Hall of Faith. They were just as human as we are and at times may have felt like giving up.

We exhibit true faith when we believe God will fulfill His promises, even in the face of impossible odds.

- What situation in my life looks impossible to me right now?
- Do I truly believe God will keep His promises to me?
- *Lord, my faith is weak at times. Help me remember these faithful people and take courage.*

The Many Facets of Faith

"But without faith it is impossible to please him."
- Hebrews 11:6

The heroes of faith in Hebrews 11 serve as role models for faithful followers today. We will consider various facets of faith portrayed in this chapter.

In Enoch's life we see *faith's walk*. His life was a simple but profound testimony in that "he pleased God." He was taken to heaven without dying.

We see *faith's work* in Noah's choosing to obey God's command to build the ark, even though it seemed foolish and he was mocked by his neighbors. His obedience saved his family.

Abraham took *faith's journey* when he left his home, not knowing where he was going. He knew the God who asked him to go would keep His promises.

Sara experienced *faith's fruitfulness* when she had a child after many years of barrenness. God had promised Abraham a son, and at first Sara doubted and laughed, as she was long past the age of child bearing. But afterward she believed and was rewarded with a baby.

Faith's loyalty is exhibited in the life of Moses as he "refused to be called the son of Pharaoh's daughter," even though he was raised in Pharaoh's household. By renouncing royalty, he was "choosing rather to suffer affliction with the people of God, than to enjoy the pleasures of sin for a season." He became a great leader of the Israelites, leading them out of slavery in Egypt toward the Promised Land.

Rahab was saved by *faith's deliverance* when she was rescued by the Israelites before they destroyed the city of Jericho. She repented of her immoral life and expressed her faith in God when she welcomed the Israelite spies sent in to investigate the city. She trusted God to spare her and her family, and became a part of the Israelite nation and an ancestor in the lineage of Jesus.

Through faith these people understood that God is and that He is faithful in keeping His promises. By faith they led lives of committed surrender to Him, enduring the hardships and enjoying the blessings that go with such a life of service. Is it possible to live the same kind of faithful life today? Absolutely.

- In what areas does my faith need to be strengthened?
- Do I believe it is possible to have this kind of faith today?
- *It is not enough to just know about this faith. Lord, help me to live it.*

God, Our Director

"Whom having not seen, ye love…ye see Him not, yet believing, ye rejoice with joy unspeakable."
- I Peter 1:8

A friend shared with me a testimony of something God had brought to her attention. She had always been intrigued with the saying "God is my Co-pilot." It brings to mind a picture of someone sitting next to us, ready to help if we need it. But God is so much more than that! He is the Director of our lives from before we were born to eternity. Unseen, too often unnoticed, quietly, but always with perfect love, He is directing our lives. Every second, every minute, 24/7, He is sitting there directing. Pushing this button, pulling that lever, using this foot pedal, touching that key, flipping this switch, on and on, every second of our lives!

Noah heard God, listened to His prompts, felt His nudges, and responded to His voice. Moses did too, as well as Paul…and John…and many others recorded in the Bible. At one point, Jesus' disciples saw Him go up to Heaven. They knew He was up there! Out of sight, maybe, but fully directing their lives. We don't have that particular visual reassurance, but the same Holy Spirit which He sent to the believers at that time also lives in us today. He nudges, prompts, and directs us. Everything that happens in our lives is directed or permitted by God, and He does it all with a pure love for us. In Him we live and move and have our being. (Acts 17:28) How do we respond to this love and direction? Do we even notice Him? We are His children and He loves us passionately. How could His directing of our lives possibly not be for our good? Once we know and truly believe this concept, it should become embedded in our hearts and applied daily to every detail of our lives. The more we seek His will and listen watchfully for His direction, the easier it is to recognize the leading of the Spirit. Then our hearts will overflow with love and praise for Him as He works out the multi-faceted details of our lives.

- In the midst of earthly troubles, do I remember that God is directing even this and that His ways are perfect?
- Do I stifle the gentle promptings of the Spirit or obey them with joy?
- *Lord, let me be awake, responsive, watching, for Your nudges and for your guidance.*

Read: Matthew 14:22-33 September 11

Why Do You Doubt?

"O thou of little faith,
wherefore didst thou doubt?"
- Matthew 14:31

Jesus had just performed the miracle of feeding the five thousand. He sent the crowd away and told His disciples to take the ship and go on to the other side of the sea. He then went up into a mountain to rest and pray. Sometime during the night, Jesus noticed that the disciples were having trouble. The wind had come up and was tossing the boat around. So Jesus went to them, walking on the water. It was dark, and when the men saw Him coming they were terrified, thinking it was a ghost! Hearing the familiar voice of their Master and Friend must have been quite comforting. Peter, in fact, was so relieved that he impulsively said, "Lord, if it be thou, bid me come unto thee on the water." And Jesus answered him, "Come."

Then Peter, in a tremendous act of faith, climbed over the side and down out of the boat and walked right across the water toward Jesus. He was doing just fine until he looked away from Jesus and considered what he was doing. When he focused on the big waves and the strong wind, he panicked. Beginning to sink, he cried out, "Lord save me!" And immediately Jesus reached out and caught him, saying, "O thou of little faith, wherefore didst thou doubt?"

How do you suppose Jesus said that? Was He disgusted with Peter? Did he speak in a scolding voice? I don't think so. I think He spoke reassuringly to restore Peter's faith.

We may think Peter was acting foolishly and should have had more faith, but how different are we? We certainly live through some storm-tossed times---whether it's a major trial or just the daily burdens that get us down. When Jesus seems far away, we focus on the wind and waves around us. Our faith falters and we begin to sink. Where are you right now? Are you in the boat without Jesus, riding out the storm? Are you walking on the water with your focus on Jesus? Or are you sinking? When you cry out to Jesus, he immediately reaches out to catch you, holding you above the waves and lovingly asking why you are doubting. Guiding you back into the safety of the "boat," the winds grow quiet and peace is restored to your soul. Don't let the storms of life sink you. Keep your focus on Jesus!

- Do I trust Him enough to follow Him, even out of the boat?
- Am I keeping my focus on Jesus, or am I looking around at the waves and starting to sink?
- *Lord, help me to keep my eyes on You and catch me when I begin to sink!*

Helping My Neighbor

"Greater love hath no man than this,
that a man lay down his life for his friends."
- John 15:13

Recently, a tsunami devastated coastal regions of many countries. Thousands of people were killed. Many others lost their homes, possessions, and loved ones. Villages were swept right off the earth by the enormous tidal waves. The incredible devastation was astounding. In the aftermath, disease and sickness were rampant as suffering people tried to rebuild their lives. Food and medical supplies were scarce, and water was contaminated.

At other times, we've read stories of devastating wars, fires, earthquakes, or epidemics; each taking an overwhelming toll on the population.

In each case, however, stories emerge of selfless individuals who put their lives on the line to help the victims of these catastrophes. One story tells about nuns from a mission deep in Zaire who risked their lives to help victims of a new disease with ghastly symptoms and a 90% death rate. Workers in medical labs went without sleep and regular mealtimes, disrupting their family lives to find out what kind of disease they were dealing with. They were willing to "lay down their lives for their friends."

Reading or hearing about these dedicated heroes can make us wonder about ourselves. Many of these people do not profess to be Christians, yet they are willing to make great personal sacrifices to help their fellow men. Am I, as a Christian woman, ready to go to the lengths they do to help my "neighbors?" When was the last time I skipped a meal or lost any sleep to spend time in prayer for someone I knew was struggling? We likely won't actually have to die for someone, but there are other ways of sacrificial giving. Just simply spending the time with a sister who needs a listening ear, or a day helping to clean a house for someone to move into can be a loving sacrifice of time and energy. While supporting and encouraging someone who is going through a stressful time can be emotionally draining, it can also be a real blessing to both of you. Financial sacrifice involves giving to those in need even when you are not sure how you are going to pay all the bills. God sees all and knows when our sacrifices are truly from the heart. He will richly bless those who willingly and sacrificially give from the storehouse of His provision.

- How willing am I to give when it requires personal sacrifice?
- Does God want me to express sacrificial love to someone today?
- *Lord, fill me with Your love and make me willing to "give until it hurts," however You direct me.*

Grapes

"I am the vine, ye are the branches: He that abideth in me, and I in him, the same bringeth forth much fruit: for without me ye can do nothing."
- John 15:5

There is an area of southern Michigan which has acres of vineyards. We enjoy driving through there in the fall. It's a feast for the senses to see the beautiful clusters of purple grapes hanging among the deep green leaves. And the sweet aroma of ripe grapes hangs in the air for all to enjoy.

If we were to stop and walk over for a closer inspection, we would find that the healthy grapes are being produced by a branch that is firmly attached to a vine. There may be places where the branch is damaged, not properly fastened to the vine. Any grapes growing on a damaged branch are shriveled, ugly, and sour. These grapes and their ailing branches will likely be cut off and destroyed by the keeper of the vineyard.

Jesus said He is the vine and we are the branches. Our lives should be firmly rooted in Him and producing good grapes. These are described in Galatians 5:22-23 as being the fruit of the Spirit. *Love, joy, peace, long suffering, gentleness, goodness, faith, meekness, and temperance...* If we are not firmly attached to the Vine, we may find our lives producing sour grapes instead. Shriveled fruits of hatred, bitterness, impatience, unkindness, envy, and other negative feelings not only rob us of our joy but also hinder our relationship with the Lord. As we stay connected to the True Vine by communicating with Him through Bible study and prayer, we can experience the true joy of producing good fruit.

- As I meditate on my daily life, do I see any sour grapes that need to be pruned out?
- Am I willing to submit to the process of removing the bad fruit?
- *Please prune the bad fruit out of my life, Lord. My heart desires to produce only fragrant fruit for You.*

September 14 *Read: John 15:1-16*

Connections

"As the branch cannot bear fruit of itself, except it abide in the vine; no more can ye, except ye abide in me."
- John 15:4

Jesus wants us to stay connected to Him, the True Vine. Living things of nature stay connected to their source of life in a variety of ways, some by attaching to a vine, some to a trunk, and some to roots in the ground.

We, too, can stay connected to our Source of Life in various ways.

PRAYER: Prayer is vital to a healthy connection. Thus we communicate our praise, thoughts, desires, and concerns to God. Even though He already knows all, He wants us to talk with Him. "Praying always with all prayer and supplication…" (Ephesians 6:18)

STUDY: God speaks clearly to us through His Word. To really know him and stay connected we must make Bible study part of our daily life. Second Timothy 2:15 tells us we should study to show ourselves approved unto God…"

FELLOWSHIP: We need the fellowship of other believers to help us stay focused, centered, and connected to the Vine. Hebrews 10:25 says we are not to forsake the assembling of ourselves together, but we are to admonish and encourage one another as we worship God collectively in Spirit and in truth… God can speak to us through our fellow-believers.

The fruit will grow, and we will experience life to its fullest as we stay properly connected to our Source of Life, the True Vine.

- Do I consider prayer, Bible study, and fellowship a vital part of my life?
- What could I do to strengthen these connections?
- *Lord, show me the ways in which I could strengthen the connections I have to You, the True Vine.*

Love Is Sweeter

"Lest any root of bitterness springing up trouble you."
- Hebrews 12:15

I was angry and hurt. My child had been wronged. Cruelly so. He was crushed, and I felt bitter toward all who were involved.

But as the days went on and my feelings subsided, God spoke to me. I could hang on to my feelings. Let them settle down into a dark corner of my heart. Life would go on, and I would hardly know they were there.

However, someone may later mention their names. Or perhaps those people would do something else I didn't like. Then those feelings would come alive and flare up, causing bitterness to well up. I may say unkind things that I would later regret. If I wished, I could choose that route.

OR...I could choose to forgive. I could confess those feelings as sin, allowing God to cleanse my heart and change those ugly feelings into love and compassion for those same people.

I chose to forgive. He cleansed my heart and filled me with His love and compassion.

A small root of bitterness can grow into a huge "tree" that casts a shadow on even our closest relationships. Allowing disappointments to grow into resentment, or holding grudges over things from the past, can result in all kinds of ugly sins---dissension, jealousy, immorality, and depression, to name a few.

God is able and ready to heal the hurt that causes bitterness to take root. And life is much sweeter with love in our hearts than with bitterness.

- Am I harboring negative feelings toward anyone?
- When I retain bitterness, am I influencing my children to do likewise?
- *Lord, I know bitterness cripples my testimony for You. Forgive me, and help me to keep it out of my heart.*

God, Our Power Source

"But we have this treasure...that the excellency of the power may be of God and not of us."
- II Corinthians 4:7

What is this treasure Paul is talking about in verse seven? In verse six he refers to creation when God said, "Let there be light" and there was light. (Genesis 1:3) Today, however, He doesn't command light to shine out of the hearts of His believers. Instead, He Himself shines in our hearts, illuminating our lives so that others around us can see His glory.

This is a beautiful picture. We are like lighthouses for God. A lighthouse without a power source is just a building. It may have a large clear bulb in good working condition, a switch with all the proper wires, and even an able keeper of the light to flip the switch, but until the connection is made, it's just a lighthouse. Once the current is flowing from the power source to the bulb, the lighthouse becomes a shining beacon, guiding ship captains through perilous waters to safety.

If we, as keepers of this earthly "Lighthouse," stay connected to the Power Source, our lives become a shining light to those who observe us. We may be able to help guide a struggling friend through troubled waters. We may never know exactly how God's Power shining through us influences others. If we don't keep our connection in good repair, however, our Light will dim or go out, and we won't be an effective lighthouse in God's Kingdom.

This Light is a precious treasure and should be protected as carefully as any other costly keepsake. It is an eternal treasure that will bless our lives and others when we stay connected to Jesus, our true Power Source.

- Am I an active lighthouse in my everyday life?
- How could I allow the Light to shine more clearly through me?
- *Lord, make my life a shining illumination of Your love and power.*

Earthen Vessels For God

"But we have this treasure in earthen vessels, that the excellency of the power may be of God, and not of us."
- II Corinthians 4:7

Have you ever wondered why God made humans out of dirt? He could have used wood as there were plenty of trees in the Garden of Eden. He could have formed man from rocks or some precious metal, if He had chosen to. Wouldn't we be much stronger? Just think of how much we could do for God with the treasure of His power within us, if we weren't such frail creatures. Paul tells us, however, exactly why God chose to put His treasure in earthen vessels. "That the excellency of the power may be of God and not of us."

We know that Satan also has power, and without God we are weak and unable to withstand his attacks. He sends all kinds of trials into our lives to trip us up and cause us to stumble and fall. We are troubled and perplexed, persecuted and cast down, but we are not distressed or in despair. We are not destroyed, and we are never forsaken. With the greater power of God sustaining us, we don't give up.

Paul may have been thinking of Gideon and his small army with trumpets and empty pitchers with lamps inside when he wrote this passage. When the pitchers were broken, the lamps shone brightly and terrified the enemy. So it is with us as Christians. Only when our self-will is broken and we are fully yielded to God, can His Gospel and glory shine through us in all its radiance. Then we stand firm and strong, like beaming lighthouses overcoming the darkness, as God's Light shines through us.

- Do I see myself as a weak creature needing God's help every day?
- What area of my self-will still needs to be broken to allow His light to shine more brightly?
- *Lord, I'm just a weak human creature, but I desire to be a shining light for You.*

The Overlooked Gift

"But covet earnestly the best gifts."
- I Corinthians 12:31

The package going into the mail didn't look like much--- it was just a small brown box. A few days after "Rose" mailed it, her friend called, asking if she had sent her something. The mailman had left a notice since she had been out, and the package would not fit in her mailbox. Two weeks later, Rose had not heard anything more about the gift and finally asked her friend if she had been in to the post office to pick it up. It was a bit surprising to find out that she hadn't. She knew her friend had been out doing lots of Christmas shopping and other errands, but by now it was several days past Christmas. Finally however, several days later, her friend called to thank her for the hand-made gift. The next day it occurred to Rose that the book she had sent in the same box had not been mentioned. Inquiring about it later, her friend admitted that she had not even seen it in the bottom of the box!

"Now what," Rose wondered, "does all of this tell me about my friend? Or, could there possibly be a lesson here for me?" The book she had sent was about learning to rejoice in every situation. It was the important part of the gift, and it had been overlooked. Then she wondered how many times we receive gifts from our Father that we are slow to pick up? Once we finally have it in our possession, do we just take the light stuff off the top and overlook the better gift underneath? If we are given a gift of money, food, or other items, do we just take it for granted, or are we truly thankful for the love in the hearts of the givers, and God who supplies all things? Are we slow to pick up the Bible and read God's Word? Do we just read through quickly or do we dig a little deeper, looking for the treasures He has hidden there for us? Are our prayers said hurriedly or do we take the time to listen for the guidance in God's answers? God's gifts should be picked up promptly, and we should look for all of the blessings hidden in the package!

- Do I recognize and pick up God's gifts as He makes them available to me?
- How could I change my attitudes or habits to discover more of what God has for me in these gifts?
- *Lord, I desire to never overlook the most important part of the gifts You so graciously give to me.*

Be Bold For Him

"As long as I am in the world,
I am the light of the world."
- John 9:5

As we read through the account of this blind beggar whom Jesus healed, we can see that he becomes bolder about his Healer as the story unfolds. The leaders at that time had made it clear that no one was to have anything to do with anyone who called Jesus the Messiah. When the man came back from the pool of Siloam able to see, his neighbors and others who had seen him begging were understandably puzzled. To their questions of how it had happened, he answered rather vaguely, "A man that is called Jesus made clay…" (v. 11)

Later, standing in front of indignant Pharisees, he was asked again how it was that he had received his sight. Since Jesus had broken their Sabbath Day tradition of rest by healing on the Sabbath, the Pharisees said, "This man is not of God…" (v. 16) But the healed man answered, "He is a prophet." Still skeptical, the Jews asked his parents if he was really their son who had been blind. They said that he was but, being afraid of the Jews, they told them to talk to him. So once again, they asked the man how he had been healed. By this time, he must have been a bit weary of the same questions over and over. He asked them why they would want to hear it again when he had already told them and they didn't listen. Then, very boldly, he asked, "Will ye also be his disciples?" (v. 27) This angered the Jews, but the man rebuked them saying "If this man were not of God, he could do nothing." (v. 33) Angrily the Jews cast him out of the temple. Meeting Jesus later, the healed man confessed his belief and worshiped Him.

As we courageously answer questions about miracles Jesus has done in our lives, we may suffer persecution too. People may also be more interested in how than in Whom, but like the beggar, we don't need to know how our lives are miraculously changed. We just need to know Who has changed us. The longer we experience life in Christ, the more we grow in grace and the more confident we become in the One who has healed us. Others may not accept us, but Jesus will. We may lose friends, jobs, or status as we share who Jesus is, but remember, no one can take away what He has done for us!

- Do I recognize what Jesus does for me as miracles from Him?
- Am I courageous enough to share Jesus with others, risking rejection?
- *Lord, give me boldness in proclaiming Your goodness to others.*

September 20 *Read: Psalms 46*

God, Our Comforter

"I, even I, am he that comforteth you."
- Isaiah 51:12

D*oes Jesus care when my heart is pained, too deeply for mirth or song?* As parents, we had received two staggering blows, just a day apart, and my spirit was crushed. And the timing, I thought, could not have been worse. We were facing our Love Feast at church, a weekend with lots of company, short nights, and much serving.

"It's too much, Lord," I cried. "I just can't do it. Why did all this have to happen now? How can I possibly function properly, performing my many duties over the weekend, through this pain? Don't you care?" Of course I knew He cared, but I desperately needed to feel it.

Oh yes He cares, I know He cares... And by the end of the weekend I felt it, too. The guests He sent to us had gone through some of the same struggles we were experiencing. We were blessed with a healing evening of heart-to-heart sharing and caring, forming a deep bond of friendship. The weekend was filled with inspiring messages, blessed fellowship, and encouraging words from our church family and friends. We were lifted above the despair, feeling deeply the comfort and love that God blesses His people with when He knows we are hurting. What I had thought was bad timing was actually good timing. God does care, and His timing is always perfect. His comfort is available to us in many forms, and He knows just what we need to get us through any painful circumstance.

Are you struggling with circumstances beyond your control? Do you feel the timing is all wrong? Take heart! Jesus does care when you are hurting. He will comfort you, and His timing is perfect. He is the greatest source of comfort we have available.

- Do I allow God to extend His comfort to me when I'm hurting?
- In what ways has God shown His divine comfort to me at the very time I needed it?
- *Lord, I thank you that you care deeply for me and that you show it in many comforting ways.*

Open Hearts

"Whose heart the Lord opened."
- Acts 16:14

The Biblical account of Lydia is short, and we are given only a glimpse into her life. She had a business in Philippi selling purple fabrics. Since purple dye was very expensive, the cloth was quite valuable. Normally, it was worn by the wealthy or by royalty. Her business was likely profitable, making Lydia an influential business woman and enabling her to have a large house.

Paul and his companions met Lydia on a Sabbath when they went to a river outside the city where a group of women had gathered to pray. As the men began to speak to the women, Lydia listened intently and her heart was opened to receive Paul's message of Jesus Christ. Soon after that, she and all the members of her household were baptized.

This is a little story with a big message. Lydia was a good example to us in several ways. She pursued the Truth by going to the gathering place on the Sabbath day. She heard the Truth as she listened intently. She accepted the Truth and was baptized. Then, living out her faith, she cared for the missionary team in her home during the rest of their stay in Philippi.

We don't know how Lydia felt that Sabbath Day morning. Maybe she was tired and was tempted to just stay home, but she went. We know how easy it is to let a multitude of other thoughts crowd out the speaker's words at times, but she listened. We don't know how much she understood of Paul's teaching about Jesus and His plan of salvation, but she accepted it. And despite the drudgery sometimes accompanying a life of giving and serving, Lydia willingly and gladly served by welcoming the mission team into her home.

This account says the Lord opened Lydia's heart to hear His message, but Lydia had to be ready and willing for her heart to be opened. How is your heart when you go to hear the Word of the Lord preached and explained? Is it open and ready to hear what God has for you? Are you ready to apply what you hear to your life and serve where you are called? Be a Lydia with an open and ready heart!

- Am I willing to honestly examine my heart and allow God to show me where it is still closed to Him?
- In what areas do I need help to be more fully open to His teaching?
- *Lord, open my heart as You did Lydia's and teach me what You want me to know.*

September 22 *Read: Acts 16:11-15*

Is My Heart Open?

"Whose heart the Lord opened."
- Acts 16:14

We don't know much more about Lydia's life except what we learn from the history and culture of the area at that time. Though we don't know her struggles and heart issues, they may not have been a lot different from those common to all women. How can we know whether our hearts are open to Jesus? Honestly asking and answering the following questions may make us more receptive to His work in our hearts.

Am I quick to confess when I sin?

Do I consistently obey God's commands?

Do I seek forgiveness from those I have wronged?

Do I readily extend forgiveness to those who have wronged me?

Do I seek to resolve conflict as quickly as possible in my relationships?

Does my daily schedule reveal that God is first in my life?

Does my life show consistent evidence of the fruit of the Spirit?

Are my conversations pure and above reproach?

Am I faithful in praying for the needs of others?

Do I rejoice when others are praised and my efforts go unnoticed?

If these questions expose areas of your heart that may be closing off your relationship with God, remember that He promises to restore those who sincerely return to Him. An open heart is receptive to His blessings and eager to channel His blessings into the lives of others.

- Can I ask myself these questions and answer them honestly?
- Am I willing to ask God to help me open the closed areas even though it may be painful?
- *My desire is for an open heart before You, Lord. Make me willing to allow You to transform me into Your likeness.*

Comfort Through A Song

"I will sing of mercy and judgment:
unto thee, O Lord, will I sing."
- Psalm 101:1

I was lying in bed early one morning unable to sleep because my mind was too busy. Things hadn't been going well and I was discouraged. My relationship with my husband was stuck on a snag. It seemed our children were forgetting everything we had tried to teach them. Life on the farm was a drag with no relief in sight. The housework was overwhelming, and I felt hopelessly behind. So, I wondered, what's the point? Maybe just giving up would be easier. Where can a mother go to resign? Is it possible to just check out and be done?

Slowly it dawned on me that a hymn was going through my mind over and over. I focused on it and realized that, without even thinking about it, I was silently singing: *"Have you a heart that's weary, tending a load of care?"* I was awed as I realized that God was speaking to me. *"Do you know my Jesus? Do you know my friend? Have you heard he loves you, and that He will abide 'til the end?"**

Oh. I had totally lost my direction. Life is full of struggles, that's just a fact. But we don't have to despair! Jesus wants us to know Him and He longs to be our Friend. (John 15:14, 15) He loves us and has promised to never even leave us, much less forsake us. (Hebrews 13:5) As I meditated on the words of the hymn and let God's love soak into my heart and soul, life didn't look quite so bleak. Marital snags can be unraveled, and children's amnesia is generally temporary. I got up, ready to tackle the housework and appreciating the advantages of our life on the farm.

This was not the first time God had spoken to me through a song. I am not a musician, but I do enjoy singing. It's good to memorize hymns as well as Scripture. The more you sing, the more hymns and portions of hymns you will have committed to memory. Then, God can bring them to your mind as needed for comfort, reminders, or direction. So, sing! Memorize the words and meditate on them. And next time you have a song running through your mind, concentrate on it and see if God is speaking to you through it.

- Am I willing to listen when God wants to speak to me through hymns?
- How can I cultivate a singing spirit and memorize hymns that speak to me?
- *Lord, remind me to sing as I go about my daily work and to meditate on and memorize what I'm singing.*

 Read: Colossians 2

Treasures of Wisdom And Knowledge

"In whom are hid all the treasures
of wisdom and knowledge."
- Colossians 2:3

Paul was struggling deeply with concern for the believers at Colossae and Laodicea, even those he hadn't met. He longed for them to join together in loving fellowship, shunning the false teachings of the day. He knew that as they grew in understanding of the Christian faith, they would be more firmly grounded and less likely to be deceived by "enticing words." He wanted them to learn to know Jesus because "all the treasures of wisdom and knowledge" are hidden in Him.

These treasures are also available to us today. But what are these treasures? Knowledge can be defined as understanding the truth and wisdom as the ability to apply the truths we have learned. These treasures are hidden from unbelievers. They are hidden in Christ, and even a Christian must truly know Christ to tap into these riches.

As Christian women, going about our daily lives, it's extremely important that we stay close to the Lord, communing with Him daily during our quiet time. We need these treasures of knowledge and wisdom as we train and teach our children, support our husbands, or interact with others. It can be frustrating and disappointing to be constantly interrupted or to have our devotional time fall by the wayside time after time. But God understands the care of small children, or other duties, and He honors our desire to seek Him. As we come to know Him in a deeper way, we are less likely to be lured into the world's way of doing things. His treasures are available and worth all the time and effort it takes to find them.

- Do I have a desire to find these riches that are hidden in Christ?
- How could I go about seeking these treasures at a deeper level?
- *Lord, thank You for providing these riches for us and give me a greater desire to seek them and apply them.*

Preparing Your Altar

"Let us draw near with a true heart
in full assurance of faith."
- Hebrews 10:22

On top of Mount Carmel, in the presence of all Israel, Elijah challenged the prophets of Baal to a contest. After he gave them instructions, the prophets of Baal built an altar and placed their sacrifice on it. All day long they called on their god to send fire, as they leaped upon the altar and cut themselves. They received no reply.

Then it was Elijah's turn. To build his altar he used twelve stones, the number of the tribes of Israel. He dug a trench around the altar and put wood and the sacrifice on it. Then he had twelve barrels of water poured over the altar, soaking everything and filling the trench. When he called on his God, his prayer was answered by fire from heaven which burned up everything, even the water in the trench. This show of God's amazing power convinced the people that the Lord is God.

Before asking God to send the fire, Elijah had spent time carefully preparing his altar. How carefully do we prepare the altar of our hearts before coming to God with our requests? Do we spend time daily in His Word and strive to put the truths we learn into practice? Do we confess our failings and keep our hearts cleansed of unconfessed sin? Although denying our own will and yielding to God's leading are difficult at times, they are essential to keeping our hearts right before God.

Then, as God sent fire from Heaven to consume Elijah's sacrifice, so He will fill us with the fire of His Spirit, thus enabling us to worship and serve Him acceptably.

- Can I honestly examine my heart to see if it's properly prepared?
- In what ways does the altar of my heart need attention?
- *Lord, I dedicate the altar of my heart to You and ask You to fill me with Your Spirit today.*

Restored Image

"Therefore if any man be in Christ...old things are passed away; behold, all things are become new."
- II Corinthians 5:17

"Your camera is here; you may come and pick it up," the lady from the camera shop said.

"It's done? It's in? I can come get it?" In disbelief, my friend spoke without stopping. After her little one had accidentally kicked her camera off the bed, breaking it, she had been told it would take four to six weeks to have it fixed. Now, four months later, she finally got her camera back. She wasn't real happy, however, that there was now an ugly gouge in the part they had worked on, and she was appalled and frustrated when, after taking just one picture, the camera wasn't working right again. Calling the troubleshooting hotline, she received an apology and was advised to take the camera back in.

As she hung up the phone, she turned angrily to her husband and fired. "I just want to throw this camera! I hate it! I'm sorry I ever bought it, and if they don't fix it, I'll never buy another camera there again!" Gently, her husband advised her not to throw the camera. He encouraged her to calm down and slipped off to pray for her. She then realized that she had not prayed at all about this camera—after all it was just a material possession, and God has more important things to think about... doesn't He? Then, knowing that God does care, she prayed about her broken camera.

Returning to the camera shop the next morning, she and her husband explained to the owner what had happened. He disappeared to the back of the store to check it out, and shortly returned to tell them the camera should not be acting like that, and he would replace it. Then he took a brand new camera off the shelf and handed it to her! Their mouths dropped open, and they looked at each other in astonishment. Sincerely thanking the owner, they left.

Looking at the new camera in her hands, my friend felt as though she really did not deserve it. It was brand new with no gouges or scars. As she studied it, she saw her own sinful nature. Broken, scarred, and gouged, she didn't feel like she was worth much in God's eyes. But Jesus, in His love and mercy, had restored her to His image through His blood! "Behold, all things are become new." What a beautiful promise. Will we accept it for ourselves?

- Do I believe Jesus has forgiven me and made me into a new creature?
- Am I willing to accept the gifts He offers?
- *Lord, I thank You for Your promise to me and that You are willing and able to do just what You promise.*

Safe In The Arms Of Jesus

"Hold thou me up, and I shall be safe."
- Psalm 119:117

The wind was brisk as we stood around the grave site on a chilly November day. The life of 48-year-old Lawrence, husband and father, had been snatched away in a tragic traffic accident as he was driving his semi-truck several hundred miles away from home.

As the minister was speaking words of comfort to the family and friends gathered there, he told us of a touching incident that had happened in his home the very morning of the accident. His little two-year-old daughter had made an unexpected, "out of the blue," comment. To her mother she said, "Lawrence is my buddy." This was unusual because she tended to be somewhat clingy and didn't warm up to many outside her family. Lawrence, however, loved children, and recently while the minister's family was visiting in his home, he had made a special effort to win this little girl's confidence. By the end of the evening, she was sitting on his lap. Now, in her little mind, he remained her buddy.

The minister went on to paint a beautiful picture of why he thought this had happened. To his little girl, this kind man's lap and arms were a safe place to be. She was content to rest there for awhile, sheltered and secure. And he reminded us that this is just what Jesus wants to be for us; a safe place, a shelter where we can rest through the storms of life. Cares and trials on every side threaten to overwhelm us, but Jesus is always there with open arms and a safe "lap." He is our Friend (John 15:14), and longs for us to accept the full measure of His love. And as we reflect that love, we also become a safe friend for those around us.

- How can I represent Jesus in a way that attracts others to Him?
- For what situations in my life today could Jesus provide the shelter I need?
- *Lord, I thank you for being that safe place we can always count on.*

September 28 *Read: Luke 10:30-37*

The Unneighborly Neighbor

"And when he saw him,
he passed by on the other side."
- Luke 10:31

When reading through the story of the Good Samaritan, it's easy to despise the priest and the Levite. How despicable to simply ignore someone who is hurting! We would never do such a thing...or would we? Why did those men walk on by? Maybe there is more to it than we first think. Their jobs were in the temple and to remain ceremonially clean, they could not touch a dead body. Even if this man was not dead, he was obviously badly hurt. What if he were to die while they were caring for him? Then they would be unable to do their jobs and perhaps they would not be paid. They were not medical people and may not have even known how to bind up wounds. Possibly they feared that the thieves were still lurking nearby, waiting for another victim. We are not told what their reasons were, and it's easy to think the worst.

But what about us? When we are prompted to visit a lonely shut-in; send a card of encouragement or thanks; or say a few words to a sister who is hurting, do we stifle the urge? Do we think, "Oh, I couldn't help anyway, I hardly know her." Or, "I might say the wrong thing, and besides, I really don't have the time." When I fail to stop and help someone in need, how different am I from the priest and Levite? Yes, it might make me late. It may cost me some money, or damage my pride. Maybe there really isn't much I can do, and it's possible that I may be hurt. But if I truly love my neighbor as Christ loves me, I will put aside my own desires and do what I can to help.

- Do I truly care about others as much as I care about myself?
- How willing am I to move out of my comfort zone to help someone else?
- *Lord, help me to rise above my excuses and be a good neighbor to those I encounter.*

The Good Neighbor

"But a certain Samaritan...
had compassion on him."
- Luke 10:33

The Samaritans were despised by the Jews. The Jews considered themselves pure descendants of Abraham, while the Samaritans were a mixed race coming from intermarriage between the Jews and Gentiles. They were considered unfit for a proper Jew to associate with. This traveling Samaritan was undoubtedly aware of how he was regarded by the people in the area where the traveler was attacked. But that didn't stop him from having compassion on one who needed help. Although the wounded man was a stranger, the Samaritan cleansed and bound up his wounds, put him on his own mount, and took him to an inn. He took care of the man overnight, and the next day he paid his own money to the host to see that the man was cared for.

What should we learn from this Samaritan? How often do we help someone who is different than ourselves, especially someone who has treated us badly? Do we reach out to those with different customs, different skin colors, or different backgrounds? Or is it easier to assume that their own people will take care of them? If we were traveling in a foreign country, would we help those in need, or would we be satisfied simply to be sightseers? How can we justify a lack of love and compassion in the face of need? Jesus teaches me that the neighbor I am to love as myself is anyone, regardless of race, beliefs, or social background, who has a need that He wants me to meet. Whether that neighbor is close by or far away, Jesus would tell us, "Go, and do thou likewise."

- Do I have a heart full of compassion, and a willingness to help others?
- How can I reach out to someone today?
- *Lord, help me truly to love my neighbor as much as I love myself.*

September 30 *Read: Mark 5:21-43*

The Hem Of His Garment

"And He said unto her, Daughter,
thy faith hath made thee whole; go in peace."
- Mark 5:34

The poor woman in this story was desperate. She had " had an issue of blood twelve years." Under Jewish law, the bleeding made her ritually unclean, which meant that anyone touching her would become unclean also. She was forced to live like a leper, excluded from most social contacts. Longing to be healed, she had spent all her money going from doctor to doctor, possibly enduring some pretty drastic treatments. But instead of being healed, she "rather grew worse." And then she heard about Jesus! Hope springing anew, she found Him in a crowd of people. I wonder if she felt some panic when Jesus started off for Jairus' home before she could get to Him. She must have been fearfully aware that touching anyone, including Jesus, would make that person unclean. But she also knew that if she could just touch Jesus she would be healed. Desperately, she pushed her way through the crowd, reached out and "touched His garment." Imagine, after all she had been through, the feeling of being instantly healed! But she was also afraid when Jesus turned and asked who had touched Him. Bravely, she fell at His feet, however, and told Him the whole story. Rather than being upset with her, Jesus consoles her by calling her "Daughter" and bids her go in peace. He made it clear that it was her faith, not just her touch, that had healed her.

And so it is with us. True faith involves action. We can be ever so near to Jesus, but until we reach out in faith and "touch the hem of His garment," we won't be healed. How sad if we were to let fear or a lack of faith keep us from approaching Him with our problems.

- Am I exercising faith which reaches out to trust Jesus, and experiencing His favor?
- What problems do I have today that I could be healed of by "reaching out and touching Jesus?"
- *Lord, I praise You for healing this woman, and I long to have the faith that she had.*

October

The Shepherd Psalm, Part I

"The Lord is my shepherd."
- Psalm 23:1

---

*The Lord is my shepherd, I shall not want...*As a shepherd keeps constant watch over his flock, day and night, so Jesus takes care of His people and provides for them.

He maketh me to lie down in green pastures... The shepherd is responsible to make sure the sheep have an ample supply of food. A lush green pasture is the first choice for feeding. God has given us an abundance of spiritual food in His Word, which should be our first choice for reading.

*He leadeth me beside the still waters...*Sheep are afraid of moving water and need a quiet pool for quenching their thirst. We also need a quiet place to drink regularly of the Living Waters.

*He restoreth my soul...*A shepherd will search far and wide to find a lost sheep and bring it back to the fold. Our Heavenly Father longs also to restore a wayward, hurting soul back into peaceful fellowship with Him.

*He leadeth me in the paths of righteousness, for His name's sake...*In Bible lands, a shepherd would occasionally have to lead his flock along a narrow path between two unfenced grain fields. He didn't dare let the sheep get into the fields, or he would have to pay the damages. Our shepherd can safely lead us in "right paths" too, if we keep our focus on Him and off all the temptations around us.

- Am I truly allowing Jesus to be the Shepherd of my life?
- Do I have a quiet place in which to drink daily of the Living Waters?
- *Lord, give me the desire to seek You daily and to allow You to lead me along right paths.*

October 2 *Read: Psalm 23*

The Shepherd Psalm, Part II

"And I will dwell in the house of the Lord forever."
- Psalm 23:6

Yea, though I walk through the valley of the shadow of death, I will fear no evil: for thou art with me... taking sheep through a valley is dangerous. A shepherd must be on the lookout for evil beasts, sharp rocks, and uneven footing. Jesus has promised to be with us through the valleys in our lives, keeping us from the evil one.

Thy rod and thy staff they comfort me...A shepherd uses his rod and a staff to defend, rescue, or guide the sheep. We have the tools of Scripture and Holy Spirit to guide and comfort us.

Thou preparest a table before me in the presence of mine enemies...God invites us to feast from His table and nourishes us with His life-giving Word.

Thou anointest my head with oil...A shepherd commonly treats the wounds of his sheep with olive oil. When we are hurting, Jesus anoints us with the soothing oil of His loving presence.

My cup runneth over...Staying close to the Shepherd brings blessings that spill over into the lives of others.

Surely goodness and mercy will follow me all the days of my life...As we follow our Shepherd, He will sprinkle our days with His goodness and His mercy.

And I will dwell in the house of the Lord forever...If we stay close to our Shepherd and are careful not to stray from Him, we can stay safe and enjoy eternity with Him in Heaven!

- Am I staying close to the Shepherd through Bible study and prayer?
- Do I trust God to take me through the valleys and the shadows?
- *Lord, my desire is to trust You as my Shepherd and to dwell in Your House forever.*

Eclipse

"Neither shall thy moon withdraw itself:
for the Lord shall be thine everlasting light."
- Isaiah 60:20

As we stood at the window one cold night, we had a fascinating view of the moon during a total lunar eclipse. As the earth's shadow slowly covered the moon, I had to think of how much my life is like that at times. How easy it is to allow the shadow of daily life come between me and God. My daily devotions can become hurried and routine; a task to get done quickly or perhaps even skipped so that I can get on to the rest of my over-crowded agenda for the day. My prayer time gets short and rushed, too. It can be easy to push aside a prompting to pray for someone or to call a sister and ask how she is doing. Am I really too busy to stop and write a note of encouragement to one who is ill or lonely? I may get impatient with a phone call or an unexpected visitor when I "don't have time for that!"

As the moon slowly came into view again, I was reminded that I can make a conscious choice to let the Light shine in my life again, too. I can *slow down* and take the time to read, pray, and listen. As I respond to God's promptings, I will find the shadow disappearing from my life, too. When we take the time for someone else, God blesses that person and us at the same time.

- Is my spiritual life undergoing an eclipse right now?
- What do I need to do to clear the shadows from my life today?
- *Lord, the shadows roll in so quickly. Help me keep them out of my life by staying close to You.*

Read: Psalm 27

Traveling Woes

"I will instruct thee and teach thee in the way which thou shalt go: I will guide thee with mine eye."
- Psalm 32:8

We were driving together in three vehicles to visit a family living in Michigan's Upper Peninsula. The plan was to stay together for the ten-hour drive, but it wasn't long until...you guessed it...we lost the others. They made an unexpected turn as we went flying past the exit. Eventually we got turned around, but we couldn't find them, and we weren't sure we were even on the right track. Our cell phones worked only sporadically, and our road map was out-dated. But worst of all was the fog. We couldn't have seen them if we were right behind them anyway!

Sometimes life can seem like that. We feel lost. The prayer connections to Heaven seem sporadic and full of static. Our Biblical "road map" seems confusing, and our vision is clouded by a thick fog of uncertainty.

Our lead driver assured us by phone that we were on the right path, and we finally caught up with them. The rest of the trip was uneventful, and we had an enjoyable visit before heading home again.

We can be assured that if we seek our Heavenly Guide, He will lead us in the right direction. Our Biblical road map will never become outdated, and God is able to lead us right through the fog. Our job is to follow in faith, believing that He will lead us safely to our destination. We will then be *Home* with no need to make a long return trip. The trials along the way may be tough and the road long, but the eternal glory will be well worth it.

- When I feel lost, am I willing to follow God's leading, even though the way ahead seems cloudy?
- How could I better allow Him to lead me through today?
- *Lord, the way does get long and confusing at times. Thank You for your promise to lead us safely Home.*

Jesus Calms The Storm

"And He said unto them, Why are ye so fearful?
How is it that ye have no faith?"
- Mark 4:40

The Sea of Galilee is 680 feet below sea level and surrounded by hills. Winds sweeping down the Jordan Valley intensify close to the sea causing unexpected and violent storms. The disciples with Jesus were experienced fishermen and probably thought they had things under control as the wind began to blow. But they soon realized that this was not just an ordinary squall. As the waves crashed over the edge of the boat and even began to fill the boat with water, the disciples panicked. They must have been frantically trying to bail out the water, as the storm threatened to destroy them all. Finally, they desperately looked for Jesus and found Him sleeping peacefully in the back of the ship. Awakening Him and shouting above the storm, they asked incredulously, "Master, carest thou not that we perish?"

I can picture Jesus getting up calmly and saying, "Relax my friends, where is your faith?" Then, He "rebuked the wind and the sea; and there was a great calm." The disciple's fear must have turned to absolute amazement as they stood there taking in the miracle and wondering how He had done that! They hardly comprehended that their humble passenger was actually the Creator and Sustainer of the universe.

We face many storms in life, some ordinary trials of daily living, and some tempests that threaten to sink our ship. They can involve our health, affecting our ability to work. Or maybe a relationship is suffering, and you don't know how to mend it. Finances can quickly become worrisome when there's not enough money to go around. The home, the workplace, or school can all be the source of overwhelming discouragement or despair. Raising and training children is a challenge on a good day. Bad days can feel like the ship is going down and maybe even make us wish it would! The loss of a loved one can take away the strength and even the desire to keep on. We can get up in the morning to face an ordinary, average day and soon find our "feet getting wet" as the waves of life begin to rise. We work hard at bailing ourselves out, rather than seeking Jesus right away. But as the storm rages, and we find ourselves up to our necks in water, where do we go? Many times we panic, hurrying to Jesus crying, "Don't You care?!" But, of course, Jesus cares! He's just waiting for us to ask for His help. Then, He speaks to the storm raging in our hearts, and the tempest stills. Though the circumstances may not change, the peace in our hearts will be unmistakable.

- What storm(s) am I facing today?
- Have I gone to Jesus for the peace He alone can give, or are you trying to bail yourself out?
- *Lord, forgive me for my lack of faith and still the storm raging in my heart just now.*

Life Abundant - The Person

"I am come that they might have life and
that they might have it more abundantly."
- John 10:10

Who is this ***Person*** who promises us a life so abundantly full of purpose and passion? In John 10 the very words of Jesus show us clearly that He is the One, the only One, who can give us life and give it *more abundantly.* Anyone else claiming to have this power is like a thief climbing over the wall into the sheepfold to harm the sheep.

Jesus says here that He is the ***Door***. (vv. 7, 9) He is the ***WAY*** to salvation and to life sustaining pastures. (v. 9) Lush pasture is very important for healthy sheep. It is where they find food and rest. Through Jesus we find nourishment in the written Word. We can rest in comfort and security as we feed daily on His Word and trust Him to work His will through our lives.

Jesus is the ***Good Shepherd***. (vv. 11, 14) A good shepherd cares more about his sheep than one who is hired to watch out for them. He knows his sheep intimately and will protect them to the point of dying for them. Jesus knows us better than we know ourselves. He loves us so deeply that He gave His life for us on the cross. He hasn't hired someone to watch over His people. He doesn't even sleep or take vacations! He doesn't push us into following His plan, either, but gently leads us as a shepherd leads his sheep. Sheep will follow the voice they recognize, and they will trust their shepherd to lead them to safety in times of danger. Trusting our Shepherd to faithfully lead us in the way of ***TRUTH,*** and protecting us in times of hardship and danger will bring a security and peace that passes all understanding!

Jesus is the ***Son of God.*** (v. 36) He is equal to God in every way. (v. 30) Through Him we have eternal life. Not only will we not perish, but no one is able to "pluck us out of His hand." (v. 28) As believers, we *become* His hand, part of the body of Christ, serving others in His name and for His glory. No one can take that away from us. We will have ***LIFE*** and have it abundantly as we follow our Good Shepherd, the ***Person*** of this abundant life, feeding from the green pastures of His Word. While we can have life in Jesus, an individual personal relationship with Him is absolutely essential for the richness of the *more abundant life* that He came to give each one of us. Don't settle for just *life,* ask Jesus to show you the way to a *more abundant life* than you even knew was possible!

- How well do I know Jesus, the *Person* of the more abundant life?
- What steps could I take to learn to know Him better and follow Him more closely?
- *Lord, I long to know You as my Good Shepherd. Show me the Way; lead me to the green pastures for food and rest.*

Life Abundant - The Purpose

"That I may know Him, and the power of His resurrection."
- Philippians 3:10

That I might SEE Him... (Mark 10:46-52) Bartimaeus was a blind beggar, but he heard the commotion as Jesus approached, heard who it was that was coming, and began to cry out loudly. He called Jesus the "Son of David" indicating that he *saw* Jesus as the Messiah. He begged for mercy, *seeing* hope in His touch. When Jesus asked the man what he wanted, he cried out, "Lord, that I might receive my sight." (v. 51) Jesus healed him immediately, and he followed Jesus, glorifying Him. Although Bartimaeus was blind physically, yet he *saw* in his heart who Jesus was and what He could do.

What about us? Do we see Jesus as our Savior, compassionately waiting for us to ask Him for restored sight? He is waiting to give us renewed clearness of vision and to heal us of our blindness.

That I might HONOR Him... (John 12:1-8) To honor someone means to show them great respect and admiration; to praise them publicly. Mary did this when she anointed Jesus' feet with the costly ointment and wiped them with her hair. One of the guests did not appreciate what she had done, but Jesus commended her.

How should we honor Him? We can praise Him through singing, worship, and testimony. We can respect His supreme power by choosing to trust Him with our marriages, our children, our work, our money, our health, and with our service to others for His glory. We can be brave, like Mary, and honor Him even when others don't understand or they criticize what we are doing. He is worthy of all praise and honor! Let us honor Him in every area of our lives!

That I might WALK with Him... (John 5:1-15) The man at the pool of Bethesda had been lame for thirty-eight years. His problem had become a way of life. He must have been astonished when Jesus walked up to him and told him to get up and walk. After all those years of immobility, his first step had to be an incredible step of faith. He may have even found it a bit frightening. What a thrill it must have been, though, to be walking, no longer dependent on others!

The purpose of this abundant life is not only for us to *see* and *honor* Jesus. To fully experience the richness of a life abundant, we must *walk* with Him. At times, it can be scary. Often it's easier just to let someone else carry the load. Sometimes we're astonished at what He asks us to do! But He does not just give us instructions and then leave us to flounder. He makes us whole in Him, and then walks right along with us.

- Do I have a true heart-felt desire to know Him better, experiencing the more abundant life?
- What can I do today to see Him more clearly, honor Him more fully, and walk more closely with Him?
- *Lord, fill my heart with a desire to experience the fullness of this more abundant life and the blessings that go with it.*

 Read: Luke 17:11-19

Life Abundant - The Passion

"Arise, go thy way:
thy faith hath made thee whole."
- Luke 17:19

Passion can be described as intense emotion such as love, joy, hate, or anger. It can also be intense enthusiasm - a keen interest in a certain subject or activity. Some people are full of passion, living life to the fullest whatever they are doing or feeling. Others are unfeeling; living a calm, detached, numb sort of life. Most of us are somewhere in between.

Live in faith! The ten lepers in this story knew the passions of sorrow, worry, and torment. They had felt the passions of disgust and rejection from others. When they saw Jesus coming into their village, they must have suddenly felt the unfamiliar passion of hope. As they stood off to the side and cried out to Him, Jesus responded. At that time if a leper thought he was healed, he was to show himself to the priest; the only one who could declare him clean. Jesus sent these men to the priest *before* they were healed. They didn't wait around, however, wondering what he meant...*they went!* They responded immediately in faith and were healed on the way.

Be thankful! While the faith of these men is admirable, unfortunately, only one of them remembered to be thankful. The others were so focused on themselves that they didn't take time to thank Jesus, maybe didn't even think about it. The one who returned was the only one who learned that it was his faith which had made him whole. God doesn't demand thankfulness, but He is pleased with it and uses our response to teach us more about Himself.

Be joyful! This one man who turned back to Jesus didn't just thank Him quietly and leave again. He praised Jesus with a *loud voice* and fell down at His feet thanking Him passionately. His joy in being healed knew no bounds! God gives us joys, big and small, all through our days. From seeing our children walking in His way to enjoying the beauty of a butterfly, we can be thankful and rejoice in His goodness.

Be passionate! The more intimately we get to know Jesus, the more passionate our love for Him grows. As our love deepens, our life in turn becomes more passionate. We grow more burdened at the sin and suffering around us. We long to see others experiencing this more abundant life that is available to all of us. We learn to know Him better through Bible study and prayer. We find Him answering as we believe He will respond to our needs. As we thank and praise Him for all He has done, we find ourselves becoming more passionate, radiating out to those whom God brings into our lives.

- Does my life show a passion for Jesus?
- How could I begin to cultivate more passion in my heart?
- *Lord, I confess I don't always feel this passion for You. Please give me the desire and wisdom to grow in this area.*

The River Of Life

"There is a river, the streams whereof
shall make glad the city of God."
- Psalm 46:4

As flows the rapid river, with channel broad and free...We sometimes sing this hymn comparing our life to a river. We find it fascinating to stand at the bank of a river and observe what is happening. After a hard rain, a river may be churning wildly, frothing and boiling as it makes its angry dash to the sea. At other times, it sings calmly and merrily as it flows gently along. A river picks up debris, tossing it about, and either depositing it along the way, or letting it settle to the bottom. Years of flowing water wears sharp edges off a stone, polishing it to a shiny smoothness.

So life is onward flowing...At times our lives are in a turmoil, feeling out of control as we're swept along in the current. Other times, when life is calm, we have joy in our hearts and a song on our lips. Unless we are watchful, however, we pick up debris along the way--branches of bitterness, leaves of discontent, and feathers of doubt. We can prayerfully toss them aside, or let them settle to the bottom of our hearts to build up dams of resentment. As we flow through life, we can allow God to refresh us by His Word, so that we bear more abundantly the fruit of the Spirit. (Galatians 5:22, 23) And as a river finally reaches its destination, so we will reach ours. Heaven awaits! Keep your eyes on the goal and allow God to chart the course along which the river of your life will flow. How glorious to gather at the river of life with the saints of all ages!

- Is the river of my life flowing along calmly, or is it needlessly churning in turmoil?
- What pieces of debris do I need to toss aside?
- *Thank You Lord, for the times my life flows smoothly and for Your help when it does not.*

Hymn by Samuel Francis Smith

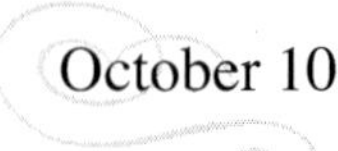

 Read: II Timothy 2:14-26

A Lesson From The Turkeys

"And the servant of the Lord must not strive;
but be gentle unto all men...patient."
- II Timothy 2:24

As my friend was driving down a country road one day, she saw a group of wild turkeys crossing the road ahead. Slowing down to allow them safe passage, she watched as the turkeys waited on each other, patiently encouraging the little ones along. Glancing back at them in her rear view mirror as she drove away, she thought about how we, as Christians, could take a lesson from the turkeys.

While these birds were simply acting out their God-given instincts, God has blessed us humans with a free will. We have a choice. Will we choose to encourage each other in our walk with the Lord? Are we ready to forgive one another when we fail, as we all do at times? What about me? Do I love my sister the way Jesus would have me love her, waiting patiently for her to grow in the Lord? Or would I rather just leave her behind as a lost cause, because she doesn't meet my standards? Do people look at me and see Jesus? Can I look in a mirror and see Jesus?

Unlike a turkey's instincts, our actions begin in our hearts. Keeping a clean heart and a clear conscience before the Lord requires a daily examination of self. Repentance and confession of sin, followed by acceptance of God's ready forgiveness will bring peace and joy. This joy will be reflected as our love for Jesus gives us the desire to patiently wait on and encourage our fellow believers in Christ. Let's take a lesson from the turkeys!

- What is my level of patience with my church family or other Christians?
- Is my heart clean so that I can effectively reflect the love of Jesus?
- *Lord, show me where I need to change my attitudes in relating to other people.*

Aging Gracefully

"The hoary head is a crown of glory,
if it be found in the way of righteousness."
- Proverbs 16:31

There is a nursing home in a town about thirty miles from us. Living in that home is a little old lady with snow white hair. She either sits in a wheel-chair or lies in her bed, day after day. She has suffered two strokes which affected her speech, making much of what she says impossible to understand. Her legs no longer hold her up and her right arm doesn't work properly. She is 93 years old. She is my great aunt, and she is beautiful.

Often when I walk into her room, her Bible lies open in front of her at the place she has been reading. She grips my hand in heart-felt appreciation as we pray together before I leave. Her sweet, caring spirit and unselfish manner draw others to her like a magnet. The staff treats her with love and respect. She's always been a special person, and her recent trials haven't changed that.

As I give her a hug and bid her goodnight, I have to wonder…what will *I* be like if I live to be 93? I've heard that as we age, we grow to be *more* like we are *now*. A sobering thought! God says in Proverbs that if we walk in the paths of righteousness, our old age will be a crowning glory. And He promises to be ever near us, leading us in those paths. Let's keep our eyes and minds on Him as He leads us Home!

- Am I cultivating a sweet, caring spirit in my daily life?
- Or am I headed down the path to becoming an unhappy, bitter old woman?
- *Lord, help me to keep growing into the kind of person You want me to be.*

October 12 *Read: II Kings 4:8-37*

Our Guest Chamber

"Search me, O God, and know my heart."
- Psalm 139:23

In II Kings 4:8-37, we read the story of the Shunammite woman who often had Elisha stay in her home as a guest. Perceiving that he was a holy man of God, she asked her husband to build a small chamber on the wall and to furnish it for Elisha's use.

We each have a "guest chamber" too. The chamber is your heart, and the Guest desiring to occupy that chamber is Jesus. Is the guest chamber of your heart available to Jesus? Or is it cluttered with busyness and other interests. How is it furnished? The Shunammite woman put a bed, a table, a stool, and a candlestick in her little chamber. Is your chamber comfortable and usable? Or is it dreary with discontent and cold with a lack of compassion? Is the table of your heart clean and ready to be written on? Or is it littered with crumbs of doubt, puddles of pride, or smears of self-righteousness? How about the lighting? Is your chamber illuminated with the love of Jesus, or is it dark with unconfessed bitterness and unforgiveness?

Maybe it's time to give our guest chamber a good cleaning and refurbish it to be as inviting to our important Guest, as the Shunammite woman's chamber was to Elisha. God blessed the woman for her kindness to Elisha by rewarding her with a son. He will also bless us as we open our hearts to welcome Him.

- What is the condition of my heart today?
- Is Jesus a welcome guest?
- *Lord, show me the areas of my heart that need to be cleaned for you.*

Being An Overcomer

"Who is he that overcometh the world but he hath believeth that Jesus is the Son of God?"
- I John 5:5

One Sunday morning in the middle of winter, our minister shared with us in his opening message that he had not had a good week. On one day it was ten degrees outside and ten degrees inside his shop. It seemed everything he tried to use broke, and because of the cold, motors would not run. One thing after another, everything that could go wrong, did. It got to the point where he was wondering "God, whose side are you on here, anyway?" But as he was thinking about the week and meditating on Scripture, he realized that his spiritual armor had become loose and had lost some of its protectiveness. As a result, he was feeling defeated.

How easily we become defeated. Some days all we have to do is get up and begin our day! It's not quite so easy to live victoriously. But as believers in Jesus Christ, we have power in Him to live as overcomers. First, by an abiding faith in Jesus as the Son of God. (vv. 4, 5) Second, by love, which demonstrates our victorious faith as we live out our love and service for God and others in practical ways. (v. 2) And third, by our joyful obedience to God's Word, which bears testimony to our genuine love for Him. (v. 4) God enables us to live as overcomers as we live our lives in His will.

- In what ways do I feel defeated?
- How can I put God's plan into action, and live as an overcomer?
- *Lord, help me to live your way and become an overcomer by your power.*

Frost In The Garden

"Be watchful, and strengthen the things which remain, that are ready to die."
- Revelation 3:3

It was early spring but warm enough for my gardener friend to set out some tender little plants in her garden. One morning soon after, however, a glance out her window registered frost on the car. Frost! She sprang into action. Throwing on some warm clothes, she rushed out the door and hooked up the hose (hallelujah--it wasn't frozen!), and sprayed those tender plants before the sun hit them and killed them. Whew! Saved them. A quick response had averted the danger.

How quick are we to respond when a friend has been hit with the frost of depression or discouragement? Do we sense the danger and make an effort to help? Prayer can melt the frost of discouragement, *if* we've kept the hose clear so that our communication with God is not blocked. We can help thaw the frost as we respond to the Spirit's promptings to send a card, make an encouraging phone call, or provide some practical help.

Maybe it would be better to think ahead and avoid such frosty close calls. Some of those plants will likely die from the frost in spite of the water. It will come too late. In that case, it would have been better to pay attention to the air temperature and sky conditions, or to check a weather forecast. If frost seemed a possibility, better to cover the plants with paper or plastic, give the cold frame extra protection, or even bring the houseplants back into the house. We could at least drain the hose to make sure it won't freeze.

What about the danger of frost in my own life? Do I take precautions to prevent it? Too easily, we do things that put us in the way of temptation. Do we pay attention to what we say, the way we say it, and the tone of our voice? What we do with our time, where we go, and what we think about can all be frosty dangers. We need to keep our hose drained of sin so we can pray for help just as soon as there is a need!

- How can I increase the warmth of compassion to avert frostbite in the life of a friend?
- Do I need to clear my prayer hose of any hindrance?
- *Lord, open my eyes to the needs of my friends and let the warmth of your love flowing through me avert a killing frost in someone else's life.*

What Will You Be?

"Let my mouth be filled with thy praise and with thy honour all the day."
- Psalm 71:8

Grandma Grace was 96 years old when she died. She spent her last months in a nursing home in her Michigan hometown. She had had a stroke, and her mind was failing as her body slowly shut down. She enjoyed her visitors but, now and then, would talk to them about the pigs rooting around on the floor! These "pigs" didn't upset her; they were just there, proof of the dementia that was overtaking her mind.

At other times, however, Grandma Grace's mind was on heaven. She had lived a godly life, and that aspect of her thoughts shone through, even though her mind was failing. She would talk about going Home and would ask her guests what color they would like for their room to be. She wanted to get their rooms ready for them when she got to heaven and insisted they tell her what color she should make them. They were amused when she talked about the pigs in the room and a bit amused at her insistence in knowing their favorite colors, too. But they were also touched and impressed that even though her mind was not nearly as sharp as it used to be, Grandma Grace was still thinking about heaven and confident that she would be going there soon. They wondered if heaven would be on her mind at all if she had not lived her life for the Lord, serving Him for the purpose of someday spending eternity with Him. Grandma Grace was a living, breathing testimony of a life lived for Christ.

What do you think you or I might be talking about when we get old? Understandably, some of us might be talking about diapers, laundry, storybooks, cooking, cleaning, band-aids, and exhaustion! Would we also talk about Jesus, what He's done for us, and our desire to spend eternity with Him? Or would we be more likely to spew out grudges, harsh words, criticism, anger, and bitterness? The way we are living, or more accurately *thinking* now, just may affect the way we relate to people when we are old, and our minds are failing. Regardless of how busy we are, Jesus can have the preeminence in our thoughts when we talk to Him, praise Him, and teach our children about Him as we go about our daily work. Filling our minds with thoughts of Jesus now can help guard against ugly thoughts and speech in later years. We, too, can be a testimony of a life lived for Christ.

- What do my thoughts focus on most during my days?
- Will my thoughts still be centered on Jesus if someday I lose the proper function of my mind?
- *Lord, remind me to keep my thoughts and actions focused on You now and for the rest of my life.*

A Testimony Is Born

"Even as the testimony of
Christ was confirmed in you."
- I Corinthians 1:6

The longer I listened to the touching testimony of the speaker, the greater the desire became to use his story in a devotional for this book. But that, I thought, was a slim possibility. I don't use personal testimonies without permission and we were in a large crowd of people. How would I ever get to him and besides, this was a well-known speaker; where would I ever find the courage to actually talk to him?! So I prayed, "Lord, this is Your book. If You want this testimony in it, you'll have to provide me with a (very clear!) opportunity to speak to him *and* the courage to do it."

After dismissal, we were enjoying the visiting and I forgot all about my prayer. After the crowd thinned out, however, I walked out into the main entrance area and there, right in front of me and all alone, was the speaker. ("Now for the courage, Lord!") I thanked him for his sharing, and explained my request for a written copy of his testimony, and permission to use it. He was very gracious and willing, and asked that I write down my name and address and put it in the donation box for the tapes he had available. He would find it there, put something together for me, and mail it.

Three months later, thinking he had forgotten, I was surprised and pleased to get a phone call from him. Then another chapter to the story unfolded. When He was ready to record his testimony, my name and address had somehow gotten lost in the shuffle, and he had no idea who I was, or where I lived, or how to get in touch with me. After much searching and "dead end streets," he prayed, "Lord, I'd like to do this for her, so if it's Your will, You'll have to find her for me!" Soon after that, he found the missing address in the bottom of a box. With no idea how it got there, or why he had even looked there, he just thanked God for it and gave me a call to see if I was still interested. Of course I was. We worked out the details, and soon I had a copy of his story in my hands. (Testimony follows in tomorrow's meditation.)

Sometimes we may think God is not really interested in the small details of our lives, but He is indeed interested, and He cares. He wants to show Himself strong on our behalf. We should never underestimate the power of God in our lives, and not be afraid to share our encouraging testimonies of that power with others.

- Do I believe God is interested in my life, and that He cares about me personally?
- In what ways has He shown me lately that He is able to work out the small details of my daily life?
- *Lord, open my eyes that I might see Your greatness and Your love for me.*

Fill Me With Love
(Testimony Written By Amos Raber)

"Inasmuch as ye have done it unto one of the least of these my brethren, ye have done it unto me."
- Matthew 25:40

About the time John came to work for us, I decided I wanted to operate more with love. So I asked the Lord to fill me to be a vessel He could use to reach out to others. Not long after that, John began to get under my hide and everything he did irritated me. I knew my feelings were not right. This really bothered me, and finally I began to feel I was slipping away from the Lord. Early one morning, the Lord woke me up, and I felt a heavy burden to pray. "Lord, what is wrong and what can I do?" I prayed.

Suddenly, in my mind, I saw Jesus. Then he disappeared, and John's face popped up. Then I felt the Lord speak to me and say, "Amos, you prayed for more love, and I sent this young man into your life. You thought he was just an irritation, but actually, it was Me. I gave you a chance to show how much you love Me, but you pushed Me back and walked off."

I wept, heartbroken, and said, "Lord, You were there, and I missed you. Please, Lord, give me another chance. I want to give John a hug and tell him I love him. The next day I went to work, and though I felt some reluctance to befriending John, I made a difference. I gave him some chances to talk, and I discovered that he was a very broken man and that he needed help. But when I thought about my promise to give John a hug, pride moved in and the fear of what someone else might think or say stopped me. It was easy to promise, not so easy to do. I missed a number of opportunities to keep my promise to the Lord.

Then came the last day on the job for John. I walked out into the parking lot with him that afternoon. It was a perfect opportunity, but when I got there, I couldn't do it. I just stuck my hand out and said, "John, I want you to know that I care about you, and I'll be praying for you." I walked away and the Lord spoke to me. "You missed Me again."

I turned around cold in my tracks. John was just turning to walk off, too, and I saw a lost and lonely look on his face. I said "Jesus, I'm not going to miss You again." Then I called, "John!" and I walked back over to him. "I want to give you a hug," I said, "and I want you to know that I love you in Jesus." John's face lit up in surprise and gratitude as he hugged me back, and I had the overwhelming feeling that I had just given Jesus a hug and had told Him how much I loved Him. Jesus will put people into our lives to see how we react. I don't have this all conquered. It's a prayer matter and a real challenge. What are we doing with this challenge? *Amos Raber*

- Is there a challenging person in my life that needs to feel Jesus' love through me?
- How could I show this person that Jesus loves her and so do I?
- *Lord, fill me with Your pure love and guide me in ways to show it to those around me, even those who seem unlovable.*

Read: Ephesians 4:17-32

Are We There Yet?

"And thou shalt remember all the way which the Lord thy God led thee."
- Deuteronomy 8:2

Little Shawn was born with a severe birth defect. His tiny feet were bent back and under so that when he walked, if he ever did, he would be walking on the tops of his feet. As a small baby, he spent many hours in surgery and wore corrective casts on his feet and legs. By the time Shawn was three, his condition was improved to the point that he could walk without help. The only lingering problem still needing correction was one foot that turned in. One day while Shawn and his daddy were out shopping, a woman expressed sympathy for his handicap and commented on how much could be done for such crippling. His daddy just smiled and said, "You should have seen him before!" Shawn isn't "there" yet, but he's well on the way and he's come a long way.

Shawn's Uncle Will is not a traveler. Home is his favorite place to be, but now and then he doesn't have a choice but to take a trip. He told us one time what it's like when he and his family travel. Someone will soon ask, "Are we there yet?" And one of the children will answer, "No, Dad, we're just at the stop sign at the end of our road." And after awhile someone asks again, "Are we there yet?" And they'll answer, "No, Dad, it's a three hour trip and we've only been gone half an hour." And so on until they finally arrive and can get out of the car…until time to return home when the scene will be repeated.

Like Shawn and Uncle Will, we're on a journey. It's a rough journey sometimes with various "surgeries" to cut out growing tumors of pride, or bitterness; to clean up festering wounds of anger or envy; or to correct bad habits and turn them in the right direction. We may ask often, "Are we there yet?" The way grows weary, and we long to arrive at our destination. But patience and perseverance are a must on this journey. Little Shawn's endurance of all the pain and trial he's been through will be worth it in the end when he's able to walk normally rather than being crippled. Uncle Will's journey ends up back at home in spite of the tiring hours of travel. Weathering the struggles and pain of life can make us more patient, more compassionate, and more Christ-like. If we are criticized or discouraged about where we are in our spiritual life, we should be able to smile and say, "You should have seen me before!" Keep your mind and heart turned to Jesus. He'll smooth the way and walk beside you. Are we there yet? No, but we're on our way!

- Do I view my life as a journey that will be worth all the trials here?
- What defects do I have that Jesus would like to heal?
- *Lord, the journey does get tiring. Help me to endure bravely the trials along the way and to keep my eyes on You.*

Lions

*"Thy God whom thou servest continually,
he will deliver thee."
- Daniel 6:16*

Lions are ferocious beasts. They can weigh 300 to 400 pounds, stand three and one-half feet tall, and measure nine feet long. They run in packs of 35-40, and have excellent night vision, smelling, and hearing. They eat an average of 75 pounds of food a day. If they're not sleeping, they're thinking about their next meal. Lions kill to live.

We don't have to be concerned about being thrown into a den of lions today, but there are many other "lions" that we do need to be aware of. They can be just as ferocious and deadly as the lions in Daniel's den. It was only by the grace of God that those lions didn't kill Daniel. And God's grace can keep us safe from these "lions."

The lion of ***contemporary culture*** is very powerful. Some workplaces forbid their employees to speak of anything pertaining to Christianity. Public schools have outlawed prayer. The thinking that "everyone else is..." affects mature Christians as well as young people. We're all tempted at times to give in to the pressures of the culture we live in. Feeding this lion, however, can kill our *commitment* to witnessing for Jesus.

The lion of ***halfhearted worship*** is probably more common than we like to admit, possibly even in our own lives. How often do we sit in a worship service with our minds on anything and everything but the songs we are singing and the message we are hearing? This lion can quickly kill our *devotion* to serving the Lord.

Materialism is a lion that stalks, attacks, and devours its victims. It is never satisfied, craving more and more to fill the emptiness in its life. It effectively kills *contentment* to feed its raging hunger.

Many more lions stalk us daily. ***Bitterness, pride, anger, fantasies, addictions, laziness, hatred, self-pity, and more*** roar through our days, intending to destroy us. Is Daniel's God still able to deliver us today? Yes. This same God that we serve continually *will deliver us*.

I would like to challenge you to take a sheet of paper and a pen right now, and make a list of things from which God has delivered you. Make another list of "lions" you are currently being delivered from and then the things you would like to be delivered from in the future. Share your list with a friend or tuck it away for later reference. And don't forget to ***praise God*** for His miraculous works in your life!

- Am I willing to search out the "lions" in my heart and life?
- Do I recognize the work of God in delivering me from strangling strongholds in my life?
- *Lord, give me the wisdom to identify the "lions" and the courage to destroy them with Your help.*

October 20 *Read: John 6:1-15*

God Knows What He Is Doing

*"And this he said to prove him:
for he himself knew what he would do."
- John 6:6*

It was meal time for the large group of people who were following Jesus, with seemingly no way to feed them. Jesus took the opportunity to test Philip's faith by asking him where they could buy bread. Philip would have known where to get food, as they were not far from his hometown of Bethsaida, and he immediately began to figure the enormous cost. Jesus knew, however, that there was no human solution to the problem, and He also knew what He was going to do about it. He knew there was a little boy in the crowd who had two small fish and five little barley loaves. He knew there was a powerful miracle just waiting to happen. He was about to strengthen the faith of Philip and the other disciples.

This miracle did not begin to happen until the little boy had willingly ***surrendered*** his lunch to the disciples. It certainly wasn't much, considering the more than 5,000 hungry people waiting for food, but it was all Jesus needed. The miracle didn't continue until the disciples ***obeyed*** His command to pass out the bread and fish to the people, even though it seemed impossible to feed everyone. After the people were all satisfied, twelve *baskets* of leftovers were gathered up!

Miracles happen when we are willing to *surrender* the little we have in the way of money, time, talents, possessions, or whatever else we may have that can be used in His service. Miracles continue when we are willing to *obey* His commands, even when the expected outcome looks absolutely impossible to us. We limit what God can do in and through us when *we* decide what is and what is not possible. God already knows what He is going to do and how things will turn out. We can rest in His promises and allow our faith to be strengthened through the tests that come our way. As we *surrender and obey,* we will have occasion to give God the glory for the miracles He performs.

- What do I have that God wants me to dedicate to His service?
- Do I believe God can take my small offering and perform a miracle with it?
- *Lord, my offering isn't much, but I surrender it to You to use as You will.*

Kill That Sin

"But if ye shall still do wickedly,
ye shall be consumed."
- I Samuel 12:25

God chose Saul to be Israel's first king, even though he was not a particularly religious young man. He was not, however, a proud and arrogant man at that time. When Samuel gathered the people together to choose a king, Saul already knew he was the one but instead of coming forward, he "hid himself among the stuff." (I Samuel 10:22) But as time went on, pride began to grow in Saul's heart. When Saul's son Jonathan attacked and destroyed a Philistine military post, Saul took all the credit for it. (I Samuel 13:3, 4) Then, with the Philistine army approaching and the men of Israel scared and scattering, Saul tired of waiting on Samuel to come. He offered the burnt sacrifice himself. This was against the law, and Samuel was upset. Then came the time when God told Saul to go and smite the Amalekites, totally destroying everything they had. Instead, Saul showed disrespect for God by saving the enemy king and the best of the animals. It was too much. Samuel was grieved, and God regretted that He had ever made Saul king. Saul lost his kingdom and his relationship with God deteriorated. In his last battle with the Philistines, Saul and his sons were killed. Saul was a king, chosen of God to rule the Israelites. He was handsome and wealthy and could have spent his life in obedient service to God, being a blessing to the people and being blessed by God. But he didn't kill the first sins that crept into his heart. His life ended in disgrace. He died in defeat on the battlefield, a disappointment to God and a failure as a king. *By not killing the sin in his life, his sin killed him.*

Saul is a sad example of what can happen to us if we allow sin to grow in our lives. Don't let it happen to you. Kill those first sprouts of sin by confessing them to God and allowing Him to forgive you and cleanse your heart. Stay alive spiritually by killing the sin before it kills you!

- Do I have sprouts of sin in my life that need to be killed today?
- What about full grown sins that need to be weeded out lest they become even bigger?
- *Lord, I know that these sins aren't always easy to see. Please reveal them and help me to destroy them.*

Read: II Peter 1

A Professor's Approach

"The same came therefore to Philip... saying, Sir, we would see Jesus."
- John 12:21

An essay in a literature text tells about the teaching methods of a certain professor. He was quite thorough in instructing his biology class. One of his students was especially eager to learn all the professor could teach him. The first lesson of the course included examining a preserved fish without cutting into it. After looking it over for about ten minutes, the student was sure he knew all he needed to know about his smelly subject. But, at the insistence of the teacher, he ended up spending three whole days with his fish; looking, studying, probing with his fingers, drawing, and periodically discussing his findings with the professor. Years later, he still had an intimate knowledge of that type of fish. All without ever cutting into it.

How does that compare with our study of the Bible? We read it through and figure we know what we need to know about God and about what Jesus has done for us. Our prayers "work," and we enjoy the worship and fellowship at church. We weather a few storms and life goes on. But think about it. If it takes three days of intense study to learn what can be learned from a dead fish without even cutting it up, how long would it take to learn all we need to know about a living God? And beyond the learning, what about the riches that are available when we dig into the Word and study further? There is much more to learn about a fish than just studying the outside. Likewise, there's much more to learn about God than just reading through His Word. As studying the outside of a fish is the gateway to a deeper understanding of the make-up and life of that particular kind of fish, reading the Bible is just the beginning of a rewarding study of God and the life and character of Jesus. Spending additional time to become intimately acquainted with God and His will for our lives is certainly worth the added effort.

- Am I spending time studying the Bible rather than just dutifully reading through it?
- Do I have a desire to learn more about God and His will for my life?
- *Lord, I want to know You and to delight in studying and meditating on Your Word.*

God Has Not Forgotten You

"Call upon me in the day of trouble:
I will deliver thee, and thou shalt glorify me."
- Psalm 50:15

Asaph, the writer of Psalm 77, was not a wicked man. He was a Levite, from Israel's priestly line. He was a singer and a choir director. (1 Chronicles 25:1) He even wrote psalms full of instruction for God's people. But at the time he wrote the 77th Psalm, Asaph was in a pit of depression. He was beyond comfort (v. 2), and could not sleep or even speak. (v. 4) Verses 7-9 show us the depth of his despair. He seemed to conclude that God had forgotten him and would no longer answer his prayers.

Could Asaph's story possibly describe your own spiritual battle? He was a godly, praying, faithful man. He loved God's Word and taught it to others. But now he was facing a terrible despair. Unfortunately, Asaph's experience is not unusual for believers like you and me. This is not a way of life but simply a state of being overwhelmed because Satan has come in like a flood. Circumstances pile up until we are pressed beyond our endurance. Although we may escape actual depression, we may need to face a staggering disappointment or frustration because things are not working out as we had hoped. We begin to wonder how we will ever get through this downward spiral.

Asaph emerged from his despair with a song and so can you! Asaph thought back on all the wonderful things God had done for him. He meditated on the goodness of God and spoke of it to others. In time, his words became a song of praise and admiration for God and what He had done for all of the children of Israel.

During a time of walking through the valley of depression, I hesitantly confided in a sister that I trusted to understand. It was a great source of comfort and healing as she shared with me that she had walked the same path and did, indeed, understand. Sometime later, I was able to share that understanding and encouragement with a younger sister who was struggling. We both found a measure of God's healing love as we shared our stories and our pain.

Dear sister, God has not forgotten you in your deep, dark trial. As you become the focus of the Holy Spirit's comfort, you become more effective in providing comfort and victory for other hurting people. What an incredible calling!

- Do I truly feel in my heart that God has not forgotten me during the hard times?
- What great things has God done for me in the past that could be a comfort to others now?
- *Lord, help me to remember that You have a purpose in the dark times I go through.*

 Read: Text Passages (below)

The Wrecks Of Time

"We glory in tribulations also:
knowing that tribulation worketh patience."
- Romans 5:3

The Temptation and Fall (Genesis 3) - One of the greatest "wrecks of time" occurred in the Garden of Eden. Adam and Eve were enjoying a life of perfection in a beautiful garden when they gave in to the temptations of Satan and ate the fruit God had specifically told them not to eat. They paid a terrible price for their disobedience, suffering shame and fear, being sent out of their beautiful home, and causing a curse to be put on all creation.

The Flood (Genesis 7:17-24) - The Great Flood destroyed all the living things God had created. The people brought this "wreck" upon themselves by their wickedness. They also paid a dreadful price of death for all the wicked.

The Tower of Babel (Genesis 11:1-9) - Pride and defiance caused the people living at this time to want to make a name for themselves and prevent being scattered over the earth as God intended for them to be. They went to great effort to build this tower that would reach all the way to heaven and fulfill their own desires. But God was not pleased. He stopped the building project by confusing the people's language, which eventually caused them to scatter over the earth, and the great tower became an abandoned, crumbling "wreck of time."

Modern day buildings - It's not unusual, as we drive through the countryside today, to see old, neglected buildings in a state of disrepair and decay. Old weathered barns lean precariously and buildings that were at one time valuable and useful are now collapsing and possibly even creating a hazard zone.

Has your *life* ever seemed like a "wreck of time?" Do you feel forsaken, overwhelmed, fearful, and deceived? Like your life is one big hazard zone? One hymn in our church hymnal speaks of glorying in the cross of Christ which towers over the wrecks of time. Whether the "wreck" happened a long time ago, or is going on in your life right now, we can know and feel the peace that results from Jesus' death on the cross for us. Although the crucifixion scene was dark and ugly, the light and love that radiates from it is beautiful and lasts forever. Take your "wrecks" to Jesus. He can heal your heart and lead you through the "clean up" time, turning the wrecks into something beautiful that will make your service for Him more effective in the future.

- Am I learning from the "wrecks" in my life those lessons God wants to teach me?
- In what ways could I use my experiences to help others?
- *Lord, show me how to bring my "wrecks" to you and allow you to begin the healing in my heart.*

Water Into Wine

"But seek ye first the kingdom of God…
and all these things shall be added unto you."
- Matthew 6:33

Jesus performed His first miracle in Cana. He and His disciples had been invited to a wedding there. When the wine ran out, breaking an unwritten rule of hospitality, the governor of the feast had an embarrassing problem on his hands. Jesus' mother came to Him seeking help. At His command, the servants filled six empty pots to the brim with water, each pot holding 20-30 gallons. Immediately, the water became wine of such high quality that the governor was surprised and wondered where it had come from. It was unusual for the best wine to be served last at a wedding feast.

Jesus can "turn the water into wine" in our lives, also. Visiting with other families, individuals, or lonely, elderly shut-ins becomes sweeter when we share testimonies of God's goodness and spend time in prayer together. The load of daily duties lessens as we lift our voices in hymns of praise while working. Long miles of travel shorten when we recite Scripture, sing, or pray for loved ones. We become less weary in serving our families and others if we remember that, as we serve them, we are serving Jesus. Just as the good wine was not depleted at the wedding, neither will it be depleted in our lives as we "seek first the kingdom of God and His righteousness." And as the best wine was saved until last, the best is yet to come in the lives of Jesus' true followers.

- Do I believe in the power of Jesus to turn water into wine?
- In what ways could I more diligently seek Him in my daily life?
- *Lord, my heart's desire is that you miraculously transform me, so that my life will refresh others.*

Only Two Nights

"For to me to live is Christ,
and to die is gain."
- Philippians 1:21

Our minister's 94-year-old mother lived alone in the little country house that she had lived in for many years. She was a spry, little lady, witty, and a delight to visit with. As her health failed, she slowed down, needing to use oxygen and a wheel chair, and spending more time in her comfortable recliner. She enjoyed crocheting beautiful afghans until her fingers stiffened too much for fine work. She looked forward to visitors; the home health care nurses who came to take care of her needs and especially her family, who stopped by often to check on her, mow the yard, and see to other things that needed attention. She anticipated her 95th birthday, thinking she just might make it! But her faith was strong and she also longed to escape from her worn out body and fly away to Paradise. She knew her time on earth was short and spoke of her desire to go Home and be with the Lord. She often said, "It is well with the Lord."

About a month before her birthday, on a Saturday, her body began to shut down. As her family gathered, she told them she would be going home soon and they were not to be sad. "In two nights I'll be gone" she said confidently. Throughout the afternoon she sang hymns of heaven in anticipation of arriving at her glorious Home. She had always had a beautiful voice and loved to sing. On Sunday afternoon, while dozing in her wheelchair, she suddenly sat up and began crying, saying over and over how beautiful that was. Her son asked her what she was seeing, and she tried to explain a vision or glimpse into Heaven, how she could see the other side, and the Lord giving her assurance. "That was beautiful, thank-you, Jesus, for letting me see that, but I didn't see the end of the tape," she said. (They guessed that what she was seeing was something like viewing a video tape.) "I want that in my memorial service," she told them, "pass it on!" Through the night and the next day, her heart rate slowed, and on Monday afternoon, she died. "Only two nights" she had told them. Two nights later, she was gone. And her family is now honoring her desire to "pass it on."

How would you feel if you knew you had only two days to live? Would you be saying "It is well with the Lord?" Would you have the deep peace and assurance that this dear, old lady had? Would you sing hymns and say, "I'm ready to go?" How would you feel if you knew you had only two days to live?

- Am I at peace with God and man, ready to die at any time?
- What do I need to do to be ready for the end of my life here on earth?
- *Lord, please show me any area of my life that needs to change, so that I will be ready for Your call.*

Precious Pearls Of Truth

"Unto you therefore which believe He is precious."
- I Peter 2:7

There are many things in life that we may consider precious. Our children, loving family relationships, and friends are precious to us. We have memories of precious moments to think back on. Costly items, such as rare coins, rare china, antique furniture, and cars may be precious to us. There are precious metals of gold and silver, and precious stones such as diamonds and rubies.

But Peter, in his two letters had a different concept of what is truly precious. In I Peter 1:7, he tells us that the *trials* we go through in life are more precious than precious metals that will perish. These trials will end, but they can strengthen us in our spiritual life if we will allow them to. In I Peter 1:18 he again refers to precious metals that cannot redeem us. Only the precious *blood* of Jesus can do that. Jesus is called a precious *living stone*, rejected by men, but chosen by God. (I Peter 2:4) Jesus is referred to as a precious *corner stone* in 1 Peter 2:6. Men reject Jesus because they want to build their own lives, but if we build upon Him, we "shall not be confounded" (or put to shame). *Jesus* is precious to those who believe. (I Peter 2:7) Peter talks of a precious *faith*. (II Peter 1:1) If we have obtained this precious faith in Jesus, then we are acceptable to God no matter who we are. We then receive the most valuable privilege in the world, that of living in the presence of God forever. In II Peter 1:4, we read of the precious *promises* that are given to us. The promises we receive from our Heavenly Father are based on His integrity and will surely be fulfilled in His own time. The promises of being born again and adopted as His children and of enjoying eternal life in Heaven are priceless. When we think of the price that was paid to redeem us so that we can partake of these precious promises, we should be filled with love and praise, proclaiming the name of our Lord Jesus. Just what *is* more precious to you? The material things in life or the blood of Jesus and the life that is promised through Him?

- When I think of precious things, do I think of my material possessions, or of spiritual things?
- What do I have in my life that may be more important to me than the things of Jesus?
- *Lord, I desire to "set my affections on things above," and I ask You to show me how truly precious You are.*

Rejoicing In Tribulation

"As sorrowful, yet alway rejoicing."
- II Corinthians 6:10

As we read about the struggles and hardships of Job, we find it hard to see that he had any reason at all to rejoice. I wonder how I would feel if, in one day's time, I lost all of my children (an unbearable thought in itself), all of my income and possessions, even my health. Would I feel joyful? I'm afraid not. Job lost all of his children and his wealth, then developed painful boils from head to foot. And to top it all off, his wife advised him to "curse God and die." Then his friends came with their depressing advice and criticism. Job wished he had never been born. (3:3) He didn't know about the meeting between God and Satan (1:6-12), and he felt that God Himself was against him. We can hardly imagine a more sorrowful condition.

But "in all this Job sinned not." Job was viewing his circumstances through God, rather than trying to see God through his pain. I have, at times, cried out "Where are You, God?" in the midst of a dark time. But seeing our trials through Jesus is the only way to experience true joy in suffering. Reflecting on the unspeakable suffering Jesus endured for us produces in us an assurance that since our faithful high priest "ever liveth to make intercession for us," we can triumph over suffering. Because of Job's steadfast confidence in God's integrity, he was able to declare unflinchingly, "For I know that my redeemer liveth and that He shall stand at the latter day upon the earth." (Job 19:25) Joy in suffering is an attitude that will help further the cause of Christ rather than causing someone to stumble by our bitterness or hopelessness. Job was able to rejoice through an incredibly dark time. Can we do the same?

- Am I willing to allow God to show me the joy in tribulation rather than focusing on my trials?
- Do I spend time in prayer, Scripture reading, singing or sharing with others when I am down?
- *Lord, reveal to me the steps I need to take to feel the joy You have for me in dark times.*

Restoring Relationships

"Be ye kind one to another…forgiving one another, even as God for Christ's sake hath forgiven you."
- Ephesians 4:32

There had been a lot of conflict between Jacob and Esau. Jacob had fled his homeland years ago, as Esau was plotting revenge. Now he was ready to go back home and make restitution with his brother.

The last time Jacob had seen his brother, Esau had wanted to kill him. As he traveled toward his homeland, Jacob learned that Esau was actually on his way to meet him, with four hundred men. Jacob was terrified! He didn't know Esau's plans and prayed desperately for divine protection. He sent servants ahead with gifts of animals hoping to gain Esau's favor. He must have trembled fearfully when he saw Esau coming toward him. But he bravely went ahead, bowing low seven times, showing the sign of respect given to a king in those days. He went all out in giving gifts to Esau, in his attempt to dispel any thoughts of revenge. However, time and prayer were already affecting attitudes, and Esau was also ready to restore the relationship. We can only imagine the feelings that must have passed between the two brothers as they came together in a joyful reunion. Esau ran to meet Jacob, and they embraced and wept. What a beautiful scene that must have been as the healing tears flowed and Esau met Jacob's family for the first time. And we can only imagine, also, the freedom the brothers felt as they let go of their bitterness and wrapped the cloak of forgiveness around each other. It must have taken a great amount of courage for the brothers to put the past behind them and choose to forgive.

Have you ever been so angry with someone you wished she were dead? Have you ever known you needed to forgive someone, but you really didn't want to? You wanted to hang on to that anger, and (admit it!) you wanted revenge. Well, you wouldn't actually want to kill her. You wouldn't even want to hurt her very badly. But you surely wouldn't mind seeing her hurt a little! I think we've all been there to one extent or another. But think about it. All the time you're fuming and sputtering and having one-sided "piece-of-my-mind" conversations with her in your head, she doesn't even know it. She is going about her daily business, and you are actually hurting no one but yourself. When we choose to forgive someone, it doesn't make her right, but it sets us free. Yes, forgiveness is a choice. When we truly forgive, we release our adversary from all accountability. When we choose to forgive those who have wronged us, we can experience a blessed freedom and the sweetness of a restored relationship.

- Am I holding onto bitter feelings toward someone I need to forgive?
- What wrongs have I committed that I need to make right in order to restore this relationship?
- *Lord, this is not an easy thing to do, and I desperately need Your help to work through this forgiveness process.*

 Read: Luke 10:25-37

Thieves

*"The thief cometh not but for to steal,
and to kill, and to destroy."
- John 10:10*

Have you ever stopped to think about the thieves in your life that are stealing something very valuable from you? These vicious robbers want to steal the sweet peace God has given you.

When the man in the story of the good Samaritan was going to Jericho, he "fell among thieves." These evil men wounded him, took his clothes (and, I would imagine, any money he had with him) and left, leaving him lying beside the road half dead. These thieves had the mindset that, "*what's yours is mine and I'm taking it.*" The priest and the Levite who came along, saw the man, and "passed by on the other side," had the attitude that *"What's mine is mine and I'm keeping it!"* They weren't interested in defiling themselves by touching this unclean Jew, or risking their safety if the robbers were hiding nearby. The Samaritan, however, had a different approach. Without thinking of himself, he tended to the wounded man with the mind that *"what is mine is yours and I will gladly share it with you."*

Satan will use the trials in your life, large or small, to steal your peace with tormenting thoughts of "what if..." or WHY did this have to happen to me? He will make the small trials seem big, and the big trials seem huge. He'll try hard to keep your mind on the struggles and the pain, keeping you from looking to Jesus for your help and comfort. Personal sin is another thief of peace. The guilt that comes as a consequence of sin will keep you awake at night and trouble your mind during the day. Even the sins of others can be a major robber of a peaceful heart. When the sinful actions of others affect your own life, it's not easy to keep your focus on Jesus and trust Him to work things out for your good.

Healing the wounds inflicted by these thieves is often painful. The man in the story likely had a painful recovery, but he was soothed by the loving care of the Samaritan and the innkeeper. The wounds we receive from the thieves of trials, sin, and others can be painful, too. Even the healing can be painful, but our Good Samaritan, Jesus, will never "pass by on the other side." He will meet us where we are to bind up our wounds, pouring on the oil and wine of His love and forgiveness. As we focus on Him rather than on our pain, as we confess our sin and claim His promises to meet our every need, we will heal from our wounds, and the thieves will have lost the victory.

- Are thieves in my life destroying the peace in my heart?
- Do I fully believe that Jesus has already won the victory over these thieves and will carry me to victory, too?
- *Lord, reveal to me any thieves in my life and pour on the oil of Your love to heal the wounds, making me whole again.*

Protection

"Put on the whole armour of God that ye may be able to stand against the wiles of the devil."
- Ephesians 6:11

I had been through a few experiences I felt resulted from being spiritually unprotected. Times that I had not prayed, had not put on the "whole armour of God" before rushing into my day.

This led to a deeper interest in this passage in Ephesians. As I studied it and prayed through it one morning, I began to wonder. Just how do you do this? How can we, as Christian women, put on the whole armour of God?

As I meditated on it, and discussed it with my church sisters, it became clear to me. We can't. God can! Our job is to read and memorize Scripture. (Reciting Scripture is a powerful tool against Satan.) And to pray fervently each day-- To "pray without ceasing." Then God will enable us to stand on the truth. He will give us peace and courage to live a life of righteousness. He will send experiences to increase our faith. All of which works together as His armour, making us strong to stand against the wiles of the devil. Satan knows his time is short. "As a roaring lion, he walketh about, seeking whom he may devour." (I Peter 5:8) We can't afford to be without this protection!

- Do I take time to put on the armor of God each morning?
- Do I understand the importance of this protection?
- *Lord, open my heart to the danger of being unprotected in this evil world and help me to be prepared for each day.*

November

The Whole Armor Of God, Part I

*"Finally, my (sisters), be strong in the Lord,
and in the power of his might."
- Ephesians 6:10*

Paul tells us that in the Christian life we are not fighting our battles against other people. Even though it *seems* like our problems are caused by others, we are actually engaged in a battle with Satan. He is a vicious fighter whose goal is to steal, to kill, and to destroy. He wants to convince you that you are helpless and hopeless. We know, however, that God is stronger, and we can depend on His strength and the armor He gives us to bring us victoriously through these battles.

Let's examine these pieces of armor a little more closely. First of all, God tells us to *stand*. We won't be ready for the battle if we're sitting or lying down spiritually.

Then He provides us with a *strong belt of truth*. Satan is nothing but a pack of lies that can sometimes actually sound true. He spreads them through the mouths of other people, romance books and other reading material, billboards along the highway, and through many of the entertainments the world has to offer. I've heard a minister say that we need to be alert constantly to these lies, and immediately "throw the cold waters of truth on the fires of temptation." Quench the temptations before Satan can burn you.

The *breastplate of righteousness* protects our hearts. The heart is the center of all our emotions and trust. Satan wants us to think we are worthless and that God is not trustworthy. But God's love for us is secure. We don't ever need to fear that God doesn't care about us or love us. When we live a life of uprightness and integrity, we can wear the breastplate of God's approval with confidence.

Next, we put on the *shoes*. Now our feet are "shod with the preparation of the gospel of peace." This gives us a desire to share the good news of the Gospel. Although we are invading enemy territory, we find safety in following the feet of Jesus. He will be with us as we talk about Him and openly share what He has done for us and can do for others. We don't need to be afraid of what others might think. Jesus' love draws people to Himself, and He wants others to feel that love through each of us.

Now we have a good start in preparing for the battles of life. God provides the armor; it's up to us to use it!

- Do I understand the purpose of these pieces of armor and how God wants me to use them?
- Do I have a true desire to make use of God's protection at all times?
- *Lord, I thank you for your wonderful gift of armor. Please show me how to use it in my life each day.*

The Whole Armor Of God, Part II

"Praying always with all prayer and supplication in the Spirit...with all perseverance...for all saints."
- Ephesians 6:18

Yesterday we studied three pieces of the armor God has supplied. But God doesn't intend for us to be only partially protected, so let's go on. There are more pieces to put on!

We need to pick up the *shield of faith*. In a battle, a shield is a movable piece that is carried on the arm and used as protection against spears, arrows, or bullets. Some of Satan's attacks, such as insults, temptations, or setbacks in our plans are easy for us to recognize. But Satan has many other flaming arrows like pride, bitterness, and negative thoughts that he hurls at us, hoping to catch us unguarded. This shield of faith helps us to see our circumstances *through Jesus*. With the darts of the enemy falling around us, we can look up and say, "Lord, I believe."

A helmet is protection for the head. The *helmet of salvation* protects our minds from doubting God. Satan wants us to doubt both God and our salvation. But with this helmet of protection, we can even trust God to think for us when our minds are so clouded from the confusions of life that we can't think for ourselves.

Now, at last, we pick up the *sword of the Spirit*. It's the only weapon of *offense* in our whole suit of armor. It is the Word of God which we use to thwart the evil plans of Satan. God will bring verses to our minds to use as sword thrusts like Jesus did when He quoted Scripture to Satan in the wilderness. In order for God to bring these Scriptures to our minds, we have to have them *in* our minds. Scripture memory is essential to making this part of the armor effective.

And, finally, the soldier must be in a constant spirit of prayer. Not only private times of prayer in our "prayer closet," but quick brief prayers in any situation we meet throughout the day. Prayer should be a habit that comes from the heart. Formal prayers, recited without any thought for their meaning, are no help in the combat against the hosts of hell. Our fellow soldiers in this battle need our prayers, too.

This suit of armor may sound heavy and cumbersome, but it actually makes the battle easier and the burden lighter. Going into the battle bathed in prayer and fully protected by God's armor, we will experience the miraculous deliverances and the blessings of victory God has for us along the way.

- Am I protected by the full armor of God at all times?
- Does my prayer life reflect the description in Ephesians 6:18?
- *Lord, You have given us all we need as we go into battle. Help me to use it to bring glory to You.*

God's Unconditional Love

"Yea, I have loved thee with
an everlasting love."
- Jeremiah 31:3

A friend shared with me what God revealed to her after the death of their much-loved dog. She and her husband were both very attached to their pet that was only two and a half years old. It was hard to understand why he had to suffer and die at such a young age.

Why, she wondered, did losing their dog hurt so much? As she thought about it, she realized that the love of a dog for his master is unconditional. We can forget to feed them; we can beat them in anger, leave them tied up too long, or neglect them in other ways. But their forgiveness and boundless love are instant and unconditional.

Then her thoughts went to God's love for us. We sometimes abuse God. We ignore Him, forgetting to talk to Him as we rush through our day. We are disobedient to what we know He has asked of us. We grieve Him time and again, but He goes on loving us unconditionally. What does He ask in return? He wants us to love Him as passionately as He loves us. He loved us enough to die on the cross for us. In comparison, how is our love for Him? Maybe, she thought, God gave this dog to them to help them unlearn what many people learn as children-that all love is conditional. God has made it all so simple, but we mortals tend to make it so difficult. His love for us is unchanging, and He wants us to love Him the same way, showing it by yielding to His leading in every area of our daily lives.

- Do I recognize and feel God's unconditional love for me?
- How can I better return that love to Him?
- *Lord, I praise you for your love for me and desire to show my love for you each day.*

Of Dogs And Humans

"What shall we say then? Shall we continue in sin, that grace may abound?"
- Romans 6:1

A friend of mine was describing an experience she had while walking their dog one day. As the dog was extra frisky, she unhooked the leash and let her run. Thinking that it would surely wear her out and calm her down, she was surprised when it turned out the opposite! Even though the dog had run until she collapsed, the closer they got to home, the more active she became. She had not gotten the excitement out of her system as her owner had hoped.

Interestingly, soon after that, she read a story about a man competing in an Alaskan dog sled race. He had been advised to have his dogs worn out when he got them to the starting point, so that they would start out calm. He discovered, too late, that it didn't work that way. They were restless and rambunctious, making them hard to control. They had not gotten the excitement out of their systems as he thought they would.

We decided it sounded quite a bit like us humans! We indulge in something, thinking we'll get it out of our system, but end up craving more instead. Although this could mean harmful substances such as drugs and alcohol, it could also hit closer home. Like the times I sit down to read just a chapter of a good book and end up reading on and on, neglecting my duties. Or I allow myself just one chocolate to satisfy the craving and eat half the bag. Or perhaps I gaze at something in the store that I would like to have but don't really need and end up impulsively buying it.

While reading, chocolates, and shopping, like running dogs, aren't bad in themselves, the concept is clear. When sampling a temptation, it's easy to be pulled into more rather than being satisfied with a little. It's easy for something innocent to become an act of sin. We need to ask the Lord to reveal any area of hidden sin in our lives and for the courage to take the necessary steps to confess and forsake actions that are not pleasing to Him.

- What area of temptation do I need to eradicate from my life?
- Am I willing to face that area and to eliminate the temptation?
- *Lord, give me strength to stand fast against any temptations that I face today.*

Sand In My Clay

"Hath not the potter power over the clay, of the same lump to make one vessel unto honor, and another unto dishonor?"
- Romans 9:21

Our minister gave us an illustration of transforming our old sin nature into a new life in Christ. Imagine taking a popsicle stick and covering half of it with glue. Now roll it in sand until it is well coated. This is a dirty stick, just as our sin natures are imperfect before God. Then take some clay and wrap it around the sandy stick, like wrapping a robe of righteousness around a new believer. Pull out the stick and you have the ball of clay (new life) minus the sandy stick, (old life). Look closely, however, and you'll see that the stick left a definite impression in the ball. And most likely several grains of sand are still embedded in the clay.

As God works with our lives, molding us into His image, those grains of sand work their way to the surface as they would in the ball of clay. Sometimes the grains of sand in our lives are obvious. Sometimes they are still hidden deep inside where we can't see them, or we can choose not to acknowledge them. They may be in the form of pride, bitterness, anger, or impatience. Maybe they are grains of self-pity, self-righteousness, hypocrisy, or envy. These grains of sand may feel more like boulders of rock as we struggle against them. But as we allow God to remove these grains, the sin nature impression in our life will become less and less as we are molded into the image of Christ.

- Do I recognize these grains of sand as they work their way to the surface of my life?
- Am I willing to allow God to help me remove them?
- *Lord, make me a willing vessel on your potter's wheel.*

Freedom At Last

"But the day of the Lord will come as thief in the night."
- II Peter 3:10

A friend shared with me that she had recently read a book telling of the lives of a few Christian relief workers in a poverty-stricken, war-torn country. As the workers had opportunity, they shared the Gospel with the local residents. Eventually, they were arrested for this and thrown into prison. As the war came closer to the city in which the Christians were imprisoned, the prisoners heard more bombings, artillery, and anti-aircraft activity. As time went on, the Christians were moved from the first prison to another and then yet another. After awhile, they spent days in one prison and nights in another. The uncertainty and apprehension were nerve-wracking, and hope of being released rose and fell unpredictably. Finally, as the enemy armies neared the city, the captors moved the Christians out during the night, through the devastated countryside, to another prison.

As the captives tried to adjust to their new surroundings, one of them noticed their captors leaving the compound. Then, suddenly, other armed men came through the door and announced that they were free! Enemies of their enemies had overtaken the city! Can we even imagine the relief? After all the days of captivity, they were free.

Does life on earth ever feel like a prison to you? Do you feel like a captive some days with all the never-ending demands of child-care or the inflictions of a physical impairment? Perhaps you feel the stresses of home-schooling several special-needs children, or you may be in a less-than-blissful marriage situation. Are you possibly dealing with a strong-willed teen or a distressing church problem? Someday, Jesus will return, and we will be truly *free!* He has already come to free us from our sins. But someday soon He will come to free us from the struggles between our flesh and spirit, and we, like the captive Christians, will be free. Can we even begin to imagine the wonder of that? Focusing on that hope rather than on the perplexities of life provides a measure of freedom while we await His coming.

- Do I consider serving Christ as slavery or as a privilege?
- How could I increase my anticipation of Jesus' return?
- *Help me, Lord, to keep my focus on You and Your return rather than so much on my circumstances here.*

Journey To Heaven

*"That ye would walk worthy of God,
who hath called you unto his kingdom."
- I Thessalonians 2:12*

The westward movement was a difficult journey to a desired, dreamed of destination. Many of the wagon trains began their journey at Independence, Missouri, and slowly traveled west to Oregon. Traveling through deep ruts or thick sticky mud, the wagons were often damaged and had to be repaired, causing lengthy delays. Struggling to get the wagons up steep mountain passes, the loads would be lightened by leaving cherished possessions behind. Water and food became scarce in places and oxen died. Sickness and death were common, with graves needing to be dug beside the trail and sad funerals performed. But there were joys, too. Pleasant weather, a smooth trail, or new babies born along the way. They saw spectacular scenery, a profusion of flowers, and amazing wildlife. Deep bonds of friendship were formed as these pioneers traveled and struggled together for months. For most, excitement was high as they pulled away from Independence, but spirits often sagged through the long, weary journey. As they drew closer and closer to the new land, however, discouragement would turn to enthusiasm, and they were willing to press on. The journey's end would be worth the trials!

Our Christian journey to Heaven is a lot like this. We are excited and enthused as we begin our new walk with God. Days are full of sunshine as we enjoy the blessings God sends. Sometimes we become discouraged and weary, however, mired down in trials and temptations. We struggle to unburden our lives of sinful thoughts, bad habits, and ungodly traits, and to go on with a lighter heart. We weep when we lose family and friends to death. But we have joys, too. God sends many signs of His love, through Scripture, family, dear friends, nature, or pets. As we grow closer to Him and to our new Home, we press on, knowing that eternal life in Heaven will be worth all the hardships of the journey. If your days are dark with clouds of trial and discouragement, take heart! God is traveling with us every step of the way, and our destination will be worth anything we have to endure here.

- Do I see my life as a journey, taking me from birth to my eternal home?
- Do I recognize the trials as being necessary for my spiritual growth along the way?
- *Lord, I thank You for the beauty along life's way and for the trials to strengthen me.*

Backpacks And Boulders

"Bear ye one another's burdens,
and so fulfill the law of Christ."
- Galatians 6:2

Paul tells us in Galatians 6:2 that we are to bear one another's burdens. Then in verse 5, he tells us every man shall bear his own burden. It sounds as though he is contradicting himself, but the word "bear" is actually translated in two different ways here. A minister once described it as the difference between boulders and backpacks.

As we walk the pathway of our life, we may come upon fellow travelers carrying boulders on their backs. Perhaps they are grieving the loss of a loved one. Or suffering from a crippling physical problem. Maybe they are facing a troubling problem that looks impossible. We can walk with them a ways, shouldering some of the burden with prayer, words of encouragement, or kind deeds, "and so fulfill the law of Christ."

In verse 5, bearing our burdens can be likened to a backpack we carry as a disciple of Christ. We are responsible to bear what God asks of us. That may include the struggles that go with being a wife, a mother, a teacher, a servant in your home, or helping others outside the home.

At times, God asks of us an extra service or gives us an unexpected trial and our backpack becomes a boulder. Then He sends others to walk beside us, to help bear the burden until it is lightened or removed. We can resist these burdens or we can accept the help He provides to make them lighter. Pride should not keep us from accepting the assistance others would like to offer us. As we help others and as we allow others to help us, we experience God's blessings together. As we look around, most of us can find someone who needs encouragement. As you reach out to bless her life, you will be blessed also.

- Do I recognize the "boulders" in the lives of others?
- Am I willing to shoulder some of that load, and do what I can to help?
- *Lord, I want to be willing to lighten the load of others in any way you ask of me.*

To Vow, Or Not To Vow?

"But let your yea be yea; and your nay, nay; lest ye fall into condemnation."
- James 5:12

"Do you plan to go to Annual Meeting?" Our church's annual conference was to be held in a state several hundred miles away, so some would be going and others would not.

The young father of four thought briefly and then replied, "Well, if someone gives me $3000.00 and builds my barn for me, I'll go." A few days later, this young father opened a letter from his mother and discovered a check for $3000.00! She had decided to begin dividing her assets among her sons.

The next time the man talked to his friend, he told him about the check. The question came again: "Are you going to Annual Meeting, then?" When he replied that he didn't think so, his friend was surprised. "You don't think so? Doesn't the Bible say, 'It is better not to vow, than to vow and not pay?' "

After thinking that over seriously, the would-be farmer did go to the meeting. And when he was ready to build his barn later, he received help as it was needed, often from unexpected sources. By the time his cows were ready to milk, he had a barn ready to use.

How seriously do we take what we say? In Ecclesiastes, Solomon warns against making careless promises to God. It is better not to vow than to make a promise to God and not keep it or to only partially fulfill your vow. Our word should be enough without needing to say "I promise..." or "I vow..." If we are always truthful, we won't feel the need to back up what we say with a vow.

- Do I always take what I say seriously?
- Have I made any promises to God that I have not yet kept?
- *Dear God, put a watch before my lips and help me not to make any false promises.*

Holy Boldness

"Let us come boldly unto the throne of grace,
that we may...find grace...in time of need."
- Hebrews 4:16

The Bible gives us some good examples of men who came before the Lord in prayer with holy boldness.

Hezekiah (II Kings 19:1-19)--During Hezekiah's reign as king of Judah, he received a message from Sennacherib, King of Assyria, ordering him to surrender. After reading the letter and realizing that his situation was hopeless, Hezekiah took it to the house of the Lord and prayed boldly for deliverance. God honored his prayer by sending an army to attack the Assyrian capital, forcing Sennacherib to return home at once.

Joshua (Joshua 10:1-15)--Joshua and his armies were on their way to help defend Gibeon against the five kings of the Amorites. On the way, God assured Joshua that He would help them. During the battle, Joshua boldly told the sun to stand still. God honored that request, giving them more daylight time. The victory was theirs, "for the Lord fought for Israel."

Elijah (I Kings 18:16-40)--During the contest on Mount Carmel with the prophets of Baal, Elijah called boldly on God to send fire from heaven. His prayer was answered dramatically as the fire consumed everything, including the stones and the water in the trench.

These men had God's assurance of victory, but they needed to "go out and conquer." We also have the assurance of God's help, when we enlist in spiritual battle, and "go out to conquer" with prayer. (I John 15:16, John 5:14, 15) We come to Him reverently, for He is our King, but with boldness and confidence, for He is faithful in keeping every promise.

Are you facing a situation which you know you need to "go out and conquer?" Life is full of such situations but don't let them trip you up. Approach the throne of God with Holy boldness, trust Him for help, then *go out and conquer!*

- Do I portray a holy boldness in my prayers, expecting God to answer within His will?
- Are you facing a new situation in which you sense God may be calling you to go out and conquer?
- *Lord, help me to trust You enough to approach You with confidence.*

Peace Like A River

"The Lord of hosts is with us;
the God of Jacob is our refuge."
- Psalm 46:11

Meditating on the 46th Psalm, we can feel the power in God's promise to us. He is our refuge and strength. He is right beside us ("very present") when we need help. The Psalm speaks of major catastrophes. Earthquakes, mountains shaking and crumbling, oceans roaring. It also speaks of political disasters. Heathen nations raging and kingdoms toppling.

While there are wars, violence, and destruction all over the world today, how is it closer home? As Christian women, wives, and mothers, our daily concerns are more likely to be right in our own hearts and homes. It may be sickness or impending death, for us or a loved one. Fear of failure in guiding a struggling teenager, or fear of adding another baby to the family when life already seems exhausting and overwhelming. Or it could be just facing another day that looks impossible.

But... *There is a river...* Many cities have a river flowing through them, making farming possible and in many ways making life easier for the people. Jerusalem has no river. But the Psalmist writes of God Himself being a river to sustain the people's lives. Everything a river is to other cities, God is to His people.

And so He is for us today. Take time each day to "be still and know that He is God, exalting Him." You will find that He becomes a river of peace flowing through you, even in the midst of all the turmoil around you.

- Am I taking time daily to commune with God?
- What situations do I have today that I could allow God's river of peace to cover?
- *Lord, fill me with that river that You are and give me the peace that passes understanding.*

 Read: Psalm 62

Walls Of Defense

"He only is my rock and my salvation:
He is my defense; I shall not be moved."
- Psalm 62:6

In long ago days cities were built with walls around them. Some towns had two thick walls which were braced at intervals with cross-walls. These walls protected the city from its enemies and kept the city and its people from being easy targets.

As Christians, we need walls of defense around us, too. These walls protect us from the enemy's attacks and make us strong in the battle of daily life.

A good strong relationship with God is a thick protecting wall. Knowing Him intimately gives us a deep desire to avoid anything that would destroy our peace in Him. God's promises provide an inner wall of protection for us. He will never leave us (Hebrews 13:5), especially in the moment of temptation, but will provide a way of escape. (I Corinthians 10:13)

Having a plan of action when temptation hits is as essential as a cross-wall when Satan attacks. Reciting Scripture, singing, or sharing the struggle with a friend can help us resist evil.

Associating with God's people (II Timothy 2:22) gives us a desire and a strength to live a life that is pleasing to the Lord and provides a valuable source of support in our struggles.

Our character can be another cross-wall of defense. Good character is developed throughout our entire lifetime. It is strengthened by overcoming temptations and weakened by yielding. It can be torn down quickly, but it takes much longer to rebuild it.

Just as weak places or holes in city walls allow the enemy easy access to our lives, so carelessness and a lack of attention permits Satan to sneak in to destroy us. God and His Word provide walls of defense for us as we stay within the shelter of His protection.

- How strong are the walls of defense around my life?
- Am I staying within the safety of the walls of God's protection?
- *Lord, please reveal to me the weak places and give me the wisdom and the strength to fix them.*

Gold For My King

"And they sing the song of Moses...saying...
just and true are thy ways, thou King of saints."
- Revelation 15:3

We can read a story in history, around 550 B.C., about a man named Croesus who was the last king of Lydia, an old city of Asia Minor. Croesus had expanded his kingdom by conquest until he was an extremely wealthy man. Naturally this wealth caught the attention of other kings, and Cyrus of Persia, who ruled much of the known world at that time, decided to make that kingdom his own. He marched his army up to the kingdom of Croesus and captured it. He then took Croesus up to the top of the city wall to watch while Cyrus's soldiers looted the city. When Croesus showed no reaction, Cyrus asked him, "How can you be so calm? They are robbing you of all your gold!"

Croesus replied, "No, they're not. You have conquered this city. It is yours now and that's *your* gold they're stealing!" Cyrus, realizing the truth of this, immediately stopped the looting.

When we give our lives to Jesus, our King, we give all that we are, all that we have, and all that we may ever become over to His rule. We are now His servants. Why then, should we become indignant or bitter when something in our life is taken away? It is now His, and we have no claim to any of the wealth, friends, career, or even the good health that may have been ours. Those things are now in His possession, and we would do well to relinquish them, as Croesus did, into the Conqueror's hands. While King Cyrus did not show good judgment with his newly acquired bounty, we can be supremely confident that our King is able and ready to take the best care of anything we turn over to Him.

This is not an easy thing to do! It takes a deep trust that God knows what is best for us and that He will work out His will in our lives to His Glory. Not always easy, but always worth it.

- Have I truly relinquished *all* my treasure to my King?
- Do I believe that He will take perfect care of the gold that I give Him?
- *Lord, I turn my life over to You in a new way today, trusting You to use it to Your glory.*

 Read: Joshua 6

The Battle Is The Lord's

"And the Lord said unto Joshua, see,
I have given into thine hand Jericho."
- Joshua 6:2

God's plan for defeating the city of Jericho must have seemed terribly lame to Joshua. God had told him the victory would be theirs if they would follow His plan. But really, walk around the city once a day for six days and on the seventh day walk around seven times and shout?! What kind of a maneuver would that have seemed like to Joshua, a high ranking military officer? Think about it…Jericho was a symbol of military power. It was one of the oldest cities in the world, fortified with double walls up to 25 feet high. Guards on top of the walls could see for miles. What a battle plan for a seemingly invincible city!

But we don't read that there was even a moment's hesitation from Joshua or the people. They had already experienced God's deliverance at the Red Sea, the Jordan River, and all through their forty years of wandering in the wilderness. They trusted God completely to do exactly as He had said. And we know the ending of the story. After watching the Israelites march around Jericho for six days, the worried Canaanites inside the city must have thought these people were crazy. But just as God had promised, at the shouts of the people and the blowing trumpets, the walls fell inward and the city was defeated.

God's people were faced with a stronghold that looked impossible to defeat. They knew, however, before they even began, that the enemy had been defeated. God had already told them He would give the city to them. They just had to obey in faith, and the victory was won.

Do you have a Jericho in your life? Do you have a bad habit you have tried and tried to break, but you just can't seem to gain victory? Perhaps you have a relationship that's gone sour and you can't bring yourself to make the first move to repair it. Bitterness, pride, fantasies, and anger can all be strongholds, difficult to overcome. We can walk around and around our Jericho until the path becomes a deep rut and just not accomplish a thing. But we don't need to! God has already defeated our enemy, Satan, and we can overcome through Christ's power. He is waiting to give us our Jericho. Our job is to obey in faith, listening to His voice and following without question. Victory may not be immediate, but with God's help, the enemy *will be* defeated.

- Do I believe God is still willing and able to deliver me from the strongholds of my enemy?
- What strongholds can I identify in my life today that God is able to "give unto me?"
- *Lord, reveal to me any strongholds in my life and lead me in the way of deliverance from them.*

First Class

"And we have known and believed
the love that God hath to us."
- I John 4:16

First class! Standing in the airport waiting room, my friend almost laughed aloud. She did not see herself as a "first class" person and certainly would not have paid for what she considered an extravagance. Recently, her mother had died and flight arrangements had been made hastily, as there was business to attend to in connection with her mother's estate. Now she was waiting to board, but she had not yet been assigned a seat number. As other passengers left the waiting area to board the flight, she was getting a bit nervous. Finally, when the area was almost empty, her brother-in-law went with her to check on the seat number one more time. The delay lengthened as the clerk rechecked the information, but she did receive a seat number. What a relief. They were already far from home, and being stranded at an airport in a strange city was not something she cared to experience. When her brother-in-law, the experienced traveler, took a look at the ticket, he discovered to her amazement that the seat was in first class!

She really enjoyed the large seat with plenty of leg room; the gourmet meal on real china; the peace and quiet of being almost alone in the front section of the plane; and the view out the window. Although she didn't consider herself worthy of first class, her Father obviously did. She didn't have the funds to pay for it, but He gave it as a gift. In her time of grief, this completely unexpected touch of His hand was extra special. Our God delights in surprising His children with unexpected blessings. Do you recognize the gifts He gives you? Do you thank Him for them? How thankful we can be that God is interested in all the details of our days, whether they be just the usual routine, or unusual "out of your comfort zone" days. The nice "out of the ordinary" things that happen don't just "happen." They are gifts from a loving Heavenly Father.

- How could I become more aware of and thankful for God's special gifts?
- Do I recognize His gifts as blessings from Him?
- *Lord, I thank You for Your tender love and all the special ways you show it.*

Attitudes Matter!

"And this he said to prove him:
for he himself knew what he would do."
- John 6:6

When Joseph was seventeen years old, his God-given dreams were rejected by his jealous brothers and even by his loving father. From that time until he was made ruler over Egypt at age 30 (Genesis 41:46), Joseph lived through trial after trial that would have tested the faith of anyone.

Through it all, Joseph kept a good attitude. Even though his brothers hated him, he obeyed his father, going to see how they fared when they were away from home, tending the flocks. His brothers, in a fit of jealousy, wanted to kill him. They threw him into a pit and then sold him to strangers. They took him with them to a foreign country and sold him to Potiphar. But Joseph's good attitude went with him and he found grace in the sight of his master. (Genesis 39:4)

When Potiphar's wife lied and got him thrown into prison, it would certainly have been understandable if he had become angry or bitter. But it seems Joseph's attitude stayed positive, even in prison. He found favor in the sight of the prison keeper who put him in charge of the entire prison. (Genesis 39:22)

After interpreting dreams for the butler and the baker, Joseph was disappointed again when the butler forgot about him and he spent another *two years* in the prison. Then, when the Pharaoh needed to have a dream interpreted, the butler finally remembered Joseph. After interpreting the dream, Pharaoh set Joseph over all the land of Egypt, in charge of preparing for the years of famine. The best part of the story is when Joseph's family--70 souls!--is saved from the famine by Joseph himself. Now he understood God's plan.

For *thirteen years* Joseph had kept a good attitude as he surely wondered why God was allowing all these trials in his life. Now he knew that although his brothers had meant evil, God meant it all for good. Not only did he save his family and the country from starving, but the folks around him could plainly see the blessing of God in his life. Attitudes do matter!

- Do others around me see the blessing of God in my life?
- In what ways does my attitude need to change to reflect God's blessing today?
- *Keeping a good attitude isn't always easy, Lord. Thank You for Joseph's good example to us.*

God's Supermarket

"He that hath no money;
come ye, buy, and eat..."
- Isaiah 55:1

Not long ago I was doing some shopping in our local super-center. Imagine my dismay when I discovered, at the check-out counter, that I didn't have my debit card. I had no checkbook and not enough cash. Embarrassed and aggravated at myself, I told the clerk that I'd have to run out to my van and get my card. Leaving my poor mortified daughters standing there with the empty cart and waiting customers behind them, I hurried out through the parking lot. I was appalled to find that the card was not there, either. After searching the console and frantically digging through the pile of stuff that had collected between the seats, I admitted defeat and slunk back into the store. I told the young man waiting there that I would have to go get my card and come back. He kindly stashed my bags under the counter until I returned later with the missing card. It never even entered my mind to ask the clerk if I could simply have the items without paying for them. I can imagine the look on his face if I had!

God, however, has a "supermarket" overflowing with everything we need, and He invites us all to **come,** even though we have no money, **buy,** and **eat.** Nothing has a price, no money is needed, and there is no limit on any item! Along the wall are overflowing cases of the *milk* and *meat* of God's Word. In an aisle marked "Galatians Five," we find a lovely display of spiritual *fruit*. Other aisles offer bottled *oils* of forgiveness, mercy, grace, and love. *Wines* of joy and fellowship line an ornate wooden display rack. Refreshing *waters* of the Holy Spirit flow freely. There are containers of *honey* in all shapes, sizes, and flavors to sweeten daily life. We can even find healing salves and bandages for binding up wounds and broken hearts in the First Aid aisle.

The only thing necessary to shop in God's supermarket is a consciousness of our need or "thirst." Then we need to *come* (v. 1), *listen* (v. 3), and *seek God and call upon Him* (v. 6). He offers us this free nourishment that feeds our souls as we eagerly receive it. Just as we would starve physically without food, so will we starve spiritually without these daily trips to our Heavenly Father's storehouse of abundant blessings. As we feed on His Word and dine with Him in prayer and worship, we'll find our thirst being quenched with Living Water that never runs out. Praise the Lord for His mercy and kindness!

- Am I making the effort to partake of these available blessings?
- Am I remembering the thank God daily for all the free nourishment he offers to me?
- *Lord, I desire to always avail myself of, and thank You for, these thirst-quenchers that You so freely offer.*

The Sacrifice Of Praise

"By Him therefore let us offer the sacrifice of praise to God continually."
- Hebrews 13:15

This is the time of year that our thoughts turn to Thanksgiving Day. There are turkey and dressing, cranberry salad, and pumpkin pie with whipped topping. Family and friends gathering for food, fun, and fellowship; possibly adding a woodcutting party or other type of work bee. And...oh yes, we need to be thankful!

And we are thankful. It's easy to praise God for all the blessings He has given us. But what about the sacrifice of praise? In I Thessalonians 5:18, we are instructed to give thanks in everything. Everything? But Lord, am I really supposed to thank You for the struggles our son is going through in his courtship? Am I supposed to praise You for the pain and stress another son is causing us with his defiance and strong will? Do I actually need to rejoice through the personal battles of impatience, discouragement, and overeating that I can't seem to overcome? Really??

When Corrie ten Boom and her sister Betsie were in the concentration camp in Germany, there was precious little to be thankful for. With 1400 women crammed into a flea infested barracks designed to hold 400, just eight backed-up toilets, and hard wooden shelves to sleep on, it was like hell on earth. But Betsie was determined to be thankful in everything, even the fleas. They were thrilled to find out later that it was the fleas that kept the guards out of their building, giving them the freedom to hold prayer meetings and Bible studies with the other prisoners! Betsie even convinced the other women to pray for the German soldiers who would be wearing the socks they were knitting. If these women could praise God in spite of their horrible circumstances, shouldn't I be able to praise Him in my circumstances today?

- Do I truly understand the concept of the sacrifice of praise?
- Am I willing to praise Him for even the hard times in life?
- *Lord, it's not easy, but I desire to thank You for everything today, even the unpleasant things.*

A Personal Eclipse

"Let nothing be done through strife or vainglory;
but ... let each esteem other better than themselves."
- Philippians 2:3

An eclipse is an amazing happening of nature that doesn't occur very often. Scientists are able to predict exactly when an eclipse will happen and how many will happen in a certain amount of time, even in a full century. There are partial eclipses and total eclipses, depending on how the sun, moon, and earth are lined up. As the moon follows its perfect, God-designed orbit around the earth, every so often it passes directly between the earth and the sun. At that point, the moon blocks the light from the sun and casts a temporary shadow on the earth. I remember being outside during a complete solar eclipse a few years ago. The temperature dropped about ten degrees, and it became eerily dark. But, in a surprisingly short time the moon had moved on and the temperature and the light had returned to normal. This can happen many times but as the planets stay on the precise orbits that God set them on, they come through the eclipse unscathed. They continue merrily and silently on their journey none the worse for their experience.

These eclipses can actually happen on a personal level, also. They can be "partial" or "total." We can experience them from both angles; the shadowed, or the "shadower." You may think you're doing just fine in a job you enjoy, when God sends someone along to take over, who possibly does a much better job than you were doing. The light that was shining on you is dimmed and the other person is now getting the recognition. The temperature in your heart cools and life looks dim for awhile. But don't fly out of orbit! The earth doesn't shrink from the shadow but bravely stays put, waiting for the shadow to pass. God has a perfect plan for you. As you willingly stay on the path He has laid out for you, you will come out of the eclipse unharmed. The shadow will pass and the light will shine again. You may look back and see clearly why the eclipse happened. And you will know that it was God's perfect will.

On the other hand, you may be the one whom God calls to be the "shadower." It may be painful for you to have to cause that eclipse. The moon takes the full heat and bright light of the sun as it passes between it and the earth. But it doesn't shy away from or veer off its orbit; it journeys on and so can you. The same God who keeps the sun, the planets, and the stars in their courses will keep you, too, as you live out the plan He has for you.

- Is there an "eclipse" going on in my life right now?
- Does my attitude reflect the Son in the way I respond to this personal overshadowing?
- *Lord, show me clearly the way You would have me go and give me the courage to follow Your perfect will.*

Read: I Samuel 18:1-5; 19:1-7

Be A Jonathan And Keep Loving

"The soul of Jonathan was knit with the soul of David, and Jonathan loved him as his own soul."
- I Samuel 18:1

Jonathan and David seem like a rather unlikely pair to become such good friends. Jonathan was the son of a king. He was a man of war, a soldier in his father's army with some pretty impressive victories to his credit. David, on the other hand, was only a young shepherd boy. He was the youngest of twelve brothers and spent his days watching his father's sheep. We aren't told exactly how they became friends. After David had been called from the pasture and anointed by Samuel, he was called to the King's house to serve King Saul. He spent much time playing his harp to soothe the King, who was troubled by an evil spirit. Saul liked him and made him his personal armor bearer. Sometime after that, David defeated the much feared Philistine giant, Goliath. Over this time, a deep and lasting friendship developed between Jonathan and David.

Jonathan was legitimately the successor to his father's throne. He loved David so much, however, that in an amazing and touching expression of his love, he handed over his right to the kingship. He gave David his robe, his tunic, his sword, bow, and belt, indicating that he was willing to forego his rights to see David crowned instead.

As David won battle after battle, he became more and more loved and admired by the people. Jonathan was still a soldier, too, but it was David who received the praise. Jonathan could easily have regretted his decision and become bitter against David, but he didn't. As Saul became jealous and tried over and over to kill David, Jonathan's loyalty to his friend remained strong. He interceded for David, convincing his father to spare his life. He kept David informed, sometimes by prearranged signs, about what was happening with King Saul. He wept when they had to separate so that David could go into hiding. David had, in a sense, eclipsed Jonathan, but Jonathan didn't fly out of orbit. He remained on the path God had for him to follow and just kept on loving David.

Is there someone you love who has "eclipsed" you? Is it hard to keep a right attitude toward her? You don't need to become bitter or let it ruin your friendship. Ask God to give you a love for that person that overcomes the bad feelings. Support her and encourage her in what she is doing. It wasn't easy for David to be the King! It may not be easy for your friend to be in her circumstances, either. Don't give up. Be a Jonathan and just keep on loving!

- Do I continue to love someone who becomes "greater" than I am?
- How can I ask the Lord to help me improve my attitude toward people who threaten me?
- *Lord, instill in me a love that overcomes all negative or jealous feelings toward others.*

Be A Martha And Keep Serving

"But one thing is needful:
and Mary hath chosen that good part."
- Luke 10:42

The story of Mary and Martha is familiar. We hear it often: "Be a Mary, not a Martha!" I always cringe when I hear that, thinking that Martha is being treated unfairly. (I'm sure it's because I'm much more like Martha than Mary!) But really, is it so wrong to be a "Martha?" Of course not. Mary and Martha both loved Jesus and He loved both of them. Martha just got her priorities mixed up at times, just like it's easy for us to do today.

I can almost hear her. "Oh Mary! Here comes Jesus and this house is a mess! Help me quickly. We must clean up and get some supper ready; bring in fresh water and change the beds…" I can also identify with her frustration when Mary didn't help but just sat with their Guest and listened to Him speak. After all, who else was going to do the work if they didn't? Martha became so annoyed that she finally asked Jesus to tell Mary to come help her! Jesus gently told Martha that she was too worried about the work, and Mary was serving Him in a more important way. He wasn't blaming Martha for being concerned about the housework. He knew someone needed to do it. But He also knew that in her sincere desire to serve Him, she was actually neglecting Him.

Now, I'm afraid that with my "Martha" nature, I would have been upset. If a guest would say that to me, my human nature would want to say (silently, of course): "Well, fine. Forget it. We'll all go without supper!" But Martha seems to have taken the rebuke as constructive criticism and handled it well. She didn't stay annoyed at Jesus. Later, when Lazarus died, Martha heard that Jesus was coming and went out to meet Him while Mary waited in the house. (John 11:20) And another time when Jesus came to Bethany before the Passover, they fixed supper for Him and Martha served. (John 12:2)

Jesus didn't expect Martha to be just like Mary, and Martha didn't try to be. I would imagine that she set her priorities back in the right order, but she also did what God had instilled in her to do and she kept on serving. Service in love is a good thing and pleasing to the Lord. But He doesn't want us to become so busy doing things *for* Him that we don't spend time *with* Him. If God didn't create you to be a "Mary," be a "Martha." Keep Him first in your life, but be yourself and keep on serving!

- Am I so busy in my service for Him that I'm no longer fully devoted to Him?
- How can I rearrange my life so that I have more time to spend *with* Him?
- *Lord, remind me that in order to serve You effectively, I must spend time at your feet daily.*

Refreshment

"Thou preparest a table before me."
- Psalm 23:5

God is taking the pathway of my life through a stretch of wilderness. It's not fun. It's *dry*... Reading the Bible is like seeing dusty words on parched paper. It's *rocky*... The irritations of daily life trip me up and I speak sharply, reacting negatively to my family. It's *dark*... My prayers seem to bounce off the ceiling, shattering at my feet. It's *desolate*... Where are you, God? Do you care? Do you even hear my cries?

But wait! Look over there! It's a table. A beautiful table that God has prepared for me right here in the wilderness. Inviting me to pull up a chair and feast. To be served by my Lord from a bowl of *grace* (II Corinthians 12:9: "My grace is sufficient for thee.") To enjoy a slice of nourishment from the platter of *peace* (John 14:27: "Peace I leave with you, my peace I give unto you: not as the world giveth, give I unto you.") A generous helping of *mercy* (Psalm 136:1: "O give thanks unto the Lord; for he is good: for his mercy endureth forever.") A heaping spoonful of *forgiveness* (Colossians 1:14: "In whom we have redemption through his blood, even the forgiveness of sin.") And to top it all off, an overflowing goblet of *love* (Jeremiah 31:3: "I have loved thee with an everlasting love.")

I am satisfied. I am refreshed. Ready to carry on. This table and the One who prepared it are always there, ready to offer loving refreshment for weary travelers. His children are free to partake.

- As we travel through the wilderness, do we recognize the refreshment table and partake from it?
- How can I allow God to refresh me today?
- *Lord, I praise You for your grace and mercy and ask that You refresh me with Your love today.*

Be Ye Thankful

"I will offer to thee the sacrifice of thanksgiving."
- Psalm 116:17

In a sermon on the godly home, a minister told us about a couple who were headed for a divorce. All love between them had seemingly died, and they no longer saw any reason to stay together.

However, one evening Larry surprised Joann by telling her that he had a very unusual dresser. Any time he needed clean clothes, they were there. And he thanked her for keeping his clothes clean, folded, and in his dresser drawers. Another time he blessed her by thanking her for the good meals that she had been preparing all their married life. And later, for keeping the checkbook balanced. She soon realized that he really meant it, and she began to see positive things in him to be thankful for. With some effort from each of them, their marriage was turned around completely, and they no longer desired a divorce.

Expressing thanks to each other is a simple but effective way to build each other up, and can make a big difference in any relationship. And let's not forget the One who deserves our praise and thanks the most. "O give thanks unto the Lord, for he is good..." (Psalm 117:1) The more we express thankfulness, the easier it is to find things to be thankful for. We should never underestimate the power there is in blessing another's life through the simple act of giving thanks. It certainly is not always easy. David calls it "the *sacrifice* of thanksgiving."

The hardest things to be thankful for at times are the circumstances God brings into our lives. This is where the "sacrifice" of thanksgiving comes in. God tells us to give thanks in *all* things, not just the times when we naturally *feel* thankful. That can be difficult! But as we practice being thankful and make a habit of expressing our gratitude, we will experience blessings we never dreamed possible. Try it. God always blesses those who obey Him.

- How can I become more thankful?
- What difficult circumstances do I need to be thankful for today?
- *Lord, teach me to offer a "sacrifice of thanksgiving" to You, regardless of my circumstances.*

November 24 *Read: Luke 7:36-50*

Thankful For Forgiveness

"In whom we have redemption through His blood, even the forgiveness of sins."
- Colossians 1:14

I marvel at the thankfulness of the woman in this story. She was a sinful woman with a bad reputation. It must have taken an incredible amount of courage for her to go into the home of a Pharisee who knew of her and her lifestyle. But she felt such overwhelming gratitude to Jesus for having forgiven her sins, that when she heard Simon had invited Him to dinner, she went, uninvited. As Jesus reclined on the dining couch, she stood weeping in gratitude, tenderly washing His feet with her tears. She took down her long hair, which was a major social no-no in those days, and wiped His feet. She had brought an alabaster box of precious ointment which she broke open, using the ointment to anoint Jesus' feet, all the while kissing them repeatedly.

Simon was appalled, but Jesus showed him, through a parable, that this woman loved Him so much because she had been forgiven so much. Simon, who felt like he was a pretty good person and didn't need forgiveness, hadn't even shown Jesus the expected courtesies of the day.

The woman's love for Jesus was a result of the forgiveness that had already taken place. As we count our blessings, we readily think of material goods, and rightly so. But how often do we thank Him for forgiving our sins? How deep is our gratitude for His redemptive death on the cross? Are we willing to go to the house of a Pharisee to bathe the feet of Jesus with our tears of gratitude, to wipe them dry with a heart of love, and to anoint them with the oil of praise? This woman's love and thankfulness knew no bounds. How about ours?

- Am I remembering the sacrifice of Jesus with deep thankfulness?
- In what ways could I show Jesus how much I love Him today?
- *Lord, I thank You for everything You bless us with and especially for Your loving forgiveness.*

The Sovereignty Of God

"And we know that all things work together for good to them that love God."
- Romans 8:28

As I was searching for a devotional topic, God impressed on me the name of Esther. I've always liked the story of Esther and deeply admire her courage. As I was reading through the book this time, I was struck by the absolute sovereignty of God. Even though His name is not mentioned even once in the book, His control is evident throughout the events of Esther's life.

Esther was chosen from a large group of young ladies to become a queen. Mordecai overheard a plot to kill the king and saved the king's life. Not being able to sleep one night, the king had one of his record books brought in and read to him. The exact page was read that reminded him to reward Mordecai. This in turn led to Haman's plans being revealed. And in the end, Haman's plan to hang Mordecai and kill all the Jews was completely reversed. Haman was hanged, many of the enemies were slain, and the Jews were miraculously saved.

As I read, I realized that this was not only a devotional subject, but that God was speaking to me personally. Going through a rough time with one of our teenage children, it was easy to forget that God was still in control. Sometimes I wondered where He was and why He wasn't doing anything. Or at least He wasn't doing what I wanted Him to do! But through this story of Esther, He gently reminded me that He was working. He knows all the details of our lives. He knows more about the rough times than we do. He sees the end from the beginning. He hears our cries, sees our tears, and feels our pain. God is just as able to deliver us and to direct us today as He was in the days of Esther.

- Do I recognize God's sovereignty in my life?
- What situation(s) in my life should I relinquish fully into God's control?
- *Lord, I thank you that you are sovereign, and I want to yield my entire life to you.*

Relationships Designed By God: Directional Signs

"Teach me thy way, O Lord, and lead me in a plain path, because of mine enemies."
- Psalm 27:11

We all need help in our relationships at times. Marriages struggle, motherhood overwhelms, and friendships challenge. But God has provided road signs for us to follow. We just have to *see* them, *read* them, and *heed* them.

The most important sign He provides for us is a ***Map--His written Word***. His Word is "a lamp unto my feet, and a light unto my path." (Psalm 119:105) Studying this map daily will familiarize us with the Way.

We have a clear ***Path*** to follow--***His Son.*** "I am the Way…" (John 14:6) Let's follow the path He has cleared for us and beware of side trails that divert us from *The Way.*

Along the way we have a ***Guide--His Holy Spirit***. "When he, the Spirit of truth, is come, he will guide you into all truth…" (John 16:13) Staying in tune with our Guide will sweeten all our relationships.

Helping us on our journey we have ***Traveling Companions--His People.*** "For if they fall, the one will lift up his fellow…" (Ecclesiastes 4:10) Confide in a trusted godly friend when you need counsel.

God has provided us with a ***Personal Compass--Our Conscience.*** "Which show the work of the law written in their hearts, their conscience also bearing witness…" (Romans 2:15) A Spirit-enhanced conscience is a compass we can rely on to help us make right choices as we face decisions and temptations along the way.

Sometimes He gives us a ***Heavenly View*** of our journey, by allowing us to see the big map and to get a glimpse of His Sovereignty. "That men may know that thou…art the most high over all the earth." (Psalm 83:18) Watch for these Heavenly views and treasure them! They may be just the encouragement you need to keep traveling on.

And, when we need them, He provides us with ***Rest Areas*** along the way. "But they that wait upon the Lord shall renew their strength…" (Isaiah 40:31) These rest areas can be Sunday morning church services, seminars, or retreats that He leads us to, or just a refreshing visit with a friend. Allow Him to provide the rest you need for the journey.

- Am I aware of and heeding the signs God has for me in my relationship journeys?
- Which of these signs am I missing?
- *Lord, the signs are there, but sometimes they are easy to miss. Open my eyes to see and my heart to respond.*

Relationships Designed By God: Warning Signs

"And be ye kind one to another, tenderhearted, forgiving one another, even as God...hath forgiven you."
- Ephesians 4:32

Along with the direction signs God has for us along the way, He also has warning signs in place to alert us to danger in our relationships. These signs tell us we are on the wrong path and will lose our way completely if we don't heed them, turn around, and find our way back.

Loss of heart-to-heart communication, both vertically and horizontally- (1Thessalonians 5:11) Our communication with God and with one another is closely tied together. If our relationship with God slips, communication with others will likely suffer also.

Loss of quality time together- (I John 1:7) It's hard to maintain a close relationship without spending quality time together, sharing thoughts, dreams, and goals.

Loss of motivation-duty vs. desire- (Psalm 38:10) In a good relationship, serving each other and spending time together will be a desire rather than a duty to be fulfilled out of obligation.

Loss of interest in common goals-pursuing self interest-(Mark 10:37) Common goals are necessary in a working relationship. Pursuing only separate selfish interests will drive you apart instead of bringing you together.

Loss of intimacy-(Psalm 107:6,7) An intimate relationship produces a feeling of belonging and acceptance. Losing that intimacy creates loneliness and feelings of isolation.

Loss of peace and patience-(Proverbs 14:29) If you find yourself feeling unsettled and irritated, snapping at those around you, it may be a sign that something is wrong in a relationship that needs to be resolved.

Loss of financial harmony-(Proverbs 30:7-9) Disagreement on managing money, regardless of how much you have, (or don't have) is one of the main causes of discord in a marriage relationship. Ask God to provide the help you need to work through these difficulties together, possibly by consulting a Christian financial counselor or an accountant.

Warning signs are put there for a reason. We have to choose whether we are going to heed them or not. Right choices will keep us on the right path, finding joy in our relationships and peace in our hearts.

- Am I willing to pay attention to the warning signs God has provided in my relationships?
- What is God speaking to my heart that I may not want to hear?
- *Lord, give me the courage to open my heart to You and to hear what You are telling me.*

 Read: Psalm 37

Relationships Designed By God: Commitment As A Choice

"Commit thy way unto the Lord, trust also in Him, and He shall bring it to pass."
- Psalm 37:5

To commit ourselves to the Lord means to trust Him, believing He can take care of us better than we can take care of ourselves. It means to rest patiently in Him and wait for Him to work out what's best for us.

I believe God has gifted women with a special sensitivity and discernment in our relationships. This doesn't make us right or better than men, it just makes us different, the way God created us. With this sensitivity, we can have a big impact on our relationships by the choices we make. Healthy relationships are built by avoiding:

1. *... a shallow and self-serving commitment:* thinking or saying our commitment is for the good of others, when in reality, we are in it for ourselves and what we can gain from it.
2. *... a temporary mindset:* being committed only as long as everything is going our way.
3. *... a lazy commitment:* not willing to put forth effort to maintain our relationship.

Sometimes it's difficult to maintain a delicate balance of trusting in the Lord, waiting on Him and working out what we believe He's telling us to do.

David tells us in this Psalm to delight ourselves in the Lord and to commit *everything* (not just our relationships) to Him. It means entrusting everything--our lives, our families and friends, our jobs, our possessions--to His control. To delight in someone means to experience pleasure and joy in their presence. This will happen only when we know that person well. And to know a person well, we must spend time with him. To delight in the Lord, and to be able to trust Him in this way, we have to know Him and the kind of Person He is. As we learn to know Him and to delight ourselves in Him, our "delight" will spill over into our relationships and we will see a difference!

- What relationships am I involved in that I need to commit more fully to the Lord?
- Am I willing to commit everything to Him? Do I fully trust that He knows what's best for me and will work that out?
- *Lord, commitment can be a hard thing but it truly is the desire of my heart. Show me where I need to change.*

Relationships Designed By God: Commitment As A Wife

"Commit thy way unto the Lord, trust also in Him, and He shall bring it to pass."
- Psalm 37:5

If you are a wife, think back with me to your wedding day. Picture yourself standing in front of the preacher, pledging your whole life to the young man beside you. Now, how would you rate your commitment? Was it:

Shallow and self-serving? Were you thinking, "This day is for *me*. *I'm* going to be sooo happy. *I'll* never be sad or lonely again. He is going to meet all of *my* needs." I'm guessing you were focused more on *him* and *us*.

Temporary? Were you thinking: "I'm fully committed to you, my dear, as long as you realize that my way is best. If not, things won't go so well." Most likely you weren't thinking anything of the sort!

Lazy? Was your attitude: "I'm committed to you forever. I do hope you realize, however, that I expect you to take care of yourself. I don't cook or clean and I certainly don't do windows." Of course not!

At that point your commitment to your marriage relationship was deep, lasting, and pure. But time goes on. We have babies and we get tired. Our husbands are busy providing for the family. When we have rare "alone" times, Hubby falls asleep. Disagreements happen and we drift apart. Satan takes advantage of this and we may come to a point where we have to make a choice. Are we going to let him tear us apart and destroy our relationship? Or are we going to choose to *commit our ways to the Lord, trust Him, and allow Him to do His healing work?*

I clearly remember a time in our marriage that I was faced with this choice. Difficult times had taken their toll and we had lost our way. I felt desperate and alone. Early one morning I was reading and praying, and feeling like even God didn't care what happened to us. I told Him (reluctantly, I admit) that I was going to choose right then to be committed to our relationship and to trusting Him. I prayed earnestly that He would show me what to do as a Christian wife. But when He honored my prayer with an immediate answer I didn't like it. I said, "No way! I can't do that. It's too hard." But God doesn't argue, so He just waited patiently while I fussed and fumed and finally came to the point of submission, and peace. That act of obedience was not an instant fix, but it was a turning point that eventually brought us back to a restored relationship. As you face these times in your marriage, *what will your choice be?*

- Is my commitment as a wife as wholehearted as that which I expect of my husband?
- Am I willing to *completely* commit my way unto God and to trust Him?
- *Lord, take my life and let it be fully committed to You and Your will for me.*

 Read: II Timothy 1

Relationships Designed By God: Commitment As A Mother

"Commit thy way unto the Lord, trust also in Him, and He shall bring it to pass."
- Psalm 37:5

If you are a mother, think back now to the time when you first held your newborn baby in your arms. The birth is over and you're marveling at the precious, helpless infant that has finally arrived. Think about your commitment to your child at that point. How would you rate it? Was it:

Shallow and self-serving? "Baby, you are here for me. You are going to make me so happy. You are going to meet all my needs that no one else is meeting." I doubt it. You were much more concerned about the baby's needs!

Temporary? "I'm fully committed to you, Little One, until you turn two. I've heard about two-year-olds and at that point you're going to live with Grandma!" No, at that point you probably couldn't imagine life without your baby.

Lazy? "I'm here for you forever, sweetheart, as long as you can take care of yourself. I don't do diapers and I certainly don't get up at night." No of course not. You knew better than that!

At that point your commitment to your baby was as deep, lasting, and pure as it ever gets. Now, while some babies are easy to raise, others will challenge that commitment right from the beginning. And they will challenge it over and over and over through the years until there comes a time when you have to make a choice. Are you going to allow Satan to drag you into the pit of despair and destroy your relationship? That is his goal--to steal, to kill, and to destroy. Or are you going to choose to *commit your way unto God, to trust Him, and allow Him to work?*

As a mother, I have been there. I know the pain of having to make that choice, and how tempting it is to just give up and quit. But I also know that a godly mother never gives up in her heart. She keeps on loving and praying. I also know the joy and peace of making the right choice. We have seen prayers answered in amazing ways. We have seen a deep faith grow in the heart of a child who saw those answers and *knew* that God *is* and that He cares. We have seen relationships restored and thriving in our home and others, because a mother *didn't give up*. Because she chose to *commit her ways unto the Lord, trust in Him, and allow Him to bring His will to pass*. As you face these times with your children, *what will your choice be?*

- What difficult challenges am I facing in my relationships with my children?
- Do I truly believe God is trustworthy, just waiting for me to commit our relationship to Him?
- *Lord, right now I choose to commit this relationship to You. I choose to trust You to work in Your own time and way.*

December

Read: Romans 8:31-39 December 1

Relationships Designed By God: Commitment In Marriagc

"For I am persuaded that (nothing) shall be able to separate us from the love of God."
- Romans 8:38,39

Friends of ours, Jack and Julie, recently shared their testimony with our church family as we were going through a series of meetings titled "Relationships Designed by God." Neither had been raised in a Christian home. They met and married at the young ages of 19 and 17. Not long after, they began attending a small Methodist Church near their home.

As time went on, with a struggling farm implement business, they argued so much about their financial problems and his increased drinking, that their four children discussed among themselves what they'd do if their parents divorced.

As Jack was preparing to attend a relative's out-of-state funeral one day, Julie knew she was being left behind, with the children, to answer the phone calls from the bill collectors. Angry words flew back and forth until Jack stormed out the door, slamming it so hard the glass broke. Immediately Julie tossed some of his clothes into a suitcase and threw it through the broken glass, saying angrily, "And don't come back!" Jack did come back, but their relationship remained tense.

A few days later they received a brochure in the mail advertising a "Spiritual Life Retreat." Knowing this might be what they needed, Jack reluctantly agreed to attend. All weekend the music, the messages, and the friendly, loving fellowship ministered to each of them in a personal way. Flowing tears cleansed them of the anger and frustrations that had consumed them, and during the weekend they each gave their hearts to Jesus. Returning home they felt like two different people, washed in the love and peace of God and full of love for each other.

They were richly blessed as they began to attend a Bible study and go to church twice on Sunday. They were called to reach out to others through a traveling mission program, sharing their testimony and faith and leading group discussions. Their teenage children often went along, taking part in a separate youth program.

Jack and Julie will soon celebrate 58 years of marriage, with most of their children and grandchildren now serving the Lord. They admit that they are still two strong-minded people who disagree occasionally, but they praise the Lord for the difference He has made in their lives and their marriage as their Savior, Provider, and Healer.

- Do I know Jesus as my personal Savior, Provider, and Healer?
- What could I do to enhance my marriage relationship?
- *Lord, I know Your presence makes a big difference in relationships. Show me where I need Your help.*

Relationships Designed By God: Commitment To A Friend

"And let us not be weary in well doing;
for in due season we shall reap, if we faint not."
- Galatians 6:9

Diane knew God wanted her to be committed to her relationship with a needy friend, but it wasn't easy. Joy struggled physically, mentally, emotionally, and spiritually. She truly desired healing, however, and had asked Diane to be her spiritual mentor and to hold her accountable to daily Bible reading. Every morning she would call, and they would talk through her battles with suicidal thoughts and other issues that Diane simply could not comprehend. They prayed together, even though it seemed like Joy's prayers were seldom, if ever, answered. Diane knew her own attitude wasn't right, but more than once she wondered if it was time for her to just end the relationship. But God always said "No," and she made the choice to stick with it.

As the days turned into months and the months into years of daily (sometimes dreaded) phone calls, Diane began to see a difference. It was clearly apparent that Joy was committed to this, too, even though it couldn't have been easy for her, either. She began to read more than one chapter a day and seemed to comprehend that God loved her, no matter what. The Word began to speak to her and their daily sharing and prayer turned into times of real worship. When Diane suggested that she start memorizing Scripture, Joy spent over *two months* on the first verse, finally succeeding even though her medications made remembering difficult. They would talk about Heaven and agree that it would really be something to actually be there. Clearly God was working in Joy's heart, and she became an overcomer.

Then one morning, Diane received a phone call that Joy had died in her sleep. Her body was no longer able to cope with the many health problems and the variety of psychiatric medications she was on. Even though her mental and emotional health was greatly improving, and her spiritual life was growing rapidly, her body finally gave out. The relationship is over and Diane misses her. How thankful she is that she made the choice to stay committed to Joy in obedience to God's calling. She looks forward to seeing her in Heaven and tries to imagine how Joy must feel now. Imagine, after all she went through, waking up in Heaven!

- Is there a relationship to which God is asking me to commit my time and energy?
- In what ways does my attitude need to improve to be able to minister to others?
- *Lord, a high-maintenance commitment is not easy. Fill me with Your grace to fill the roles You have for me.*

Relationships Designed By God: Growing Through The Barren Times

"Thy word is a lamp unto my feet,
and a light unto my path."
- Psalm 119:105

We all go through barren times in our relationships, whether it's with family, church family, other people in our lives, or even in our relationship with the Lord.

As Elijah sat by the brook, eating food brought by ravens (an "unclean" bird) and drinking from the brook, his life and ministry were in a barren time. He had taken a shocking message to Ahab who had no defense against a drought. We don't know how long he was by the brook, but he had plenty of time to think and wonder how Ahab was reacting to what he had done. We don't know whether he was discouraged and worried, but he wouldn't have needed to be, because *God took care of him by the brook.*

When the brook dried up, God sent him to a widow (a Gentile from Jezebel's homeland) for further care. This woman had no food. She and her son expected to eat one last meal and then die. This woman was in a barren time, also. It could have looked pretty bleak to Elijah as he wondered why God had sent him here, of all places. *But God took care of them* in a miraculous way. It's hard to imagine how this woman felt as she went to fix the last of her food for Elijah. How thankful she must have been when she realized that she and her son would not die of starvation after all.

It's easy for us to become despondent, traveling through the barren times in our lives. But instead, God wants to help us grow through them. We have a wonderful tool Elijah and the widow did not have. We have God's written Word to help us through the barren times. No matter how dry and hopeless our struggles seem, we will be able to find God's hand of care if we look for it. The poor widow woman learned that God takes care of those who put him first, even in the hard times. Elijah had all he needed while the king in his palace suffered hunger.

The same God who provided for Elijah and the widow in unusual ways will also provide for us, sometimes in ways we least expect. He still performs miracles, large and small. The barren times are never easy, but with God's help, we can grow into greater Christ-likeness and into a closer relationship with Him. Remembering God's faithfulness in the barren times has a way of strengthening your faith for the next drought you may face.

- Do I have a relationship that is struggling through a barren time today?
- Am I able to fully trust God to help me through this time?
- *Sometimes the struggle is so great that I don't even know how to pray... except...Lord I'm Yours; use me.*

December 4 *Read: Numbers 6:22-27*

Speaking A Blessing

"The Lord bless thee, and keep thee."
- Numbers 6:24

The sixth chapter of Numbers closes with a beautiful blessing. The Lord was speaking to Moses, instructing him to tell Aaron and his sons to use these words to bless the children of Israel. It's a blessing straight from God we can still use today. We can share it along with a hand-shake or a hug as we part with friends and loved ones. It can be used in a letter, card, or note of encouragement. A simple "The Lord bless you and keep you," warms our hearts and binds our spirits together in bonds of love.

There is great power in the spoken word. We can see a big difference in our children when we speak blessing into their lives, rather than cursing. Speaking a blessing to our husbands in the morning such as "God bless you with a good day," can enhance our relationship and get him off to a good start. Speaking words of friendliness, kindness, and caring to neighbors and friends whose lives we touch, will allow them to see Jesus and possibly give them the desire to know Him better.

It is so important that we guard our lips. Ugly words cannot be taken back and are so often regretted. I can think of many times when I've spoken harshly to our children, words of "cursing" with no blessing to them. All the regret in the world will not retract them--or the pain I see in their eyes. Confessing, asking their forgiveness, and earnestly praying that God will delete the incident from their minds helps, but the spoken word itself cannot be deleted. We've all heard the saying, "You are what you eat." Let's change that to say "You are what you speak." Now let's think about our own lives. Am I a blessing or a curse to those around me? Which do I *want* to be? Which will I *choose* to be? With God's help we can succeed in being a blessing to those around us. The results will be more far-reaching that we may even know.

- Do I pray for God's help in guarding my lips each day?
- In what areas of my life do I need to be more diligent in speaking a blessing to others?
- *Lord, I invite You to come and be the guard to my lips, speaking a blessing to those around me.*

Read: Philippians 6:5-9 December 5

Our Purpose In Life

"As the servants of Christ,
doing the will of God from the heart."
- Ephesians 6:6

What is your purpose in life? Do you ever wonder why you are here or what your purpose in life really is? God says in His Word that we are to be servants. Servants for Him.

We do have a choice as to whom we will serve. We have two options. Just two. We can serve Satan, or we can serve God. Whichever master we yield ourselves to is the one we serve. Those who choose to serve Satan become slaves to sin. They will spiral downward in a sin-filled life which will eventually bring forth spiritual death.

We who choose to serve the Lord are not slaves! We are called into a life of righteousness--a blessed calling that brings fulfillment and satisfaction beyond measure. We experience joy and peace that the world cannot understand as we get to know our Master. Would a slave's master die for him? Not likely. But our Master died for us. And He left us a perfect example of servanthood. If you want to be like Jesus, be a servant.

Whether you are serving Him on the mission field, as an employee, or in your own home, responsibility and honesty are essential. God will receive glory from your efforts as you work hard with enthusiasm. And, while you should want to please those you serve, it is most important that you do the will of your Father in Heaven. A life of servanthood is tiring at times but it is the most fulfilling life you can live.

- Do my daily activities identify me as a servant for Christ?
- How could I better serve Him in my routine today?
- *Lord, my heart's desire is to be a servant for You. Open my eyes to the opportunities You have for me.*

A Servant's Heart

"His Lord said unto him,
Well done thou good and faithful servant."
- Matthew 25:21

Do I truly have a servant's heart? How can I tell? Let's pause and examine our hearts a moment. Be honest with yourself as you take a look inside your heart and evaluate the level of willingness to serve.

HUMBLE - Philippians 2:3 instructs us to esteem others better than ourselves. As we serve others, we need to put on the "apron of humility." Only what we do for God's glory will be of eternal benefit. If we work only to bring glory to ourselves, we ruin our witness for the Lord.

PRAYERFUL - Genesis 24 tells the story of Abraham's servant, Eliezer, going to a far country to find a wife for Isaac. Eliezer's heart was prayerful as he traveled and as he waited by the well, and God honored his prayer. His trip was successful, and Isaac was blessed with a godly wife, Rebecca, whom he loved.

LOOKING FOR OPPORTUNITIES - Galatians 6:9 encourages us not to "be weary in well doing." We need to be sensitive, listening to others, and responding to the opportunities God brings to us to help others. That means we need to be available and guard against becoming frustrated at the interruptions in our days. If we're on the look-out, God will give us opportunities to grow in servanthood. Although it takes time and energy to respond to these unscheduled calls, our expressions of love will have a great impact in the lives of others if we are willing to serve.

JOYFUL - John 15:11 Following Jesus results in fullness of joy. God has a place of service for each of us. The joy increases as we serve willingly where God has planted us. There's a blessing in serving that comes in no other way. Be alert, be available, and be willing. A servant heart seeks to discern and do the will of the Master. Don't miss out on the opportunities!

- Is my heart truly a servant's heart?
- What could I do today to be of service to another?
- *Lord, give me a genuine desire to be in Your service every day wherever You have placed me.*

God, Our Shelter

"Thou hast lifted me up,
and hast not made my foes to rejoice over me."
- Psalm 30:1

A minister tells a story about trying to make friends with two small neighbor children. The little boy was easy to win over, but the girl was not so sure. She was just three years old, and he thought she had probably never seen a man with a red beard before!

One day as the children arrived at the farm with their mother, the little girl tripped and fell into a ditch at the edge of the driveway. A large barking dog ran over, and she lay in the ditch looking up at that big dog. She was terribly frightened, of course, and as our minister friend rushed to her rescue, she leaped into his arms and clung to him. Her fear of the dog completely wiped out her fear of the man. From her place of safety, she could look at that big dog and laugh. He wasn't nearly as scary from the arms of her rescuer.

And that is just where we need to be when the big dogs of life are barking at us. Safe in the arms of Jesus. A parent or child sick enough to be hospitalized. A teenager causing us untold parental pain. A dream that's about to fall through, or a job lost unexpectedly. Financial difficulties or a hurting marriage. The loss of a loved one. Whatever trial you are facing or experiencing, Jesus wants to be your shelter, your comforter, your friend. Will you let Him?

- Am I immobilized with fear when I should trust my Savior?
- Am I willing to honor Jesus by trusting Him to protect me?
- *Lord, life can be scary, but I know You are able to be my shelter and I thank You for it.*

A Godly Woman

"Teaching us that...we should live soberly, righteously, and godly, in this present world."
- Titus 2:12

The word ***godly*** means "devoutly conforming to the will of God." ***Devout*** means to be devoted to, or given up wholly. This embraces an attitude that leads to frequent and sincere prayer and worship. ***Devoted*** means loyal and faithful, suggesting motives as impelling as a vow. To ***conform*** is to bring into harmony or agreement, to be similar or identical to. We need to be faithful in bringing our own wills into complete harmony with what God desires for our lives. Your life. My life. Now, let's look at a few aspects of being a godly woman.

To be godly women, we must love the Lord and be committed to following His plan for us. Seeking His will through prayer, Scripture, and possibly the counsel of other godly Christians is essential to knowing how God is directing us. We may sense the need for this when we are facing a crisis or a big decision with lasting consequences, but we also need His guidance in the day-to-day grind of the mundane. Sometimes the daily pressures can get us down faster than the bigger ones.

As godly women, we need to be willing to fulfill God's design for us, whether in the home as wives, mothers, homemakers; or as caregivers, teachers, office workers, or any other role in which He may have placed us. Sometimes we may chafe at our responsibilities and wish we were doing someone else's job, as it looks so much more inviting. But if we only knew, that person may be looking at us and thinking the same thing. God's will for each of us is always best.

Godly women are committed to supporting those around them. Husbands get weary and discouraged in their roles, too. They need a loving wife who prays for them, encouraging them in their service for the Lord, rather than criticizing or trying to change them. Children need to know they are loved and worth the time you spend with and for them. Elderly folks need to know they are still useful and important, a cherished part of our lives. Employers, co-workers, friends, roommates, neighbors...we all need to be supported with affirmation, rather than disheartened by unkind words or actions.

Living as a godly woman is not easy and we fail often. But God's blessings are assured as we do our best to live out His perfect plan for us in the way He has designed.

- Do I truly understand what it means to be a godly woman?
- In what areas do I need to ask God for help to improve?
- *Lord, my greatest desire is to be a godly woman, serving You in exactly the way You have planned for me.*

Our Eyes Are Upon Thee

"Be not afraid nor dismayed...
for the battle is not yours, but God's."
- II Chronicles 20:15

Jehoshaphat was afraid. He had just received a message that three unfriendly armies were headed his way. He called all of Judah together to fast and pray. They came before the Lord knowing they had "no might against this great company," and admitting they did not know what to do. "*But our eyes are upon thee,*" they prayed. (v. 12) With all of Judah standing before the Lord (even the women and children), God spoke through Jahaziel. "Be not afraid nor dismayed by reason of this great multitude; *for the battle is not yours, but God's.*" (v. 15) He tells them to "go down against them...ye shall not need to fight in this battle...stand ye still and *see the salvation of the Lord*...fear not, nor be dismayed...*for the Lord will be with you.*" (vv. 16, 17) Then Jehoshaphat and all of the others fell before the Lord, *worshiping and praising*. The next morning, before Jehoshaphat and his men went forth to meet the advancing armies, Jehoshaphat reminded them to "*believe* in the Lord your God...so shall ye prosper." (v. 20) And he appointed *singers* to praise the beauty of holiness, walking before the army as they marched toward the enemy. Remember, all of this was done *before* the battle had even begun!

And look what happened. As soon as they began singing, God set those armies against each other. They ended up killing *each other*! Jehoshaphat and his men must have been astonished when they arrived at the battle site and saw only dead bodies. There was simply nothing left to do but haul away the goods; three days of hauling the riches and precious jewels back to Jerusalem, rejoicing and praising the Lord. And Jehoshaphat's realm was "quiet: for his God gave him rest round about." What an example of spiritual warfare and full reliance on God to fight our battles.

We are not facing an enemy army as Jehoshaphat was, but every day we face temptations, pressures, and "rulers of the darkness of this world" who want to defeat us. (Ephesians 6) But, as believers, we have the power of God's Spirit in us, and He will fight for us, if we only ask for His help. And God always wins! We need to recognize as Jehoshaphat did that the battle is not ours, but God's. When we acknowledge our weaknesses, His strength can work through us. When we make sure we are following God's plan, we can ask Him for help in our daily battles. As we Trust Him, and believe in Him, we can expect to be "*established and ... so shall we prosper.*"

- What battles am I facing that God offers to fight for me?
- Do I fully believe that God will fight for me and that He *will* triumph?
- *Lord, this trusting is not easy, but I choose to give my battles to You, and praise You for fighting them for me.*

Give Up The Grudge

*"For if ye forgive men their trespasses,
your heavenly Father will also forgive you."
- Matthew 6:14*

There is a story about a Lord and a Duke who were bitter enemies. One day this Lord got the message that the Duke would be passing by his city on a certain day. Taking advantage of this unexpected opportunity, the Lord made plans for a surprise attack and shared this news with his inner company. Upon hearing this, the Chaplain tried to persuade the Lord to give up his plan. After several unsuccessful tries to change his mind, the Chaplain made one last attempt. He asked the Lord if he could meet with him for prayer in his office the next morning. He agreed and the next morning, the Chaplain asked the man to repeat the Lord's Prayer after him. They began: *"Our Father which art in Heaven, hallowed be thy name, they Kingdom come, thy will be done in earth as it is in Heaven. Give us this day our daily bread and forgive us our debts as we forgive…"* The Lord could not continue. The Chaplain then said, "You will either have to give up the grudge or give up the prayer. You cannot keep both."

Have you ever prayed the Lord's Prayer while harboring a grudge? Holding a grudge is having feelings of resentment or ill will toward someone, especially over a long period of time. I think we all have. A sobering thought when we stop to think about it. Just how quick am I to forgive?

What exactly is forgiveness? Forgiveness is the act of pardoning someone for a wrong or a mistake. Forgiveness is giving up the right to hurt back. It's canceling out the demands we may put on another--"*if* you do thus and so, *then* I will forgive you." Forgiveness is not necessarily forgetting the wrongdoing, but it is renouncing the ill will that used to accompany the memory of your pain. Forgiveness does not make the other person right but it *sets you free.*

Are we obligated to practice forgiveness? **We know** that Jesus paid the ultimate price—His life on the cross—*in forgiveness of our sins.* **We pray:** "Forgive us our debts *as we forgive our debtors.*" **We read:** *Forgive, and ye shall be forgiven.*" (Luke 6:37), and "*Vengeance is mine, I will repay, saith the Lord.*" (Romans 12:19). Not only are we commanded to practice forgiveness; we are *blessed* when we obey.

- Am I holding a grudge against anyone today?
- Do I truly believe that I must forgive in order to be forgiven?
- *Lord, this can be a hard thing to do. Give me the courage to search my heart and to thoroughly forgive.*

Of Fires And Forgiveness

*"Condemn not and ye shall not be condemned;
forgive, and ye shall be forgiven."
- Luke 6:37*

Todd's business involves restoring buildings after fire or water damage. He was called one day to give an estimate on a garage in their local town. The garage sets beside an alley, and someone had set fire to it causing a substantial amount of damage. The insurance company had already been there and had issued a check to the homeowners. Todd agreed to do the job for the amount of the insurance company's estimate.

When the job was finished, Todd contacted the owners to make sure they were satisfied with his work and to collect payment. The lady told him times were very hard for them and they would only be able to pay a fraction of the agreed-on price. He was surprised but graciously agreed to work with them. During another phone call a couple of weeks later, she told him she had sent the check but it must have gotten lost in the mail. He soon received a small payment with a note attached stating they needed the rest to keep food on the table. Over the course of time he made many calls and was assured over and over that the bill would be paid in full. They did make a few payments but each time it was only after he had called to inquire about it. Finally, he decided to just let it go and see what happened. It's been several years now and he hasn't heard anything from them.

Now this has been a bit hard to swallow. After all, Todd had spent a considerable amount of time on that garage. Besides that, they'd *had* the insurance money but now were unwilling to pay him. And to make matters worse, he has to drive right by this place on his way home from the office. It's pretty easy to look at it with a critical eye, checking the driveway for a new car or other signs that the owners are spending money elsewhere.

As time went on, Todd knew he had a choice to make. He could be angry with bitter feelings rising up every time he passed the house. He could wish for a way to "pay them back" for the unfair way they had treated him. He could berate himself for not collecting the money *before* he started the job. *Or* he could choose to forgive and set himself free from the bondage of all the negative thoughts and feelings. Todd chose to forgive. Could we do the same?

- How easy is it for me to forgive when I have been wronged?
- Is any unforgiveness hidden away in my heart?
- *Lord, show me any unforgiveness I am harboring in my heart and give me the courage to choose freedom.*

Bank Accounts

"That he would grant you, according to the riches of his glory, to be strengthened with might by His Spirit in the inner man."
- Ephesians 3:16

If you go to your local bank, there are several types of accounts you can open in your name. The money you deposit into these accounts is available for withdrawal at a later date. A checking account gives you the convenience of writing checks rather than handling the money itself. A savings account holds your money in safe-keeping until you draw out the cash as you need it. Some banks offer a money-market account that pays interest according to the amount in it. And an IRA is a retirement fund that cannot be tapped into without penalty until you reach retirement age.

As Christians, we have access to Heavenly Accounts. These accounts require no deposits, have no penalties for early withdrawal, and pay wonderful dividends. They have names such as Mercy, Peace, Grace, Compassion, Forgiveness, and Hope. We can withdraw from these accounts any quantity we need, and they will never run dry, as God lovingly supplies all we need.

Do you desire more from God? You can have it...by giving away what you've got! That is what we are here for. And as we minister to others with compassion, readily forgive, and serve with a willing heart, God will fill our accounts to overflowing. We will never give ourselves dry, and we will enjoy the dividends of rich rewards as God blesses our own lives.

- Am I tapping into my Heavenly Accounts through prayer and Bible study?
- Do I believe God is able to supply all my needs?
- *Lord, help me fully believe that You will never let my "accounts" run dry. Lord, I praise You for that!*

God Our Pilot

"For this God is our God forever and ever:
he will be our guide even unto death."
- Psalm 48:14

Our family took a trip to California for our church conference several years ago. Flying was a new experience for us, and we looked forward to it with great anticipation. At take-off time however, my feelings were quite different. Roaring down the runway at a tremendous rate of speed when you can't see out the front window is rather unnerving! I gripped the armrests during lift-off thinking, *there's no way this monstrous machine can possibly stay in the air.* But it did, and I relaxed and enjoyed the ride. I had to trust the unseen pilot to know what he was doing and to get us there safely. Landing at our destination brought the same feelings. It felt as though we were surely going to crash into some unseen obstacle. I was quite relieved when we finally stopped at the gate and could get off that plane!

Does your life ever seem like that? Like you're racing headlong into the unknown, unable to see your way through? Maybe you're clutching armrests fearing what your doctor will tell you about some test results. Perhaps you're facing an unexpected move to a strange community. Or facing childbirth, eager for the destination but apprehensive about the journey.

Whatever your situation, you have an unseen Pilot, too. Very present and real. He knows what He is doing, and He will get you there safely. It may be a smooth journey, or a rough one, full of turbulence. But as our pilot spoke to us over the intercom, so your Pilot will speak to you through His Word and the Holy Spirit. You can have peace, knowing your Pilot is at the controls.

- What flight into the unknown am I facing?
- Am I fully trusting God as my Pilot?
- *Lord, my heart wants to trust you fully. Thank you for piloting me to safety.*

December 14 *Read: John 14*

Our Mission Statement

"Verily, verily, I say unto thee, We speak that we do know, and testify that we have seen."
- John 3:11

If someone asked you about your personal mission statement, what would you say? Do you *have* a mission statement? *Should* you have a mission statement?

When Jesus was talking to Nicodemus (John 3:16), he explained to him the amazing gift of eternal life. He gave him *God's mission statement:* **"For God so loved the world, that he gave his only begotten Son, that whosoever believeth in him should not perish, but have everlasting life."**

Later (John 14:6), Jesus was speaking with his disciples about his crucifixion and ascension, assuring them that He would be back. Thomas asked Him where He was going and how to get there. Jesus answered the question *with His mission statement:* **"I am the way, the truth, and the life: no man cometh unto the Father but by me."** In the same conversation, Jesus presented to them *The Holy Spirit's mission statement:* **"But the Comforter... shall teach you all things, and bring all things to your remembrance, whatsoever I have said unto you."** (John 14:26)

As the Holy Spirit's mission is to present Jesus Christ to us, *our mission statement* should be: **to present Jesus Christ to others.** We have many opportunities to do this. Maybe God is calling you to a mission field in a foreign country...or right in your own home. Most of us "rub shoulders" with the world to one extent or another.

When my husband and I were enjoying a meal out with some friends recently, our friendly waiter became serious as we were preparing to leave. He quickly (and a bit nervously) spilled out his frustration and bitterness about his Christian life bringing only trials and grief. We were touched and felt a real urgency as we encouraged him not to give up and assured him that Jesus loved him and *would* carry him through. It was a brief, intense encounter that left us with a longing to reach out to him further. Later we wrote him an encouraging note and sent it, along with a small book, to the restaurant, hoping it will encourage him to keep on serving the Lord. We included our phone number, and although we may never know what happens to this young man, or if our efforts have made any difference, we can keep praying for him.

Should you have a mission statement? *Yes, you should!* It can make you aware of opportunities to share Jesus with others, even if it's only with a smile. You will feel God's blessing as you bless others.

- What mission field does God have for me today?
- Do I recognize the opportunities He provides for me to share Jesus with others, even in my own home?
- *Lord, open my eyes to these opportunities and give me the courage to share You with those around me.*

You Are Precious

"Since thou wast precious in my sight,
thou hast been honorable, and I have loved thee."
- Isaiah 43:4

It was not a good day. I was in the middle of a good *grump*. And I had no intention of changing any time soon. Quite frankly, I was enjoying every minute of it. Oh, I knew it wasn't right. And I knew no one else was enjoying it. You know the saying "If Mom's not happy, nobody's happy." But after a full day of grumpiness, even I was tired of it. And admittedly, rather ashamed of myself.

The next morning, still feeling ashamed and discouraged about how I'd been acting, I opened my devotional book to the day's entry, the title of which read: "You're Something Special."

"Hmph," I snorted. "I *don't* think so." *Special* didn't exactly describe how I had been acting or feeling. But as I read on, I began to realize that regardless of how I feel or act, God loves me and wants to help me triumph over every circumstance.

And that is true for you as well. Think about it. God has blessed us far beyond what we could ever deserve. Things that are for our enjoyment, beyond our necessities. Beautiful flowers of all kinds for us to enjoy. Lovely sunsets, painting the sky in blazing color. Loving, funny animals for pets and entertainment. The gift of humor, making life enjoyable, and lightening heavy moments. God delights in providing these extra pleasures in our lives. He is always ready to comfort, guide, or protect us when we need it. Whether we are patient or irritable, loving and helpful, or snappy and selfish, God's love for us prevails. We are His children, and He loves us unconditionally. We are precious to Him.

- Do I feel in my heart that Jesus loves me?
- Do I recognize all the pleasures in my life that are from Him?
- *Lord I thank You for Your love for me and for all the ways You show it.*

A Puppet Show

"I am the vine, ye are the branches. He that abideth in me, and I in him, the same bringeth forth much fruit; for without me ye can do nothing."
- John 15:5

When I was a girl in grade school, a couple would come to our school about once a year to put on a puppet show. I remember being completely entranced by the puppets as they moved across their little stage, talking and acting very much alive. It looked so real! After the show, however, the husband and wife team would bring the puppets out and show us how they worked. Every moving part of the puppet was connected to a string. Each string was attached to a cross-bar that the puppeteers held, one in each hand as they skillfully maneuvered the dolls. The puppeteers were the unseen but very real power that controlled every movement of the little wooden figures.

If we compare our lives to a puppet show, who is in control? Which cross-bar are your "strings" attached to? Are they attached to the victorious cross of Jesus? Or to the type of cross you would find in a graveyard...the cross of death, brought on by sin that snuffs out life? We desire to have God in full control of our lives, but check your "strings." Does each one have a good solid connection, from your body members to the cross-bar? Do you strive to please God in where your feet take you, and what your hands do? How about what your eyes see, and what your ears hear? Our tongues are a real challenge! But if we keep the "strings" in good repair through daily quiet time with God, we can trust Him to be the unseen but very real power, guiding us in everything we do.

- Do I have any broken "strings" that need repair?
- Which areas in my life do I need to put more fully into God's control?
- *Lord, show me any "strings" that need repair and give me the strength and courage to fix them.*

Christ In Me And I In Him

"Christ in you, the hope of glory...
every man perfect in Christ Jesus."
- Colossians 1: 27, 28

The concept of Christ in me and I in Him can be a bit confusing and hard to understand. If I am in a room, the room cannot be in me. If I am in a car, the car cannot be in me. We can illustrate this concept, however, with a sponge and water. When you put a sponge into a pail of water, it soaks the water into itself and sinks under the surface as it becomes fully saturated.

A friend of ours once needed a new sponge with which to wash his car. Not wanting to spend a lot of money, he bought a cheap sponge, took it home and dropped it into his bucket of water. When he was ready to use it, he was surprised to see the sponge still setting on top of the water. It hadn't soaked up any water at all. Trying again, he held it down longer but up it popped, still not taking in any water. A bit frustrated by this point, he held it under the water and wrung it out, twisting and breaking the air pockets and finally allowing the water to soak into the sponge. Now he could use it for its intended purpose.

As the sponge became useful by taking in water, so we become useful in Christ's Kingdom when we are filled with Him. We invite Him in when we accept Him as our Lord and Savior. We grow in Him as we read His Word, communicate with Him in prayer, and fellowship with other believers. As we become submerged and saturated in Him--fully surrendered to His control--we are ready to be used for our intended purpose--to bring glory to God through our lives and by reaching out to others.

Unfortunately, sometimes we resist. We have "air pockets" that have to be broken before Jesus has total control. It's not easy and it hurts, but God, in His great love for us, is patient and lovingly helps us get those areas broken down if we're willing to allow Him to work in us. Being filled with Him and useful in His Kingdom is worth all the "wringing out" that must precede it!

- Are there "air pockets" in my life that I need help to break?
- How could I be more saturated with Him?
- *Lord, show me the air pockets in my life and give me the courage to let You break them down.*

A Long Way From Home

"The journey is too great for thee."
- I Kings 19:7

Elijah had just experienced two great spiritual victories. He had defeated the prophets of Baal, and God had answered his prayer for rain. But now, Jezebel was so angry about her dead prophets that she was determined to kill Elijah, and he was running for his life. Finally he stopped to rest under a Juniper tree, exhausted and so depressed he wanted to die.

If we define home as "***the place where you ought to be***", we can see that Elijah was ***a long way from home***. He was ***H***ungry, ***A***ngry, ***L***onely, and ***T***ired. His courage, his journey, and his ministry had come to a ***HALT.*** Elijah was so focused on his dilemma that he couldn't see his way back home. But God didn't leave him there to blindly find his own way back. He graciously sent an angel to minister to Elijah. Notice God's treatment for this deep despondency. Rest, food, and drink, then more rest, food, and drink. This loving nourishment gave Elijah the strength to travel forty days and forty nights to the mountain where God showed Himself mighty through His still small voice. He then instructed Elijah to return to his duties, and Elijah went.

We may wonder how Elijah could end up in such a state. It's not uncommon, however, for us to experience a letdown after a spiritual high. Or maybe there's been no spiritual experience at all. Maybe you're just simply *a long way from home*. Has your courage, your journey, and your ministry come to a *HALT?* "Home" for us could be a relationship. It could be our spiritual condition, or our physical or emotional health. Can you identify with Elijah, sitting under a Juniper tree (or in your recliner), feeling like life isn't worth living? Asking "Why, Lord, is this happening to me…how much do You think I can take…don't You care?…etc." Running from your struggles, knowing you're *a long way from home* and not able to see the way back? I can. A little more closely than I like to admit.

Does God leave us to blindly find our way back? No. He gently says, "My daughter, the journey is too great for you. Partake of what I have to offer and be strengthened." And He offers us rest, food and drink. Loving rest for our souls in His very presence. Nourishing food from His living Word and the drink of sweet fellowship with a sister or other caring person. When it's time to return, you will be able to go in His strength. You are not alone! The God who took care of Elijah is waiting for you to stop, sit down, and cry out Him. Don't wait any longer!

- Where am I in my life journey? Have I drifted far from "home" in any area?
- Am I willing to accept His help to return?
- *Lord, the journey is, indeed, too great for me. Strengthen me and lead me back to the duties You have for me.*

Just Fifty-Seven Cents

"Every man according as he purposeth in his heart, so let him give...for God loveth a cheerful giver."
- II Corinthians 9:7

I recently heard the story of a little girl, living in the late 1800s, who was turned away, along with several other children, at the doors of a small church because there was "no more room." As she stood crying on the steps, a kind pastor asked her what was wrong. He then gently took her by the hand and led her to the right Sunday school class.

The little girl was greatly affected by the experience and thought about all the children who weren't able to attend Sunday school because the building was too small. She wondered how she could help them. She was from a poor family but faithfully began to save her pennies. Two years later the little girl died and her heart-broken mother found the kind pastor who had befriended her daughter on the church steps. She tearfully asked him to take care of the funeral and handed him a tattered little purse. Inside the purse, the pastor found fifty-seven cents and a note written by the little girl. "This is to make a bigger church so all the other children can come to Sunday school."

Deeply moved, the pastor knew what he had to do. He read the note to his congregation and began a building fund for an addition to the church. He sold each one of the pennies, increasing the amount greatly. Others heard about the little girl's desire and donations began to pour in from all over. Within five years the little girl's fifty-seven cents had multiplied to $250,000. That was a huge amount of money in those days and the fund continued to grow.

This is a true story and if you were to visit the city of Philadelphia today, you could see the Temple Baptist Church; various Sunday school buildings; the Temple University; and two hospitals ministering to the medical needs of people, rich and poor. All these buildings were built from the building fund that began with a little girl's offering of just fifty-seven cents.

We often tend to think our efforts for the Lord are so insignificant they couldn't possibly be of any use to Him. But they can be! Something as simple as reading a Bible story to a child, offering a comforting word to a hurting friend, or giving a friendly smile to an elderly person can begin a ripple effect that continues way beyond our knowledge. The little girl didn't live to see what God did with her fifty-seven cents. We may never know what He does with our efforts either, but He can multiply our love offerings today also.

- Do I believe God can use my efforts for Him as humble beginnings for greater things?
- What opportunities do I have today to serve Him in a small way?
- *Lord, show me how I can provide You with a simple "building fund" today.*

December 20 *Read: Philippians 4:10-20*

Illusions Or Reality

"But my God shall supply all your need according to His riches in glory by Christ Jesus."
- Philippians 4:19

A young friend of mine found a thought-provoking cartoon in the newspaper on Christmas morning. In it was a little boy sitting in a big easy chair beside a Christmas tree. He was looking up with frightened eyes at a huge, mean looking Roman soldier in armor who has obviously just come out of the fireplace. The soldier is saying "Whom was you expecting?" Down in the corner a tiny bird is answering, "Fat guy, beard, red suit…"

Looking at the cartoon she shared with me, we couldn't help but feel sorry for the scared, disappointed little boy. But really, she wondered, how often are we like him? We wait anxiously and expectantly, praying and trusting God to come through for us. We expect Him to be like the world's view of Santa Claus–big, kind, harmless, completely understanding and understandable. We're excited as we wait for Him to deliver exactly what we want. Then we're disappointed, sometimes even crushed, when life turns out like this little boy's Christmas. We may end up with a pile of "gifts," everything but what we really wanted, and we wonder why.

At this point we may start to question God. Is He really good? Does He really care about me at all? Who *is* this big scary Soldier who shows up when we're expecting jolly old Saint Nick?

Maybe the problem isn't with God at all. Maybe the problem is with our perception of God. Santa Claus isn't even real! He's a figment of someone's imagination that doesn't even exist. *God is real and true.*

We are in a spiritual battle. Our hearts and lives are in constant danger of the enemy. Santa Claus may seem safer and friendlier, but we don't need an illusion! We need a real Soldier who loves us without end and will fight for us even though we don't always feel it. God showers us with blessings and we cry over what we didn't get. Sometimes He even seems scary as we wonder what is going to happen next. He doesn't always deliver just what we *want* but He knows just what we *need* and will never fail to supply those needs at just the right time. *God will come through.* It may not be in the way we were expecting, but He *will* come through and even when life is scary, we are safe with Him.

- Do I truly believe God knows about and will supply everything I need?
- What situations in my life do I need to quit dreaming about and fully give over to Him?
- *Lord, it's so easy to build castles in the air. Help me to fully commit my life to You and allow You to be my Warrior.*

That's Impossible

*"With men this is impossible;
but with God all things are possible."
- Matthew 19:26*

Our God is Master of the impossible. There are many stories in the Bible of men and women who were faced with impossible circumstances. Some of them believed even though they didn't understand and some doubted. And I wonder, where would I be in some of these cases? Well, actually I know. Individually and as a family, we've faced things that looked impossible. I believe...but I struggle to trust. "I *know* You can work this out, Lord, but *how* are You going to manage it and *when* are You going to do it? Surely Lord, You could use my help!" But let's take a look at some of these instances that were impossible with men, but possible with God.

When the Angel Gabriel appeared to Zacharias in the temple and told him that he and Elisabeth would have a son, Zacharias was skeptical. He wondered how that could possibly be since they were far too old to have a baby. His age was bigger to him than God's promise. As a result of his unbelief, he was unable to speak until the promise was fulfilled. And it was! In due time Elisabeth had a son and they called him John. And Zacharias magnified the Lord.

During this time, Gabriel also appeared to Mary, telling her that she would be the mother of Jesus. Mary, also, was frightened and confused. She was engaged, but not married, so how could this be? But with the angel's reassurance, she submitted. She answered, "Behold the handmaid of the Lord; be it unto me according to thy word." We don't know how much she thought about the risks she was taking and what could become of her, we just know that she submitted and became the mother of our Lord. She believed, even under humanly impossible conditions.

What is happening in your life right now? Is everything going smoothly day by day? If so, thank God! The valleys come often enough. We can praise Him for the smooth stretches of road. But if you're in a valley now, how does it appear to you? Does it just simply look impossible? If it does, I encourage you to spend some time reading and meditating on these and the many other Biblical stories where God does the impossible. (Exodus 14:15-31; Joshua 6:1-27; Daniel 3:1-30; and Daniel 6:1-28 are just a few.) We can choose to continue to doubt or we can choose, like Mary, to submit to His divine plan, regardless of how we feel. Doubt muzzles our praise and destroys our testimony. As we trust Him we can praise Him, and allow Him to work the impossible in our lives.

- Am I willing for God to display the impossible through me?
- Do I fully trust God to do the impossible in the times when I see no way out of the valley?
- *Lord, I believe. Please help me to trust You completely during the dark times of my life.*

 Read: Luke 1:26-38; 2:1-7

Narrow Is The Way

"Because strait is the gate, and narrow is the way, which leadeth unto life, and few there be that find it."
- Matthew 7:14

It seems that we Americans often have a warped concept of Christianity. We think that, as followers of Jesus, our lives should be easy, going just the way we plan them. But Jesus teaches a different Way.

If we could go back in time, sit down with Mary over a cup of tea, and ask her about her life, she would tell us that being in the center of God's will isn't always easy. I imagine Mary was as excited as any young woman would be, planning to marry the man she loved. It was confusing, frightening, and--to Joseph--devastating to have Mary expecting a child before their wedding. It seemed that God had "messed up" their plans, just as it seems He does ours at times. Let's think about some of the aspects of this Narrow Way:

1. *God didn't ask Joseph and Mary-He told them.* No place in Scripture does it say the angel Gabriel asked Joseph or Mary if God's plan was OK with them. He simply told Mary what the plan was and Mary accepted it humbly and sweetly. God doesn't ask our permission, either, when His plan is different than ours. He has a detailed plan for our lives, and it's up to us whether we accept it willingly and grow through it, or fight it and become bitter.

2. *God's plan for Mary and Joseph required their submission.* Along with the shame and rejection of her condition, Mary likely had to ride a donkey to Bethlehem at the end of her pregnancy. We can only imagine the misery of a trip like that! And then--to give birth in the dark, dirty surroundings of a stable. Not long after, they were forced to flee to Egypt because the King wanted to kill their baby. *And years later*...To have your adult son hatefully mistreated and cruelly killed is something we can't even begin to comprehend.

3. *God blessed them for their obedience.* Jesus was a blessing all through His life. Mary watched and marveled at the things He said and did and pondered what others said about him. She was blessed as *"Jesus increased in wisdom and stature, and in favour with God and man."* (Luke 2:52) She watched as her son, ultimately, blessed the entire world. It's hard to imagine how she felt when she realized that her son had ***opened the door to Heaven for all who accept Him and receive Him as their Lord and Saviour.***

While God's plan for our lives may at times differ from our thinking, it is always in harmony with His wisdom and authority. When we accept it as a gift, it can have a far-reaching impact for good.

- Am I feeling the peace of being in the center of God's will for my life today?
- How may I be resisting His plan for my life?
- *Lord, this plan You have for me is hard, sometimes. Give me the grace and strength to press on in Your will.*

Walking The Narrow Way

"When thou passesth through the waters, I will be with thee...For I am the Lord thy God."
- Isaiah 43:2, 3

At a young age, our son and daughter-in-law, Mike & Anna, are experiencing one of the hard times along the "narrow way." A year after the birth of their first child, Jordan, a precious healthy daughter, they were again joyfully expecting a baby. Anna was experiencing some difficulty, as she had the first time, but with bed-rest and patience, things were looking good.

Then one evening her condition took a turn for the worse and they prayerfully headed for the hospital. After a series of tests, Anna was admitted and closely monitored. Though this was not in the plan, Mike and Anna were willing and ready to do whatever was best for the baby. Days turned into weeks of hospitalization with Baby's condition not quite dangerous but fragile. The separation from little Jordan was hard, and the days became quite monotonous. But they knew that every day increased the likelihood of a healthy baby.

Finally, after five weeks of anxious waiting, little David Michael was born 2 months early, weighing in at 3# 1 oz. Tiny, but seemingly healthy and stable. We rejoiced that all appeared well. The next day, though, plans were changed again. David's condition worsened, deteriorating rapidly, and after just 28 hours of life, little David died. There is now a fresh, tiny grave in the cemetery just a few miles from our house.

Oh, the pain and the giving up as we all struggled to accept God's plan when our plans had seemed so right. Pain and grief, mixed with feelings of joy and thankfulness that Baby David was safe in the arms of Jesus, blended into a jumble of intense emotion. Those two days and the emotional, exhausting days that followed tested our faith and endurance. Never once, however, have we heard a word of complaint or bitterness or anger from Mike & Anna. Though heartbroken, their deep faith and acceptance of God's will has carried them through and are a source of inspiration and encouragement to the rest of us. We were all richly blessed by the love and care of family, church family, and other friends as many kindnesses were shown to us during that time.

God does not ask whether His plans suit us, and living in His will demands our submission. But we are blessed as we allow Him to work out His will in our lives, and we may never know the effect our response has on others.

- How is my attitude affected when God's will turns out to be different than mine?
- Do I truly believe that He will direct my life in a way that is best for me?
- *My heart's desire is to willingly accept the plan You have for me, Lord. Forgive me when I resist Your will.*

Doubt... Or Wonder?

"Be it unto me according to thy word."
- Luke 1:38

Zacharias and Mary each received a message from God through the angel Gabriel. They were both understandably startled at the appearance of an angel, and puzzled at what they were hearing. Their messages were similar in that they were each going to have a child, and to each of them, it seemed impossible. Let's consider their reactions to this message.

Zacharias seriously doubted the angel's message. It was totally unexpected in the first place, and besides that, he and Elisabeth were *old*--way beyond the time of childbearing. His immediate focus was on the sheer impossibility of the promise. All the doubt in his heart came out in his question, *"Whereby shall I know this? for I am an old man, and my wife well stricken in years."*

Mary's situation was similar in that the angel's visit was completely unexpected and the message a seeming impossibility. She reacted with wonder rather than doubt, however, saying, *"How shall this be, seeing I know not a man?"* I can't imagine that Gabriel's explanation made things very clear to her. Her mind must have been whirling with the realization of what it would mean to be unmarried and expecting a baby. She certainly didn't understand all the implications of what was happening. She only knew that God was asking her to serve Him and in her humble, sweet spirit she responded: *"Behold the handmaid of the Lord; be it unto me according to thy word."*

Zacharias's doubt resulted in a rebuke that left him unable to speak until many months later after the baby was born. It's easy to misunderstand or doubt what God wants to do in our lives. Sometimes we think His promises are impossible, but entertaining doubts about God's Word can easily result in the sin of unbelief.

Mary didn't wait to see how everything was going to work out before offering her life to God. Even though the results appeared disastrous at that point, she submitted to His plan with willing acceptance. This plan was not easy for her, but she was ultimately blessed beyond anything we can imagine.

- Can I willingly accept God's plan for my life even when the outcome seems impossible or disastrous?
- Am I willing to submit to God as Sovereign, even when I do not understand?
- *Lord, I know that You shine brightest in impossible situations. Forgive my doubt and make me willing to serve You.*

A Christmas Miracle

"Jesus said... If thou canst believe,
all things are possible to him that believeth."
- Mark 9:23

A friend recently related a story about a small miracle that happened to them on Christmas morning. A neighbor had given them a few hens, an exotic breed that was laying colored eggs. After a few months in their barn, however, the hens had not laid a single egg. They tried different things, including more light, as they anxiously awaited those first fresh eggs, but nothing worked.

Shortly before Christmas, the young daughter excitedly told her mother she had dreamed there were two eggs in the hen house on Christmas morning. One was red and one was green! Her mother and older sister breathed prayers that she would not be disappointed. On Christmas morning, when they went out to do the chores, they were surprised and delighted to find that there were, indeed, two eggs in the nest. One was a pale green, and the other was a light rusty-red color! Two eggs, one red and one green, just like the little girl's dream. And on Christmas morning. A little miracle just for them. It was an exciting reminder to them that God cares. Not just about the big things in life, but He cares about the small things, too. And a little girl with a big dream has a growing faith that God cares about her and her family.

He cares for each one of us, and as we look for signs of His love, we find them in many little things all around us. God has many different ways of showing us He cares. Besides using other people, He often uses pets or other animals. Flowers, birds, waterfalls, and beautiful scenery in all parts of His world speak to us of His love. Evidence of His love surrounds us on every side. Believe it...look for it...and praise Him for it!

- Do I recognize God's caring in the little things and praise Him for it?
- Do I believe God does perform miracles in the lives of those who love and serve Him?
- *Lord, thank you for all the small ways you show me that you care.*

Renewal

"Create in me a clean heart, O God;
and renew a right spirit within me."
- Psalm 51:10

Recently, a friend shared with me an interesting experience. She had known for a long time that she was not reading her Bible or praying as much as usual. More and more, she was lapsing into various excuses, but ignoring the accompanying twinges of guilt that developed. Her Bible reading had become dry and meaningless. She had quit getting up early enough to have a quiet time alone. Late one night, the Lord convicted her, and she repented. She told God that if He would wake her early, she would read His Word. She begged Him to speak to her through it as He used to.

She went to sleep with that thought and sure enough, she found herself awake early the next morning. TOO early. It wasn't even five o'clock yet! "Oh Lord," she prayed, "This is just too early. Surely you don't mean now. Wake me again at six and I'll get up." Later she woke to a strange ding-ding-ding sound that she couldn't identify--not their alarm clock, or any other usual noise. She looked at her watch and the hands pointed to exactly six o'clock. *"Oh yes, Lord, that was You, wasn't it?"* she thought and smiled as she headed down the stairs.

Not only was God faithful to waken her at the exact time she had requested, but as she spent time reading an old familiar passage, it came alive to her in a way that it never had before. "Thank You, Lord," she prayed, "for renewing my spirit in a way that only You can."

- Do I sense myself slipping away from my first love?
- Is my spirit in need of a renewal?
- *Lord, help me to always put You first and to stay in close communion with You.*

Focusing On Jesus

"Looking unto Jesus the author and finisher of our faith."
- Hebrews 12:2

As Peter impulsively climbed out of the boat and walked across the water toward Jesus, we can picture him looking directly into the Master's eyes. His focus was on Jesus rather than on his own feet. One wonders if he was even aware of actually walking on the water. But, we know that he looked away for a moment, became aware of the howling wind and the high waves, and started to sink. We can only imagine the panic he must have felt as he started to go down. When he cried out in fear, however, Jesus immediately reached out and caught him.

We know that to get through a tough situation victoriously we must keep our focus on Him. It's easy to hear or to give that advice, but what exactly does it mean to "focus on Jesus?" Especially, what does it mean to me?

Diane has a precious memory of her late husband Jim gazing at her from his end of the table. With eight children in their family, there would often be lots of other activity in the room, but when he looked at her, she would see his love for her shining in his eyes. After Jim was gone, Jesus showed Diane that, in the midst of the turmoil that life can become, He looks at her with that same expression in His eyes. For her, "focusing on Jesus" means closing her eyes and picturing that look in her mind. The blessing and peace she feels in His presence is priceless.

We likely will never walk on water, but we all walk through hard times in our lives. How easily we focus on the waves and winds of difficult circumstances. Looking around and feeling like we are sinking, our faith wavers and we wonder how we'll ever stay afloat. If we want to come through these situations victoriously, however, we must keep our focus on Jesus. His power is far greater than any problem.

Faltering faith doesn't necessarily mean we have failed. Peter was afraid, but instead of panicking, he looked straight at Jesus for help. Just as Jesus was the *only One* who could help Peter out of his dilemma, so He is the only One who can truly help us through all the dilemmas of our lives. It's our choice. Will we sink beneath the waves of despair or will we focus on Him, experiencing the peace and blessing He has for us?

- Where is my focus as I go through tough times in my life?
- Am I easily distracted by the difficulties of the situation, faltering and sinking in depression and hopelessness?
- *Lord, the waves are high and the wind is strong. Forgive me for wavering, take my hand, and lead me through.*

December 28 *Read: I John 1*

Of Courtrooms And Report Cards

"And the blood of Jesus Christ his son cleanseth us from all sin."
- I John 1:7

Recently we had the opportunity of sitting in on a courtroom session. It was a happy occasion as one of our church families welcomed three small children into their family in an adoption ceremony. It was also a serious time. The judge entered the room from a side door, in his black robe, looking stern and intimidating. In respect we were all asked to rise to our feet as he strode with purpose to his seat behind the judge's bench. After greeting those of us in attendance, he opened a folder and took out some papers. Putting on his glasses, he studied the papers intently, then began asking the prospective parents questions concerning the children they were planning to adopt. This little story has a happy ending. The questions were answered, the papers signed, and the smiling judge's little hammer came down, *"bang,"* in finality.

Now go back in your memory to your school days. Do you remember being handed a report card periodically? Maybe you opened it eagerly knowing you and your parents would be happy with it. Or perhaps you didn't open it at all, stuffing it away and hoping your parents would forget about it, too. What was recorded there was a (sometimes painfully) accurate reflection of your work at school. The marks on the card were final and could not be easily changed.

And now, picture yourself in a courtroom. You are in the defendant's chair and the Judge has entered the room. He greets you, then opens a folder with your name on it and takes out a "report card." The left side of this card has your name on it, also, and you tremble as He opens and studies it intently. Down one side of the card are listed the "subjects" you will be graded on. "Righteousness," "Holiness," "Purity," "Keeping the Word of God." If you were grading yourself, how would you do? Would you be passing any of these subjects? I think we would all be failing in all areas. But the Judge is now examining the right side of the report card. The name **JESUS** is written at the top of this side, and there is a bold **100%** beside each of your subjects on His side. And as you watch, a red stream flows down the page, washing away your failing grades. The Judge smiles as he bangs his gavel down and says, **"Forgiven!"**

The blood of Jesus erases our sins. Even though we may try valiantly, we can't even get a passing grade on our own. He understands our humanness and is ready to cleanse us from **all** unrighteousness as we confess our sins and ask His forgiveness. (I John 1:9)

- Do I understand and believe that Jesus has completely forgiven my sins, if I have repented and confessed them to Him?
- How am I doing in these subjects of godly living?
- *Lord, I thank you for your work on the cross. Help me to live a life pleasing to you at all times.*

Clothed In Righteousness

"My soul shall be joyful in my God: for He hath clothed me with the garments of salvation, He hath covered me with the robe of righteousness."
- Isaiah 61:10

We were attending an evening wedding a few days after Christmas. The church was beautifully decorated with a Christmas theme. The candlelight ceremony was lovely and, of course, the guests were all dressed in their finest. I had spent a good deal of time and effort, and I admit, a good bit of exasperation, getting everyone cleaned up and ready to go. In spite of all the stress, we were, indeed, a well-dressed family as we sat in attendance.

I began to think a little deeper about being well-dressed, however, as the minister began to compare our wedding finery to our spiritual clothing. Isaiah 61:10 says God has clothed us with the garments of salvation and covered us with the robe of righteousness as a bride and groom adorn themselves. We are to be clothed in humility for God resists the proud. (1 Peter 5:5) And Colossians 3:12-14 tells us that we, as the elect of God, are to put on mercy, kindness, humbleness, meekness, long suffering, forbearance, forgiveness, and most of all, charity.

Thinking about how our preparation time had gone before the wedding, I realized we weren't quite as well dressed as I had thought we were! We looked good on the outside, but only God could see how we looked on the inside. While it is certainly appropriate to dress in our best for a wedding, it is much more important to be sure that our inner adorning matches God's character qualities.

- Am I as concerned about my family's spiritual clothing as I am about the clothes we wear?
- In what ways does our spiritual clothing need to be mended?
- *It's easy, Lord, to be too concerned about our outer clothing, Show me your provision for our spiritual clothing.*

The Parasites Of Life

*"I am the good shepherd, and know my sheep,
and am known of mine."*
- John 10:14

Unlike many animals, sheep are very dependant creatures. Without the intervention of the shepherd, their physical well-being can be threatened by the presence of parasites. One such parasite is a tiny worm that thrives in the sheep's intestine by attaching itself to the intestinal wall and robbing the sheep of life-giving blood and nutrients. This worm is controlled by giving the sheep an oral dose of worming medicine.

One Saturday afternoon, a friend of ours and his sons had corralled their sheep in an enclosure so they could catch them one by one and worm them. It so happened that one of the young ewes, only a bit larger than a lamb, was able to escape through the gap under the bars of the gate. Despite all the shepherds' attempts, they were unable to catch the little ewe. Her quest for freedom overrode all efforts expended to catch her or to coax her back into the corral. When they tempted her with a bucket of grain, she drew near but stayed just out of reach. After much patience, one of the boys finally got close enough to grab her from behind. Startled, she struggled free again before they could get the medicine into her mouth. So they decided to leave her alone, hoping to catch her at feeding time on another day, which is what eventually happened.

Our friend shared with us that as this little episode unfolded, he thought about how many times our Shepherd tries to reach us for our betterment, and we value our selfish freedom more than the good He could bestow. Life is full of "parasites" that can easily infect us if we don't get our regular dose of medicine. Pride, greed, jealously, anger, hatred, and worry are just some of the parasites with which Satan wants to infect us. They burrow into our hearts and rob us of the vitality Jesus wants us to know. We can carry a hidden parasite around for a long time, while appearing to be in good health. It's crucial that we keep our hearts clean and healthy by daily doses of quiet time spent with God. But we also need to be aware that some around us may be struggling with a parasite of their own and finding it difficult to come near enough to receive that life-giving treatment. Has God nudged you to call a sister or friend or to write a note to someone going through a hard time? Your thoughtfulness could be just the inspiration she needs to take the final step toward the Shepherd for a healing dose of love and forgiveness. Don't turn away from a hurting heart.

- What "parasite" might be infecting my life right now?
- Am I willing to draw near enough to my Savior to receive a dose of His life-giving medicine?
- *Lord, help me to keep my heart pure with a daily dose of your tonic. Show me, also, how I can encourage others.*

The Graces Of Grace

"As every man hath received the gift,...minister the same... as good stewards of the manifold grace of God."
- I Peter 4:10

I've heard it said that grace can be defined as **G**od's **R**iches **A**t **C**hrist's **E**xpense. The ultimate gift of God's grace was given to us at Calvary when He gave His own Son to die for our sins so that we can live eternally with Him in Heaven. The gifts continue as we experience His grace on a daily basis.

In I Peter 4:10, God asks us to share this gift of grace in serving one another. The abilities God has given each of us should be used in serving others, not for our own selfish pleasure.

The Shunammite woman was called a "great woman." We can see a genuine graciousness in her character as we read through this story. Her life was graced with a spirit of ***HOSPITALITY.*** She and her husband had often hosted Elisha for a meal as he passed through the area, and she wanted to prepare a little room for him to stay in when he came. Elisha was so grateful that he asked her what he could do for her in return. He even offered to speak to the King and get her an honored position or a special favor. The woman, however, showed a sweet attitude of ***CONTENTMENT*** as she answered him, "I dwell among my own people," gently refusing the big rewards he was offering her. As a result of her contentment, she had a son, a far greater gift than an honored position with the King.

When this woman's son was a young man, he became ill and died. Naturally, his mother was devastated. She rode all the way to Mt. Carmel as fast as she could to talk to Elisha. She refused to talk to his servant, Gahazi, but took her emotional request straight to the "man of God," revealing a deep ***FAITH*** that there was no substitute for God's representative. It wasn't until Elisha himself went to her house, prayed, and laid on the child, that her son was revived.

This mother was overjoyed when Elisha called her into the room and she saw that her son was alive. Before embracing him, however, she fell at Elisha's feet, bowing to the ground in a humble spirit of ***THANKFULNESS*** for what he had done for their family.

We can grace the lives of others in many ways as we receive the manifold grace of God. When we serve others, even our own families, without selfish motives, others will see Jesus in us and will praise Him for the help they have received. In return, we are blessed by God's grace in ways we don't even expect.

- What abilities has God given me that He can use to bless others through me?
- Am I willing to use these abilities for His glory?
- *Lord, show me clearly where I can bless You with the talents You have given me.*